Palgrave Studies in the History of Social Movements

Series Editors
Stefan Berger
Institute for Social Movements
Ruhr University Bochum
Bochum, Germany

Holger Nehring
Contemporary European History
University of Stirling
Stirling, UK

Around the world, social movements have become legitimate, yet contested, actors in local, national and global politics and civil society, yet we still know relatively little about their longer histories and the trajectories of their development. This series seeks to promote innovative historical research on the history of social movements in the modern period since around 1750. We bring together conceptually-informed studies that analyse labour movements, new social movements and other forms of protest from early modernity to the present. We conceive of 'social movements' in the broadest possible sense, encompassing social formations that lie between formal organisations and mere protest events. We also offer a home for studies that systematically explore the political, social, economic and cultural conditions in which social movements can emerge. We are especially interested in transnational and global perspectives on the history of social movements, and in studies that engage critically and creatively with political, social and sociological theories in order to make historically grounded arguments about social movements. This new series seeks to offer innovative historical work on social movements, while also helping to historicise the concept of 'social movement'. It hopes to revitalise the conversation between historians and historical sociologists in analysing what Charles Tilly has called the 'dynamics of contention'.

More information about this series at
http://www.palgrave.com/gp/series/14580

Ana Stevenson

The Woman as Slave in Nineteenth-Century American Social Movements

palgrave
macmillan

Ana Stevenson
International Studies Group
University of the Free State
Bloemfontein, South Africa

Palgrave Studies in the History of Social Movements
ISBN 978-3-030-24466-8   ISBN 978-3-030-24467-5 (eBook)
https://doi.org/10.1007/978-3-030-24467-5

© The Editor(s) (if applicable) and The Author(s) 2019
This work is subject to copyright. All rights are solely and exclusively licensed by the Publisher, whether the whole or part of the material is concerned, specifically the rights of translation, reprinting, reuse of illustrations, recitation, broadcasting, reproduction on microfilms or in any other physical way, and transmission or information storage and retrieval, electronic adaptation, computer software, or by similar or dissimilar methodology now known or hereafter developed.
The use of general descriptive names, registered names, trademarks, service marks, etc. in this publication does not imply, even in the absence of a specific statement, that such names are exempt from the relevant protective laws and regulations and therefore free for general use.
The publisher, the authors and the editors are safe to assume that the advice and information in this book are believed to be true and accurate at the date of publication. Neither the publisher nor the authors or the editors give a warranty, express or implied, with respect to the material contained herein or for any errors or omissions that may have been made. The publisher remains neutral with regard to jurisdictional claims in published maps and institutional affiliations.

Cover illustration: Granger Historical Picture Archive / Alamy Stock Photo

This Palgrave Macmillan imprint is published by the registered company Springer Nature Switzerland AG.
The registered company address is: Gewerbestrasse 11, 6330 Cham, Switzerland

*Every woman in these pages worked
so that the children of the future
could share a better tomorrow.*

*To the children of today,
Benjamin Lucas Curry,
Ariana Rose Curry,
Emma Sophia Cox,
Henry Thomas Cox,
Paige Smith Zimmerman,
and Harriet Mia Murdoch.*

*These women were dreaming of
changing the world
for you.*

Series Editors' Preface

Around the world, social movements have become legitimate, yet contested, actors in local, national and global politics and civil society, yet we still know relatively little about their longer histories and the trajectories of their development. Our series reacts to what can be described as a recent boom in the history of social movements. We can observe a development from the crisis of labour history in the 1980s to the boom in research on social movements in the 2000s. The rise of historical interests in the development of civil society and the role of strong civil societies as well as non-governmental organisations in stabilising democratically constituted polities have strengthened the interest in social movements as a constituent element of civil societies.

In different parts of the world, social movements continue to have a strong influence on contemporary politics. In Latin America, trade unions, labour parties and various left-of-centre civil society organisations have succeeded in supporting left-of-centre governments. In Europe, peace movements, ecological movements and alliances intent on campaigning against poverty and racial discrimination and discrimination on the basis of gender and sexual orientation have been able to set important political agendas for decades. In other parts of the world, including Africa, India and South East Asia, social movements have played a significant role in various forms of community building and community politics. The contemporary political relevance of social movements has undoubtedly contributed to a growing historical interest in the topic.

Contemporary historians are not only beginning to historicize these relatively recent political developments; they are also trying to relate them to a longer history of social movements, including traditional labour organisations, such as working-class parties and trade unions. In the longue durée, we recognise that social movements are by no means a recent phenomenon and are not even an exclusively modern phenomenon, although we realise that the onset of modernity emanating from Europe and North America across the wider world from the eighteenth century onwards marks an important departure point for the development of civil societies and social movements.

In the nineteenth and twentieth centuries the dominance of national history over all other forms of history writing led to a thorough nationalisation of the historical sciences. Hence social movements have been examined traditionally within the framework of the nation state. Only during the last two decades have historians begun to question the validity of such methodological nationalism and to explore the development of social movements in comparative, connective and transnational perspective, taking into account processes of transfer, reception and adaptation. Whilst our book series does not preclude work that is still being carried out within national frameworks (for, clearly, there is a place for such studies, given the historical importance of the nation state in history), it hopes to encourage comparative and transnational histories on social movements.

At the same time as historians have begun to research the history of those movements, a range of social theorists, from Jürgen Habermas to Pierre Bourdieu and from Slavoj Žižek to Alain Badiou as well as Ernesto Laclau and Chantal Mouffe to Miguel Abensour, to name but a few, have attempted to provide philosophical-cum-theoretical frameworks in which to place and contextualise the development of social movements. History has arguably been the most empirical of all the social and human sciences, but it will be necessary for historians to explore further to what extent these social theories can be helpful in guiding and framing the empirical work of the historian in making sense of the historical development of social movements. Hence the current series is also hoping to make a contribution to the ongoing dialogue between social theory and the history of social movements.

This series seeks to promote innovative historical research on the history of social movements in the modern period since around 1750. We bring together conceptually informed studies that analyse labour movements, new social movements and other forms of protest from early modernity to the present. With this series, we seek to revive, within the context of historiographical developments since the 1970s, a conversation between historians on the one hand and sociologists, anthropologists and political scientists on the other.

Unlike most of the concepts and theories developed by social scientists, we do not see social movements as directly linked, a priori, to processes of social and cultural change and therefore do not adhere to a view that distinguishes between old (labour) and new (middle-class) social movements. Instead, we want to establish the concept 'social movement' as a heuristic device that allows historians of the nineteenth and twentieth centuries to investigate social and political protests in novel settings. Our aim is to historicise notions of social and political activism in order to highlight different notions of political and social protest on both left and right.

Hence, we conceive of 'social movements' in the broadest possible sense, encompassing social formations that lie between formal organisations and mere protest events. But we also include processes of social and cultural change more generally in our understanding of social movements: this goes back to nineteenth-century understandings of 'social movement' as processes of social and cultural change more generally. We also offer a home for studies that systematically explore the political, social, economic and cultural conditions in which social movements can emerge. We are especially interested in transnational and global perspectives on the history of social movements and in studies that engage critically and creatively with political, social and sociological theories in order to make historically grounded arguments about social movements. In short, this series seeks to offer innovative historical work on social movements while also helping to historicise the concept of 'social movement'. It also hopes to revitalise the conversation between historians and historical sociologists in analysing what Charles Tilly has called the 'dynamics of contention'.

At the heart of Ana Stevenson's volume on *The Woman as Slave in Nineteenth-Century American Social Movements* stands the desire to historicise an analogy that was both extremely widespread and deeply flawed. Comparing women with slaves was often deeply racist, and yet Stevenson's book shows clearly that this analogy served as an analytical framework for dealing with the 'woman question' in a great variety of different American social movements throughout the nineteenth century. Her analysis is highly perceptive in tracing the many changes that this analogy underwent over the course of the nineteenth century and across diverse social movements. Her book is also excellent at analysing the many interconnections between different social movements in using and developing the analogy between women and enslaved people of African descent.

By following the woman-slave analogy in both antislavery movements and proslavery lobbies, in women's rights movements, dress-reform movements, labour reform movements and in suffrage movements as well as, not the least, in free love movements, racial uplift movements and anti-vice movements, Stevenson reveals on the one hand the ubiquity of that analogy in nineteenth-century social movement politics in the United States. On the other hand, she traces the importance of this discourse to a great variety of different and often mutually exclusive political projects, those of political reform and those of a complete transformation of the foundations of American society.

The crucial period in which the discursive construction of the woman-slave analogy was being re-forged was the period of the Civil War and its aftermath. Transnational, transatlantic networks of reformers proved to be particularly important in using the analogy to foster their particular reform projects that invariably had to do with the intersections between race, class, and gender. Yet the writings on the intersectionality of racial, class, and gender identities that have gathered in prominence since the 1980s do not so much build on but transcend the kind of analogical thinking that was at the heart of a 'woman-as-slave worldview', as Stevenson argues in her concluding chapter. For analogical thinking historically all too often prioritised one identity over the other, in particular those of white women over those of their black sisters, and thus served ultimately a de-radicalised and racist agenda. Overall, Stevenson has provided us with tantalising glimpses of a kind of pre-history of intersectionality, one that points to as many pitfalls as to possibilities and promises. It is a major achievement of this volume to lead the reader competently and elegantly through the many reincarnations of the woman-slave analogy in America's nineteenth century.

Bochum, Germany Stefan Berger
Stirling, UK Holger Nehring

A version of Chap. 4, though substantially revised, appeared as "'Symbols of Our Slavery': Fashion and Dress Reform in the Rhetoric of Nineteenth-Century American Print Culture," *Lilith: A Feminist History Journal* 20 (2014): 5–20. Thanks to the Australian Women's History Network and the Lilith Editorial Collective for their permission to reproduce aspects of this journal article.

ACKNOWLEDGMENTS

This project has been in the making since I was an honors student at The University of Queensland in 2009, whereupon I first encountered echoes of the woman-slave analogy in the periodicals compiled in Ann Russo and Cheris Kramare's edited compendium, *The Radical Women's Press of the 1850s* (1991). Since then, I have been the beneficiary of the expertise and kindness of scholars who have championed my work from near and far, including Chris Dixon, Sarah Pinto, Michelle Arrow, Sharon Crozier-De Rosa, Susanne M. Klausen, Clare Corbould, Lisa Featherstone, Julie Husband, and Frances M. Clarke. This book could not have been written without the confidence Ian Phimister placed in my work. I am profoundly grateful for the opportunities afforded me by the International Studies Group at the University of the Free State, South Africa. My thanks also to my editor, Camille Nurka, for her unparalleled insights as I came to the end of this project.

Studying the United States from abroad for the better part of a decade has been a challenging enterprise that would not have been possible without the support of the School of History, Philosophy, Religion, and Classics (now the School of Historical and Philosophical Inquiry) at The University of Queensland; New England Regional Fellowship Consortium; Australia and New Zealand American Studies Association; Organization of American Historians; and, most especially, the International Studies Group at the University of the Free State. I deeply appreciate the feedback I received from seminars at the Schlesinger Library, Harvard University; Massachusetts Historical Society; American Cultures Workshop, United States Studies Centre, The University of Sydney; Wits History Workshop,

University of the Witwatersrand; History Department Seminar Series, Stellenbosch University; and A Workshop in Transnational Feminism/*Atelier sur le féminisme transnational*, L.R. Wilson Institute for Canadian History, McMaster University.

The gratitude I owe my family, friends, and colleagues is global in its dimensions, spanning Australia, South Africa, and the United States. I have always benefited from the love and encouragement of Janet and Colin Stevenson, Luca Stevenson, and Noreen Rossall. More broadly, I am indebted to the generosity of the Stevenson, Rossall, Bristow, Hardwick, Jarvis, and Forbes families. My thanks especially to Alana Piper, Jon Piccini, Sheilagh Ilona O'Brien, Gemmia Burden, Kate Ariotti, Duncan Money, Cornelis Muller, Kate Law, Abraham Mlombo, Danelle van-Zyl Hermann, Ana Rita Amaral, Lazlo Passemiers, Clement Masakure, Admire Mseba, David Patrick, Rebecca Swartz, Jacqueline-Bethel Tchouta Mougoué, and Kristin Allukian; Ilse le Roux, Tari Gwena-Masakure, Judy King, and Angelica Litaole; and Katherine Cox, Amanda Acutt Harvey, Philippa Kerr, Joan Palmes, Tui Trezise, Megan and Adam Zimmerman, Ashton Fagg and Lucy Galea, Christopher Ham, Megan Doney, Patience Matlala, Gertrude Nakibuule, Gillian Busch, and Howard and Katherine Munro.

My acknowledgments would not be complete without due appreciation for the baristas whose expertise has fueled this book, from Merlo Coffee UQ in Brisbane to Adda Coffee & Tea House, Tazza D'Oro CMU, Artisan Café, and Arriviste Coffee Bar in Pittsburgh, and the Royal Roastery, Stereo Café, and Urban Brew in Bloemfontein.

And my thanks, finally, to the love of my life—my husband—who is no tyrant.

Contents

1 Women's Rights, Feminism, and the Politics of Analogy   1

Part I   Transatlantic Social Movements   21

2 "All Women are Born Slaves": Antislavery, Women's Rights, and Transatlantic Reform Networks   23

3 "Bought and Sold": Antislavery, Women's Rights, and Marriage   69

Part II   Between Public and Private   115

4 "Tyrant Chains": Fashion, Antifashion, and Dress Reform   117

5 "Degrading Servitude": Free Labor, Chattel Slavery, and the Politics of Domesticity   159

Part III The Politics of Slavery and Emancipation   205

6 "Political Slaves": Suffrage, Anti-suffrage, and Tyranny   207

7 "*Slavery Redivivus*": Free Love, Racial Uplift, and
    Remembering Chattel Slavery   257

8 "Lady Emancipators": Conclusion   301

Bibliography   311

Index   345

Abbreviations

AASS	American Anti-Slavery Society
AERA	American Equal Rights Association
AFAAS	American and Foreign Anti-Slavery Society
AWSA	American Woman Suffrage Association
BFAAS	British and Foreign Anti-Slavery Society
FLRA	Female Labor Reform Association
NAACP	National Association for the Advancement of Colored People
NACW	National Association of Colored Women
NAWSA	National American Woman Suffrage Association
NDRA	National Dress Reform Association
NEWC	New England Women's Club
NWP	National Woman's Party
NWSA	National Woman Suffrage Association
WNLL	Woman's National Loyal League
WWA	Working Women's Association

List of Figures

Fig. 2.1	Hiram Powers, *The Greek Slave*. Alamy, Image ID: D2XWBM. Artokoloro Quint Lox Limited/Alamy Stock Photo	24
Fig. 2.2	John Tenniel, "The Virginian Slave," *Punch* 20 (1851): 236. © Punch Limited	25
Fig. 2.3	William Blake, "Europe supported by Africa & America" (London, Johnson and Edwards, 1796). Alamy, Image ID: MMGW37. The Picture Art Collection/Alamy Stock Photo	36
Fig. 3.1	"The Tyrant," c. 1840–1880. Library Company of Philadelphia, Comic Valentine Collection, 12.19	82
Fig. 3.2	"Eliza: Uncle Tom's Cabin" (New York: A.S. Seer's Union Square Print, 1886). Library of Congress, Theatrical Poster Collection	100
Fig. 4.1	Frank Beard, "A slave to Fashion's tyrant laws," c. 1869. Library Company of Philadelphia, Comic Valentine Collection, 10.4	121
Fig. 4.2	"Amelia Bloomer, Originator of the New Dress," *Illustrated London News* (27 September 1851): 396. The Victorian Web, http://www.victorianweb.org/art/costume/bloomer.html	130
Fig. 4.3	"Woman's Emancipation," *Harper's New Monthly Magazine* 3 (August 1851)	132
Fig. 4.4	"The Slave of Fashion," *Harper's Bazaar* XI, no. 16 (April 1878): 256. Home Economics Archive, Research, Tradition and History, Cornell University	155
Fig. 5.1	*Slavery as it exists in America: Slavery as it exists in England* (Boston: J. Haven, c. 1850). Library Company of Philadelphia, Print Department, Political Cartoons, P.9675	164

Fig. 5.2	William H. Helfand, "You think no doubt you're quite the style," c. 1840–1880. Library Company of Philadelphia, Comic Valentine Collection, 17.16	202
Fig. 6.1	"The Two Platforms," 1866. Library Company of Philadelphia Print Department, Political Cartoons: 1866–1868, 9387.F	222
Fig. 6.2	National American Woman Suffrage Association, "Abraham Lincoln" (Grand Rapids: The Cargill Co., 1910). Catherine H. Palczewski, Postcard Archive, University of Northern Iowa, Cedar Falls, IA	253
Fig. 6.3	Nina Allender, "Great Statues of History," *Suffragist*, January 1915. Wikimedia Commons	254
Fig. 6.4	National Association for the Advancement of Colored People, *Crisis: A Record of the Darker Races* 10, no. 4 (August 1915). Brown University, The Modernist Journals Project	255
Fig. 7.1	"Circassian Beauty," c. 1865. Wisconsin Historical Society, Image ID: 109430	262

CHAPTER 1

Women's Rights, Feminism, and the Politics of Analogy

The analogy between woman and slave has a long historical lineage. Countless philosophers, political theorists, social reformers, legislators, and cultural commentators have been prompted to ask: Are women, in fact, slaves? This seems an extraordinary, even offensive, question to contemplate today. It strikes at the heart of ongoing debates about the heterogeneous category of "woman" as it elides the historical reality that free women were the beneficiaries of freedom; enslaved women were not, and racist gender conventions routinely disregarded the womanhood of enslaved and colonized women. But this question has nonetheless preoccupied social movements, as it constantly generated answers that have proved as clear as they have been indistinct. Generations of reformers, who grasped for the words to call attention to the great evils they sought to combat, believed that discourses of slavery created a productive and provocative site of meaning. This logic aligned far more closely with the political claims of white women than it did women of color, yet this question was not contemplated exclusively by white women. What this book describes as the *woman-slave analogy* obtained currency across a vast spectrum, gaining a particularly powerful hold over social, cultural, and political imaginaries across the long nineteenth century. Its meaning never truly fixed, the woman-slave analogy has provoked reflection as much as a sense

© The Author(s) 2019
A. Stevenson, *The Woman as Slave in Nineteenth-Century American Social Movements*, Palgrave Studies in the History of Social Movements, https://doi.org/10.1007/978-3-030-24467-5_1

of misunderstanding and frustration. Since historians and other scholars continue to struggle with the legacy and implications of analogy in feminist thought, these questions remain as relevant as ever today.

The Woman as Slave in Nineteenth-Century American Social Movements offers a reappraisal of the woman-slave analogy, a rhetorical device that has provoked the interest and astonishment of historians and feminist theorists since the 1970s. At the center of such evaluations have been incisive examinations of how this comparison was, at best, structurally untenable, and at worst, deeply racist. Prior to the twentieth century, however, the validity of such claims was rarely—if ever—explored thoroughly.[1] Was the universal "woman" enslaved, or was she not? Preoccupied with this question, many reformers asked themselves: How could she be emancipated? To answer in the affirmative was to support social reform and perhaps even the radical transformation of society. But to deny the slavery of woman was often to uphold the legal, political, and social status quo, from chattel slavery to women's subjugation. Too many theorists and commentators across the centuries have embraced discourses of slavery to analyze the condition of women for historians to dismiss the woman-slave analogy as a rhetorical impasse.

The woman-slave analogy gained particular prominence in the United States during the antebellum era, prior to the Civil War. It proliferated in a culture dominated by the antislavery movement and the "Sisterhood of Reforms"—a term that encapsulated the deep connections between antebellum social movements—to produce a worldview premised on the idea that the position of women was no better nor any freer than that of enslaved people of African descent.[2] The women's rights reformer Paulina Wright Davis, for example, believed that the "analogy that exists between the conditions of women, and of the negro race in the United States, is so close, that slavery and caste apply to the one as well as to the other."[3] Such statements, however, must almost always be read with the invisible adjective *white* as a preface to the noun *woman*. But the woman-slave analogy also became enmeshed in an impulse that unified these social movements: first to identify and then to eliminate all forms of oppression. It was in this

---

[1] See: Kari J. Winter, *Subjects of Slavery, Agents of Change: Women and Power in Gothic Novels and Slave Narratives, 1790–1865* (Athens: University of Georgia Press, 1992), 1–16.

[2] Thomas Wentworth Higginson, *Cheerful Yesterdays* (Boston: Houghton, Mifflin and Company, 1898), 119–120.

[3] "Pecuniary Independence of Woman," *Una*, December 1853.

context that many reformers unreflectively described different forms of oppression as different states of "slavery." However, both the critics and the architects of the status quo embraced comparable rhetoric. For proslavery ideologues, lawmakers, and other commentators, the specter of emancipation—for either enslaved people or women—implied the overhaul and inversion of the social fabric. A woman-as-slave worldview thus influenced a diversity of perspectives toward the woman question.

This book is the first to develop a history of the woman-slave analogy in the United States, exploring its changing meanings and implications across nineteenth-century social movements. It analyzes the ideological foundations of this rhetoric alongside the competing political projects to which it was dedicated. By tracing the transformation of the woman-slave analogy across the long nineteenth century, this book considers how and why various reformers and their contemporaries embraced or rejected a woman-as-slave worldview. In doing so, it places the ideas of those who supported women's rights alongside those who did not. Many of the white reformers who mobilized the woman-slave analogy articulated racist, nativist, and elitist sentiments, yet others—both simultaneously and paradoxically—used this rhetoric to express a growing awareness of the connections between gender, race, and class. And those who questioned the validity of this rhetoric anticipated the conclusions of later scholarship. The woman-slave analogy emerges as a radical but fundamentally imperiled theoretical framework for debating the woman question.

THE POLITICS OF ANALOGY

In 1977, historian William H. Chafe remarked: "Probably no analogy has been used more frequently by both scholars and women's rights advocates than that between sex and race."[4] For at least two decades prior, scholars and intellectuals across a variety of humanities disciplines, from history and literature to political science, had intermittently reflected on the politics of espousing an analogy between sex and race—or its earlier incarnation, woman and slave. Some accepted the logic of each analogy. Building on the work of Joseph K. Folsom and Gunnar Myrdal (who, in 1944, had described women's oppression as "A Parallel to the Negro Problem"), an influential 1951 article by Helen Hacker systematically codified what she

---

[4] William H. Chafe, *Women and Equality: Changing Patterns in American Culture* (New York: Oxford University Press, 1977), 45.

perceived as the similarities and differences between women and African Americans, finding the relationship to be "historical, as well as analogical."[5] Most later scholars developed a far more critical approach. This was a crucial intervention, given that the 1960s and 1970s witnessed the reemergence of the sex-race analogy amongst feminist activists and women's liberationists.

Key figures responded to the debate by condemning the use of analogy, especially in the emerging fields of women's history and African-American history.[6] Chafe appreciated the need to focus on the diversity amongst women as much as their commonalities as a class. The analogy with race, he averred, had been—and could continue to be—productive to the extent that it illuminated parallels that would expose the nature of social control. The sex-race analogy might therefore be a catalyst for instigating social change.[7] Other historians, however, became too preoccupied with women's commonalities as women—sometimes with little to no attention to the effects of diversity or free versus enslaved status. This coincided with a particular interest being espoused among many emerging feminist historians: to recover the lives of their nineteenth-century foremothers, from abolitionists and women's rights reformers to suffragists. Blanche Glassman Hersh, for example, described the "double connotation" of what she termed the "slavery of sex," a rhetorical phenomenon she observed amongst abolitionist women. But her analysis took these women's proclamations far too literally and uncritically. This concept, Hersh argued, was used in "feminist-abolitionist rhetoric to denote the parallel positions of women and slaves: black women were enslaved by chains and codes; all

---

[5] Helen Hacker, "Women as a Minority Group," *Social Forces* 30 (1951): 60–69. For example, see: Joseph K. Folsom, *The Family and Democratic Society* (New York: John Wiley & Sons, 1943), 623–624; Gunnar Myrdal, *An American Dilemma: The Negro Problem and Modern Democracy* (New York: Harper & Brothers Publishers, 1944), Appendix 5; Helen Matthews Lewis, "The Woman Movement and the Negro Movement: Parallel Struggles for Rights" (Doctor of Philosophy, University of Virginia, 1949). For a fuller analysis of the genealogy of this rhetoric across the twentieth century, see: Serena Mayeri, *Reasoning from Race: Feminism, Law, and the Civil Rights Revolution* (Cambridge, MA: Harvard University Press, 2011).

[6] For example, see: Linda La Rue, "The Black Movement and Women's Liberation," *The Black Scholar* 1, no. 7 (1970): 36–42; Catharine Stimpson, "'Thy Neighbor's Wife, Thy Neighbor's Servants': Women's Liberation and Black Civil Rights," in *Woman in a Sexist Society: Studies in Power and Powerlessness*, eds. Vivian Gornick and Barbara K. Moran (New York: Basic Books, 1971).

[7] Chafe, *Women and Equality*, 3–4, 45–78.

women were the slaves of creed and custom, imprisoned within the traditional concept of woman's sphere."[8]

Pioneer feminist historian Gerda Lerner presented the misuse of analogy as an ethical dilemma for feminist historians. This was a crucial methodological intervention for the analysis of nineteenth-century women reformers, as the archival recovery of their lives revealed that their embrace of the woman-slave analogy had been prolific. Lerner herself was an early biographer of Sarah Grimké and Angelina Grimké, the sisters from South Carolina, who had become influential abolitionists and women's rights reformers during the 1830s. Both embraced the woman-slave analogy with vigor, making Lerner all too aware of their particular rhetorical proclivities. The "slave comparison," as she described it, "obviously was a rhetorical device rather than a factual statement." However, if feminist historians were to take these women's words too literally, then it might be wrongly interpreted as fact rather than rhetoric. This interpretation also had the potential to position women primarily as "victims of oppression," a perspective she believed should not be the "*central* aspect of women's history." The Grimké sisters, however, were far less victimized than the enslaved women in their midst. Lerner stressed that equating women's oppression, particularly that of slaveholding women, with enslaved people was to disregard the "real plight of the slave":

> All analogies—class, minority group, caste—approximate the position of women, but fail to define it adequately. Women are a category unto themselves; an adequate analysis of their position in society demands new conceptual tools.[9]

The implication was that, without due caution, feminist historians could be at risk of perpetuating a woman-as-slave worldview in their own historical prose.

---

[8] Blanche Glassman Hersh, *The Slavery of Sex: Feminist-Abolitionists in America* (Urbana: University of Illinois Press, 1978), vii. For some later examples of this problem, see: Kathleen Barry, *Susan B. Anthony: A Biography of a Singular Feminist* (New York: New York University Press, 1988), Chapter 6; Richard Sears, "Working Like a Slave: Views of Slavery and the Status of Women in Antebellum Kentucky," *Register of the Kentucky Historical Society* 87, no. 1 (1989): 1–19, esp. 16.

[9] Gerda Lerner, *The Majority Finds Its Past: Placing Women in History* (New York: Oxford University Press, 1979/2005), 4–5, 117–118, 28, 31.

The problem of analogy remained a key methodological question. Describing Sarah Grimké's famous salutation, "Thine in the bonds of womanhood," from her *Letters on the Equality of the Sexes, and the Condition of Women* (1837), historian Nancy F. Cott outlined an important paradox. "'Bonds' symbolized chattel slavery" to Grimké, who intentionally endowed her phrase with a "double meaning": "womanhood bound women together even as it bound them down."[10] Although historians, literary scholars, and feminist theorists appreciated this paradox, they increasingly emphasized the degree to which "feminist abolitionists," as antebellum women reformers have often been described, expressed racism through their use of the woman-slave analogy. White women reformers habitually privileged a sense of gender identity over cross-class or cross-racial coalitions with either people of color or working-class women, often willfully overlooking crucial differences between the situation of free white women and African Americans, both enslaved and free.[11] Black feminist and critical race theorists, especially, intervened by emphasizing the degree to which deep imbalances of power were intrinsic to the formation of this analogy. As bell hooks and Angela Y. Davis stressed, the use of analogy effectively disregarded the experiences of the women of color who were actually enslaved across the eighteenth and nineteenth centuries.[12] Others realized that "victimologies" offered the impression that women had "*only* been victims*" throughout history, enabling the problematic assumption

[10] Nancy F. Cott, *The Bonds of Womanhood: "Woman's Sphere" in New England, 1780–1835* (New Haven: Yale University Press, 1977), 1.

[11] Robert L. Allen and Pamela P. Allen, *Reluctant Reformers: Racism and Social Reform Movements in the United States* (Washington: Howard University Press, 1974), 133, 136–138; Chafe, *Women and Equality*, 51–58; Hazel V. Carby, "White Woman Listen! Black Feminism and the Boundaries of Sisterhood," in *The Empire Strikes Back: Race and Racism in 70s Britain*, ed. Centre for Contemporary Cultural Studies (London: Routledge, 1982); Jean Fagan Yellin, *Women and Sisters: The Antislavery Feminists in American Culture* (New Haven: Yale University Press, 1989), 29–96; Nancie Caraway, *Segregated Sisterhood: Racism and the Politics of American Feminism* (Knoxville: University of Tennessee Press, 1991), 134–148; Karen Sánchez-Eppler, *Touching Liberty: Abolition, Feminism, and the Politics of the Body* (Berkeley: University of California Press, 1993); Kathleen M. Brown, "Brave New Worlds: Women's and Gender History," *William and Mary Quarterly* 50, no. 2 (1993): 317; Carla L. Peterson, *"Doers of the Word": African-American Women Speakers and Writers in the North* (New Brunswick: Rutgers University Press, 1995), 51.

[12] bell hooks, *Ain't I a Woman: Black Women and Feminism* (Boston: South End Press, 1981), esp. 2, 7, 126; Angela Y. Davis, *Women, Race & Class* (London: The Women's Press, 1981), esp. 32–33. See also: Paula J. Giddings, *When and Where I Enter* (New York: HarperCollins, 1984, 2009), esp. 60–70.

that women "cannot be effective social agents on behalf of themselves or others."[13] Such a conclusion was misleading, other historians revealed, because the power and agency enjoyed by elite slaveholding women meant that most plantation mistresses operated as the oppressor rather than the oppressed.[14] Feminist scholars have been right to condemn this rhetoric, among their forebears as much as their contemporaries, as racism was central to the foundations of feminism in the United States.[15]

Increasingly, feminist scholars began to challenge assumptions about the universality of womanhood, highlighting that women's experiences have been far from homogeneous. "The idea of 'common oppression' was," according to hooks, "a false and corrupt platform disguising and mystifying the true nature of women's varied and complex social reality."[16] This had important implications for the analysis of analogy. Too great a preoccupation with the situation of "women and Blacks"—a phenomenon philosopher Elizabeth V. Spelman describes as the "ampersand problem"[17]—essentially overlooked black women, as Gloria T. Hull, Patricia Bell Scott, and Barbara Smith's classic work, *All the Women Are White, All the Blacks Are Men, but Some of Us Are Brave: Black Women's Studies* (1982), demonstrated.[18] Spelman pointedly observed how odd it would be to proclaim that women were "'treated like slaves' if they *were* slaves."[19] Questions about the ethics of such comparisons began to be extended beyond either woman and slave or sex and race. "The group experience of slavery and lynching for blacks, genocide for Native Americans, and military conquest for Mexican-Americans and Puerto Ricans," sociologist Deborah King emphasized, "is not substantively

---

[13] Sandra G. Harding, ed. *Feminism and Methodology: Social Science Issues* (Bloomington: Indiana University Press, 1987), 5, 11.

[14] See: Thavolia Glymph, *Out of the House of Bondage: The Transformation of the Plantation Household* (New York: Cambridge University Press, 2008); Stephanie E. Jones-Rogers, *They Were Her Property: White Women as Slave Owners in the American South* (New Haven: Yale University Press, 2019).

[15] Louise Michele Newman, *White Women's Rights: The Racial Origins of Feminism in the United States* (New York: Oxford University Press, 1999).

[16] bell hooks, *Feminist Theory: From Margin to Centre* (Boston: Beacon Press, 1984), 44.

[17] Elizabeth V. Spelman, *Inessential Woman: Problems of Exclusion in Feminist Thought* (Boston: Beacon Press, 1988), Chapter 5; Lerner, *The Majority Finds Its Past*, 28–31.

[18] Gloria T. Hull, Patricia Bell Scott, and Barbara Smith, eds. *All the Women are White, All the Blacks are Men, but Some of Us are Brave: Black Women's Studies* (New York: The Feminist Press, 1982).

[19] Spelman, *Inessential Woman*, 9–10.

comparable to the physical abuse, social discrimination, and cultural denigration suffered by women."[20]

Yet, as historiographical debates worldwide suggest, the woman-slave analogy was far from singular. As historian Suzanne Miers astutely observes, "Slavery is arguably the most misused word in the English language."[21] Examples of the disingenuous and misleading use of analogy abound across world history. What exactly constitutes slavery or labor exploitation has proven particularly controversial, as indentured servitude, bonded labor, debt peonage, convict labor, and other forms of unfree labor have repeatedly been described in terms of chattel slavery.[22] The arts and sciences were so influenced by the social construction of race and gender during the nineteenth century that dangerous scientific parallels emerged.[23] Since the mid-twentieth century, analogies between African Americans and women or race and sex, and civil rights and feminism or black power and women's liberation, have proven highly mutable.[24] Both sides of the late-twentieth-century abortion debate, for example, came to embrace chattel slavery as an analogy for the rights of the unborn in the United States.[25] Even today, some commentators draw misleading links between the contemporary refugee

---

[20] Deborah K. King, "Multiple Jeopardy, Multiple Consciousness: The Context of a Black Feminist Ideology," *Signs: Journal of Women in Culture and Society* 14, no. 1 (1988): 45. For the emergence of a related analogy, see: Ana Stevenson, "The Gender-Apartheid Analogy in the Transnational Feminist Imaginary: *Ms.* Magazine and the Feminist Majority Foundation, 1972–2002," *Safundi: The Journal of South African and American Studies* 19, no. 1 (2018): 93–116.

[21] Suzanne Miers, "Slavery: A Question of Definition," *Slavery & Abolition: A Journal of Slave and Post-Slave Studies* 24, no. 2 (2003): 1.

[22] Clive Moore, *Kanaka: A History of Melanesian Mackay* (Port Moresby: University of Papua New Guinea Press, 1985); David Neal, "Free Society, Penal Colony, Slave Society, Prison?" *Australian Historical Studies* 22, no. 98 (1987): 497–518; Surendra Bhana, "Indenture in Comparative Perspective," *Safundi: The Journal of South African and American Studies* 9, no. 2 (2008): 215–224; Clare Anderson, "Convicts and Coolies: Rethinking Indentured Labour in the Nineteenth-Century," *Slavery & Abolition: A Journal of Slave and Post-Slave Studies* 30, no. 1 (2009): 93–109.

[23] Sander L. Gilman, "Black Bodies, White Bodies: Toward an Iconography of Female Sexuality in Late Nineteenth-Century Art, Medicine, and Literature," *Critical Inquiry* 12 (1985): 204–242; Nancy Leys Stepan, "Race and Gender: The Role of Analogy in Science," *Isis* 77, no. 2 (1986): 261–277.

[24] Chafe, *Women and Equality*, 45–78; Spelman, *Inessential Woman*, Chapter 3; Lisa M. Hogeland, "*Invisible Man* and Invisible Women: The Sex/Race Analogy of the 1970s," *Women's History Review* 5, no. 1 (1996): 31–53; Mayeri, *Reasoning from Race*.

[25] Debora Threedy, "Slavery Rhetoric and the Abortion Debate," *Michigan Journal of Gender & Law* 2 (1994): 3–26.

crisis and the transatlantic slave trade.[26] When placed together, such a multiplicity of concepts reveal just how conceptually ambiguous and even substantively harmful the use of analogy can be—among activists and scholars alike.

So how can analogy be understood as a historically informed linguistic concept? To the extent that it is a familiar political strategy, analogy is thought to be cognitively, linguistically, and intellectually commonplace. Cognitive science and psychology suggest that the ability to make analogies and understand analogical reasoning lies at the foundation of all human concepts, rendering analogy the "fuel and fire of thinking."[27] Linguistically, analogy relates to metaphor. According to linguist Jonathan Charteris-Black, "metaphors come into being when there is a *change* in how a word is *used*," meaning a word is embraced metaphorically when applied in a manner that is distinct from its dictionary definition. Metaphors frame the interpretation of politics by eliminating alternative perspectives; they are effective because they "provide cognitively accessible ways of communicating policy through drawing on ways of thinking by analogy."[28] But this does not make all literary devices equal. Metaphors that facilitate the understanding of a "conceptual point" can be useful; however, if and when they begin to "stand-in for the concept itself," metaphors become dangerous.[29]

And what of the changing historical contexts in which discourse is produced? Literary scholar Karen Sánchez-Eppler describes discourse as referring to "any historically specific structure of assertions, vocabularies, categories, and beliefs," thus explaining the coexistence of "[chattel] slavery (the fact of bondage) and the discourse of slavery (the pattern of statements, definitions, and beliefs that both enables the fact of bondage and mediates subsequent accounts of it)."[30] Thus, slavery became a discourse through which commentators of differing political persuasions described imbalances of power. For clarity, this book will use *chattel slavery* to

---

[26] Yogita Goyal, "The Logic of Analogy: Slavery and the Contemporary Refugee," *Humanity: An International Journal of Human Rights, Humanitarianism, and Development* 8, no. 3 (2017): 543–546.

[27] Douglas Hofstadter and Emmanuel Sander, *Surfaces and Essences: Analogy as the Fuel and Fire of Thinking* (New York: Basic Books, 2013), 1.

[28] Jonathan Charteris-Black, *Politicians and Rhetoric: The Persuasive Power of Metaphor*, 2nd ed. (Basingstoke: Palgrave Macmillan, 2011), 31–32, 331.

[29] Peter Kwan, "The Metaphysics of Metaphors: Symbiosis and the Quest for Meaning," *UMKC Law Review* 71, no. 2 (2002): 328.

[30] Sánchez-Eppler, *Touching Liberty*, 9.

describe the institution that became entrenched across the Americas and *slave emancipation* to refer to the collective implications of the Slavery Abolition Act of 1833, the Emancipation Proclamation of 1863, and the Thirteenth Amendment of 1865. In contrast, it will use *slavery* and *emancipation* to refer to examples of analogy or metaphor.

During the nineteenth century, reform and popular cultures embraced incredibly expansive descriptions for what might constitute a state of slavery. The meaning of slavery has encompassed multiple conditions, yet reformers remained aware that there were differences between slavery as a literary device and chattel slavery itself. However, nineteenth-century scholars and scientists routinely elided the brutality and dehumanization of chattel slavery. Later twentieth-century historical revisionism demanded a complete reappraisal of the American South, newly emphasizing the degree to which chattel slavery engendered the powerlessness and social death of enslaved people of African descent.[31] This necessitated an ever more careful approach to slavery as a concept. Ideas about slavery were caught up in the changing usage of the word itself—the point at which Charteris-Black describes metaphor as becoming "a feature of language use or 'discourse.'"[32] At least some of the contention surrounding the woman-slave analogy is borne of the interpretative gulf between nineteenth-century reformers and twentieth-century scholars.

As feminist scholars began to realize the enduring influence of analogical reasoning in feminist thought, a problem of terminology emerged collectively—if inadvertently. The most comprehensive study to date is Jean Fagan Yellin's book, *Women and Sisters: The Antislavery Feminists in American Culture* (1989), which describes the process whereby the supplicant slave and liberated woman, epitomized in the 1830s' "Am I Not a Woman and a Sister" abolitionist emblem, influenced nineteenth-century visual culture. However, Yellin did not settle on a discrete term to encapsulate this rhetorical phenomenon. Chafe had envisioned the comparison between women and chattel slavery as a subset of—rather than a distinctive precursor to—what he termed the "sex/race analogy."[33] What Lerner described as the "slave comparison" and Hersh as the "slavery of sex" has

---

[31] Orlando Patterson, *Slavery and Social Death* (Cambridge, MA: Harvard University Press, 1982).
[32] Charteris-Black, *Politicians and Rhetoric*, 31–32.
[33] Chafe, *Women and Equality*, 45–78.

1 WOMEN'S RIGHTS, FEMINISM, AND THE POLITICS OF ANALOGY   11

since been captured in ever more complicated terminology.[34] Other examples include the "slave metaphor," the "analogy of slavery," the "metaphor of bondage," the "analogy between race and gender," the "slavery paradigm," the "discourse on the relationship between the white woman and the slave," the "intersecting rhetorics of feminism and abolitionism," the "analogy of white women's lack of rights to slavery," the "analogy of 'the slavery of sex,'" an analogy of "racialized sufferings," "marriage-equals-slavery rhetoric," the "analogy between the wife and the slave," the "race and gender/sex analogy," the "racial analogy," and the "woman-as-slave analogy," among many others.[35]

As this overview indicates, the nineteenth-century rhetorical phenomenon has not been the focus of any single historical analysis. Collectively, these different terms evoke a lack of precision about the central concerns that were being considered via analogy. Did reformers focus on women in general or married women in particular? White women, or all women? Chattel slavery specifically or racial oppression more broadly? This is symptomatic of a rich but somewhat repetitive field of study, to which this book brings greater clarity. A new analytical framework can simplify that which is already in existence. The *woman-slave analogy* is both a descriptor and a criticism of a particular historical and rhetorical phenomenon: the comparison between women and enslaved people of African descent, as it

---

[34] Lerner, *Majority Finds Its Past*, 352; Hersh, *Slavery of Sex*, vii.

[35] Ellen Carol DuBois, *Feminism and Suffrage: The Emergence of an Independent Women's Movement in America, 1848–1869* (Ithaca: Cornell University Press, 1978), 32; Davis, *Women, Race & Class*, 33; Elisabeth Griffith, *In Her Own Right: The Life of Elizabeth Cady Stanton* (New York: Oxford University Press, 1984), 111; Kathryn Kish Sklar, "'Women Who Speak for an Entire Nation': American and British Women Compared at the World Anti-Slavery Convention, London, 1840," *Pacific Historical Review* 49, no. 4 (1990): 467; Elizabeth B. Clark, "Matrimonial Bonds: Slavery and Divorce in Nineteenth-Century America," *Law and History Review* 8, no. 1 (1990): 31; Sánchez-Eppler, *Touching Liberty*, Chapter 1; Vron Ware, *Beyond the Pale: White Women, Racism, and History* (London: Verso, 1992, 2015), xxi; Peterson, "*Doers of the Word*," 51; Vikki Bell, "On Metaphors of Suffering: Mapping the Feminist Political Imagination," *International Journal of Human Resource Management* 24, no. 4 (1995): 509; Nancy F. Cott, *Public Vows: A History of Marriage and the Nation* (Cambridge, MA: Harvard University Press, 2000), 67; Marilyn Yalom, *A History of the Wife* (New York: Perennial, 2001), 194; Malini Johar Schueller, "Analogy and (White) Feminist Theory: Thinking Race and the Color of the Cyborg Body," *Signs: Journal of Women in Culture and Society* 31, no. 1 (2005): 66; Estelle B. Freedman, *Redefining Rape: Sexual Violence in the Era of Suffrage and Segregation* (Cambridge, MA: Harvard University Press, 2013), 56; Sabine Broeck, *Gender and the Abjection of Blackness* (Albany: State University of New York Press, 2018), 50.

was embraced across the long nineteenth century. Following the conclusions of other feminist scholars, this term seeks to emphasize that the majority of commentators were concerned with the situation of women—and, implicitly, white women—before that of enslaved people or free people of color. However, it also gestures to the fact that these considerations were inherently connected. This term alludes to how reformers both envisioned and criticized the social construction of womanhood as engendering the slavery of women in all aspects of life—not just in marriage, but from birth to death.

Existing scholarship is also shaped by three major shortcomings: first, it overlooks the ubiquity of discourses of slavery in antebellum culture; second, it supposes that the rhetoric of white women reformers was singular, often suggesting that they alone mobilized the woman-slave analogy; and third, it largely assumes that the application of this rhetoric was explicitly metaphorical and, as such, remained static over the course of the nineteenth century. Historians have not been sufficiently attentive to the possibility that some reformers mobilized the woman-slave analogy in an attempt to expose the very real but nonetheless differing sites of legal, social, and political subjugation experienced by free and enslaved women from different regional, racial, and class backgrounds. Nor have they considered the degree to which the rise of chattel slavery and its demise after the Civil War influenced the worldview that underpinned the formation of this analogy. After the Civil War, a far from insignificant proportion of white women's rights reformers may have convinced themselves that women were, in fact, a literally "enslaved" class, a departure that casts the events of the Reconstruction era in a whole new light.

Since so many nineteenth-century reformers considered a woman-as-slave worldview to be so very thought-provoking, their proclamations need to be taken seriously. To understand each of these influences, this book connects the mobilization of the woman-slave analogy during the antebellum era to its changing manifestations in the immediate postbellum era and beyond.[36] As much as racism was central to the ideological foundations of the woman-slave analogy, this rhetoric also prompted

---

[36] David Roediger calls for the analysis of such rhetoric to extend beyond the antebellum era and to 1870. David Roediger, "Race, Labor, and Gender in the Languages of Antebellum Social Protest," in *Terms of Labor: Slavery, Serfdom, and Free Labor*, ed. Stanley L. Engerman (Stanford: Stanford University Press, 1999), 170.

reformers to think about gender, race, and class in ways which scholars are yet to fully scrutinize.

A WOMAN-AS-SLAVE WORLDVIEW

The woman-slave analogy existed alongside and often in conflict with the cultural veneration of womanhood. However, a cohesive, if asymmetric, rationale lay behind the comparison between forms of subordination grounded in gender and race because nineteenth-century political ideology sought to determine what constituted citizenship and who could be considered a full citizen. During the 1830s, when women tentatively stepped into the public sphere to become the rank-and-file of the "Sisterhood of Reforms," their contributions and achievements were both controversial and contested. Although white women were imbued with a high degree of cultural power and enjoyed the benefits of citizenship, all women remained legally, politically, and socially disenfranchised. Many white women and at least some African Americans found in these hypocrisies a parallel with the legal, political, and social discrimination against enslaved people of African descent.

The subjugation of free women, however, was manifestly not slavery. But those who embraced the woman-slave analogy were not always focused on the realities of chattel slavery. The institution's habitual exploitation and dehumanization rendered the comparison tenuous and highly problematic—not least because of its inaccuracy.[37] Some legal scholars and contract theorists, however, identify certain points of comparison more tenable than others. Between the seventeenth and nineteenth centuries, the legal parallels between husband and wife, parent and child, master and slave offered the foundations for patriarchal society.[38] Married women, children, servants, and the enslaved were perceived to lack self-ownership and so had a comparable legal status.[39] So, when Paulina Wright Davis asserted in 1855 that the "law regards the husband as 'master and owner,'"

---

[37] For the lives of enslaved women of African descent, see: David Barry Gaspar and Darlene Clark Hine, eds. *More Than Chattel: Black Women and Slavery in the Americas* (Bloomington: Indiana University Press, 1996).

[38] For patriarchy and its various meanings, see: Carole Pateman, *The Sexual Contract* (Stanford: Stanford University Press), Chapter 2.

[39] Sandra L. Rierson, "Race and Gender Discrimination: A Historical Case for Equal Treatment under the Fourteenth Amendment," *Duke Journal of Gender Law & Policy* 1, no. 89 (1994): 89–117; Reva B. Siegel, "Home as Work: The First Woman's Rights Claims

her analysis was not mere hyperbole.[40] This is not to overstate the validity of the comparison, however, for although a fine legal line differentiated the status of free women from that of enslaved people, the social and cultural implications of this difference were profound and absolute.[41]

Many commentators nonetheless embraced discourses of slavery to describe that which *was*—and *was not*—chattel slavery. As this institution began to define the meaning of racial "otherness" in the United States, chattel slavery became the catalyst, the signifier; in becoming a discourse unto itself, slavery as a concept became a referent, the signified.[42] Sometimes this language could be completely or very nearly abstracted from chattel slavery; and at other times, it was intrinsically and directly linked to actual institutions across the American South, the Caribbean, and even the Ottoman Empire and beyond. In the early republic, antislavery advocates identified the increasing racial specificity of chattel slavery at the same time as embracing the obliqueness of discourses of slavery, applying the latter to describe sin and religious experiences as much as love and desire, dreams, and stimulants.[43] "There is no slavery of the body and mind," antebellum health reformers concluded, "equal to that of the opium taker."[44] In the process, enslaved people of African descent became "surrogate selves," mediating what Toni Morrison describes as the lure and elusiveness of human freedom.[45] The "Slave [is] a happy man compared with the drunkard," claimed the temperance, women's rights, and dress reformer Amelia Bloomer in 1850.[46] This sentiment echoed through a later novella, Frances Ellen Watkins Harper's *Sowing and Reaping: A Temperance Story* (1877), which continued to embrace discourses of slavery to describe dependency on alcohol. Historians have too often separated the woman-slave analogy from a historical moment when it was one among many expressions of such reform rhetoric.

Concerning Wives' Household Labor, 1850–1880," *Yale Law Journal* 103, no. 5 (1994): 1100; Pateman, *The Sexual Contract*, 119–120.

[40] P.W. Davis, "Woman's Rights Convention in Boston," *Lily*, November 1855.
[41] Broeck, *Gender and the Abjection*, 37–38.
[42] Sánchez-Eppler, *Touching Liberty*, 9.
[43] David Brion Davis, "Declaring Equality: Sisterhood and Slavery," in *Women's Rights and Transatlantic Antislavery in the Era of Emancipation*, eds. Kathryn Kish Sklar and James Brewer Stewart (New Haven: Yale University Press, 2007), 14.
[44] "Horrors of Opium Eating," *Water-Cure Journal* (from the *Sun*), 1 January 1846.
[45] Toni Morrison, *Playing in the Dark: Whiteness and the Literary Imagination* (New York: Vintage, 1993), 7.
[46] "Slavery and Intemperance," *Lily*, May 1850.

David Roediger describes this phenomenon as a "'Down with all slavery!' position"—a position that could, in practice, be quite difficult to maintain. Antebellum abolitionism taught that chattel slavery was the harshest category of oppression and most reformers and other antislavery sympathizers were deeply critical of chattel slavery. However, at least some of the proponents of a broader definition of slavery might equivocate about the abolition of chattel slavery itself.[47] Despite these differences, many antebellum reformers espoused a more unequivocal commitment to antislavery principles—if not always to immediate abolitionism—than their contemporaries. This made antislavery an anathema to anti-abolitionists, proslavery ideologues, and lawmakers, who instead used discourses of slavery to justify social hierarchy, including the enslavement of people of African descent and the subjugation of women. Such polyvalence reveals the competing political projects to which a woman-as-slave worldview could be dedicated, including progressive, moderate, and even conservative ideals. Each of these differing and competing perspectives contributed to the expansive meanings that came to be associated with discourses of slavery.

Those who embraced a woman-as-slave worldview assumed it would be widely understood if not necessarily accepted. An address by a reformer or a lawmaker might only make a brief exclamation about the slavery of woman—either in elegiac acceptance or indignant condemnation—and expect their conclusions to be easily comprehensible. Others developed more detailed, rigorous, and extended comparisons of the condition of women versus that of enslaved people. As early as the 1860s, such assertions began to be redefined in terms of a comparison between sex and race rather than just woman and slave. A less emphatic expression of this logic occurred through comparisons between social movements, particularly abolitionism and the women's rights movement. To more fully appreciate how the woman-slave analogy operated, it is necessary to consider the myriad ways in which reformers, proslavery ideologues, and other commentators embraced each of these approaches.

As a result, the woman-slave analogy offered countless reformers a framework through which to begin to consider the relationship between different forms of oppression. Recent scholarship suggests that the

[47] David R. Roediger, *The Wages of Whiteness: Race and the Making of the American Working Class* (London: Verso, 1991, 2007), 82.

inextricable connections between gender, race, and class were "powerfully theorized" during the antebellum era.[48] In her analysis of the sexual contract and feminist responses to traditional contract theory, Carole Pateman comes closest to conceptualizing the comparison between slavery and the status of women as a theoretical approach. Since its earliest articulations, Sabine Broeck also argues, the "infamous and persistent use of the analogy of 'women' with and as 'slaves'" has been at the center of feminist thought. This intellectual tradition has long made claims to women's full humanity by aggressively constructing "a philosophical, political, and sociomaterial line between 'woman' and 'slave,' between 'human' and 'thing.'" Such rhetoric provided what Broeck describes as "a springboard for white women to begin theorizing a catalogue of their own demands for an acknowledgement of modern, free subjectivity as antagonistic to enslavement."[49] However, while some scholars concede that the woman-slave analogy did offer what might be considered an analytical or theoretical framework, the full implications of this recognition remain obscured.

It is challenging to reconsider the woman-slave analogy as an analytical or theoretical approach because the logic that informed it was deeply racist and irrevocably flawed. But it is exactly because the woman-slave analogy was so inadequate that it must be reconsidered as having offered nineteenth-century reformers the foundations for a theoretical framework. Not all attempts to theorize oppression have been successful; indeed, those who embraced the woman-slave analogy to pursue radical political projects were perhaps mostly unsuccessful in realizing their aims. In order to better appreciate its limitations, it is therefore important to consider the woman-slave analogy as a theoretical framework on its own terms. This book does not condone such rhetoric, nor does it make any attempt to reclaim, recover, or advocate the woman-slave analogy as a redeemable product of feminist thought. But it does suggest that scholars aim to move beyond centering analyses around its palpable racism to discover what else these myriad reformers might have been trying to say, through what amounted to rhetorical strategies that now appear both unprincipled and

---

[48] Lori Merish, *Archives of Labor: Working-Class Women and Literary Culture in the Antebellum United States* (Durham: Duke University Press, 2017), 10, Chapter 4.

[49] Broeck, *Gender and the Abjection*, 17, 39. For scholarship which inspired this analysis, see: Hortense Spillers, "Mama's Baby, Papa's Maybe: An American Grammar Book," *Diacritics* 17, no. 22 (1987): 64–81; Saidiya V. Hartman, *Scenes of Subjection: Terror, Slavery, and Self-Making in Nineteenth-Century America* (New York: Oxford University Press, 1997).

opportunistic. For even despite such severe limitations, the woman-slave analogy was mobilized with such persistence and determination that it actually emerged in contexts that might appear surprising.

A greater diversity of reformers both condoned and promoted a woman-as-slave worldview than historians and feminist scholars have previously appreciated. This reflects the fact that the American literary tradition is neither "exclusively white or black in its subject matter or in the historical experience it refracts," as literary scholar Ann duCille argues; such a false dichotomy obfuscates what are, in fact, "complex and interlocking cultural and linguistic phenomena."[50] These conclusions can be extended beyond antebellum literary culture to the realm of reform discourse. To this end, important and unexpected parallels emerge between the rhetoric of nineteenth-century reformers from different backgrounds. "Has woman *no* rights? Is she the *natural* slave of man?" one correspondent asked a temperance and women's rights periodical in 1852.[51] It is perhaps contrary to expectation to discover that similar questions were sometimes posed and comparable conclusions reached in the abolitionist print culture of African Americans. Only months later, *Frederick Douglass' Paper*, edited by the famous self-emancipated abolitionist Frederick Douglass, offered similar remarks about the 1852 women's rights convention in Syracuse, New York: "It is well said by someone, 'as woman was the first, so will she be the last slave.' May God speed the day of universal emancipation!"[52] This suggests that African Americans could and did use discourses of slavery in discussions about women's rights—the rights chattel slavery annihilated—in a manner that was both familiar and distinct.

One scholar suggests that African-American women "rarely formulated" such arguments, yet they did so with more frequency than might reasonably be expected.[53] Importantly, African-American women did not experience any sense of confusion about the meaning of chattel slavery or the implications of liberation from the "metaphorical slavery" that so many free white women espoused.[54] Such references to chattel slavery were grounded in historical fact, not analogy or metaphor, because, as Evelyn

---

[50] Ann duCille, *The Coupling Convention: Sex, Text, and Tradition in Black Women's Fiction* (New York: Oxford University Press, 1993), 8–9.

[51] Jane Frohock, "Maine Ahead on Woman's Rights," *Lily*, June 1852.

[52] J.T., "The National Woman's Rights Convention at Syracuse," *Frederick Douglass' Paper*, 17 September 1852.

[53] Newman, *White Women's Rights*, 6.

[54] Yellin, *Women and Sisters*, 79. See also: Giddings, *When and Where I Enter*, 70.

Brooks Higginbotham argues, black and white women constructed and represented their gendered identities in "very different, indeed antagonistic, racialized contexts."[55] However, as free and self-emancipated women of color began to consider the degree to which certain gender conventions also inhibited their freedom, the woman-slave analogy gained a degree of influence. This occurred more frequently in the postbellum than the antebellum era, but examples of both emerge. Importantly, it was a qualified advocacy of such rhetoric: African-American women mobilized discourses of slavery primarily to analyze chattel slavery and its gendered legacies for freedwomen. In their own voices, as well as by quoting others, some African Americans participated, however fleetingly, in the perpetuation of a woman-as-slave worldview.

The woman-slave analogy was never simply a one-way comparison; it offered an analytical and theoretical framework that was constantly being contested, reimagined, and reconfigured. As Carla L. Peterson emphasizes, the prevalence of analogy in the antebellum era is particularly instructive. Analogy can be said to imitate the "similarity between two unlike entities," Peterson explains; it "allows the speaker to select the term with which to compare the chosen object or idea and, in the process, to emphasize one particular feature over all others." Functioning "as a form of explanation," analogy finds the "same cause" to have "given rise to the similarity of features." This is the point at which its effectiveness collapses, for "analogy often seeks to suppress what does not fit; and yet, since similarity never means exact sameness, difference always remains."[56] It was this very sense of sameness that preoccupied the majority of white women, severely undermining their ability to look beyond their own situation in advocating women's rights. However, at least some of their black and white contemporaries discovered in their own expression of the woman-slave analogy a greater awareness of the existence of many different forms of oppression.

The Woman as Slave in Nineteenth-Century American Social Movements seeks to historicize the use of the woman-slave analogy across the long

---

[55] Carla L. Peterson, "'And We Claim Our Rights': The Rights Rhetoric of Black and White Women Activists before the Civil War," in *Sister Circle: Black Women and Work*, eds. Sharon Harley, and the Black Women and Work Collective (New Brunswick: Rutgers University Press, 2002), 131; Evelyn Brooks Higginbotham, "African-American Women's History and the Metalanguage of Race," *Signs: Journal of Women in Culture and Society* 17, no. 2 (1992): 258.

[56] Peterson, "'And We Claim Our Rights'," 139.

nineteenth century. It analyzes the changing meaning of this rhetoric through the antislavery, women's rights, dress reform, labor reform, suffrage, free love, racial uplift, and anti-vice movements. As this book reveals, women and men, black and white, enslaved and free, from the most famous and infamous reformers to the rank-and-file, championed a woman-as-slave worldview. It emphasizes the voices of individuals across the social strata, from different racial, cultural, and regional backgrounds who both supported and rejected women's rights. The woman-slave analogy was an undoubtedly racist construction, but it was also significant insofar as it offered the foundations of a theoretical framework that facilitated fierce debates about the woman question.

This book remains mindful of the continuities that shaped the mobilization of this rhetoric, particularly the racism that always remained at its foundations, while also tracing the implications of its transformation.[57] The Civil War and its aftermath were central to the shifting meanings that came to be associated with the woman-slave analogy; and the transformation that occurred followed a counterintuitive logic. During the antebellum era, a sense of the connections between gender, racial, and class oppression was engendered not through abstract allusions to many different states of slavery, but rather, through a direct interrogation of chattel slavery's brutality. When the woman-slave analogy appeared in isolation from a broader consideration of the institution's systemic abuses, reformers and other commentators more willfully overlooked the subjugation of enslaved people of African descent. Increasingly emphatic expressions of this rhetoric emerged during the Civil War era because, as far as the majority of free whites were concerned, slave emancipation had solved the problem of chattel slavery. Hereafter, white suffragists, free love advocates, and anti-vice reformers mobilized the woman-slave analogy in an ever more opportunistic manner. Across the Reconstruction era and beyond, white reformers collectively developed the most racist and virulent expressions of this rhetoric yet. Quite the opposite was true of African-American reformers, who consistently used discourses of slavery to explore the connections between race, gender, and class, always remaining attentive to the historical reality of chattel slavery and its unfinished legacy.

---

[57] On the need for feminist historians to remain mindful of both continuity and change in women's history, see: Judith M. Bennett, *History Matters: Patriarchy and the Challenge of Feminism* (Philadelphia: University of Pennsylvania Press, 2006).

This book is divided into three parts: Transnational Social Movements; Between Public and Private; and The Politics of Slavery and Emancipation. Each subsequent chapter is structured around a theme that loosely corresponds with a social movement: antislavery, marriage, fashion, labor, suffrage, and sex. Chapter 2 analyzes how women in transatlantic antislavery networks reimagined a claim that had been pioneered amongst previous generations of literary women: that all women were born to slavery. As Chap. 3 reveals, abolitionists, women's rights reformers, and proslavery commentators all mobilized discourses of slavery to criticize or embrace the patriarchal norms of marriage. Chapter 4 considers the process whereby reformers began to theorize fashion, as the rank-and-file began to embrace the rhetoric that more famous reformers propagated in their advocacy of dress reform. As Chap. 5 illustrates, labor reformers, especially working-class and African-American women, used discourses of slavery to consider the rigors of both capitalist exploitation in the North and chattel slavery in the South. Turning to the question of women's enfranchisement and universal suffrage in the wake of slave emancipation, Chap. 6 considers the manner in which suffragists used the woman-slave analogy to approach the political debates of the Reconstruction era. Chapter 7 traces the analogy's transformation across the nineteenth century by exploring the free love, racial uplift, and anti-vice movements. Finally, Chap. 8 concludes by situating the woman-slave analogy as a precursor to and locus for some of the contestations and provocations that prompted later feminist theoretical approaches to the analysis of gender, race, and class.

The Woman as Slave in Nineteenth-Century American Social Movements assembles a particularly unsettling vision of feminism's past. This history of the woman-slave analogy illuminates the shifting trajectories of this particularly fraught rhetorical strategy and highlights the waves of consternation it caused. However, at least some of its adherents championed a woman-as-slave worldview in an attempt to understand the connections between many forms of oppression. This rhetoric might be better analyzed not only as an asymmetric literary device or reform strategy, but also in terms of the political ideology of those who embraced it. Who used the woman-slave analogy to pursue radical politics? Who, in turn, embraced a woman-as-slave worldview to maintain the status quo? And whose perspectives transformed over the course of the nineteenth century? These insights have implications for our understanding of women's history, the history of women's rights movements, and intersectional feminist activism in the twenty-first century.

PART I

Transatlantic Social Movements

GOD save each Female's Right,
Show to her ravish'd fight
Woman is Free;
Let Freedom's voice prevail,
And draw aside the vale,
Supreme Indulgence hail,
Sweet Liberty.

Think of the cruel chain,
Endure no more the pain of slavery: –
Why should a tyrant bid;
Her providence assign'd
Her soul to be confin'd,
Is not her gentle mind
 By virtue led?

A voice re-echoing round,
With joyful accents found,
"Woman is Free;
Assert the noble claim,
All selfish arts disdain;"
Hark how the note proclaim,
"Woman is Free!"

By a Lady, "Tune—*God Save America*,"
Philadelphia Minerva I, no. 37 (1795)

CHAPTER 2

"All Women are Born Slaves": Antislavery, Women's Rights, and Transatlantic Reform Networks

In the decades prior to the Civil War, a sculpture wrought by Hiram Powers, an American living in Europe, captured the imagination in Britain and the United States. Completed in Florence across 1843–1844, this sculpture depicted a young Greek Christian woman captured in the Greek War of Independence and about to be sold in a Turkish bazaar. Provocative due to her chains, controversial due to her nudity, and unsettling due to her whiteness, *The Greek Slave* (Fig. 2.1) became a celebrated example of the era's penchant for ideal sculpture. First exhibited in London in 1845, *The Greek Slave* achieved even greater fame and adulation during its 1847–1848 American tour. Handbooks and art reviews offered a guide for interpreting the sculpture's nudity, encouraging spectators to consider her plight in terms of her physical vulnerability and resounding spiritual fortitude.[1]

But these were not the only interpretations *The Greek Slave* provoked. When it was displayed in the Crystal Palace as part of the American exhibit at the Great Exhibition, London's *Punch* made a connection that many bourgeois spectators would not. Its 1851 cartoon, "The Virginian Slave" (Fig. 2.2), though satirical, did not feature a white European woman but

[1] See: Joy S. Kasson, *Marble Queens and Captives: Women in Nineteenth-Century American Sculpture* (New Haven: Yale University Press, 1990), Chapter 3.

© The Author(s) 2019
A. Stevenson, *The Woman as Slave in Nineteenth-Century American Social Movements*, Palgrave Studies in the History of Social Movements, https://doi.org/10.1007/978-3-030-24467-5_2

Fig. 2.1 Hiram Powers, *The Greek Slave*. Alamy, Image ID: D2XWBM. Artokoloro Quint Lox Limited/ Alamy Stock Photo

rather an enslaved woman of African descent.[2] Few had previously been willing to extend their disdain for the enslavement of a European woman to the horrors of chattel slavery in the American South. Others were inspired to a different response, seeing in this ideal sculpture a powerful analogue for women's subjugation to men. When the abolitionist and women's rights reformer, Lucy Stone, had witnessed *The Greek Slave* during its American tour, she reflected on how it "stood in the silence, with fettered

[2] John Tenniel, "The Virginian Slave," *Punch* 20 (1851): 236.

Fig. 2.2 John Tenniel, "The Virginian Slave," *Punch* 20 (1851): 236. © Punch Limited

THE VIRGINIAN SLAVE.
INTENDED AS A COMPANION TO POWER'S "GREEK SLAVE."

hands and half-averted face—so emblematic of women."[3] While Stone was moved to consider the situation of free women, Frederick Douglass' abolitionist newspaper, the *North Star*, contemplated the situation of enslaved women everywhere. "*Chains*! CHAINS! on limbs so human!" one correspondent admonished. "*[A]ll slave girls are* GREEK, and *all slave masters* TURKS, wicked cruel and hateful; be … their country Algiers or Alabama,

---

[3] Alice Stone Blackwell, *Lucy Stone: Pioneer of Women's Rights* (Charlottesville: University Press of Virginia, 1930), 89.

Congo or Carolina, the same."[4] *The Greek Slave* emerged as the popular personification of the complex rhetorical impulses being articulated across Europe and the United States to describe the subjugation of women.[5]

These were just some of the transatlantic contestations that contributed to the changing meaning of the woman-slave analogy. Across the sixteenth and seventeenth centuries, the slavery analogy had become a distinctive feature of European philosophy. "Man is born free; and everywhere he is in chains," Jean Jacques Rousseau declared in 1762.[6] These proclamations were at once connected to and surprisingly abstracted from actual institutions of chattel slavery. While men's capacity for freedom offered the foundations for the social contract, the sexual contract was one of subjection for women. As Carole Pateman argues, the sexual contract dictated that "women are not born free; women have no natural freedom."[7] Gradually, European women began to contemplate the degree to which the slavery analogy might be an apt description of their own situation. To not be free, however, did not—and does not—automatically represent a state of slavery. Soon, the claims of European philosophers diverged from the visions espoused by people of African descent, whose own writings sometimes reflected upon the loss of freedom.

This chapter considers the process whereby abolitionist women in the United States became preoccupied with the woman-slave analogy. It charts how, by the 1830s, their interpretation had become explicitly linked to chattel slavery, especially in the American South. However, women's emerging awareness of their own lack of freedom had not always been so precisely expressed in terms of chattel slavery as a racialized institution. Across the previous centuries, the slavery analogy had gradually gained explicitly racial connotations. This transformation occurred alongside the expansion of the transatlantic slave trade, the racialization of chattel slavery as an institution, and the founding and expansion of Britain's colonies in North America. Hereafter, greater proximity to or distance from chattel slavery came to shape how reformers mobilized the woman-slave analogy in transatlantic antislavery discourse and beyond.

[4] S.F.W. Bloomfield, "The Greek Slave," *North Star*, 3 October 1850.
[5] See: Jean Fagan Yellin, *Women and Sisters: The Antislavery Feminists in American Culture* (New Haven: Yale University Press, 1989), Chapter 5.
[6] Jean Jacques Rousseau, *The Social Contract & Discourses*, trans. G.D.H. Cole (New York: E.P. Dutton and Company, 1762, 1782, 1913), 6.
[7] Carole Pateman, *The Sexual Contract* (Stanford: Stanford University Press, 1988), 6.

Men Are Made for Liberty, and Women for Slavery

Philosophers have long found salience in the idea of slavery as representative of a total loss of autonomy. For European men, the slavery analogy emerged as a blunt metaphor to describe a generalized political subjugation. Women, too, considered the efficacy of the slavery analogy—principally to criticize the patriarchal institution of marriage, but also to deliberate the extent to which their subjugation was lifelong. Mary Astell, for example, responded to her contemporaries by penning what would become a famous adage: "*If* all men are born free, *how is it that all women are born slaves?*"[8] But these analyses were initially only connected to actual institutions of chattel slavery inconsistently. Ideas first constructed around abstractions soon became more connected to the transatlantic slave trade or chattel slavery in European colonies around the world. As early as the seventeenth century, Kathryn Kish Sklar and James Brewer Stewart argue, some women began to understand "their own emancipation in terms that drew on their understanding of [chattel] slavery as a gendered institution."[9] But as European women began to insist that they had been born to slavery, African women recalled being born to freedom.

Many nineteenth-century reformers insisted that women's history had been a history of slavery. Bold assertions appeared in Lydia Maria Child's *Brief History of the Condition of Women: In Various Ages and Nations* (1835) and Thomas Low Nichols' *Woman in All Ages and Nations* (1849).[10] These somewhat propagandistic analyses proved neither inconsistent nor wholly incompatible with the conclusions of later historians. In the ancient world, David Christian observes, greater disparities around class, occupation, and gender emerged following the institutionalization of social hierarchy and the market economy; and women's subordination developed alongside concepts such as the state, taxation, and slavery.[11] Feminist historians also speculate about the emergence of slavery as an institution in ancient societies. According to Gerda Lerner, patrilineal

---

[8] Mary Astell, *Some Reflections Upon Marriage* (London: R. Wilkin, 1700/1706), Preface. See: Pateman, *The Sexual Contract*, 120–129.

[9] Kathryn Kish Sklar and James Brewer Stewart, eds. *Women's Rights and Transatlantic Antislavery in the Era of Emancipation* (New Haven: Yale University Press, 2007), xii–xiii. For the gradual racialization of chattel slavery and other forms of unfreedom across the Atlantic world, see: Seymour Drescher, *Abolition: A History of Slavery and Antislavery* (Cambridge: Cambridge University Press, 2009).

[10] For women's historical writing, see: Mary Spongberg, *Writing Women's History since the Renaissance* (Basingstoke: Palgrave Macmillan, 2002).

[11] David Christian, *Maps of Time: An Introduction to Big History* (Berkeley: University of California Press, 2005), 257, 263.

marital exchange and concubinage led to the commodification of female sexuality and reproductive capacity. Slavery evolved alongside inscriptions of power and gendered subordination, primarily from the sexual exploitation of female war captives. Even as slavery declined across medieval Europe, evidence suggests that women overwhelmingly remained in bondage.[12] "Women, always available for subordination," according to Lerner, had come to be "seen as inferior by being like slaves."[13]

In the works of ancient philosophers, too, as much as in social custom, the archetypical slave had been a woman.[14] Classical philosophy believed in a dichotomy between the mind and body, attributes that were respectively gendered as male and female. This influenced ideas about biological difference and self-sovereignty, traits considered essential for democratic engagement. The participation of women and enslaved people in civil society was curtailed, partially because they were perceived to lack self-sovereignty. Yet, in these ancient societies, the wives of citizens were imbued with a degree of privilege and security that was not extended to enslaved women and men. Deeply influenced by classical thought, later Enlightenment philosophers routinely failed to make such an important distinction between different classes of women, especially married women, and enslaved people.[15] This omission had enduring consequences for the development of a woman-as-slave worldview.

The Enlightenment cultivated a blossoming debate about the nature of freedom. Philosophers began to use the slavery analogy to condemn the tyranny of sovereign rulers, as well as to assert the natural freedom with which men were born. However, the dichotomy between mind and body continued to exclude women from Enlightenment ideals. Political authority was deemed artificial, but domestic authority and women's subjection to men were believed to be natural. This justified patriarchal hierarchy in a private realm to be structured by "a Master of a Family with all the subordinate Relations of Wife, Children, Servants, and Slaves, united under

---

[12] Susan Mosher Stuard, "Ancillary Evidence for the Decline of Medieval Slavery," *Past and Present*, no. 149 (1995): 3–28.

[13] Gerda Lerner, *The Creation of Patriarchy* (New York: Oxford University Press, 1986), Chapter 4, esp. 77–78, 100.

[14] Seymour Drescher and Stanley L. Engerman, eds. *A Historical Guide to World Slavery* (New York: Oxford University Press, 1998), xii.

[15] Elizabeth V. Spelman, *Inessential Woman: Problems of Exclusion in Feminist Thought* (Boston: Beacon Press, 1988).

the Domestic Rule of a Family," as John Locke articulated in 1690.[16] Women were believed to be incapable of participating in the social contract; a lack of reason made women unable to transcend sexual desire, contract theorists argued, so women could not act as individuals. Men, in turn, having overcome the rule of the father, had the reason necessary to uphold civil laws fraternally. This, Pateman argues, meant that men had an interest in maintaining the sexual contract, wherein women's sexual subjugation was a necessary but rarely considered antecedent to the social contract.[17]

The legal establishment increasingly inscribed the permanent minority of married women. Most clearly described in Sir William Blackstone's *Commentaries on the Laws of England* (1765–1769), coverture granted husbands near-absolute control of their wives' person and property. Significantly, Blackstone interspersed a chapter detailing his own thoughts on marriage between two other key chapters: "Of Master and Servant"; "Of Husband and Wife"; and "Of Parent and Child."[18] The expansion of women's legal disabilities also shaped cultural attitudes toward women. Alan Macfarlane describes the practice of "wife selling," an English public ritual where a woman could be "taken to a public place, perhaps with a halter round her neck," and "auctioned" to the highest bidder (usually prearranged), who would "buy" her and thereby become her husband. A response to stringent marriage laws, this informal and legally ambiguous practice became a popular method for obtaining *de facto* divorce, for it ensured divorce and remarriage in a single act that maintained patriarchal authority.[19]

The transatlantic slave trade created something of a moral and economic paradox for Enlightenment philosophers concerned with the nature of freedom. Across the seventeenth century, the violent capture and transportation of Africans from the coast of West Africa expanded to supply the

---

[16] John Locke, *Two Treatises of Government* (London: Awnsham and John Churchill, 1698), Section 86, 228. See also: Locke, *Two Treatises*, Section 82, 226.

[17] Pateman, *Sexual Contract*, 102–103.

[18] William Blackstone, *Commentaries on the Laws of England*, Vol. I (Oxford: Clarendon Press, 1765).

[19] Alan Macfarlane, *Marriage and Love in England: Modes of Reproduction, 1300–1840* (Oxford: Blackwell, 1986), 226–227; Pateman, *Sexual Contract*, 121–122. For later examples in the United States, see: "Treatment of Women," *Lily*, January 1851; "Wife Whipping Legal in this Country," *Woodhull and Claflin's Weekly* (from *Woman's Journal*), 9 September 1871; "Woman at Auction," *Woodhull and Claflin's Weekly* (from *New York Sun*), 29 March 1873.

Americas with enslaved labor.[20] Some Europeans remained unconvinced of the morality of the slave trade or chattel slavery. As the Baron de Montesquieu observed, the European massacre of Native Americans led to the enslavement and transportation of Africans who were then forced to labor in the Americas.[21] However, any uneasiness about chattel slavery and its violation of natural rights constituted an exception amid the transportation of enslaved peoples to British, Spanish, French, Dutch, and Portuguese colonies. Locke, for example, while not a slaveowner personally, held stock in the Royal African Company, a corporation with a monopoly on the slave trade.[22] "Every freeman," he believed, should have "absolute power and authority over his negro slaves, of what opinion or religion soever."[23] As emerging scientific theories about racial difference rationalized the enslavement of Africans, the philosophers and reformers who embraced the slavery analogy gradually became more influenced by chattel slavery's transformation into an explicitly racialized institution.

It was in this context that European women began to embrace the slavery analogy for their own purposes in the literary public sphere, often in a manner quite abstracted from chattel slavery itself. Literary women initially used discourses of slavery to express concerns about the institution of marriage, especially the injustice of coverture, and the inferiority of girls' education. Karen Offen describes how Madeleine de Scudéry, a seventeenth-century French novelist and central figure in salon culture, described women's experience of marriage as analogous to slavery. Although some of de Scudéry's early novels were set amongst ancient slaveholding cultures, they did not emphasize any real connection between the slavery analogy and actual histories of bondage.[24] Some British women likewise described marriage as well as politics in similar terms. As power, liberty, and slavery became subjects of public debate during the English Civil War

[20] David Brion Davis, *Inhuman Bondage: The Rise and Fall of Slavery in the New World* (Oxford: Oxford University Press, 2006); Drescher, *Abolition*; Manisha Sinha, *The Slave's Cause: A History of Abolition* (New Haven: Yale University Press, 2016).

[21] Baron de Montesquieu, *The Spirit of the Laws*, eds. and trans. Anne M. Cohler, Basia C. Miller, and Harold S. Stone (Cambridge: Cambridge University Press, 1748/1989), 250.

[22] Pateman, *Sexual Contract*, 71; Drescher, *Abolition*, 77.

[23] "The Fundamental Constitutions of Carolina, Drawn Up by John Locke, March 1, 1669," in *The Colonial Records of North Carolina*, Vol. I: 1662–1712, ed. William L. Saunders (Raleigh: P.M. Hale, 1886), 204.

[24] Karen Offen, "How (and Why) the Analogy of Marriage with Slavery Provided the Springboard for Women's Rights Demands in France, 1640–1848," in *Women's Rights and Transatlantic Antislavery*, 59–73.

of 1642–1651, women began to reconsider their own status.[25] Men "usurped a Supremacy to themselves," playwright Margaret Cavendish, the Duchess of Newcastle, claimed in 1653, a supremacy maintained through a "Tyrannical Government" that rendered women "more and more enslaved."[26] Why, Astell went on to ask in *Some Reflections Upon Marriage* (1700), should women receive an "ill Education and unequal Marriage," only to become "yok'd for Life" to the "Will and Pleasure of an absolute Lord and Master?"[27] Addressing their own concerns, as women, this use of the slavery analogy remained more or less abstracted from the contemporaneous expansion of chattel slavery in the colonial enterprise.

Discourses of slavery, therefore, developed in the context of the "problematic of slavery" as it existed in transatlantic literary, cultural, and political discourse.[28] Rarely did the proclamations that women were born to slavery—or, as Cavendish declared in 1662, "Men are made for *Liberty*, and *Women* for *slavery*"[29]—allude to actually enslaved persons. Antislavery literature, in contrast, was dedicated to denouncing chattel slavery as it existed in European colonies. Only from about 1670 onward did British women begin to look toward these colonies to secure "political self-empowerment" through what Moira Ferguson describes as "Anglo-Africanism." This was a popular "colonialist discourse about slavery that unwittingly intensified negative attitudes toward Africans in general and slaves in particular." For British women to mediate an "unconscious sense of social invalidation, through representations of the colonial other," enslaved peoples became representationally objectified, marginalized, silenced, pitied, and controlled.[30] As an antislavery ethos expanded across the eighteenth century, discourses of slavery were increasingly

---

[25] Jerome Nadelhaft, "The Englishwoman's Sexual Civil War: Feminist Attitudes towards Men, Women, and Marriage 1650–1740," *Journal of the History of Ideas* 43, no. 4 (1982): 555–579.

[26] Margaret Cavendish, *The World's Olio*, 2nd ed. (London: A. Maxwell, 1653/1671), Preface.

[27] Astell, *Some Reflections*, 3–4.

[28] Carl Plasa and Betty J. Ring, eds. *The Discourse of Slavery: From Aphra Behn to Toni Morrison* (Oxon: Routledge, 1994), xiii.

[29] Margaret Cavendish, *Orations of Divers Sorts, Accommodated to Divers Places* (London: 1662), 183.

[30] Moira Ferguson, *Subject to Others: British Women Writers and Colonial Slavery, 1670–1834* (New York: Routledge, 1992), 4–6.

counterpointed by discourses of abolition.[31] Yet, as Srividhya Swaminathan and Adam R. Beach emphasize, many British writers still "invoked slavery to describe a variety of states, both physical and metaphorical, without the kind of careful acknowledgment of difference in forms of enslavement and unfree labor that scholars are so careful to note today."[32]

The few women of African descent to emerge in the literary public sphere perceived chattel slavery quite differently. Phillis Wheatley, an enslaved woman and poet, gained transatlantic fame with the London publication of *Poems on Various Subjects, Religious and Moral* (1773). Wheatley treated the themes of slavery and freedom in a manner distinct from either her antislavery or literary contemporaries.[33] In contradistinction to the many European women who believed themselves to have been born to slavery, some of Wheatley's poems implied that she had not, in fact, been born enslaved. At least a century earlier, Europeans had been alerted to the possibilities consequent upon this crucial difference. An immensely popular novel by Englishwoman Aphra Behn, *Oroonoko; or, The Royal Slave* (1678), was the first novel by a woman; its title character becomes horrified at the prospect of his child being born into chattel slavery.[34] Something similar was evoked in Wheatley's 1773 poem to the Earl of Dartmouth. Describing "from whence my love of Freedom sprung," Wheatley told of how she was "snatched from Afric's fancied happy seat," finally imploring: "Can I then but pray/Others may never feel tyrannic sway?"[35] Since Wheatley became enslaved as a child, after being captured and transported to colonial North America, her writings indicated that she was not, in fact, born to slavery.

The 1790s constituted the moment at which the idea of slavery could no longer be so easily abstracted from institutionalized chattel slavery around the world. Slavery became at once both "fact and metaphor," as

---

[31] Brycchan Carey, Ellis Markman, and Sara Salih, eds. *Discourses of Slavery and Abolition: Britain and its Colonies, 1760–1838* (Basingstoke: Palgrave Macmillan, 2004).

[32] Srividhya Swaminathan and Adam R. Beach, eds. *Invoking Slavery in the Eighteenth-Century British Imagination* (Farnham: Ashgate, 2013), 1.

[33] Glenna Matthews, *The Rise of Public Woman: Woman's Power and Woman's Place in the United States, 1630–1970* (New York: Oxford University Press, 1992), 50.

[34] Vron Ware, *Beyond the Pale: White Women, Racism, and History* (London: Verso, 1992, 2015), 51.

[35] "To the Right Honorable William, Earl of Dartmouth, His Majesty's Principal Secretary of State for North-America," in *The Collected Works of Phillis Wheatley*, ed. John Shields (New York: Oxford University Press, 1988).

R.S. White describes it.[36] Yet the slavery analogy continued to be employed in a manner both abstracted from and in direct reference to chattel slavery. Although the women who challenged the *"Liberté, égalité, fraternité"* proclaimed by the French Revolution largely turned to these abstractions, at least one influential figure also embraced an antislavery ethos. In 1792, Olympe de Gouges finalized her antislavery play, *L'Esclavage des Noirs* (*Black Slavery*). Initially conceptualized in 1784 for the *Comedie française* as a subdued narrative of "oriental" slaves, de Gouges reimagined her play as an outright antislavery narrative recounting the escape of "negro" slaves. The play's transformation did not exhibit purely opportunistic abolitionism, however; it represented what Gregory S. Brown describes as de Gouges' "deliberate self-fashionings" prior to the French Revolution.[37]

Only one year previous, de Gouges had penned her *Déclaration des droits de la femme et de la citoyenne* (*Declaration of the Rights of Woman and the Female Citizen*). This constituted a response to the *Déclaration des droits de l'homme et du citoyen* (*Declaration of the Rights of Man and the Male Citizen*), drafted in 1789 by General Lafayette, Thomas Jefferson, and Honoré Mirabeau. In 1791, de Gouges sought to extend the rights of man to women, as well as to instigate a separate discussion about women.[38] "What advantage have you received from the Revolution?" she asked:

> Woman, wake up; ... discover your rights. ... Enslaved man has multiplied his strength and needs recourse to yours to break his chains. Having become free, he has become unjust to his companion.[39]

While de Gouges' antislavery and women's rights philosophies seemingly informed each other, her works also reveal the degree of inconsistency with which many commentators embraced discourses of slavery.

---

[36] R.S. White, *Natural Rights and the Birth of Romanticism in the 1790s* (Basingstoke: Palgrave Macmillan, 2005), Chapter 6.

[37] Gregory S. Brown, "The Self-Fashionings of Olympe De Gouges, 1784–1789," *Eighteenth-Century Studies* 34, no. 3 (2001): 383–401.

[38] Joan Wallach Scott, "French Feminists and the Rights of 'Man': Olympe De Gouges' Declarations," *History Workshop* 28 (1989): 9–10.

[39] Olympe de Gouges, "The Declaration of the Rights of Woman, 1791," in *Women in Revolutionary Paris, 1789–1795: Selected Documents*, eds. Darline Gay Levy, Harriet Branson Applewhite, and Mary Durham Johnson (Urbana: University of Illinois Press, 1979), 92. Original: "*Femme, réveille-toi ... reconnais tes droits. ... L'homme esclave a multiplié ses forces, a eu besoin de recourir aux tiennes pour briser ses fers. Devenu libre, il est devenu injuste envers sa compagne. Ô femmes! ... Quels sont les avantages que vous avez recueillis dans la Révolution?*"

In the years following the French Revolution, Englishwoman Mary Wollstonecraft made significant contributions to the transformation of the slavery analogy. Her most famous work, *A Vindication of the Rights of Woman* (1792), mobilized this rhetoric to criticize women's subjugation, leading one scholar to argue that "it is not an exaggeration to say that [slavery] serves as an interpretative and organizational device of the text." Analogy and metaphor acted as the "figurative layer" which underwrote the *Vindication*'s philosophical and moral arguments to create both "internal coherence [and a] sense of urgency."[40] Wollstonecraft explored themes of love and marriage, education and reason, politics and fashion. Women "may be convenient slaves," she argued, "but slavery will have its constant effect, degrading the master and the abject dependent." Men, in turn, were prone to "act like a tyrant, and tyranny" would, Wollstonecraft observed, "ever undermine morality." Although the majority of her analysis was abstracted from chattel slavery, she periodically experimented with more direct overtures to other tyrannical institutions. Speaking at one point of the "husband who lords it in his little harem," Wollstonecraft went on to ask: "Is one half of the human species, like the poor African slaves, to be subject to prejudices that brutalize them[?]"[41] Chattel slavery in the European colonies offered what many literary women saw as an increasingly concrete comparison for women's oppression.

For Wollstonecraft, the slavery analogy offered a more apt description of the condition of women than it did either for the condition of men or for humanity more generally. While her earlier work, *A Vindication of the Rights of Men* (1790), had referred to slavery only five times, her more famous 1792 work contained more than 80 references to slavery; what Ferguson describes as "a metonymic chain of the tyrannized" included, for Wollstonecraft, both women and enslaved people of African descent. By invoking the Eastern harem alongside colonial chattel slavery, Wollstonecraft emerged as "a political pioneer, fundamentally altering the definition of rights and paving the way for a much wider cultural dialogue."[42] Yet, in making this connection, she also contributed to bringing the slavery analogy into an ever more

---

[40] Himani Bannerji, "Mary Wollstonecraft, Feminism and Humanism: A Spectrum of Reading," in *Mary Wollstonecraft and 200 Years of Feminisms*, ed. Eileen Janes Yeo (London: Rivers Oram Press, 1997), 229–232, 239–242.

[41] Mary Wollstonecraft, *A Vindication of the Rights of Woman* (London: J. Johnson, 1792), x–xi, 158, 330.

[42] Moira Ferguson, "Mary Wollstonecraft and the Problematic of Slavery," *Feminist Review* 42 (1992): 82, 92, 98–99.

unambiguous dialogue with chattel slavery. Wollstonecraft, like so many other European literary women, would constantly focus her analysis on free white women at the expense of the experiences of actually enslaved people. Thus, this feminist foremother laid the foundations for later expressions of the woman-slave analogy, which, as Sabine Broeck suggests, would become ever more grounded in a violently anti-Black imaginary of an enslaved, abjected African.[43]

The connections being established amongst literary women soon emerged in visual culture. William Blake's 1796 engraving, "Europe Supported by Africa and America," portrayed each woman as an analogue for her continent to inscribe a connection between colonial, racial, and gender oppression. Historians offer multiple and sometimes competing interpretations of this engraving. Originally published in John Gabriel Stedman's South American travel diary, it presented the continents, "equal and interlinked," as the three Graces of Greek mythology.[44] For Blake, slavery represented "a paradigm for all injustice": existing as it did at the core of all unequal relationships, slavery was the one term that could fully encapsulate the violation or loss of natural rights.[45] Saree Makdisi finds ambiguity in this engraving, suggesting that it can be read as "a critique of a world system based on inequality and brutal exploitation," rather than "as evidence that Blake supported [chattel] slavery."[46] However, European women were not exploited in the same manner as enslaved people, even if they remained restricted by the social, cultural, and political structures identified by women such as Astell and Wollstonecraft. As Anne K. Mellor emphasizes, the women of color are cuffed by metal armbands that recall the slave's fetters, while the lone white woman wears a valuable necklace. It is Europe that is "supported" by Africa and the Americas, not vice versa; thus, European women are sustained by African and Native American women. It was on account of the labor and sexual exploitation of enslaved

---

[43] Sabine Broeck, *Gender and the Abjection of Blackness* (Albany: State University of New York Press, 2018), 55–67.

[44] Clare Midgley, *Women Against Slavery: The British Campaigns, 1780–1870* (London: Routledge, 1992), 29.

[45] White, *Natural Rights*, 169, 182.

[46] Saree Makdisi, *William Blake and the Impossible History of the 1790s* (Chicago: University of Chicago Press, 2003), 256.

Fig. 2.3 William Blake, "Europe supported by Africa & America" (London, Johnson and Edwards, 1796). Alamy, Image ID: MMGW37. The Picture Art Collection/Alamy Stock Photo

and Indigenous women that so many European women could enjoy the privileges they did possess (Fig. 2.3).[47]

In binding all together by a plant-based cord, did Blake seek to portray each woman and her continent as equally oppressed? Or did he seek to identify and criticize the interconnections in between? These possibilities spoke to the increasingly polyvalent meanings that discourses of slavery were developing on the eve of the nineteenth century. Soon, discourses of

[47] Anne K. Mellor, "Sex, Violence, and Slavery: Blake and Wollstonecraft," *Huntington Library Quarterly* 58, no. 3/4 (1995): 357–358.

slavery would be routinely mobilized in reform discourse as well as to express conservative and anti-reform perspectives. By the end of the eighteenth century, British reformers were no longer relying solely on "a univocal white woman-black male slave analogy," Clare Midgley suggests. Rather, reform discourse was increasingly shaped by "a 'triple discourse' of slavery" that might reference enslaved Africans in British colonies, or Orientalist discourses about women in Eastern harems, or colonized and Indigenous women in "savage" societies.[48] As revealed so powerfully by Hiram Powers' ideal sculpture, *The Greek Slave*, this polyvalence was becoming equally true in the United States. For Americans, however, the analogy between women and enslaved people in the American South or the Caribbean held greater credence.

Antislavery advocacy culminated in the abolition of the transatlantic slave trade in 1807, followed by the British Empire's Slavery Abolition Act of 1833. The broadening use of the woman-slave analogy in transatlantic reform discourse occurred in conjunction with these achievements. In 1834, the British antislavery movement gathered at a men's reception to commemorate the first anniversary of Emancipation Day. The celebration, Midgley notes, also observed the recent wedding of Priscilla Buxton, who had been co-secretary of the London Female Anti-Slavery Society and confidante to her father, the parliamentary antislavery leader Thomas Fowell Buxton. During this event, one man toasted that the bride "might long rejoice in the fetters put on that day as well as over those which she had assisted to break."[49] At a moment when women's rights reformers were seeking to reconfigure marriage as a site of women's oppression, antislavery men embraced discourses of slavery to applaud antislavery principles while simultaneously advocating the relative subjugation of women.

As the British Empire moved away from enslaved labor and toward other forms of free but deeply coercive labor, the British reformer and travel writer Harriet Martineau observed what she believed to be crucial differences between chattel slavery in the United States and slavery in the Egyptian harem. Her earlier work, *Society in America* (1837), had discussed abolitionist women and cultivated a woman-as-slave worldview. A decade later, in an 1847 letter, Martineau described what she perceived

---

[48] Clare Midgley, "British Abolition and Feminism in Transatlantic Perspective," in *Women's Rights and Transatlantic Antislavery*, 129; Bannerji, "Mary Wollstonecraft," 229–234.
[49] Anna Gurney and Sarah Buxton's Journal, 1834, Buxton Papers: Vol. XII, 111–113, Anti-Slavery Papers, Rhodes House Library, in Midgley, *Women Against Slavery*, 80, 100.

as slavery in its different forms. Envisaging that, upon leaving the United States, she had "seen the last [she] should ever see of Slavery," Martineau was surprised when she "next saw Slavery in a hareem at Cairo." The latter was "more favorable," she believed, since "much of the Slavery of the East" was "owing to the institution of polygamy."[50] Two years later, Martineau's letter was published in *The Liberty Bell*, a popular American antislavery gift book that had been sold at the Boston Anti-Slavery Bazaar since 1839. At century's end, during his own travels across Europe and Northern Africa, abolitionist Frederick Douglass used discourses of slavery to make similar comments about the forms of oppression he observed amongst Egyptian women.[51]

One of the outcomes of women being denied their history, Gerda Lerner argues, was that many "had to argue as though no woman before her had ever thought or written."[52] The constant re-emergence of the slavery analogy amongst literary women illustrated their need to begin again and again as much as it highlighted a transformation in their use of both the slavery analogy and discourses of slavery. Although this rhetoric facilitated a greater awareness of the subjection of women in an increasingly interconnected world, it seldom precipitated European women's self-identification with enslaved people of African descent. The abstractions of Enlightenment philosophy and the specificity of antislavery discourse thus offered European women a language through which to describe their own situation under patriarchy. As Wollstonecraft's posthumous novel asked: "Was not the world a vast prison, and women born slaves?"[53] Such proclamations were both racially exclusionary and inherently meant to describe women who were, in fact, free. In North America, however, where chattel slavery was a more immediate part of everyday life, abolitionist women began to foreground the situation of enslaved people of African descent.

[50] "Letter: From Harriet Martineau, London, July 9, 1847," in *The Liberty Bell*, ed. Friends of Freedom (Boston: National Anti-Slavery Bazaar, 1849), 45–47.
[51] Leigh Fought, *Women in the World of Frederick Douglass* (Oxford: Oxford University Press, 2017), 257.
[52] Gerda Lerner, *The Creation of Feminist Consciousness: From the Middle Ages to Eighteen-Seventy* (New York: Oxford University Press, 1993), 166.
[53] Mary Wollstonecraft, *Maria; or, The Wrongs of Woman* (Philadelphia: James Carey, 1798/1799), 22.

The Abolitionist Sisterhood and the "Woman Question"

European women seldom had any direct exposure to chattel slavery, which was largely restricted to the geographically remote imperial colonies. The situation was quite different in North America's colonial outposts. As the British colonies became reliant on the transatlantic slave trade across the seventeenth and eighteenth centuries, chattel slavery became an ever more visible and entrenched institution. One of the most significant demographic implications was that people of African descent became far more populous in North America and the Caribbean than in Europe.[54] This meant that, in colonial North America, even the abstracted use of the slavery analogy was more closely informed by an awareness of the institution. Since chattel slavery became central to public debate across the antebellum era, more direct and unambiguous allusions to this racialized institution shaped the rhetoric of nineteenth-century social movements.

During the American Revolution of 1765–1783, many colonists embraced discourses of tyranny and slavery with vigor. According to Bernard Bailyn, slavery represented the "absolute political evil" in eighteenth-century political discourse. Revolutionary ideals about a tyrannical government's capacity to enslave free colonists seemed insubstantive or overly radical in Britain, but took on far greater force in the thirteen colonies. Not merely rhetorical, slavery characterized an ultimate state of compulsion. To many colonists, Bailyn argues, the enslavement and degradation of Africans represented "a more dramatic, more bizarre variation of the condition of those who had lost the power of self-determination."[55] Questions about the nature of slavery thus led to questions about the nature of freedom.[56] Each existed in terms of what François Furstenberg describes as a continuum. The colonists understood the possibility of political slavery not

---

[54] Recent historians attest to the long history of Africans in Europe, see: T.F. Earle and K.J.P. Lowe, eds. *Black Africans in Renaissance Europe* (Cambridge: Cambridge University Press, 2005); Catherine Molineux, *Faces of Perfect Ebony: Encountering Atlantic Slavery in Imperial Britain* (Cambridge, MA: Harvard University Press, 2012); Miranda Kaufmann, *Black Tudors: The Untold Story* (London: Oneworld Publications, 2017); Olivette Otele, *African-Europeans: An Untold History* (London: Hurst Publishers, 2019).

[55] Bernard Bailyn, *The Ideological Origins of the American Revolution* (Cambridge, MA: Harvard University Press, 1967), esp. 232–246.

[56] David R. Roediger, *The Wages of Whiteness: Race and the Making of the American Working Class* (London: Verso, 1991/2007), 28.

merely as a metaphor; "its conceptual force lay in the parallel with the 'other': the African slave."[57]

Political discourse influenced the few commentators who began to ponder the question of women's rights in colonial North America. The existence of many different forms of coercion and subjugation encouraged some to consider women's experiences as yet another site of oppression, as coverture continued to replicate the legal and patriarchal hierarchy of marriage and the family.[58] American women initially followed the trends that had been established amongst European women of previous generations, whose references to tyranny had been political and whose use of the slavery analogy remained essentially abstracted from chattel slavery. "I desire you would Remember the Ladies," Abigail Adams famously implored her husband, the founding father John Adams, in 1776. "Do not put such unlimited power into the hands of the Husbands," she wrote. "Remember all Men would be tyrants if they could."[59] In the early years of the Republic, other women began to expand upon what Adams had described as men's unbridled tyranny. As early as 1790, Judith Sargent Murray expressed the belief that "woman's form" should not denote a "weak, a servile, an inferior soul."[60] A 1795 poem, moreover, denounced the "tyrant" man to jubilantly declare: "Woman is Free."[61]

Antebellum reformers continued to use abstracted discourses of slavery to describe all manner of conditions, from intemperance to religious experiences. However, the prominence of chattel slavery in political debate meant that such pronouncements could always be directly related back to the institution itself. Bailyn suggests that later generations lost the expansive meanings that had been associated with "slavery" during the eighteenth century.[62] But perhaps this expansiveness did not become quite so elusive—at least not for reformers, who continued to draw on discourses of

[57] François Furstenberg, "Beyond Freedom and Slavery: Autonomy, Virtue, and Resistance in Early American Political Discourse," *Journal of American History* 89, no. 4 (2003): 1295–1330.

[58] Nancy F. Cott, *Public Vows: A History of Marriage and the Nation* (Cambridge, MA: Harvard University Press, 2000), Chapter 1.

[59] Abigail Adams to John Adams, 31 March 1776, *Adams Family Papers: An Electronic Archive*, Massachusetts Historical Society.

[60] Judith Sargent Murray, "On the Equality of the Sexes," *Massachusetts Magazine*, Vol. II (Boston: I. Thomas and E.T. Andrews, 1790).

[61] By a Lady, "Tune—*God Save America*," *Philadelphia Minerva*, 17 October 1795, in Danny O. Crew, *Suffragist Sheet Music* (Jefferson: McFarland & Company, 2002), 8–9.

[62] Bailyn, *Ideological Origins*, 233.

slavery in myriad contexts, including political slavery, wage slavery, and sexual slavery. As an antislavery ethos gained more adherents after the 1830s, chattel slavery increasingly became a "touchstone" for measuring dependence and degradation.[63] Indeed, as Manisha Sinha suggests, chattel slavery became the "benchmark of oppression," for the antebellum labor movement as much as for abolitionists.[64]

The rise of the abolitionism in the 1830s would provide white women in the United States with the opportunity to connect their own situation more explicitly with the enslavement and emancipation of enslaved people of African descent. This decade witnessed the emergence of a cross-racial network of hundreds of female antislavery societies across the northern states, as corollaries to organizations such as the American Anti-Slavery Society (AASS), established in 1833 and led by William Lloyd Garrison. The antislavery movement afforded women a degree of political participation. Julie Roy Jeffrey describes the women who constituted this movement's rank-and-file as the "great silent army of abolition." Their efforts followed women's earlier contribution to the British antislavery movement. As early as the 1780s, British women had operated in female-only societies which organized boycotts and petitioning campaigns. The *Liberator*, edited by Garrison, cited the earlier success of these female anti-slavery societies to support women's efforts in the United States.[65] Garrison and his followers quickly distinguished their approach from previous mass antislavery protest. Inspired by British Quaker Elizabeth Heyrick's controversial pamphlet, *Immediate, Not Gradual Abolition* (1824), and black Bostonian David Walker's *Appeal to the Colored Citizens of the World* (1829), the *Liberator* advocated the immediate abolition of chattel slavery from its first issue in 1831.[66] Ordinary abolitionist women, black and white, became central to sustaining this unpopular cause in the decades before the Civil War.

Abolitionist women developed a rhetoric of "sisterhood" amid a cultural milieu preoccupied with chattel slavery. Jean Fagan Yellin describes how the "Am I Not a Woman and a Sister?" emblem became famous

---

[63] Roediger, *Wages of Whiteness*, 20. See also: Marcus Cunliffe, *Chattel Slavery and Wage Slavery: The Anglo-American Context, 1830–1860* (Athens: University of Georgia Press, 1979).

[64] Sinha, *Slave's Cause*, 347.

[65] Julie Roy Jeffrey, *The Great Silent Army of Abolition: Ordinary Women in the Antislavery Movement* (Chapel Hill: University of North Carolina Press, 1998), 24–25.

[66] Midgley, *Women Against Slavery*, 111–112; Davis, *Inhuman Bondage*, 237, 255–260.

amongst these women by 1836. It appeared on such diverse ephemera as antislavery tokens, as the masthead for the *Liberator*'s Ladies' Department, and as a cover vignette for Lydia Maria Child's book, *Authentic Anecdotes of American Slavery* (1838). The emblem's specter of the enslaved black female supplicant transformed antislavery discourse. It not only became integral to how white abolitionist women considered the abuses of chattel slavery, but it also informed their own experiences of subjugation, as women. This encouraged some to develop a growing sense of self-identification with the experiences of enslaved people of African descent. However, these realizations continued to be informed by assumptions about racial hierarchy, as white abolitionist women often envisaged themselves as the liberators of enslaved women.[67] The development of a woman-centered abolitionism enabled questions about the morality of chattel slavery to be turned toward other political questions, including what became known as the "woman question."

The antislavery movement concurrently called attention to the violence, pain, and suffering that chattel slavery engendered to effect sympathy for enslaved people of African descent.[68] Antislavery societies embraced biblical commands, especially: "Remember them that are in bonds, as bound with them; and them which suffer adversity, as being yourselves also in the body." Hebrews 13:13 encouraged abolitionists and other antislavery advocates to challenge themselves to practice anti-racism, which often amounted to romantic racialism. "As 'we remember them in bonds as bound with them,' we find we have so much to do, much even for ourselves," the Anti-Slavery Convention of American Women attested in 1838. "[H]ow slow were we to feel the truth that all men are indeed 'born free and equal'?"[69] For many abolitionist women, however, cultivating sympathy for enslaved people also offered what Gay Gibson Cima describes as a route toward full citizenship. Some women began to develop a sense of self-identification with enslaved people, scholars argue, as this process also enabled them to envision their own emancipation from a patriarchal social order.

[67] Yellin, *Women and Sisters*, 12–26, esp. 17–22.

[68] Elizabeth B. Clark, "'The Sacred Rights of the Weak': Pain, Sympathy, and the Culture of Individual Rights in Antebellum America," *Journal of American History* 82, no. 2 (1995): 463–493; Margaret Abruzzo, *Polemical Pain: Slavery, Cruelty, and the Rise of Humanitarianism* (Baltimore: Johns Hopkins University Press, 2011).

[69] "Address to Anti-Slavery Societies," in *History of Pennsylvania Hall, which was Destroyed by a Mob, On the 17th of May, 1838* (Philadelphia: Merrihew and Gunn, 1838), 133.

Through their appropriation and (mis)use of the Hindu concept of "metempsychosis," which referred to the passage of the soul at death into another body, Garrisonian women who supported the immediate abolition of chattel slavery proposed a sympathetic "bond" between free women and enslaved people.[70]

The Quaker poet Elizabeth Margaret Chandler first advocated metempsychosis as a means by which abolitionists could perform this deeper sense of sympathy.[71] Her 1831 article "Mental Metempsychosis," first published in Benjamin Lundy's *Genius of Universal Emancipation*, encouraged imaginative, intellectual, and bodily self-identification with enslaved people of African descent. Chandler challenged her fellow abolitionists to "imagine themselves for a few moments" in the slave's "very circumstances, to enter into his feelings, comprehend all his wretchedness, [and] transform themselves mentally into his very self," so as to elicit "compassion." Asking abolitionists to "let the fetter lie" with "weight upon their wrists," Chandler inspired women to exercise this practice of self-identification so as to engender sympathy with the enslaved.[72] But metempsychosis, Cima argues, did not encourage abolitionists literally to think of themselves as a slave; rather, it encouraged action through "a particular kind of *critical and partisan* spectatorship, distance, and self-judgement, as well as an activated awareness of another's material circumstances."[73] This practice could both challenge and reinforce patriarchal ideas about women's moral superiority: metempsychosis emphasized gender identity at the expense of challenging free white women to consider the crucial differences between their own experiences, as women, and those experiences that were defined by racial discrimination or chattel slavery.[74]

The abolitionist phenomenon of metempsychosis was not strictly limited to white abolitionist women, however. Cima suggests that African-American women, in fact, critically transformed the practice. Philadelphia abolitionist Sarah Forten, whose poetry often appeared in the *Liberator*, centered

---

[70] Gay Gibson Cima, *Performing Anti-Slavery: Activist Women on Antebellum Stages* (Cambridge: Cambridge University Press, 2014), 2, Chapter 1; Yellin, *Women and Sisters*, 12–14. This concept would later influence poets such as Ralph Waldo Emmerson and Walt Whitman, see: John Michael Corrigan, *American Metempsychosis: Emerson, Whitman, and the New Poetry* (New York: Fordham University Press, 2012).

[71] Cima, *Performing Anti-Slavery*, 68–72.

[72] "Mental Metempsychosis," *Genius of Universal Emancipation*, 1 February 1831.

[73] Cima, *Performing Anti-Slavery*, 21–22; Yellin, *Women and Sisters*, 12–14.

[74] Yellin, *Women and Sisters*, 23–26.

her analysis not on the feelings of white abolitionists but on the experiences of the enslaved. As increasingly stringent laws targeted free blacks in the North, more African Americans came to realize their own embodied vulnerability.[75] In an 1832 address to the Female Literary Society of Philadelphia, Sarah Mapps Douglass pursued even more direct connections between herself and enslaved people. Douglass reflected on how important it was "to stir up in the bosom of each ... [a] feeling of deep sympathy for our brethren and sisters, who are ... held in bondage the most cruel and degrading—to make their cause our own!" Imagining the "oppressor lurking" just beyond her "own peaceful home," Douglass envisaged "his iron hand stretched forth to seize me as his prey, and the cause of the slave became my own."[76] This address appeared in the *Liberator*, under the Ladies' Department's "Am I Not a Woman and a Sister" emblem, to further link Douglass' body with that of the slave. Douglass effectively reconfigured metempsychosis from Chandler's vision of sympathy with the enslaved to having sympathy first for oneself and then with enslaved people.[77]

After the emergence of Sarah and Angelina Grimké within the antislavery movement, the AASS found that the woman question became increasingly contentious. Born to slaveholders in Charleston, South Carolina, both sisters had been slaveowners as children. As young adults, their growing commitment to Quakerism and the principles of antislavery encouraged the Grimké sisters to abandon their Episcopalian and slaveholding roots. By the late 1820s, Sarah had left Charleston to join the Orthodox Quakers of Philadelphia's Arch Street Meeting-House, soon to be followed by her younger sister. Even before Chandler's 1831 poem, Angelina herself had engaged in metempsychosis-like episodes in her own diary.[78] A growing personal disquiet toward chattel slavery led Angelina to the Philadelphia Female Anti-Slavery Society (established in 1833, the same year as the AASS). After hearing of the mob violence that followed an 1835 address by British abolitionist George Thompson, Angelina wrote an impassioned letter to Garrison. Unbeknownst to its author, he published this letter in the *Liberator* almost immediately. This precipitated a backlash among the Grimkés' Quaker friends

[75] Cima, *Performing Anti-Slavery*, 72–81.
[76] "Mental Feasts," *Liberator*, 21 July 1832. For authorship, see: Marie Lindhorst, "Politics in a Box: Sarah Mapps Douglass and the Female Literary Association, 1831–1833," *Pennsylvania History: A Journal of Mid-Atlantic Studies* 65, no. 3 (1998): 263–278.
[77] Cima, *Performing Anti-Slavery*, 91–122.
[78] Yellin, *Women and Sisters*, 29–32.

and slaveholding family, while also launching Angelina's abolitionist career. The Grimké sisters became the only women in attendance at the AASS's Agents' Convention in November 1836. Held in New York City under the tutelage of abolitionist firebrand Theodore Dwight Weld, the Agents' Convention aimed to train new touring agents on behalf of the AASS.[79] Angelina expressed a deep concern for the situation of enslaved women, both in her *Appeal to the Christian Women of the South* (1836) and in an 1837 address to northern women that was published the following year. Enslaved women should be seen as "our country women," Grimké implored in *An Appeal to the Women of the Nominally Free States* (1838), for "*they are our sisters*; and to us, as women, they have a right to look for sympathy with their sorrows, and effort and prayer for their rescue."[80]

The Grimké sisters soon embarked upon a series of "parlor talks" in private homes on behalf of New York City's newly formed Female Anti-Slavery Society. Many expressed a keen interest in their oratory. In a series of well-received addresses, they denounced chattel slavery and discussed theological questions, political arguments, and racial prejudice in both the North and South. But the prospect of women speaking in public outraged some abolitionists, especially men. Women's right to public speech quickly became controversial because it contravened the cult of true womanhood: a cultural idea based on women's capacity for purity, piety, domesticity, and submissiveness.[81] The welcoming atmosphere the Grimké sisters later experienced from the Boston Female Anti-Slavery Society led them to tentatively brook the question of women's rights during their abolitionist addresses. But their success generated more spectators and came with far greater scrutiny. When the Grimkés began to address "promiscuous" audiences—mixed gatherings of women and men—they encountered even more hostility, especially from clergymen unwilling to offer church venues for their

---

[79] Gerda Lerner, *The Grimké Sisters from South Carolina: Pioneers for Women's Rights and Abolition* (Chapel Hill: University of North Carolina Press, 1967/2004); Robert H. Abzug, *Passionate Liberator: Theodore Dwight Weld and the Dilemma of Reform* (New York: Oxford University Press, 1980), 151–152.

[80] Angelina Grimké, *An Appeal to the Women of the Nominally Free States*, 2nd ed. (Boston: Isaac Knapp, 1838), 21.

[81] Barbara Welter, *Dimity Convictions: The American Woman in the Nineteenth Century* (Athens: Ohio University Press, 1976). For the controversies surrounding women's public speech, see: Caroline Field Levander, *Voices of the Nation: Women and Public Speech in Nineteenth-Century American Literature and Culture* (New York: Cambridge University Press, 1998); Mary Kelley, *Learning to Stand & Speak: Women, Education, and Public Life in America's Republic* (Chapel Hill: University of North Carolina Press, 2006).

lectures.[82] Yet, as southerners, former slaveholders, and Quakers, the Grimkés vocally defended their moral imperative to speak out against chattel slavery. Chandler herself had expressed this ethos, asking: "When woman's heart is bleeding,/Shall woman's voice be hush'd?"[83]

In response to the controversy, the Grimké sisters more thoroughly integrated their perspectives toward the woman question into their private correspondence, public addresses, and published works. Their experiences in abolitionist settings contributed to what they envisaged as the nucleus of the woman-slave analogy. "I feel as if it is not the cause of the slave only [for] which we plead, but the cause of woman as a responsible moral being," Angelina wrote to a friend. "[O]ur whole sex needs an emancipation from the thraldom of public opinion."[84] Her deeply felt commitment to abolitionism, informed by a strategic analysis of the woman question, led Angelina to conclude that the "rights of the slave and of woman blend like the colors of the rainbow."[85] The Grimkés offered the most public avowal of their convictions, but were far from alone. "The [Grimké] sisters found obstacles so multiplied in their path, that they considered the establishment of women's freedom of vital importance to the anti-slavery cause," Child reflected in an 1839 letter to Garrison:

> "Little can be done for the slave," said they, "while this prejudice blocks up the way." They urged me to say and do more about women's rights, nay, at times they gently rebuked me for my want of zeal. I replied, "It's best not to *talk* about our rights, but simply go forward and *do* whatsoever we deem a duty. In toiling for the freedom of others, we shall find our own." On this ground I have ever stood; and so have my anti-slavery sisters.[86]

---

[82] Lerner, *Grimké Sisters*, 107–145; Susan Zaeske, "The 'Promiscuous Audience' Controversy and the Emergence of the Early Woman's Rights Movement," *Quarterly Journal of Speech* 81, no. 2 (1995): 191–207.

[83] "Think of Our Country's Glory," in *The Poetical Works of Elizabeth Margaret Chandler: With a Memoir of Her Life and Character*, ed. Benjamin Lundy (Philadelphia: Lemuel Howell, 1836), 64.

[84] Angelina Grimké to Jane Smith, 29 May 1837 and 25 July 1837, in *Women's Rights Emerges within the Antislavery Movement, 1830–1870: A Brief History with Documents*, ed. Kathryn Kish Sklar (New York: St Martin's Press, 2000), 111, 117.

[85] Catherine H. Birney, *The Grimké Sisters: Sarah and Angelina Grimké; the First American Women Advocates of Abolition and Woman's Rights* (Boston: Lee and Shepard, 1885), 203.

[86] Lydia Maria Child to William Lloyd Garrison, 2 September 1839, in *Lydia Maria Child: Selected Letters, 1817–1880*, eds. Milton Meltzer and Patricia G. Holland (Amherst: University of Massachusetts Press, 1982), 47.

Child would enact these very principles during her tenure as the editor of the AASS's *National Anti-Slavery Standard* in the early 1840s.[87]

While both sisters would address the woman question through the lens of abolitionism, Sarah Grimké espoused a particular affinity for women's rights. Her *Letters on the Equality of the Sexes, and the Condition of Woman* (1837) advocated the religious, social, legal, and political equality of women and men in the United States and around the world. One of her central conclusions established that women were "much in the situation of the slave." This qualifier—"much"—is important, because it revealed Grimké's sense of the sameness as well as the difference in situation: all women could be *like* slaves, but not all women were literally enslaved.[88] This was a point which Grimké labored. "I do not wish by any means to intimate that the condition of free women can be compared to that of slaves in suffering, or in degradation," she continued. Her analysis of the legal condition of women revealed that they enjoyed "very little more liberty, or power, in some respects, than the slave." The *Letters* emphatically stressed that American women must not "forget [their] brethren and sisters in bondage," lest they fail to "assert [their] privileges" as free women and "perform [their] duties as moral beings." But Grimké realized that free women remained severely curtailed in doing so, not least because coverture ensured the "very being of a woman, like that of a slave, is absorbed in her master."[89]

The valediction to each of Sarah Grimké's *Letters*, "Thine in the bonds of womanhood," evoked what Nancy F. Cott describes as a "double meaning": the bonds of friendship and sisterhood amongst women and the bonds of chattel slavery.[90] The first of the *Letters*, however, was actually signed more explicitly: "Thine for the oppressed in the bonds of womanhood, SARAH M. GRIMKE."[91] As her writings collectively attest, Grimké comprehended

[87] Yellin, *Women and Sisters*, 56–61.

[88] Hélène Quanquin, "'There Are Two Great Oceans': The Slavery Metaphor in the Antebellum Women's Rights Discourse as a Redescription of Race and Gender," in *Interconnections: Gender and Race in American History*, eds. Carol Faulkner and Alison M. Parker (Rochester: University of Rochester Press, 2012), 82; Nancie Caraway, *Segregated Sisterhood: Racism and the Politics of American Feminism* (Knoxville: University of Tennessee Press, 1991), 136–138.

[89] Sarah Grimké, *Letters on the Equality of the Sexes, and the Condition of Woman: Addressed to Mary S. Parker* (Boston: Isaac Knapp, 1837/1838), 33, 82, 40, 42, 75.

[90] Nancy F. Cott, *The Bonds of Womanhood: "Woman's Sphere" in New England, 1780–1835* (New Haven: Yale University Press, 1977), 1.

[91] Grimké, *Letters*, 15.

that enslaved people and women faced largely different, but sometimes similar, forms of oppression. Both, however, were structurally connected across all aspects of society. And as oppressed as free women may be, their comparative privilege provoked a moral responsibility to advocate abolitionism. As Gerda Lerner observes, Sarah Grimké constructed a "social theory on the basis of comparing two kinds of systems of oppression."[92]

The Grimké sisters effectively pioneered the wider use of the woman-slave analogy amongst abolitionist women in the United States. Historians have long been fascinated by their explicit comparison between the situation of free women and enslaved people of African descent, especially insofar as the antislavery movement became what one scholar describes as a "consciousness-raising experience."[93] But, as Ellen Carol DuBois asks, to what degree did this reform strategy represent "political rhetoric" or "historical process"? Did the Grimké sisters and their contemporaries embrace discourses of slavery simply because they were already abolitionists, or because their abolitionism effected a new consciousness of their own lack of rights, as women? When historians emphasize too great a connection between the antislavery and women's rights movements on account of what these women said, DuBois argues, this ignores the importance of the earlier reformist efforts toward benevolence and moral reform in the 1820s.[94] However, the degree to which abolitionists and women's rights reformers would come to mobilize this rhetoric suggests that it might be more productively seen as a product of both political rhetoric and historical process. One historian suggests that it was "[l]ogic and experience" that propelled Sarah toward "a systematic analysis of why women were treated as an oppressed class."[95] As Angelina began to extend her own realizations about chattel slavery to the situation of women, another suggests, enslaved people came to "represent what she concluded was her own oppression as a woman, the oppression of all women, and woman's struggle for liberation."[96]

---

[92] Gerda Lerner, *The Feminist Thought of Sarah Grimké* (New York: Oxford University Press, 1998), 24.

[93] Blanche Glassman Hersh, *The Slavery of Sex: Feminist-Abolitionists in America* (Urbana: University of Illinois Press, 1978), vii.

[94] Ellen Carol DuBois, *Feminism and Suffrage: The Emergence of an Independent Women's Movement in America, 1848–1869* (Ithaca: Cornell University Press, 1978), 31–32.

[95] William H. Chafe, *Women and Equality: Changing Patterns in American Culture* (New York: Oxford University Press, 1977), 25.

[96] Yellin, *Women and Sisters*, 32.

An analysis of these shifting meanings and implications reveals that, although the Grimkés never truly disregarded the plight of enslaved people, many of their contemporaries certainly would. Perhaps the most important conclusion, as Hélène Quanquin observes, is that the Grimké sisters seemed to remain wary of the ambivalence at the heart of the comparison. Both women, but Sarah especially, tried not to position one institution—chattel slavery or women's subjugation, especially in marriage—as worse than the other. Yet the woman-slave analogy would be mobilized in a manner that was far from consistent, even amongst abolitionist women themselves.[97] Historians find deep insincerity in any claims to a universal sisterhood, as white abolitionist women ultimately developed a feminist consciousness that sidelined experiences relating to race and class.[98] Shirley J. Yee questions the degree to which white women were able to transcend their own racism and even begin to understand the concerns of women of color, when so many conceived of the lives of enslaved people as nothing more than "a handy rhetorical device."[99] The normalization of the woman-slave analogy offered abolitionist women the opportunity to highlight the hypocrisy of their male counterparts; but this tendency, as so many historians assert, also directed attention away from chattel slavery itself. As more and more women reformers came to embrace a woman-as-slave worldview, the interdependent concerns the Grimké sisters espoused began to dissipate.

The rapid embrace of the woman-slave analogy across the 1830s must be evaluated in terms of the critical departure that metempsychosis represented. Metempsychosis played a significant role in the transformation of the woman-slave analogy because the practice encouraged abolitionist women to directly connect the antislavery movement, immediate abolitionism, and the prospect of slave emancipation to their own embodied experiences. Through their self-identification with enslaved people, women reformers began to move away from philosophical abstractions about slavery and toward an analysis that was absolutely grounded in chattel slavery itself. Indeed, it was in the context of chattel slavery that "abstract ideas about equality and individual rights gained real social meaning."[100] Although most early

---

[97] Quanquin, "'There Are Two Great Oceans'," 82, 78.
[98] Yellin, *Women and Sisters*, 25.
[99] Shirley J. Yee, *Black Women Abolitionists: A Study in Activism, 1828–1860* (Knoxville: University of Tennessee Press, 1992), 136, 148.
[100] Ellen Carol DuBois, "Outgrowing the Compact of the Fathers: Equal Rights, Woman Suffrage, and the United States Constitution, 1820–1878," *Journal of American History* 74, no. 3 (1987): 840.

abolitionist women did not lose sight of the exploitation of enslaved people of African descent, the subsequent appropriation of the woman-slave analogy by a whole generation of women's rights reformers would transform the use of this rhetoric even further.

THE WORLD'S ANTI-SLAVERY CONVENTION OF 1840

The American Anti-Slavery Society (AASS) was dedicated to the immediate abolition of chattel slavery and denounced the American Colonization Society, which was founded in 1817 and advocated that any manumitted people be repatriated to West Africa. However, the debates surrounding the woman question precipitated an organizational schism, when the election of four women to the AASS's executive committee in 1839 left some abolitionist men outraged. The following year, the American and Foreign Anti-Slavery Society (AFASS) formed as a male-only organization led by Arthur and Lewis Tappan and Henry B. Stanton. The breakaway AFASS, which only allowed women to create female auxiliaries, also diverged from the AASS in terms of its growing desire to pursue antislavery within electoral politics.

The hostility surrounding the woman question intensified at the World's Anti-Slavery Convention in 1840. This was a singular event that brought British, American, and European antislavery advocates together in London. The convention was hosted at the Masonic Hall under the auspices of the newly formed British and Foreign Anti-Slavery Society (BFASS). An event which hosted 500 delegates and attracted 5,000 visitors over nine days, the World's Convention welcomed antislavery luminaries such as Englishman Thomas Clarkson, Irishman Daniel O'Connell, and Americans William Lloyd Garrison and Lucretia Mott. Both the AASS and the AFASS sent delegates, causing an unanticipated hurdle to quickly surface: the first days of the World's Convention became mired in discussion not about the abolition of chattel slavery but about the presence of the seven women who arrived alongside Mott and Garrison as part of the AASS's delegation.[101] In consequence, the World's Convention would

[101] The account draws on: Donald R. Kennon, "'An Apple of Discord': The Woman Question at the World's Anti-Slavery Convention of 1840," *Slavery & Abolition: A Journal of Slave and Post-Slave Studies* 5, no. 3 (1984): 244–266; Kathryn Kish Sklar, "'Women Who Speak for an Entire Nation': American and British Women Compared at the World Anti-Slavery Convention, London, 1840," *Pacific Historical Review* 49, no. 4 (1990): 453–499; Maurice Bric, "Debating Slavery and Empire: The United States, Britain and the World's Anti-Slavery Convention of 1840," in *A Global History of Anti-Slavery Politics in the Nineteenth Century*, eds. William Mulligan and Maurice Bric (Basingstoke: Palgrave Macmillan, 2013).

rehearse the very same internal organizational strife over the woman question that the AASS had witnessed across the previous decade.

The World's Convention was an event that Margaret McFadden describes as "a vivid watershed of women's internationality." When confronted by the possibility that women would be excluded from the proceedings, the AASS delegates likely held the recent experiences of the Grimké sisters uppermost in their minds. At the center of the controversy was Lucretia Mott, an influential Quaker abolitionist from Philadelphia. Her allegiance to Garrisonian abolitionism made her more radical than many other antislavery advocates, while her association with Hicksite Quakers, who had split from their American Orthodox brethren in 1827, made British Orthodox Quakers uneasy. Mott was also central to the emerging transatlantic network of women's rights advocates. During the World's Convention, she established a burgeoning friendship with the young, newly married Elizabeth Cady Stanton. Although the Grimké sisters were not in attendance, Mott brought copies of their latest abolitionist tracts to her friends as she traveled around Britain.[102]

What was really at issue at the World's Convention? Although the AASS had recently experienced similar controversies about race and gender, many of its delegates had become far more used to gender-mixed, cross-racial antislavery gatherings by 1840. The problem, then, as many AASS delegates saw it, was gender-based hypocrisy. The BFASS had only been formed in 1839, under the leadership of British Quaker Joseph Sturge. A month prior to the World's Convention, its London Committee resolved to accept male delegates only; and the AFASS, an organization far more ideologically aligned with the BFASS than the AASS, was in agreement.[103] Since the World's Convention welcomed men from all antislavery factions, the American women were "excluded as women, not merely as Garrisonians." Indeed, the woman question had not disrupted the British antislavery movement, suggesting that the controversy which erupted in London reflected women's "greater integration" within American abolitionism.[104] The debate that precipitated this decision was defined by a

[102] Margaret H. McFadden, *Golden Cables of Sympathy: The Transatlantic Sources of Nineteenth-Century Feminism* (Lexington: University Press of Kentucky, 1999/2015), Chapter 1, esp. 15, 18. For the Hicksite-Orthodox split, see: Carol Faulkner, *Lucretia Mott's Heresy: Abolition and Women's Rights in Nineteenth-Century America* (Philadelphia: University of Pennsylvania Press, 2011), Chapter 3.

[103] Kennon, "An Apple of Discord," 245–248.

[104] Sklar, "Women Who Speak," 462–464; Kennon, "An Apple of Discord," 253.

growing sense of the theoretical weight of the woman-slave analogy as well as an increased willingness to compare exclusion based on race to exclusion based on gender.

Kathryn Kish Sklar suggests that Mott's diary offers insight into the AASS women's experiences at the World's Convention. As some of the event's most influential figures, these women embodied the burgeoning connections between abolitionism, women's rights, and the era's other social movements, including temperance and moral reform.[105] On the antislavery world's stage, the prospect of women's exclusion from antislavery advocacy offered a rationale for women's rights because the discussion of enslaved people's oppression "elicited a parallel to the subordinate position of women, a parallel not all reformers were willing to make."[106] Mott's diary revealed the degree to which some AASS delegates pursued this comparison to advocate that women be included as full delegates. However, the comparison was not grounded in analyses of a similarity of status, per se; rather, it proclaimed that neither women nor enslaved people of African descent should be excluded from the civil and political public sphere.

Some American delegates used analogy to respond to and protest the exclusion of the AASS women, thus drawing attention to the prejudices that flourished even amongst antislavery advocates. Before the World's Convention, Mott endeavored to convince Joseph Sturge of the "inconsistency of excluding Women Delegates," especially when "E. Heyrick—a woman" had inaugurated the cause of immediate abolition only 16 years previous. To advocate the inclusion of both, Mott then compared the exclusion of women to that of people of color. However, Samuel Jackman Prescod, a free-born mixed-race Jamaican delegate, believed "it would lower the dignity of the Convention and bring ridicule on the whole thing if ladies were admitted." Mott replied, insisting that "similar reasons were urged in Pennsylvania for the exclusion of colored people from our [antislavery] meetings—but had we yielded on such flimsy arguments, we might as well have abandoned our enterprise." While the African-descended men to whom Mott referred were free, the gradual or recent abolition of chattel slavery in the northern states and the Caribbean meant this freedom may have only been achieved quite recently. Similarly, Boston clergyman Nathaniel Colver considered "[w]omen constitutionally unfit

---

[105] Sklar, "Women Who Speak," 463; McFadden, *Golden Cables*, 18.
[106] Kennon, "An Apple of Discord," 245.

for public or business meetings," so Mott regaled him of how "the colored man too was said to be *constitutionally* unfit to mingle with the white man." When Sarah Pugh penned a protest on behalf of the AASS women delegates from Pennsylvania, she situated women as "co-equals in the advocacy of Universal Liberty."[107]

The women's protest would be to no avail. On the first day of the World's Convention, the AASS women were effectively silenced by being relegated to the gallery.[108] When debate broke out, the proceedings were completely sidetracked by the woman question. In protest, Wendell Philips expressed how women had long been admitted to Massachusetts antislavery societies on principle.[109] The AASS, he attested, had "interpret[ed] 'friends of the slave' to include women as well as men." Phillips further infused his radical abolitionism with republicanism and American exceptionalism. If American abolitionists did not accept the custom of denying "colored brethren into our friendship," he asked, why should the World's Convention "yield to a parallel custom or prejudice [against women] in Old England?"[110] In beginning to advocate a body politic that was not exclusively white, some AASS men also criticized the BFASS and AFASS ideal: a body politic that was male.

Although some American and British delegates were displeased about the women's exclusion from the World's Convention, these men nonetheless participated in the proceedings. Phillips, for example, served alongside an AFASS delegate as one of the convention's secretaries. George Thompson, who had benefitted from the assistance of female antislavery societies when faced with mob violence in the United States only years earlier, also equivocated. However, when Garrison, delayed on account of the transatlantic voyage, finally arrived at the convention four days late, he joined the women in the gallery and sat silently in solidarity. Other elite British and French spectators such as Lady Byron wandered through the gallery to witness the "exiled Americans," engaging in erstwhile "performances of solidarity" which would haunt the

---

[107] Frederick B. Tolles, ed. *Slavery and "the Woman Question": Lucretia Mott's Diary of Her Visit to Great Britain to Attend the World's Anti-Slavery Convention of 1840*, Supplement No. 23 to the *Journal of the Friends' Historical Society* (Haverford: Friends' Historical Association, 1952), 22–28. See: Sklar, "Women Who Speak," 466–467.

[108] Kennon, "An Apple of Discord," 249.

[109] Sklar, "Women Who Speak," 467–468.

[110] *Proceedings of the General Anti-Slavery Convention: Friday, June 12th, to Tuesday, June 23rd, 1840* (London: British and Foreign Anti-Slavery Convention, 1841), 24, 36.

proceedings.[111] Also joining the women were black Boston abolitionist Charles Lenox Remond, Rhode Island Quaker William Adams, and Nathanial Peabody Rogers, editor of the *Herald of Freedom* in Concord, Massachusetts.[112]

The AASS women who had been excluded as delegates, as well as those who witnessed the events, articulated the hypocrisy they perceived amongst abolitionist men. Mott wrote a bemused letter to Maria Weston Chapman, organizer of the Boston Anti-Slavery Bazaar since 1835, which pointedly divulged that the "name of [the] 'World's Convention' was merely a 'poetical license'—(alias a rhetorical flourish)" to describe the racially inclusive gathering of men. Since the event was not entitled to such a name, she declared, "a 'World's Convention' has yet to be held."[113] Writing to the Grimké sisters, Stanton similarly mocked the pretense of refusing "any delegates that were sent to the world's convention." Relaying a message from Mott, she encouraged both women to continue to "speak out for oppressed woman," as "a great struggle is at hand & ... all the friends of freedom for woman must rally round the Garrison standard."[114] Some even used discourses of slavery to make sense of their remembrances. Later that year, a poem entitled "England's Usages" appeared in the AASS's *National Anti-Slavery Standard*:

> Usage bade its servants, they,
> Slaves unto Usage! must obey,
> To spurn their woman—slaves away!
> O, deep servility! They say
> "As England does, so too must we
> As here in England's realm we be." ...
> A *woman* rules Britannia—yet
> Freedom's champions in her council met,
> The chains of slavery to unbind
> From limb and soul of all mankind,
> Spurn woman's faithful heart away,

---

[111] Cima, *Performing Anti-Slavery*, 167.
[112] Faulkner, *Lucretia Mott's Heresy*, 97.
[113] Lucretia Mott to Maria Weston Chapman, 7 July 1840, in *British and American Abolitionists: An Episode in Transatlantic Understanding*, ed. Clare Taylor (Edinburgh: Edinburgh University Press, 1974), 103–104.
[114] Elizabeth Cady Stanton to Sarah Grimké and Angelina Grimké Weld, 25 June 1840, in *The Selected Papers of Elizabeth Cady Stanton and Susan B. Anthony*, Vol. I, ed. Ann D. Gordon (New Brunswick: Rutgers University Press, 1997), 10–11.

> Because, forsooth! they must obey
> Britain[n]ia's usages! ...
> She may not speak? no; woman's heart
> Its light and warmth may not impart
> In Freedom's Council—tho' the call
> Was sung throughout the world, for all
> The friends of those in thrall!
> It bade not *slaves themselves* to come!
> *Is she not such?* Let slaves be dumb,
> Whatever in her bosom glows,
> Whate'er she feels, whate'er she knows,
> Her "woman-lips" may not reveal
> Before her *lords!*[115]

The woman-slave analogy—"*Is she not such?*"—thus emerged to make sense of the World's Convention. In her diary, Mott had also described the British custom of excluding women from antislavery proceedings as "English usage."[116] Other remembrances were shaped by observances about American exceptionalism and the difference between monarchy and republicanism that had been aired during the proceedings.

Use of the woman-slave analogy intensified in later remembrances, especially amongst those who emerged as women's rights reformers. Three years later, Scottish woman Marion Reid, who had been "shocked" at the American women's exclusion, published *A Plea for Woman* (1843).[117] In her preface, Reid quoted Percy Bysshe Shelley's 1817 poem, *The Revolt of Islam*, asking: "Can man be free, if woman be a slave?"[118] This question obliquely considered whether women were born to slavery. An epigraph such as this is both commentary and substance; it is a peritext which is secondary to, but still an important aspect of, a literary text.[119] By citing famous literary figures (often men) in this manner, nineteenth-century women deliberately placed themselves within what they perceived as an

---

[115] E.M., "England's Usages," *National Anti-Slavery Standard*, 27 August 1840. See: Kennon, "An Apple of Discord," 256.

[116] Faulkner, *Lucretia Mott's Heresy*, 98.

[117] Susanne Ferguson, "Foreword," in *A Plea for Woman*, ed. Marion Reid (Edinburgh: Polygon, 1843/1988), viii.

[118] Marion Reid, *A Plea for Woman: Being a Vindication of the Importance and Extent of Her Natural Sphere of Action* (New York: Farmer & Daggers, 1845), Preface. See: Midgley, *Women Against Slavery*, 163.

[119] Andrew Bennett and Nicholas Royle, *An Introduction to Literature, Criticism and Theory*, 4th ed. (London: Routledge, 1960/2014), 5.

illustrious literary tradition.[120] Not only did women reformers frame their treatises with famous poems; many chose poems that centered around discourses of slavery. Child's *Brief History* had similarly featured an epigraph from Lord Byron's 1814 poem, *The Corsair*:

> I am a slave, a favored slave
> At best, to share his splendor, and seem very blest;
> When weary of these fleeting charms and me,
> There yawns the sack, and yonder rolls the sea.
> What! am I then a toy for dotard's play
> To wear but till the gilding frets away?[121]

Increasingly, women's rights reformers recited the few quotations that were both sympathetic to women's oppression and could also legitimate a woman-as-slave worldview. This had a reverberating effect, even in marginalia. When British Quaker Anne Knight annotated the preface to her own copy of Reid's book, she proclaimed, "No! Emancipate her then!"[122]

In the coming decades, the World's Convention remained a critical moment for those women who had been in attendance. Mott, for example, would sign her letters to British Quaker abolitionist Elizabeth Pease with the salutation, "I am thine with a sister's freedom."[123] The event left an especially deep impression on Stanton, a young, newly married woman who developed a life-changing friendship with Mott during these weeks.[124] After revisiting the proceedings of the World's Convention in 1852, Stanton wondered how, back in 1840, she had "sat there quietly and listened" to the resolutions. The intervening years had witnessed her growth as a women's rights reformer as well as her ever-increasing uptake of the woman-slave analogy. The passage of time led her to realize that antislavery men, the "champions of freedom, the most progressive men of the nineteenth century, [had] denied women the right of free speech in an

---

[120] Nina Baym, *Woman's Fiction: A Guide to Novels by and About Women in America, 1820–70*, 2nd ed. (Urbana: University of Illinois Press, 1978/1993), xvii.

[121] L. Maria Child, *Brief History of the Condition of Women: In Various Ages and Nations*, Vol. I (New York: C.S. Francis & Co., 1845), Preface.

[122] McFadden, *Golden Cables*, 20.

[123] Kennon, "An Apple of Discord," 257.

[124] Elisabeth Griffith, *In Her Own Right: The Life of Elizabeth Cady Stanton* (New York: Oxford University Press, 1984), Chapter 3; Michael P. Farrell, *Collaborative Circles: Friendship Dynamics and Creative Work* (Chicago: University of Chicago Press, 2001), Chapter 6; Faulkner, *Lucretia Mott's Heresy*, Chapter 6.

antislavery convention," she confided to Susan B. Anthony. But it also directed her toward an increasingly racist application of the woman-slave analogy. "If Sambo had been cast out of the convention for any reason," she again mused in 1852, "I wonder if Wendell Phillips and George Thompson would have coolly remarked on his discomfiture, 'Well, he is as happy outside as in!'"[125]

By 1840, the woman-slave analogy had become central to this very particular transatlantic dialogue about women's rights within the antislavery movement. The Grimké sisters began to use the woman-slave analogy at a moment during the early 1830s when their commitment to abolitionism was greater than their interest in women's rights. But the expression of these ideas differed on the other side of the Atlantic. During the World's Convention, it became more of a strategic response to the controversy surrounding women's emergence into the antislavery public sphere. "In London as so often in the United States," Sklar observes, "arguments about women's status derived from analogies with the status of black persons." But Mott arguably offered less an analogy than a criticism of the hypocrisy of excluding both people of color and women from public debate—either in England or New England. Still, any "analogy between race and gender" could be particularly "potent" in London, where people of African descent "appeared as exotic outsiders" on account of profound demographic differences between Britain and the United States.[126]

Contesting the Woman-Slave Analogy

"The prolonged slavery of woman is the darkest page in human history," read Volume I of the *History of Woman Suffrage* (1881), edited by Elizabeth Cady Stanton, Susan B. Anthony, and Matilda Joslyn Gage.[127] This assertion reflected the degree to which nineteenth-century women's rights reformers and suffragists came to believe that women were indeed born to slavery. "Held always and everywhere in a state of subordination," Paulina Wright Davis had similarly averred in 1853, woman

---

[125] Elizabeth Cady Stanton to Susan B. Anthony, 2 April 1852, in *Elizabeth Cady Stanton as Revealed in Her Letters, Diary and Reminiscences*, Vol. II, eds. Theodore Stanton and Harriot Stanton Blatch (New York: Harper & Brothers, 1922), 40–41.
[126] Sklar, "Women Who Speak," 466–467.
[127] Elizabeth Cady Stanton, Susan B. Anthony, and Matilda Joslyn Gage, eds. *History of Woman Suffrage* [hereafter *HWS*], Vol. I (Rochester: Susan B. Anthony, 1881), 13.

remained "an unchanged slave."[128] Yet, as more women's rights reformers embraced the woman-slave analogy, other reformers began to question their conclusions.

After Margaret Chandler's premature death in 1834, "Mental Metempsychosis" was republished in *The Poetical Works of Elizabeth Margaret Chandler* (1836). This compilation made the principles of metempsychosis again available to abolitionists at a moment when the Grimké sisters were taking to the lecture circuit and the AASS was about to witness its schism over the role of women. Not only did abolitionist women write about their personal experiences of metempsychosis; they sometimes even enacted its principles in their addresses. Although Cima suggests that black and white abolitionists engaged in these performances of sympathy at antebellum antislavery gatherings, few—if any—formerly enslaved people were regularly present in such settings during the 1830s. At these events, abolitionist women would "'excite' themselves to a higher level of engagement" with chattel slavery by imagining themselves in the circumstances of enslaved people.[129] Although metempsychosis did not encourage abolitionists to take the process of self-identification literally, this crucial sense of distance may not have always been realized by individuals whose dedication to the cause became increasingly fervent.

In the years after the World's Anti-Slavery Convention, the antislavery movement offered women such as Abby Kelley personal fulfillment as well as a greater sense of the restrictions on their own lives. Kelley's pursuit of metempsychosis suggests that, for some abolitionists at least, these personal experiences of metempsychosis may have been taken far more literally than Chandler might have imagined. In 1841, Kelley wrote to fellow abolitionist Nathanial Peabody Rogers of her inner world:

> When I ... become myself the slave—when at such a moment I feel the fetters wearing away the flesh and grating on my bare ankle bone, when I feel the naked cords of my neck shrinking away from the rough edge of the iron collar, when my flesh quivers beneath the lash, till, in anguish, I feel portions of it cut from my back; or when I see ... the brutish and drunken overseer lay his ferocious grasp upon the person of my sister and drag her to his den of pollutions—ah! when I see the fires of liberty going out in her bosom[.] ... [W]hen I witness all the unutterable abominations that

---

[128] "The Moral Character of Woman," *Una*, 1 June 1853.
[129] Cima, *Performing Anti-Slavery*, 53–55, 137–247.

spring from slavery, myself reduced to slavery by … a sanctified Doctor of Divinity, who … robs me of my heart's blood and lays his iron grasp upon my immortal soul.[130]

Biographer Dorothy Sterling describes this passage as symbolic of the "wellsprings of her growing oratorical power." In "a kind of self-hypnosis," she suggests, Kelley "had *become* the slave."[131] Musings such as these were not wholly limited to private reflections between friends and coadjutors. As an AASS lecturer alongside Frederick Douglass in 1841 and again across 1842–1843, Kelley sometimes responded to racist pejoratives not by distancing herself from the controversy of chattel slavery but by claiming an imaginative connection between herself and African Americans, particularly enslaved women.[132]

In each instance, Kelley's body had effectively supplanted the enslaved body as a site of suffering without actually contributing to the reduction of that suffering.[133] A similar expression of metempsychosis occurred a decade earlier, when the abolitionist Rev. John Rankin attempted to convince his slaveholding brother to manumit his enslaved property. "I myself was a slave," Rankin wrote, envisaging his wife and children "being whipped, at the pleasure of a … capricious master."[134] Yet, even as Rankin sought to encourage his brother to acknowledge enslaved people's humanity, this process still allowed the beneficent abolitionist who earnestly opposed chattel slavery to participate in what Saidiya V. Hartman describes as the essential "fungibility of the captive body."[135] But Rankin could be confident in his status as a minister and as an abolitionist man. The same could not be said for abolitionist women such as Kelley, whose efforts were quickly contested if they stepped beyond the movement's rank-and-file or the expectations of feminine decorum.

[130] Abby Kelley to N.P. Rogers, 8 July 1841, New-York Historical Society, in Dorothy Sterling, *Ahead of Her Time: Abby Kelley and the Politics of Antislavery* (New York: W.W. Norton & Company, 1991), 132–133.
[131] Sterling, *Ahead of Her Time*, 132, 133; Yellin, *Women and Sisters*, 49–50.
[132] Fought, *Women in the World*, 77–78; Sterling, *Ahead of Her Time*, 135–136, 142–144.
[133] Hartman, *Scenes of Subjection*, 19–20.
[134] John Rankin, *Letters on American Slavery* (Boston: Garrison & Knapp, 1833), 55–56.
[135] Hartman, *Scenes of Subjection*, 17–23. Hartman does not describe this passage in Rankin's letter as an expression of metempsychosis.

What can the ideal of practicing metempsychosis with a degree of critical distance mean, given the simultaneous transformation of the woman-slave analogy across the 1830s and 1840s? Abolitionist women were concerned with the abuses of chattel slavery, yet their reformist principles were also piqued by the "social ordering of power whereby women are kept in a perpetual state of subjection to physical, emotional, and economic exploitation by men."[136] Metempsychosis was buttressed by the long history of embracing discourses of slavery to condemn different forms of oppression, most especially on the part of foremothers such as Mary Wollstonecraft. Thus, when abolitionist women went on to consider their own experiences, as women, any pretentions to critical distance appear to have collapsed—at least temporarily, if perhaps not constantly. This allowed abolitionist women and their fellow reformers to extend the idea that women were born to slavery quite literally to themselves.

The manner in which abolitionist women pursued forms of metempsychosis increasingly elided any of the clear and important distinctions between what it meant to be an enslaved person of African descent and what it meant, as a free white woman, to advocate on their behalf. Many women's rights reformers had formative experiences in the antislavery movement. Susan B. Anthony, for example, an abolitionist and temperance advocate, later became one of the century's most preeminent suffragists. In an 1857 AASS address, she used metempsychosis to entreat her spectators to "make the slaves [*sic*] case our own." Asking her spectators to "feel that it is ourselves, and our 'kith & our kin,' who are despoiled of our inalienable right to life, liberty & the pursuit of happiness," Anthony implored that "could we but feel for the slave, as bound with him;—… and love him as ourself, [*sic*]—… how easy would be the task of converting us all to abolitionism."[137] There is little to suggest that Anthony's embrace of metempsychosis definitively ended with the abolition of chattel slavery in 1865. Across the next 50 years, the question of who exactly could be considered a slave or an enslaved class became increasingly slippery epistemic territory among women reformers, especially for suffragists such as Anthony and Stanton.

---

[136] Kari J. Winter, *Subjects of Slavery, Agents of Change: Women and Power in Gothic Novels and Slave Narratives, 1790–1865* (Athens: University of Georgia Press, 1992), 5.

[137] Susan B. Anthony, "Make the Slave's Case our Own," Speech for Tour for American Anti-Slavery Society, c. 1857, 2, 3–4, 8, 10, Susan B. Anthony Papers, Schlesinger Library.

In contrast, although the enslaved poet Phillis Wheatley herself had been born to freedom, most enslaved people of African descent were indeed born enslaved, especially following the abolition of the transatlantic slave trade. Antebellum slave narratives and other antislavery literature, which gained popularity in the transatlantic literary public sphere, solemnly attested to this reality. Many slave narratives began with the phrase "I was born," a literary convention through which self-emancipated African Americans asserted the full humanity of enslaved people of African descent.[138] Slave narratives penned by formerly enslaved women were less numerous but no less influential than those authored by men. However, self-emancipated women attested to the singularity of their own gendered experiences of chattel slavery. As Harriet Jacobs insisted: "Slavery is terrible for men; but it is far more terrible for women."[139] By offering testimonies of the lived experience of chattel slavery, slave narratives again demonstrated that enslaved people were born into slavery and free women were not.

As the woman-slave analogy gained greater prominence amongst abolitionists and women's rights reformers, the use of discourses of slavery began to create some controversy. Highly influential abolitionists, especially Frederick Douglass, expressed uncertainty about the implications of using such rhetoric to describe that which was not chattel slavery. In 1843, when antislavery lecturer John A. Collins suggested that the concept of private property was enslaving and perhaps worse than chattel slavery, Douglass and fellow black abolitionist Charles Remond objected.[140] Douglass also questioned the legitimacy of the slavery analogy during his 1845–1846 tour of the British Isles. Addressing spectators in Glasgow, Scotland, Douglass "denied" the notion of the laborer's wage slavery. "What was slavery?" he asked. "Let one who has experienced it in his own person tell ... the difference between American slavery and what, by the misuse of the term, was called slavery" in Britain. Nor did disenfranchisement necessarily constitute slavery, Douglass continued, "otherwise all women were slaves," as they were "universally deprived of this right." What was meant by slavery needed to be mindfully

---

[138] James Olney, "'I Was Born': Slave Narratives, Their Status as Autobiography and as Literature," *Callaloo* 20 (1984): 46–73.

[139] L. Maria Child, ed., *Incidents in the Life of a Slave Girl* (Boston: The Author, 1861), 119.

[140] Fought, *Women in the World*, 80–81.

connected to that which defined chattel slavery. This, he emphasized, was "the mark of the slave-driver's lash," "to be bought and sold in the market," and to have "all the powers of the mind of a man," yet still be considered property.[141]

It would seem to follow that, on account of his disapproval of the liberal manner in which some of his fellow reformers mobilized discourses of slavery, Douglass would express equal reticence toward those who promoted the woman-slave analogy. Yet, as his own women's rights advocacy reveals, this was not entirely the case. In 1848, Douglass attended the first women's rights convention in Seneca Falls, New York. The 1776 Declaration of Independence had excluded women, enslaved, and Indigenous people from its purview; however, it also offered an important model upon which many abolitionists and women's rights reformers built.[142] "We hold these truths to be self-evident, that all men *and women* are created equal," the Declaration of Sentiments and Resolutions, penned by Stanton and adopted by the convention, unequivocally asserted.[143] Douglass was quickly convinced of the need for women's rights and, alongside Stanton, became one of the few delegates to support the controversial demand for women's enfranchisement. In his support for women's rights and women's enfranchisement, Douglass would periodically embrace the woman-slave analogy well into the 1880s.

After the 1848 women's rights convention, Douglass published an editorial about its proceedings in his new abolitionist newspaper, the *North Star*. Aware that such a subject would likely incite "the fury of bigotry and the folly of prejudice," he offered a rationale for women's rights by drawing an analogy with the gradual success of the antislavery movement. "Many who have at last made the discovery that the negroes have some rights," Douglass emphasized, "have yet to be convinced that women are entitled to any." Although he did not begin his personal association with the AASS until 1841, Douglass went on to recall the organization's earlier

---

[141] Frederick Douglass, "An Account of American Slavery: An Address Delivered in Glasgow, Scotland, on January 15, 1846," *Glasgow Argus*, 22 January 1846, in *The Frederick Douglass Papers: Series One—Speeches, Debates, and Interviews*, Vol. I, eds. John Blassingame and C. Peter Ripley (New Haven: Yale University Press, 1979), 131. Thanks to Julie Husband for recommending this speech.

[142] Furstenberg, "Beyond Freedom," 1295–1296; Judith Wellman, "The Seneca Falls Women's Rights Convention: A Study of Social Networks," *Journal of Women's History* 3, no. 1 (1991): 9–37.

[143] Declaration of Sentiments and Resolutions, 19–20 July 1848, Elizabeth Cady Stanton and Susan B. Anthony Papers Project, Rutgers University.

controversies. Referring either to the AASS's 1839–1840 schism, the controversy surrounding the World's Convention, or both, he claimed:

> Eight years ago, a number of persons of this description actually abandoned the anti-slavery cause, lest by giving their influence in that direction they might possibly be giving countenance to the dangerous heresy that woman, in respect to rights, stands on an equal footing with man. In the judgment of such persons the American slave system, with all its concomitant horrors, is less to be deplored than this *wicked* idea.[144]

To support the women's cause, Douglass pursued an analogy between social movements rather than between women and enslaved people.

Women's rights reformers also mobilized this analogy between social movements. "We are the abolitionists of slavery among women," Davis declared of women's rights reformers in 1853, "and demand emancipation on the soil, not colonization on the clouds."[145] Davis and her coadjutors often described their movement and its goals in terms of antebellum abolitionism. Only days after these remarks appeared in her women's rights periodical, *Frederick Douglass' Paper* republished Davis' comments. "Well and happily said, every word of it," the latter editorialized.[146] This rejoinder evoked no sense of frustration that discourses of slavery should also be used to advocate women's rights, as long as its abolitionist mission was not obscured. Both the *North Star* and *Frederick Douglass' Paper* published excerpts of the proceedings and resolutions from women's rights conventions. Douglass' abolitionist newspapers would circulate—if not always fully endorse—the use of the woman-slave analogy among his fellow women's rights reformers.

Other antebellum reformers, however, soon began to question the efficacy of the woman-slave analogy, either for the benefit of women or enslaved people of African descent. This was epitomized in an infamous exchange between Jane Grey Swisshelm, the antislavery journalist and editor of Pittsburgh's *Saturday Visiter*, and the abolitionist and women's rights reformer Parker Pillsbury.[147] Following the 1850 women's rights convention in Worcester, New York, Swisshelm insisted that the "question of color had no right to a hearing." In a move that echoed—but inverted—

---

[144] "The Rights of Woman," *North Star*, 28 July 1848. See: *HWS*, Vol. I, 74–75.
[145] "The Moral Character of Woman," *Una*, 1 June 1853.
[146] "WOMAN," *Frederick Douglass' Paper*, 10 June 1853.
[147] See: Sklar, ed. *Women's Rights Emerges*, 191–196.

the concerns expressed by both the BFASS and AFASS at the World's Convention 10 years earlier, Swisshelm said: "One thing at a time!" "Many a man," she continued, "is in favor of emancipating every Southern slave, and granting the rights of citizenship to every free negro, who is by no means agreed that his wife or mother should stand on a political equality with himself." Deeply aware of how social reform could divide as well as unite, Swisshelm saw her approach as pragmatic. Other men and women were "anxious for the elevation of woman," she concluded, but "hate 'the niggers' [*sic*] most sovereignly. Why mingle the two questions?"[148]

The depth of concern that Douglass and Swisshelm expressed toward the use and misuse of language signaled, if to differing ends, the degree to which the woman-slave analogy had permeated social movement discourse by 1850. "Sex and color were emerging as the roots of two mutually exclusive political movements," Martha S. Jones observes; many reformers were unconvinced that the difficult questions surrounding race and gender could be adequately addressed by a single social movement.[149] The *North Star* published Pillsbury's reply to Swisshelm, in which he emphasized the situation of African-American women. "That ANY woman [*sic*] have rights," he acknowledged, "will scarcely be believed; but that colored women have rights, would never have been thought of, without a specific declaration."[150] Like Stanton and Anthony, with whom he would work closely during the 1860s and 1870s, Pillsbury became a lifelong proponent of the woman-slave analogy.

Swisshelm, however, remained unconvinced. Although she, like Pillsbury, was sympathetic to both causes, Swisshelm continued to believe that it was "bad policy" to bring the reforms together. "The women of this glorious Republic are sufficiently oppressed without linking their cause to that of the slave. The slave is sufficiently oppressed without binding him to the stake which has ever held woman in a state of bondage," she argued. Two years earlier, Douglass himself had similarly alluded to what amounted to a constant concern for many reformers. Abolitionism and women's rights appeared exceedingly radical to antebellum onlookers in

---

[148] Jane Grey Swisshelm, *Saturday Visiter*, 2 November 1850.

[149] Martha S. Jones, *All Bound Up Together: The Woman Question in African American Public Culture, 1830–1900* (Chapel Hill: University of North Carolina Press, 2007), 92.

[150] Parker Pillsbury, "Woman's Rights Convention and People of Color," *North Star*, 5 December 1850.

isolation, let alone together. "Nothing can ever persuade us that the union of the two questions has not injured both," Swisshelm reflected, an exceptional assertion in a reform culture that had become mired in rationales that were grounded in discourses of slavery.[151] In spite of these criticisms, a woman-as-slave worldview became central to envisioning what reformers were increasingly perceiving as many different forms of oppression.

The 1850s is often described as the moment when women's rights reformers began to transform their activism on behalf of others into activism on behalf of themselves. The woman-slave analogy had also become a "staple of feminist rhetoric," soon gaining greater prominence and circulation in the new women's rights periodicals such as Amelia Bloomer's *Lily*, Davis' *Una*, and Lydia Sayer Hasbrouck's *Sibyl*.[152] At the same time, however, some women's rights reformers remained reticent to establish an actual organization. The 1852 women's rights convention "rejected a proposal for a national women's rights society on the grounds that formal organizations 'fetter and distort the expanding mind.'"[153] These reservations were expressed by none other than Angelina Grimké Weld, the former abolitionist who had personally experienced the full force of the AASS's organizational structure during the 1830s.

What one scholar describes as the "improbable connection" between women's status and that of enslaved people of African descent constituted a revelation for many women reformers, one that enabled fellow reformers and their spectators to finally comprehend the reality of women's situation.[154] The proceedings of women's rights conventions during the 1850s attest to the prominence of the woman-slave analogy as much as to the consternation it could cause. President Asa Mahan, of the coeducational Oberlin College, Ohio, questioned the use of discourses of slavery, either with respect to the governor and the governed or husband and wife.[155] Most reformers, however, were far less critical of this rhetoric. As another reformer, Rev. Thomas Wentworth Higginson, implored: "The only

---

[151] Jane Grey Swisshelm, "Woman's Rights and the Color Question," *Saturday Visiter*, 23 November 1850.

[152] Yellin, *Women and Sisters*, 129.

[153] DuBois, *Feminism and Suffrage*, 51; Angelina Grimké Weld, *HWS*, Vol. I, 540–542.

[154] Quanquin, "'There Are Two Great Oceans'," 82.

[155] *Proceedings of the National Women's Rights Convention, Held at Cleveland, Ohio, on Wednesday, Thursday and Friday, October 5th, 6th, and 7th, 1853* (Cleveland: Gray, Beardsley, Spear, 1854), 185–186.

demand of our female reformers is to be set free."[156] However, while the reality of women's situation was indeed dire, it was not, in fact, chattel slavery. The failure to adequately communicate this distinction would plague white women's rights reformers across the nineteenth century.

Only infrequently did African-American women's perspectives about the women's rights movement gain circulation during the 1850s. However, as women such as Sojourner Truth, Frances Ellen Watkins Harper, Anna Julia Cooper, Pauline E. Hopkins, and Mary Church Terrell achieved greater prominence, they did not always refute the ways in which their contemporaries embraced discourses of slavery. In fact, on some occasions, each seemed to purposefully respond to white women's proclamations by using similar rhetoric. Thus, African-American women used discourses of slavery not to proclaim that all women experienced oppression equally, but to highlight their own experiences. "We are all bound up together in one great bundle of humanity," Harper insisted in 1866, "and society cannot trample on the weakest and feeblest of its members without receiving the curse in its own soul."[157] For Harper, being "bound up together" did not mean all peoples experienced the same degree of oppression in the same manner; rather, it meant emancipation needed to be collective.[158]

Across lives dedicated to social reform, the women who had been present at the World's Convention would bring different perspectives to their use of the woman-slave analogy. Lucretia Mott had used the comparison to illustrate the hypocrisy of the World's Convention, a criticism based upon the exclusion of women in contrast to the inclusion of men of African descent. In its aftermath, Marion Reid returned to the long-held notion that women were born to slavery. And increasingly, Elizabeth Cady Stanton employed the woman-slave analogy to ever more racist ends—to advocate for the inclusion of white women but, effectively, the exclusion of African-American men and women. These tensions would persist across the nineteenth century. When reminiscing again in 1898, Stanton continued to find it "remarkable" that "abolitionists, who felt so keenly the wrongs of the slave, should be so oblivious to

---

[156] Thomas Wentworth Higginson, *Woman and Her Wishes; an Essay: Inscribed to The Massachusetts Constitutional Convention* (Boston: Robert F. Wallcut, 1853), 26.

[157] "We Are All Bound up Together," 1866, in *A Brighter Coming Day: A Frances Ellen Watkins Harper Reader*, ed. Frances Smith Foster (New York: The Feminist Press, 1990), 217–219.

[158] Jones, *All Bound Up Together*, 1–3.

the equal wrongs of their own mothers, wives, and sisters," when both were accorded a "similar legal status."[159]

Conclusion

Lucy Stone found in *The Greek Slave* a figure "emblematic of women," yet the foundations for her personal insight were far from new. On the cusp of the nineteenth century, Mary Wollstonecraft had transformed how women might approach the slavery analogy. Decades later, Sarah Grimké, Angelina Grimké Weld, and countless others would share in a transatlantic reform culture inspired by the political theory of John Locke and Wollstonecraft herself, as well as the immediate abolitionism of William Lloyd Garrison.[160] Having discovered Wollstonecraft's writings only recently, antebellum abolitionists and women's rights reformers found not only a foremother but also a philosophical and rhetorical progenitor with whom they imagined themselves to be in dialogue.[161] In effect, metempsychosis offered abolitionist women the opportunity to dramatize what they read in *A Vindication of the Rights of Women* (1792). Yet, while Wollstonecraft could only ever imagine the existence of enslaved peoples in far-flung colonies, the Grimké sisters lived in the midst of chattel slavery, in ease and privilege, on account of their exploited labors. Wollstonecraft offered this new generation parallels that were all the more tangible in their own historical moment on the other side of the Atlantic.

Through their preoccupation with the woman-slave analogy, most white women reformers cultivated the sense of sameness that Carla L. Peterson identifies.[162] Some of their contemporaries, however, would take another path. At the beginning of the Civil War, Harriet Jacobs again challenged white abolitionists and women's rights reformers to remember

---

[159] Elizabeth Cady Stanton, *Eighty Years and More: Reminiscences 1815–1897* (New York: T. Fisher Unwin, 1898).

[160] Alison M. Parker, *Articulating Rights: Nineteenth-Century American Women on Race, Reform, and the State* (DeKalb: Northern Illinois University Press, 2010), 6.

[161] Eileen Hunt Botting and Christine Carey, "Wollstonecraft's Philosophical Impact on Nineteenth-Century American Women's Rights Advocates," *American Journal of Political Science* 48, no. 4 (2004): 707–722; Kennon, "An Apple of Discord," 259–260.

[162] Carla L. Peterson, "'And We Claim Our Rights': The Rights Rhetoric of Black and White Women Activists before the Civil War," in *Sister Circle: Black Women and Work*, eds. Sharon Harley and the Black Women and Work Collective (New Brunswick: Rutgers University Press, 2002).

that they had not, in fact, been born to slavery: "O virtuous reader! You never knew what it is to be a slave; to be entirely unprotected by law or custom; to have the laws reduce you to the condition of a chattel, entirely subject to the will of another."[163] African-American reformers would embrace discourses of slavery to highlight the plight of all enslaved people as well as the rights of women, while working-class women developed criticisms of capitalist labor exploitation. Other commentators and lawmakers, in turn, mobilized this rhetoric to support and perpetuate the patriarchal and racial status quo. Across the coming decades, the woman-slave analogy would proliferate across the women's rights, dress reform, labor, suffrage, free love, racial uplift, and anti-vice movements.

[163] *Incidents in the Life of a Slave Girl*, 86.

CHAPTER 3

"Bought and Sold": Antislavery, Women's Rights, and Marriage

The analogy between marriage and chattel slavery was the most common expression of the woman-slave analogy. To describe a free woman as being "bought and sold" was to indicate the lack of autonomy she experienced in courtship and marriage. In 1850, women's rights reformer Elizabeth Cady Stanton concluded: "A married woman is not supposed to have any legal existence. She has no more absolute rights than a slave on a southern plantation."[1] Describing the heroine's fate in a popular proslavery novel published the same year, Caroline Lee Hentz also wrote of how marriageable women were "bought and sold like a negro slave."[2] Stanton's interpretation, shaped by the legal and political imperatives of the women's rights movement, rejected the laws relating to marriage and, to a lesser extent, chattel slavery. But Hentz's interpretation accepted the status quo of chattel slavery and developed a criticism of the subjugation of privileged white women in marriage alone. Though similarly phrased, each was informed by vastly different political perspectives.

Many abolitionist women evinced a corporeal self-identification between themselves and enslaved people of African descent across the 1830s, a decade during which their efforts in the antislavery movement

[1] E.C.S., "Why Must Women Vote," *Lily*, May 1850.
[2] Caroline Lee Hentz, *Linda; or, the Young Pilot of the Belle Creole* (Philadelphia: T.B. Peterson & Brothers, 1850), 104.

© The Author(s) 2019
A. Stevenson, *The Woman as Slave in Nineteenth-Century American Social Movements*, Palgrave Studies in the History of Social Movements, https://doi.org/10.1007/978-3-030-24467-5_3

were increasingly contested. Abolitionists and women's rights reformers developed a criticism of marriage that principally challenged white men's dominance. At the center of what Karen Sánchez-Eppler describes as the "intersecting rhetorics of feminism and abolitionism" existed an acknowledgment that the physical differences attributed to women and Africans proscribed any claims to personhood beyond the norms of white masculinity. Much antislavery literature, she argues, presented the two institutions—marriage and chattel slavery—not simply as analogous but, in fact, as "coextensive and indistinguishable." Yet the lived experiences of free women and enslaved people of African descent were, of course, vastly different. While the "identifications of woman and slave, marriage and slavery may [have] occasionally prove[d] mutually empowering," Sánchez-Eppler concludes, the comparison more often tended toward "asymmetry and exploitation."[3]

However, antislavery and proslavery white women were far from alone in using the woman-slave analogy to inform their analysis of the marriage relation. By examining the perspectives of abolitionists, self-emancipated African Americans, and women's rights reformers alongside that of proslavery commentators, this chapter offers a comprehensive sense of the connection many Americans saw between marriage and chattel slavery. How, then, did discourses of slavery—for example, yokes, fetters, chains, bondage, and shackles, as well as tyranny—shape discussions about marriage and its legal implications, as much as its legal absence? The degree to which abolitionist women engaged with metempsychosis suggests that their use of discourses of slavery could be less metaphorical and more literal than has previously been accepted. As more antislavery and women's rights reformers came to interpret their courtships and marriages in these terms, many found the personal to be political in their own unions. However, in contrast to the white women reformers who often used antislavery tropes to examine their own situation, black and white abolitionists embraced discourses of slavery to articulate concerns about the lack of legal marriage among enslaved people of African descent. The analogy between marriage and chattel slavery was also exceedingly common in proslavery thought, extending to the letters and diaries of elite southern women as much as to popular culture. Yet, unlike northern reformers, southern women consistently used this rhetoric to endorse rather than to question chattel slavery.

---

[3] Karen Sanchez-Eppler, *Touching Liberty: Abolition, Feminism, and the Politics of the Body* (Berkeley: University of California Press, 1993), 14–16.

Each of these rhetorical traditions continued, but also began to undergo a conceptual revision, in the era of slave emancipation.

This chapter begins to chart the transformation in the use of the woman-slave analogy, a conceptual shift that will be explored throughout this book. The approach of many women reformers actually began to change in the wake of the Fugitive Slave Law of 1850. Some began to discuss the plight of the "fugitive wife," a new trope that depicted unloved or battered women attempting to flee husbands and fiancés from whom they ultimately cannot escape. This literary device appeared with ever greater frequency in the decades following the Civil War. The fugitive wife, postbellum women's rights reformers and free love advocates argued, faced a worse fate than enslaved people of African descent during the antebellum era. This represented the foundations for an important shift, as many antebellum reformers had rejected chattel slavery as much as women's subjugation in marriage. After the abolition of chattel slavery, rather than remaining attentive to oppression derived from gender, race, and class, the fugitive wife trope allowed some reformers to begin to refocus their attention toward the situation of white women alone.

A Lighter Yoke to Wear?

The marriage contract began to be redefined as the foundations of family property rights as early as the fourteenth century.[4] Uniquely indissoluble as a contract, it continued to be based on a fundamental power imbalance between contractors well into the nineteenth century and beyond.[5] In spite of the reality of economic necessity, women appeared to enter a voluntary contract when they married. Chattel slavery, however, was inherited matrilineally and was more obviously coercive. As Nancy F. Cott emphasizes, the "pairing of unequals" was the most striking feature of both institutions, as power and superiority worked to construct independence and dependence.[6] The notion of woman as property was enduring but also constantly contested in love, marriage, and the passing of the

---

[4] Carole Pateman, *The Sexual Contract* (Stanford: Stanford University Press, 1988), 154, 180–181.

[5] Amy Dru Stanley, *From Bondage to Contract: Wage Labor, Marriage, and the Market in the Age of Slave Emancipation* (Cambridge: Cambridge University Press, 1998), 4, 8.

[6] Nancy F. Cott, *Public Vows: A History of Marriage and the Nation* (Cambridge, MA: Harvard University Press, 2000), 62.

married women's property acts—and perhaps most especially amongst social reformers.

Marriage based upon romantic love gained greater importance by the late eighteenth century and would become widely accepted as an antebellum cultural ideal.[7] This process promoted women's autonomy, although perhaps only inadvertently because the notion of "falling in love" was predicated on spiritual affinity.[8] According to Chris Dixon, antebellum reformers hoped to revolutionize marriage and envisaged companionate marriage as an ideal that diverged from the institution's legal and patriarchal hierarchy.[9] Many believed that true individualism could be found through true marriage. "In the true marriage relation," Lucretia Mott reflected in 1875, "the independence of the husband and the wife is equal, their dependence mutual, and their obligations reciprocal."[10]

But these new romantic ideals were in conflict with the legal and social realities of marriage. The sentimental emphasis on romantic love did not blind women to the fact that marriage was often contracted for economic reasons.[11] Many women embraced discourses of slavery to describe feelings about their own unions. Largely abstracted from ideas about chattel slavery, these musings had far more to do with women's consciousness of their restrictions in a patriarchal society. Women could begin to come to terms with their loss of independence after marriage because, unlike the discourse of romantic love, discourses of slavery allowed wives and husbands to interrogate the marriage relation critically.[12] The 1802 diary of northerner Mary Orne Tucker, for example, considered "proper motives" alone

---

[7] Karen Lystra, *Searching the Heart: Women, Men, and Romantic Love in Nineteenth-Century America* (Oxford: Oxford University Press, 1989); Elizabeth Maddock Dillon, *The Gender of Freedom: Fictions of Liberalism and the Literary Public Sphere* (Stanford: Stanford University Press, 2004).

[8] Steven Seidman, *Romantic Longings: Love in America, 1830–1980* (New York: Routledge, 1991), 31.

[9] Chris Dixon, *Perfecting the Family: Antislavery Marriages in Nineteenth-Century America* (Amherst: University of Massachusetts Press, 1997).

[10] Lucretia Mott quote clipping, 1875, Lucretia Coffin Mott—Biographical material and memorabilia (1873–1930, n.d.), Garrison Family Papers—Series IX: Wright Family, Sophia Smith Collection.

[11] Nancy F. Cott, *The Bonds of Womanhood: "Woman's Sphere" in New England, 1780–1835* (New Haven: Yale University Press, 1977), 76–77.

[12] Amy Dru Stanley, "Conjugal Bonds and Wage Labor: Rights of Contract in the Age of Emancipation," *Journal of American History* 75, no. 2 (1988): 478.

to render women "insensible of the bondage" of marriage. Otherwise, matrimony could prove "a galling chain":

> *Souls* must be *kindred* to make the bands silken[.] ... I rejoice that the knot which binds me was not tied with any mercenary feelings, and ... my heart is under the same *sweet* subjection as my *hand*.[13]

Sometimes, men paying suit even used discourses of slavery to allay their sweethearts' fears. To assure his fiancée that she was no "prisoner," one southerner wrote that "no compulsion, no fetters but such as Love shall forge ... bind you to the engagement."[14] However, as women became increasingly aware of the gendered restrictions of marriage, they were not always convinced by such entreaties. As another northerner reflected in 1819, "It is but seldom husbands bring/A lighter yoke to wear."[15]

Abolitionists and women's rights reformers developed more direct and expansive criticisms of marriage. Many embraced companionate marriage and began to place this ideal against what they viewed as its antithesis: the marriage that was inherently oppressive, they contended, constituted the slavery of women. Since the ideal of romantic love, celebrated in verse and literature, failed to reflect the institution's domestic realities, marriage rendered women "chattels personal to be used and abused at the will of a master," the unmarried Sarah Grimké argued.[16] For the abolitionist women who had gained prominence prior to marrying abolitionist men, this took on greater significance. The degree to which abolitionists employed antislavery discourse to describe their own relationships illustrated just how thoroughly their reform commitments resonated across

---

[13] Mary Orne Tucker Diary, 17 April 1802, James Duncan Phillips Library, Essex Institute, in Cott, *Bonds of Womanhood*, 76–77.

[14] William Wirt to Elizabeth Gamble, 3 August 1802, William Wirt Papers, Maryland Historical Society, in Anya Jabour, "'No Fetters but Such as Love Shall Forge': Elizabeth and William Wirt and Marriage in the Early Republic," *Virginia Magazine of History and Biography* 104, no. 2 (1996): 216–217.

[15] Lucy Beckley Journal-Book, 1819, Connecticut Historical Society, in Cott, *Bonds of Womanhood*, 77.

[16] "Marriage," n.d., *The Grimké Sisters from South Carolina: Pioneers for Women's Rights and Abolition*, ed. Gerda Lerner (Chapel Hill: University of North Carolina Press, 1967/2004), 308. Lerner ascribes this to Sarah Grimké, although not beyond reasonable doubt, see: Lerner, *Grimké Sisters*, 297–302.

their personal lives.[17] As early as the 1830s, women reformers who were seeking to establish more egalitarian unions for themselves began to describe the marriages they considered to be inherently oppressive through ever more overt allusions to chattel slavery.

Many abolitionist women approached the institution with ambivalence. Marriage was "*sinful*," according to Angelina Grimké; it did not inspire "higher, nobler sentiments," but made the "lower passions *captive* to their will, the *latter* seemed to be *lords* over the former."[18] The Grimké sisters were deeply influenced by the abolitionist analysis of sexuality, which was tainted through its association with slaveholders' despotic abuse of power as well as patriarchal domination in marriage.[19] Upon Angelina's 1838 marriage to abolitionist Theodore Dwight Weld, the couple provocatively omitted the word "obey" from their vows, as would later reform brides such as Elizabeth Cady Stanton, Amelia Bloomer, and Lucy Stone.[20] Historians suggest that Angelina Grimké Weld's subsequent retreat into domesticity offered a cautionary tale for the difficulties of continuing a career on the abolitionist lecture circuit at the same time as becoming a wife and mother.[21] While this withdrawal from public life certainly revealed the competing tensions and attractions of domesticity, it also illustrated the degree to which many reformers believed in reforming the individual as well as the world.[22]

---

[17] Dixon, *Perfecting the Family*, 169; Hélène Quanquin, "'There Are Two Great Oceans': The Slavery Metaphor in the Antebellum Women's Rights Discourse as a Redescription of Race and Gender," in *Interconnections: Gender and Race in American History*, eds. Carol Faulkner and Alison M. Parker (Rochester: University of Rochester Press, 2012), 86–90.

[18] Angelina Grimké to Theodore Dwight Weld, 4 March 1838, in *Letters of Theodore Dwight Weld, Angelina Grimke Weld, and Sarah Grimke, 1822–1844*, Vol. II, eds. G.H. Barnes and D.L. Dumond (Gloucester: Peter Smith, 1965), 587.

[19] Dixon, *Perfecting the Family*, Chapter 6; Robert K. Nelson, "'The Forgetfulness of Sex': Devotion and Desire in the Courtship Letters of Angelina Grimke and Theodore Dwight Weld," *Journal of Social History* 37, no. 3 (2004): 664.

[20] Lerner, *Grimké Sisters*, 175–182; Elisabeth Griffith, *In Her Own Right: The Life of Elizabeth Cady Stanton* (New York: Oxford University Press, 1984), 33; Marilyn Yalom, *A History of the Wife* (New York: Perennial, 2001), 198; Joelle Million, *Woman's Voice, Woman's Place: Lucy Stone and the Birth of the Woman's Rights Movement* (Westport: Praeger, 2003), 195.

[21] Lerner, *Grimké Sisters*, 167, 181, 203–206; Katharine du Pre Lumpkin, *The Emancipation of Angelina Grimke* (Chapel Hill: University of North Carolina Press, 1974), 146–149, 166–203; Dixon, *Perfecting the Family*, 92–97.

[22] Dixon, *Perfecting the Family*, 92–93.

If, in their use of the woman-slave analogy, women reformers fostered a greater awareness of their own powerlessness as wives, then this rhetoric could also imbue men with a greater sense of their own autonomy. Prior to what they believed would be companionate marriages, some abolitionist men expressed a desire to "liberate" their fiancées and wives from family restrictions.[23] In the late 1830s, Judge Daniel Cady did not condone his daughter Elizabeth's marriage to Henry Stanton. Averse to having a radical antislavery agent in the family, Judge Cady was also uncertain of the young man's financial viability.[24] Should Elizabeth remain with her disapproving family while Henry attended the World's Anti-Slavery Convention of 1840, he wrote to his friend Gerrit Smith (also a Cady cousin), his sweetheart would be "*in chains*" by his return.[25] Soon after their marriage, however, the Stantons became ideologically divided over women's participation at the World's Convention, which is often cited as establishing, or at least inspiring, the young Elizabeth Cady Stanton's evolving commitment to women's rights.[26]

Abby Kelley, the abolitionist who had identified so deeply with the principles of metempsychosis, also believed in reforming the self in the context of courtship. "I *can* and *ought* to *discipline myself*," she decided of her feelings for fiancé, abolitionist Stephen S. Foster, during the early 1840s. Stephen's courtship repartee could not have helped allay her fears, however. "Now you are my *own*," he wrote to Abby:

> Perhaps you do not like the idea of being so thoroughly possessed by another, but I shall hold you *fast*. ... I shall henceforth claim & hold you as my *own* property. I shall now *tyrannize* over you to my heart's content so you may prepare for it & make a virtue of submission.

Of course, reformers sometimes uttered possessive sentiments with irony or as romantic repartee; yet these men conveyed a sense of ownership nonetheless. Mockingly invoking the biblical command, "wives submit yourselves unto your husbands," Stephen directed his fiancée to "surrender ... and submit quietly to my authority as a good dutiful loving wife

---

[23] Ibid., 167.
[24] Griffith, *In Her Own Right*, 30.
[25] Henry Stanton to Gerrit Smith, 17 May 1840, Gerrit Smith Papers, Syracuse University Library, in Dixon, *Perfecting the Family*, 167–168.
[26] Griffith, *In Her Own Right*, Chapter 3; Dixon, *Perfecting the Family*, 88–89; Yalom, *A History*, 198–199.

should." Antebellum reformers espoused a more comprehensive understanding of the marriage contract and its legal implications than many of their contemporaries. So, while Abby believed Stephen to be "jesting," she warned him not to "push your jokes too far." As Abby nonetheless concluded, if Stephen brought "shackles broken, whips dust-trodden" together with "a proclamation of emancipation," then she would "yield to her good knight, [who] holds her heart of hearts most truly."[27] The companionate ideal, these reformers hoped, would persist despite all else.

This rhetorical interplay only intensified between abolitionist couples across the 1850s. "Tis next to a chattel slave, to be a *legal* wife," Lucy Stone confided to her friend Antoinette Brown, who would later become her sister-in-law.[28] Much like Kelley, Stone was conflicted about her relationship with Henry B. Blackwell and the restrictions that marriage placed on women. Unlike many suitors and husbands, including other reformers, Henry desired that Lucy would maintain her individuality and reform efforts following marriage. "[M]y love shall *never fetter you* one iota," he assured her. However, when Lucy initially refused to consider his marriage proposal, Henry believed that this rebuttal was to "subject oneself to a more abject slavery than ever actually existed."[29] For Henry, marriage, the law, and chattel slavery systemically created and perpetuated forms of oppression that individuals needed to transcend. Following Lucy's consent to marry, the Stone-Blackwells created a marriage protest that renounced the legal authority vested in husbands. The document was circulated by Rev. Thomas Wentworth Higginson, their marriage officiator and fellow abolitionist, and appeared in such reform newspapers as the *Liberator*, the *Lily*, and the *Una*.[30] Its continued significance was confirmed at century's end, when the couple's suffrage newspaper, the

---

[27] Abby Kelley to Stephen Foster, 30 July 1843; Foster to Kelley, 10 August 1843; Kelley to Foster, 13 August 1843, Abby Kelley Foster Papers, 1836–1891, American Antiquarian Society, in Dorothy Sterling, *Ahead of Her Time: Abby Kelley and the Politics of Antislavery* (New York: W.W. Norton & Company, 1991), 204–205.

[28] Lucy Stone to Antoinette Brown, 9 June 1850, in *Friends and Sisters: Letters between Lucy Stone and Antoinette Brown Blackwell, 1846–93*, eds. Carol Lasser and Marlene D. Merrill (Urbana: University of Illinois Press, 1987), 72.

[29] Henry B. Blackwell to Lucy Stone, 2 May 1854; Blackwell to Stone, 12 July 1854, Lucy Stone Papers, Library of Congress, in Dixon, *Perfecting the Family*, 169.

[30] "Marriage of Lucy Stone Under Protest," *Liberator*, 4 May 1855; F.W.H., "A Marriage Under Protest," *Lily*, 15 May 1855; "Marriage of Lucy Stone Under Protest," *Una*, May 1855. This document did not have any legal standing.

Woman's Journal, venerated a reprint of the Stone-Blackwell marriage protest.[31]

Together, abolitionists and women's rights reformers normalized the woman-slave analogy in the context of a reformist criticism of marriage. As the *Lily* observed in its 1856 report about the marriage of dress reformer Mary E. Walker and Albert E. Miller, the institution was "enthralling women" with "laws and customs that give to man unlimited powers to oppress her." But, the newspaper also emphasized, "true marriage" would result in "liberty" and "happiness."[32] The rank-and-file responded to the example set by famous reform couples by penning their own marriage protests. "Freedom is our motto," one couple asserted when their vows appeared in a dress-reform periodical:

> We see nothing inviting in the track of bondage; we have no assurity that the flag of liberty floats there. Therefore, free to act and think, we have resolved never to wear the galling chains of modern legalization. We are too well aware that love comes not from chains and prison walls.[33]

For this rank-and-file couple, as for their more famous contemporaries, discourses of slavery offered what had become a normative description of marriage. By looking toward individualism as the ideal that defined "true" marriage, this couple challenged what, for many other reformers, could be an inherently oppressive institution. Constantly cited as a necessary preclusion to marriage, love was believed to establish freedom as a corollary to the slavery of woman that would otherwise be engendered.

Marriage in Antebellum Reformist Print Culture

Marriage became an object of criticism for both abolitionists and women's rights reformers, who regarded it as a form of contractual slavery. Many embraced the analogy between marriage and chattel slavery, envisaging the bondswoman as an "abject icon" representative of a total loss of self-ownership. "By defining freedom through the negative example of the female slave's subjection," Amy Dru Stanley argues, "abolitionists opened

---

[31] Lucy Stone and Henry Brown Blackwell, "Marriage Protest," *Woman's Journal*, 28 October 1893.

[32] "Unions," *Lily*, January 1856.

[33] Geo. Wellington Lewis and Harriet Wheeler Lewis, "Marriage Without Ceremony," *Sibyl*, 1 July 1857.

to question the right of women to own themselves."[34] One of the most enduring criticisms that women's rights reformers developed was the analogy between the slaveowner and the husband, a comparison indebted to the abolitionist trope of the lascivious, rapacious slaveholder. However, at least some antislavery literature problematized the analogy between marriage and chattel slavery in a manner that seldom occurred elsewhere. African Americans, for example, criticized the lack of legal marriage amongst enslaved people of African descent, as the marriage contract also signified access to civic society.

Antislavery literature established trends that would have deep consequences for the women's rights print culture that developed in the postbellum era. The fate of enslaved women was at the center of much antislavery literature, which often focused on a character archetype described as the tragic mulatta. This literary trope centered on a mixed-race character, often enslaved but sometimes precariously free, whose destiny was "overdetermined" by chattel slavery.[35] Some literary scholars view the tragic mulatta as an unfortunate concession to the white reading public; others suggest that the trope was developed strategically, especially by black abolitionists, to challenge the expectations of their northern readership and assert the full humanity of enslaved people of African descent.[36] Julie Husband suggests that the tragic mulatta became a useful representational surrogate for analyzing the degree to which sexual coercion, violence, and a lack of self-ownership characterized both chattel slavery and marriage. Often, reform literature displaced distasteful discussions about women's lack of autonomy onto this character. This resulted in an explicit narrative connection between the tragic mulatta's fate and that of her free counterpart, a married white woman.[37]

[34] Stanley, *From Bondage to Contract*, Chapter 1, esp. 26–28.

[35] Eve Allegra Raimon, *The "Tragic Mulatta" Revisited: Race and Nationalism in Nineteenth-Century Antislavery Fiction* (New Brunswick: Rutgers University Press, 2004), 5.

[36] Jean Fagan Yellin, *Women and Sisters: The Antislavery Feminists in American Culture* (New Haven: Yale University Press, 1989), 71–74; Ann duCille, *The Coupling Convention: Sex, Text, and Tradition in Black Women's Fiction* (New York: Oxford University Press, 1993), 6–7; Raimon, *The "Tragic Mulatta,"* esp. 5–25; Adélékè Adéèkó, "Signatures of Blood in William Wells Brown's *Clotel*," *Nineteenth-Century Contexts: An Interdisciplinary Journal* 21, no. 1 (1999): 115–134; Venetria K. Patton, *Women in Chains: The Legacy of Slavery in Black Women's Fiction* (Albany: State University of New York Press, 2000), 94–95.

[37] Julie Husband, *Antislavery Discourse and Nineteenth-Century American Literature: Incendiary Pictures* (New York: Palgrave Macmillan, 2010), 90.

One of the key legal differences between chattel slavery and freedom, however, was that free people could marry and enslaved people could not. Enslaved people deeply valued marital relationships despite these legal and cultural obstacles, sometimes finding fulfillment in such unions after experiences of family separation.[38] Antislavery literature explored the ambiguities that resulted from the legal differences between marriage for the enslaved and for the free. According to Tess Chakkalakal, the "slave-marriage plot" explored narratives about "non-legal unions," which ultimately "challenged what it meant to be husband and wife in nineteenth-century America."[39] While consensual, if non-legal, interracial unions could exist, coercive and non-consensual liaisons were far more frequent.[40] The discourse of seduction effaced the possibility of the rape of black women, both in the eyes of the legal establishment and on account of insidious stereotypes about lasciviousness.[41] Abolitionists responded by highlighting the prevalence of rape on southern plantations, an act slaveholders routinely used to discipline, punish, and dehumanize enslaved women while maintaining white supremacy.[42]

To illuminate the absolute power that slaveowners and other white southerners possessed, antislavery literature depicted the ill-fated consequences of interracial love under chattel slavery. Lydia Maria Child's 1842 short story, "The Quadroons," highlighted what the marriage contract's legal absence meant for enslaved women, and thus obliquely acknowledged the legal protections it did offer free women.[43] "I would not, if I could, hold you by a legal fetter," the mixed-race character Rosalie tells her white paramour, mistakenly believing in the transcendence of romantic love. The marriage contract, described as a "legal fetter," is envisaged as an impediment to romantic love; however, its absence soon proves

---

[38] Heather Andrea Williams, *Help Me to Find My People: The African-American Search for Family Lost in Slavery* (Chapel Hill: University of North Carolina Press, 2012), Chapter 2.

[39] Tess Chakkalakal, *Novel Bondage: Slavery, Marriage, and Freedom in Nineteenth-Century America* (Urbana: University of Illinois Press, 2011), 1.

[40] Cott, *Public Vows*, 42–45.

[41] Saidiya V. Hartman, *Scenes of Subjection: Terror, Slavery, and Self-Making in Nineteenth-Century America* (New York: Oxford University Press, 1997), Chapter 3; Deborah Gray White, *Ar'n't I a Woman? Female Slaves in the Plantation South*, Revised Edition (New York: W.W. Norton & Company, 1985, 1999), Chapter 1.

[42] Estelle B. Freedman, *Redefining Rape: Sexual Violence in the Era of Suffrage and Segregation* (Cambridge: Harvard University Press, 2013), 27–32; Dixon, *Perfecting the Family*, Chapter 1.

[43] Yellin, *Women and Sisters*, 72.

pivotal. The paramour, "weakened in moral principle, and unfettered by laws of the land," later abandons Rosalie and their daughter.[44] Child's focus on the protective potential of the marriage contract obscured, at least partially, the claims of those abolitionist women who saw the marriage contract as a source of their own oppression.

African-American abolitionists offered competing but not wholly incompatible interpretations of similar circumstances. William Wells Brown's novel *Clotel; or, The President's Daughter* (1853) was partially inspired by Child's short story of a decade earlier.[45] The novel narrated the fictional fate of President Thomas Jefferson's mixed-race, illegitimate daughter. It commences with the title character, her "complexion as white as most of those who were waiting with a wish to become her purchasers," standing upon the auction block:

> Why stands she near the auction stand,
> That girl so young and fair?
> What brings her to this dismal place,
> Why stands she weeping there?

Brown interpreted Clotel's exploitation as ironic because of her whiteness and reprehensible due to her legal vulnerability. Although Clotel and her white paramour, Horatio, later embark upon "marriage," like Rosalie, she vows that should his "affections fall" or his "conscience" impel him to abandon her, she "would not, if I could, hold you by a single fetter." When Horatio later marries a wealthy white woman, Clotel rejects his invitation to remain "his real wife" and spurns him.[46] To their own peril, enslaved female characters in other antislavery literature—including Rosalie, Clotel, and Cassy from Harriet Beecher Stowe's *Uncle Tom's Cabin; or, Life Among the Lowly* (1852)—become victimized on account of what amount to non-legal unions. Both Child and Brown used discourses of slavery to describe a specific problem, namely the absence of legal protections for mixed-race and enslaved women under chattel slavery.

Antislavery literature stressed the freedoms that married women enjoyed regardless of the marriage contract. In contrast, women's rights

---

[44] Lydia Maria Child, "The Quadroons," in *The Liberty Bell*, ed. Friends of Freedom (Boston: Massachusetts Anti-Slavery Fair, 1842), 118, 222.
[45] Raimon, *The "Tragic Mulatta,"* 65.
[46] William Wells Brown, *Clotel; or, the President's Daughter: A Narrative of Slave Life in the United States* (New York: Dover Publications, 1853, 2004), 7, 1, 21, 43.

reformers became ever more inclined to pursue emphatic comparisons between matrimonial oppression and chattel slavery. This analysis departed from the ideal of romantic love and instead recast the husband in the same terms as the slaveowner. Upon marriage, Elizabeth Cady Stanton maintained, women not only lost their legal existence but also took the "name of her master": "Civilly, socially and religiously, she is what man chooses her to be, nothing more or less,—and such is the slave, and this is slavery."[47] The use of analogy enabled antebellum women reformers to both acknowledge and overlook the similarities and differences between marriage and chattel slavery.[48] Estelle B. Freedman observes the continuance of such an analysis in the postbellum era, when a column in the *Woman's Journal*, "Crimes against Women," compared the white male assailants of white women to antebellum slaveowners. However, suffragists employed this rhetoric to advocate for white women's voting rights while overlooking the degree to which emerging racist stereotypes about the black rapist were being used to deny black men's voting rights.[49]

At least some women's rights reformers considered the specific characteristics of each institution. Married women could not be "sold" or "bartered" for the husband's "pecuniary benefit," Paulina Wright Davis rationalized, making wives, in this respect, unlike enslaved people of African descent. But neither could married women change "a bad master for a better one," she reflected, because husbands retained "a slaveholder's life estate in her person." All too aware of the effective indissolubility of marriage, women's rights reformers understood just how difficult it was for women to obtain a legal separation or divorce.[50] However, women reformers did not always draw attention to the fact that enslaved people could not just arbitrarily change their master, either. Although reformers did overemphasize the implications of the marriage contract, most did not condone the abuses of either marriage or chattel slavery. Husbands not only controlled the "nominal freedom" of their wives, Davis continued, but children were "as absolutely at the disposal of her [their mother's] owner ... as are those of the slave-mother."[51] When such

[47] Stanton, "Why Woman Must Vote," *Lily*, May 1850.
[48] Carla L. Peterson, "'And We Claim Our Rights': The Rights Rhetoric of Black and White Women Activists before the Civil War," in *Sister Circle: Black Women and Work*, eds. Sharon Harley and the Black Women and Work Collective (New Brunswick: Rutgers University Press, 2002), 139.
[49] Freedman, *Redefining Rape*, 54–56.
[50] Christine Bolt, *The Women's Movements in the United States and Britain from the 1790s to the 1920s* (Amherst: University of Massachusetts Press, 1993), 23.
[51] "Pecuniary Independence of Woman," *Una*, December 1853.

Fig. 3.1 "The Tyrant," c. 1840–1880. Library Company of Philadelphia, Comic Valentine Collection, 12.19

ideas entered popular culture, however, the intent was to satirize rather than condemn the possibility that men could be tyrants or the burgeoning analysis that the husband was, essentially, a slaveowner (Fig. 3.1).

As Stanton gained prominence as a women's rights reformer, she would come to dwell on ever more specific comparisons between the condition of married women and chattel slavery. Since women were "given in marriage like an article of merchandise," Stanton maintained, the "rights of humanity are more grossly outraged at the altar than at the auction block of the slaveholder; because … [nothing] can secure … her individual rights, her social equality."[52] While her perspective toward marriage "aroused antagonism,"

[52] "Letter from Mrs. E.C. Stanton," *Sibyl*, 1 February 1857.

even amongst her peers, some historians suggest that her constant recourse to comparing the husband and wife to master and slave amounted to "a logical extension of the views of most feminists."[53] It was only really logical, however, due to the degree to which antebellum women's rights reformers had, by the 1850s, utterly convinced themselves of the comparison between marriage and chattel slavery.

Ultimately, Stanton contributed to the development of "a language of individual liberty that acted as a catalyst for social change," Elizabeth B. Clark argues. However, her enthusiasm for the comparison between marriage and chattel slavery narrowed her perception of the condition of women and "dictated an appeal to a specific sort of legal remedy," one that would ultimately shape as much as inhibit the aims of the women's rights and suffrage movements.[54] As biographer Lori Ginzburg argues, the narrative of chattel slavery and emancipation served, for Stanton, "primarily as a lesson in women's own status, degradations, and rights."[55] But if the perceived applicability of the woman-slave analogy had become increasingly commonplace, few other antebellum reformers were willing to claim that marriage, as an institution, was worse than chattel slavery. This would change following the Civil War, a point at which Stanton's use of the woman-slave analogy not only became increasingly central to her own expression of racism but also more symptomatic of how other reformers, especially suffragists, approached the woman question.

The women's rights literature of the 1850s extended the analyses that abolitionist and women's rights reformers had developed of their own matrimonial unions. However, the use of the woman-slave analogy herein sometimes went far beyond what most contemporaries might have considered to be this rhetoric's logical conclusions. The legal implications of the marriage contract and its specific similarities to chattel slavery had gradually come to define how many women's rights reformers envisaged all marriages. Laura Curtis Bullard's novel *Christine; or, Woman's Trials and*

---

[53] Blanche Glassman Hersh, *The Slavery of Sex: Feminist-Abolitionists in America* (Urbana: University of Illinois Press, 1978), 102.

[54] Elizabeth B. Clark, "Matrimonial Bonds: Slavery and Divorce in Nineteenth-Century America," *Law and History Review* 8, no. 1 (1990): 26.

[55] Lori D. Ginzberg, *Elizabeth Cady Stanton: An American Life* (New York: Hill and Wang, 2010), 47, 162–164. See also: Angela Y. Davis, *Women, Race & Class* (London: The Women's Press, 1981), 70–86; Sue Davis, *The Political Thought of Elizabeth Cady Stanton: Women's Rights and the American Political Traditions* (New York: New York University Press, 2010), 223–225.

Triumphs (1856) reveals the degree to which this analogy had been normalized, even amongst the women's rights movement's rank-and-file. It is significant that Bullard does not appear to have been especially involved in reform culture until the 1860s; she would succeed Susan B. Anthony at the editorial helm of the *Revolution* approximately 15 years after the publication of her novel.[56] The woman-as-slave worldview that the little-known Bullard had imbibed as a younger woman was expressed in her 1856 novel—but with a twist.

At the end of *Christine*, Bullard's title character, a middle-aged woman long dedicated to her career as a women's rights reformer, weds her estranged first love on his deathbed. However, as the newlywed Philip begins to recover, the couple's marriage vows become a reality. Rather than anticipating matrimonial bliss, each character inadvertently concludes that their union will be inherently oppressive—a state of slavery, for the wife in particular. Christine convinces herself that the "chain that bound him to her was galling." While her presence was "valuable" and "delightful" as a nurse, "as a wife it was unwelcome." Upon waking, Philip similarly believes that Christine is "unhappy under the chains I, in my selfishness, ... imposed," resolving that she "should not be my slave."[57] Although Christine only appears to have accepted this marriage proposal because her suitor seems to be at death's door, the couple do remain married; the novel thus implies that marriage and the advocacy of women's rights were, in fact, compatible.[58] But was marriage a state of slavery? Or was it not? Both characters believe that marriage was, for women, necessarily a state of slavery—a normative description of the institution, as women's rights reformers had come to understand it. However, these characters also discover themselves to be mistaken in this assumption, as their experience of their union proves otherwise. In the end, Bullard emphasized the need for companionate marriage, something which Christine and Philip ultimately find.[59]

Other reformers aimed to forsake marriage altogether. Free love advocates, who were often antislavery sympathizers, routinely used discourses

---

[56] Denise M. Kohn, "Laura Jane Curtis Bullard (1831–1912)," *Legacy: A Journal of American Women Writers* 21, no. 1 (2004): 74–82.

[57] Laura Curtis Bullard, *Christine; or, Woman's Trials and Triumphs* (New York: De Witt & Davenport, 1856), 377, 380–381.

[58] Kohn, "Laura Jane Curtis Bullard," 75.

[59] Karen Tracey, *Plots and Proposals: American Women's Fiction, 1850–1890* (Urbana: University of Illinois Press, 2000), 126.

of slavery to describe marriage. Their focus on sexuality meant free lovers—or "sex radicals," as Joanne E. Passett describes their intellectual project and reform ethos—considered the oppression of women in marriage to be a more urgent concern than chattel slavery. Francis Barry, a purveyor of free love publications who also initiated a free love community of Berlin Heights, Ohio, was a regular contributor to the *Lily* and later to Stanton and Anthony's suffrage newspaper, the *Revolution*.[60] "Marriage is the slavery of woman," Barry wrote to the *Lily* in 1855. "Marriage does not differ, in any of its essential features, from chattel slavery."[61] After the Civil War, free lovers would begin to most fully develop the position that Stanton had aired in 1850: that marriage was worse than chattel slavery. As Barry himself concluded in 1868: "When women are no longer owned, when men are no longer slaveholders (and this will be when the *system* is abolished) then, and not till then, will ... women be recognized and treated as equals."[62] But free love advocates often took this position much further than any of their women's rights predecessors. In an address she gave on many occasions, Victoria Woodhull offered a rationale for free love in these very terms:

> The marriage law is the most damnable ... the most consummate outrage on woman—that was ever conceived. Those who are called prostitutes, ... are free women, sexually, when compared to the slavery of the poor wife. They are at liberty, at least to refuse; but she knows no such escape. "Wives, submit yourselves to your husbands," is the spirit and the universal practice of marriage.[63]

Some free lovers even expressed the belief that a "loveless union" constituted what Ezra Heywood, Stanton, and others described as the "legalized prostitution of marriage."[64]

---

[60] Joanne E. Passett, *Sex Radicals and the Quest for Women's Equality* (Chicago: University of Illinois Press, 2003), 1–2, 13, 59–90, 174.
[61] Francis Barry, "The Marriage Institution," *Lily*, 15 July 1855.
[62] Francis Barry, "The Marriage Institution," *Revolution*, 7 May 1868.
[63] "Tried as by Fire; or, The True and the False, Socially," n.d., in *Selected Writings of Victoria Woodhull: Suffrage, Free Love, and Eugenics*, ed. Cari M. Carpenter (Lincoln: University of Nebraska Press, 2010), 218.
[64] E.H. Heywood, *Cupid's Yokes: Or, the Binding Forces of Conjugal Life* (Princeton: Co-Operative Publishing Co., 1877), 8, 21–22; E.C.S. "Marriage and Divorce," *Revolution*, 22 October 1868.

Some antislavery literature problematized the analogy between marriage and chattel slavery because it clarified the protections that the marriage contract could offer free women. Such realizations did not often enter personal reflections about marriage or other expressions of the woman-slave analogy. Yet, while abolitionists envisaged the bondswoman as the apex of a loss of self-ownership, women's rights reformers and free love advocates increasingly made the same conclusions about free, married women. Even so, some women's rights literature questioned—perhaps even parodied—the belief that marriage was, for wives, always and invariably a state of slavery.

MARRIAGE AND SLAVEHOLDING IN PROSLAVERY THOUGHT

Abolitionists and women's rights reformers used the woman-slave analogy to condemn the power of slaveholders over enslaved people, of husbands over wives, and emphasize the need for self-ownership among enslaved people and free women. Proslavery commentators, by contrast, embraced the analogy between marriage and chattel slavery to justify both institutions and maintain the status quo. Nancy F. Cott argues that the convergence of antislavery and proslavery rhetoric offered "renewed prominence to the comparison between the wife and the slave." Enlightenment philosophy had established relationships of domination and subordination grounded in the hierarchies of master-servant, parent-child, and husband-wife. The analogy that resulted, between married women and enslaved people, was less a critique and more an account of the perceived inferiority of both. The "positive good" thesis worked to demonstrate that chattel slavery was a sadly inescapable institution, yet one that remained reciprocally beneficial in a civilized society. In response to immediate abolitionism, southern slaveholders sought to further "domesticate" chattel slavery through benevolent paternalism: if marital and racial subordination were foreordained by God and nature, women and enslaved Africans had certain rights and duties within the family.[65]

Why, though, did southern men compare the situation of their wives to that of their enslaved property? William Harper's 1838 "Memoir on Slavery," published in the *Southern Literary Journal*, sought to justify such a position. "*Servitude* is the condition of civilization," he opined, suggest-

---

[65] Cott, *Public Vows*, 60–66; Larry E. Tise, *Proslavery: A History of the Defense of Slavery in America, 1701–1840* (Athens: University of Georgia Press, 1987/2004), 101.

ing that no one, in fact, was free. But if neither master nor slave were free, some individuals were certainly more free than others. Harper acknowledged the possibility that "cruelties" could be inflicted by "brutal husbands on their wives; of brutal parents ... on children; of brutal masters on apprentices," but justified chattel slavery in terms of these domestic power relations. "Wives are protected from their husbands, and children from their parents," he declared. "The relation of Master and Slave, when there is no mischievous interference between them, is ... naturally one of kindness."[66] What Harper positioned as a positive good were exactly the social relations that abolitionists and women's rights reformers criticized.

Southern proslavery commentators produced ever more rigorous defenses of chattel slavery across the 1850s. "The Slave Institution at the South" could "dignify the family," the future Confederate officer Christopher G. Memminger asserted in 1851: "Each planter is in fact a Patriarch—his position compels him to be a ruler in his household."[67] Some southerners qualified love in terms of these hierarchical relationships. "A man loves his children because they are weak, helpless and dependent; he loves his wife for similar reasons," the social theorist and proslavery commentator George Fitzhugh reflected:

> He ceases to love his wife when she becomes masculine or rebellious; but slaves are always dependent, never the rivals of their master. Hence, though men are often found at variance with wife or children, we never saw one who did not like his slaves, and rarely a slave who was not devoted to his master.[68]

The perceived commonalities between enslaved people of African descent and women were simultaneously extended to ideas about race and gender more generally. Scientific thought in Europe and the American South began to establish the theory of polygenesis, which advocated the absolute separation between the races, to support a white supremacist racial hierarchy. Based largely around the science of craniometry, scientific men expanded upon

---

[66] William Harper, "Memoir on Slavery," *Southern Literary Journal* 3, no. 2 (1838): 87, 89–90.

[67] C.G. Memminger, *Lecture Delivered Before the Young Men's Library Association of Augusta, April 10th, 1851* (Augusta: W.S. Jones, Newspaper, Book and Job Printer, 1851), 14.

[68] George Fitzhugh, *Sociology for the South, or the Failure of Free Society* (Richmond: A. Morris, 1854), 246–247.

an analogy between race and gender to describe these characteristics as innate and validate the inferiority of both.[69]

Not all white southern women were convinced of the desirability of the society their contemporaries advocated, at least not in all its particulars. Like their northern counterparts, southern women periodically embraced abstracted discourses of slavery, often in private, to contemplate the social and domestic hierarchy borne of marriage.[70] Some rejected marriage altogether, if perhaps only tentatively. As one woman confessed to her diary in 1827, "the sweets of independence are greatly preferable to that *charming servitude* under a lord and master."[71] But this rhetoric was not always so completely abstracted from chattel slavery itself. When Susan Dabney Smedes recalled the antebellum experiences of her mother, she concluded, in 1887, that "the mistress of a plantation was the most complete slave on it."[72] Why did elite southern women, who were so deeply invested in the privilege of the southern lady, liken their situation to those whose enslavement made their social status possible?

This is a paradox that has not been lost on historians. Ann Firor Scott views the comparison that plantation mistresses made between themselves and their enslaved servants to have occurred too frequently to be purely rhetorical. The palpable discontent and sense of constraint among elite southern women, she argues, destabilized plantation society and its patriarchal social structure.[73] This remains a point of historiographical

---

[69] Stephen Jay Gould, "American Polygeny and Craniometry before Darwin: Blacks and Indians as Separate, Inferior Species," in *The "Racial" Economy of Science: Toward a Democratic Future*, ed. Sandra Harding (Bloomington: Indiana University Press, 1993); Nancy Leys Stepan, "Race and Gender: The Role of Analogy in Science," *Isis* 77, no. 2 (1986): 261–377. Nell Irvin Painter emphasizes the need to describe these nineteenth-century conclusions as science, not pseudoscience, so as to "note the qualifications of yesterday's scientists (rather) than to brand as mere 'science' their thought that has not stood the test of time." Nell Irvin Painter, *The History of White People* (New York: W.W. Norton & Company, 2010), x.

[70] Catherine Clinton, *The Plantation Mistress: Woman's World in the Old South* (New York: Pantheon Books, 1982), 34.

[71] Elizabeth Ruffin Diary, 26 February 1827, Southern Historical Collection, University of North Carolina Library, in Elizabeth Fox-Genovese, *Within the Plantation Household: Black and White Women of the Old South* (Chapel Hill: University of North Carolina Press, 1988), 255.

[72] Susan Dabney Smedes, *Memorials of a Southern Planter* (Baltimore: Cushings & Bailey, 1887), 191.

[73] Anne Firor Scott, *The Southern Lady: From Pedestal to Politics, 1830–1930* (Chicago: University of Chicago Press, 1970), 50, 17, 72.

contention, however, on account of the degree to which slaveholding women were the beneficiaries of the material comforts of the plantation. For southern ladies, benevolent paternalism often intersected with the demands of domesticity.[74] Some historians situate chattel slavery as mandating the "subordination of all women, both black and white, to masterhusbands whose behavior ranged from benevolent to tyrannical, but always within a patriarchal context."[75] Others challenge such a perspective. Thavolia Glymph finds cross-racial gender identification to have been impossible exactly because of racial hierarchy on the southern plantation. Since the plantation mistress was the "feminine face of paternalism," Glymph argues, she could not be a victim of chattel slavery; she was not encouraged to identify with her enslaved property, who endured the brunt of patriarchal and paternalistic authority.[76]

The prominence of the woman-slave analogy amongst elite southern women thus remains something of a contradiction. As Stephanie McCurry suggests, women's subordination bore much of the "ideological weight of slavery, providing the most concrete example of how public and private distinctions were confounded in political discourse and culture."[77] The disparity between the ideal of the southern lady and the rigors of household management led some elite southern women to question men's dominance.[78] But it rarely encouraged them to develop a criticism of chattel slavery itself or sympathize with enslaved people of African descent in anything other than a superficial or passing manner. Mary Boykin Chestnut, for example, did not feel a deep loving companionship with her husband, the lawyer, planter, and secessionist James Chestnut, Jr. This led

---

[74] Marli F. Weiner, "The Intersection of Race and Gender: The Antebellum Plantation Mistress and Her Slaves," *Humboldt Journal of Social Relations* 13, no. 1/2 (1986): 374–386.

[75] Jacqueline Jones, *Labor of Love, Labor of Sorrow: Black Women, Work, and the Family, from Slavery to the Present* (New York: Basic Books, 1985), 25.

[76] Thavolia Glymph, *Out of the House of Bondage: The Transformation of the Plantation Household* (New York: Cambridge University Press, 2008), 4, 23; Fox-Genovese, *Within the Plantation Household*, 132.

[77] Stephanie McCurry, "The Two Faces of Republicanism: Gender and Proslavery Politics in Antebellum South Carolina," *Journal of American History* 78, no. 4 (1992): 1251–1252.

[78] Scott, *The Southern Lady*, Chapter 3; Clinton, *The Plantation Mistress*, Chapter 2; Glymph, *Out of the House of Bondage*, Chapter 1.

her to meditate upon the institution of marriage throughout her life.[79] "There is no slave, after all, like a wife," Chestnut confided to her diary, a month after the outbreak of the Civil War. Only months earlier, she had felt "faint, seasick" after witnessing an enslaved woman be sold on the auction block: "It was too dreadful. I tried to reason. 'You know how women sell themselves and are sold in marriage, from queens downwards, eh? You know what the bible says about slavery, and marriage. Poor women, poor slaves.'"[80]

Among southern women and northern women reformers, these incongruent analyses of the analogy between marriage and chattel slavery generated contradictory interpretations in antebellum popular literature. It offers insight into the approaches that novelists from different backgrounds brought to their interpretation of women's subjection in marriage. Literary representations of slaveholding women challenged the prevailing perception that they accepted matrimonial and household dependence more willingly than enslaved women.[81] These criticisms, however, remained imbued in a proslavery narrative; but they were also influenced by the cultural impact of the antislavery movement and abolitionist discourse. Russ Castronovo identifies a literary countertradition wherein proslavery women novelists imitated the slave narrative to reflect upon their own condition under patriarchy. However, these novelists routinely failed to appreciate that chattel slavery was central to the production of their class position. The heroines in what Castronovo describes as the "stolen slave narrative" express little sense of a shared oppression with enslaved people because they have no interest in deconstructing their own racial or class-based privilege.[82]

Caroline Lee Hentz and E.D.E.N. Southworth were some of the foremost popular novelists of the antebellum era. A northerner who migrated to the Upper South with her husband, Hentz was sympathetic to chattel slavery. Southworth, in contrast, a northerner who embraced an antislavery ethos, lived primarily in the antebellum slaveholding capital of

---

[79] Mary A. DeCredico, *Mary Boykin Chestnut: A Confederate Woman's Life* (Lanham: Rowman & Littlefield Publishers, 1996), 19–22.

[80] Mary Boykin Chestnut, Diary, 9 May 1861; 4 March 1861, in *A Diary from Dixie: Mary Boykin Chestnut*, ed. Ben Ames Williams (Boston: Houghton Mifflin Company, 1905, 1949, 1980), 49, 11.

[81] Fox-Genovese, *Within the Plantation Household*, 96.

[82] Russ Castronovo, "Incidents in the Life of a White Woman: Economies of Race and Gender in the Antebellum Nation," *American Literary History* 10, no. 2 (1998): 239–265.

3 "BOUGHT AND SOLD": ANTISLAVERY, WOMEN'S RIGHTS, AND MARRIAGE 91

Washington, D.C. Influenced by the national drama of chattel slavery and abolitionism that shaped the era's literary sentimentalism, their novels explored the experiences of elite women on slaveholding plantations.[83] Both women published extensively during the 1850s, often with T.B. Peterson & Brothers of Philadelphia. This was a commercial firm that profited from a broad contemporary interest in the slavery debates, without needing to make too fine a distinction between one position or another.[84] While the "stolen slave narrative" certainly produced best selling fiction, Hentz in particular needed to placate the competing interests of the literary marketplace: northern printing presses; a broad readership (regardless of region); and the cultural surveillance that demanded southerners protect and defend the South.[85] Both women used essentially similar literary conventions and rhetorical strategies to characterize the domestic lives and courtships of elite southern women; however, the personal worldview of each shaped their narratives. Ultimately, while Hentz was solely concerned with the experiences of marriage among slaveholding women, Southworth criticized the oppression of both women and enslaved people of African descent.

Hentz echoed the many southern women who used discourses of slavery solely to understand their own oppression. Cindy Weinstein suggests that *The Planter's Northern Bride* (1854), Hentz's proslavery response to Stowe's *Uncle Tom's Cabin*, revealed that one of her broader literary imperatives was to "undermine altogether the differences between slavery and freedom."[86] Her novels brought this proslavery analysis of the master-slave relationship to her criticism of the husband-wife relationship. Hentz's novel *Linda; or, The Young Pilot of the Belle Creole* (1850) portrayed the "despotism of Mrs. Walton," a character whose merciless treatment of her adolescent stepdaughter is constructed through direct references to chattel slavery. When Mrs. Walton arranges for Linda to marry her son to retain the family plantation, Linda implores her stepmother to take her fortune instead. "I wish I were the poorest girl in the south-west, if I must be bought and sold like

---

[83] Shirley Samuels, ed. *The Culture of Sentiment: Race, Gender, and Sentimentality in Nineteenth-Century America* (New York: Oxford University Press, 1992).

[84] Carl Ostrowski, "Slavery, Labor Reform, and Intertextuality in Antebellum Print Culture: The Slave Narrative and the City-Mysteries Novel," *African American Review* 40, no. 3 (2006): 499–500.

[85] Tracey, *Plots and Proposals*, 50–53.

[86] Cindy Weinstein, *Family, Kinship, and Sympathy in Nineteenth-Century American Literature* (Cambridge: Cambridge University Press, 2006), 69.

a negro slave," she objects, only to be reproached for addressing her stepmother with less respect than "a single slave on the plantation." Although Linda and Mrs. Walton both acknowledge that enslaved people can be sold against their will, Hentz has her characters consider the implications of this reality no further. Whipped and coerced into lodgings "scarcely thought good enough for a slave," Linda revolts against such "tyranny" and actively protests the marriage.[87] This proslavery depiction of the despotic mistress anticipated Harriet Wilson's slave narrative, *Our Nig: Sketches from the Life of a Free Black, in a Two-Story White House, North, showing that Slavery's Shadows Fall Even There* (1859), which would come to epitomize this character archetype in antislavery literature.

Hentz was primarily concerned with the experiences of young belles rather than their enslaved property. Novels such as *Linda*, however, also considered the social differences between marriage and chattel slavery. Hentz alluded to the fact that privileged white women could hope to avert the sexual commodification of arranged marriages; indeed, Linda does not consent to be "trafficked away in this vile manner."[88] Expecting patriarchal and legal authority to work in her favor, Linda appeals to her father and the legal system. The latter, in particular, is only possible because this character is personally empowered, has access to sympathetic legal representation, and retains the rights unmarried women were accorded. But her attempt fails; the law actually leaves Linda even more vulnerable, a realization that encourages her to flee her father's plantation. Hentz, like Lydia Maria Child and William Wells Brown, illuminated how patriarchal legal structures disadvantaged women; but unlike Child and Brown, Hentz expressed no concern for how this reality both extended to, and was often compounded for, free women of color or enslaved people of African descent.

Another of Hentz's novels, *Eoline; or, Magnolia Vale; or, the Heiress of Glenmore* (1852), depicted the character of Mr. Glenmore, an affluent patriarch, attempt to enforce a marriage between his daughter and the neighboring planter's son. When Eoline refuses and seeks employment as a music teacher at a female academy, her father cannot abandon the "despotism in his bosom" despite the social disapproval he fears. As Chestnut herself would record in her diary, "every man objects to any despot but himself."[89] Although Glenmore asks himself whether his daughter should

[87] Hentz, *Linda*, 102–106.
[88] Ibid., 105.
[89] Chestnut, 25 February 1861, in *A Diary from Dixie*, 7.

"be made a musical drudge, a hireling, a slave," he enforces the marriage nonetheless. Hentz praises "this noble young girl" for her refusal to "sell her birthright" and instead decide to flee her father, thus sacrificing "luxury and home, rather than barter[ing] her soul's independence, her heart's liberty ... in a traffic unsanctioned by God or man!" Unconcerned about the prospect of never marrying "after having thrown off the chains of parental despotism," Eoline considers her "independent spirit" as her "only inheritance" and finds some fulfillment as a school teacher. But Hentz also described how marrying an unworthy suitor would lead to an ill-suited union—the marriage that many northern reformers would have considered to be inherently a state of slavery—to illustrate the need for romantic love. "Chains are chains, though forged of gold," another patriarch explains to Glenmore, telling of how his daughter became a listless recluse following her own discordant union.[90]

The double proposal plot of these novels, Karen Tracey argues, allows each heroine to first reject the proposal of an arranged marriage but later accept a proposal from the same suitor. "A more equitable marriage," she continues, "grows out of courtship while remaining compatible with southern hierarchy." Since Hentz's heroines ultimately prove themselves to be trustworthy arbiters of race and class interests, her novels implied that families did not need to force their daughters to become "objects of exchange in marriage." Indeed, the character of Eoline eventually falls in love with her intended. The couple would have married, Hentz suggests, if only left to "free will." Thus, by manipulating the social hierarchies that so many proslavery southerners embraced, Hentz redefined romantic love such that her novels' conclusions "appear natural even though they paradoxically increase the heroines' autonomy and strengthen the system that confines them."[91] For Hentz, illustrating the differences between coercion and freely given romantic love revealed that which she viewed as acceptable for enslaved people—barter, trafficking, exchange—and the matrimonial practices that she considered untenable for elite white women.

In these novels, Hentz accepted and promoted common assumptions about white supremacy, black inferiority, and chattel slavery. The Jezebel stereotype, which conjured an image of black women's insatiable lust, informed her depiction of enslaved women; it meant that African-American women

[90] Caroline Lee Hentz, *Eoline; or, Magnolia Vale; or, the Heiress of Glenmore* (Philadelphia: T.B. Peterson & Brothers, 1852), 23–29, 44, 116.
[91] Tracey, *Plots and Proposals*, 54–55, 59.

faced contradictions attendant on their sexual commodification being routinely interpreted as the result of promiscuity.[92] Popular literature often mobilized these stereotypes so as to accentuate racial, gender, and class differences. Linda, for example, enacts benevolent paternalism when she embarks on a night-time expedition to a neighboring plantation to arrange a good purchase for her mammy, yet her graciousness and courteousness never extends to too great a sense of familiarity.[93] And when the enslaved character Gatty attempts to support Eoline, her mistress, when she is faced with the prospect of an arranged marriage, she is quickly silenced.[94] According to Tracey, Hentz aspired to establish the improbability of interracial or cross-class identification as much as its undesirability. However, a disobedient planter's daughter still had the potential to inspire disrespect amongst her enslaved servants. This was an outcome that Hentz attempted to quell, even as her narratives illuminated it as a possibility.[95]

The popular literature that cultivated this sense of distance between free women and enslaved people remained distinct from the ideals of most antislavery literature. The latter, to varying degrees, encouraged northern readers to imagine the prospect of cross-racial identification—and sometimes even the possibilities of collective emancipation. Southworth's novels differed from much antislavery literature in that she focused on slaveholders rather than enslaved people of African descent. Her ambivalence toward southern culture also led her to question why women should aspire to marriage as well as to doubt whether it could support them emotionally and economically.[96]

Her early novel, *Retribution: A Tale of Passion* (1856), established a parallel between mistress and slave through the character of Hester, a slaveholder with antislavery inclinations. Initially serialized across 1849 in the *National Era*, its publication offered a precedent for the serialization of Stowe's famous antislavery novel in the same newspaper only two years later.[97] *Retribution* embraced antislavery literary themes, from the

[92] White, *Ar'n't I a Woman?* Chapter 1.
[93] See: Hentz, *Linda*, 40–44.
[94] See: Hentz, *Eoline*, 25–28.
[95] Tracey, *Plots and Proposals*, 65–69.
[96] Cindy Weinstein, "'What Did You Mean?': Marriage in E.D.E.N. Southworth's Novels," *Legacy: A Journal of American Women Writers* 27, no. 1 (2010): 44.
[97] Vicki L. Martin, "E.D.E.N. Southworth's Serial Novels *Retribution* and *The Mother-in-Law* as Vehicles for the Cause of Abolition in the *National Era*: Setting the Stage for *Uncle Tom's Cabin*," in *E.D.E.N. Southworth: Recovering a Nineteenth Century Popular Novelist,*

generous slaveholder who attempts to manumit her enslaved property to the tragic mulatta whose emancipation remains incomplete prior to her planter father's death. The objections Southworth expressed toward chattel slavery, however, principally revolved around white women's subjugation in the family, as she examined the degree to which the legal oppression of chattel slavery extended to free women.[98] "Talk of woman's bondage," Hester reflects, "of woman's chains; the bondage is a bondage of protection, the chain, a chain of love."[99] This lack of attention to enslaved characters compromised the novel's explicit abolitionism, yet its narrative still reflected other antislavery literature and the sentimental tradition.

Southworth's later novel, *The Missing Bride; or, Miriam the Avenger* (1855), depicts the character of Commodore Waugh as a patriarch who believes he is entitled to arrange the marriages of his dependents. At his southern plantation, "Luckenough," which the enslaved character Crazy Nell verbally parodies as "Lock-em-up," Waugh indulges "the solitary majesty of his own demoniacal passion." When his elder niece, Edith, marries a heroic English soldier rather than the preferred Dr. Grimshaw, Waugh criticizes her for base ingratitude. Edith maintains that "honest hearts are not to be bought, or sold," but Waugh thunders: "I am no tyrant, minion, do you hear!" Waugh also repeatedly threatens his younger niece, Jacquelina, saying: "I have the greatest mind to whip her to death!"[100] Southworth sought to expose what the myth of benevolent paternalism concealed: the tyrannical behavior patriarchs directed toward their dependents.

The prospect of Jacquelina's arranged marriage leads her to ponder: "How much would such a girl as myself bring in the slave market of the Sultan's city?"[101] This character identified with the plight of enslaved women far more than any of Hentz's characters, revealing the degree to which the connections Mary Wollstonecraft, Harriet Martineau, and Hiram Powers imagined between the eastern harem, chattel slavery, and the sexualized subjugation of women persisted in the antebellum

eds. Melissa J. Homestead and Pamela T. Washington (Knoxville: University of Tennessee Press, 2012).
[98] Husband, *Antislavery Discourse*, 65–68.
[99] Emma D.E.N. Southworth, *Retribution; or, The Vale of Shadows: A Tale of Passion* (Philadelphia: T.B. Peterson, 1856), 173.
[100] E.D.E.N. Southworth, *The Missing Bride; or, Miriam the Avenger* (Philadelphia: T.B. Peterson & Brothers, 1855), 123, 129, 85–86, 110.
[101] Ibid., 275.

United States. Some abolitionist women found inspiration not only in the bondswoman who was enslaved on the southern plantation but also the European woman enslaved in the Muslim Mediterranean, a region that had offered "a rich reservoir" for orientalist imaginings of women's enslavement across the eighteenth century.[102] Yet Jacquelina's sense of identification with enslaved people was somewhat qualified, because the direct comparison her character envisages is with an orientalized—potentially even a "white"—slave rather than an enslaved person of African descent.

The manner in which northern reformers and southern proslavery novelists approached the analogy between marriage and chattel slavery, however distinct, sometimes converged more closely than might reasonably be expected. This can be observed in another of Hentz's novels, *Marcus Warland; or, the Long Moss Spring* (1852). The character of Florence is a young belle who flouts convention and actively courts her beau, Marcus. Deeply conscious of the restrictions of marriage, Florence also avoids what she views as inevitable—an engagement—for as long as possible. "I have always dreaded the idea of love," she laments, "because I know, if I once yielded to its power, I should become far more of a vassal than any slave on this broad plantation."[103] This sentiment, as Hentz expressed in an 1852 popular novel, was strikingly similar to Stanton's reflections in a women's rights newspaper only two years earlier. As Stanton herself had conjectured: "A married woman is not supposed to have any legal existence. She has no more absolute rights than a slave on a southern plantation."[104]

Both Hentz and Stanton deliberated the contradictions between the romantic ideal and the actual restrictions of marriage. Yet, here and elsewhere, Stanton, Southworth, and their fellow reformers denounced the very system of chattel slavery. In contrast, Hentz's criticism of marriage only inadvertently questioned the institution's existence; her novels instead promoted the self-realization of elite white women while embracing southern culture and its proslavery, white supremacist traditions.[105] Stanton's 1850 claim that marriage was the more egregious institution, moreover, was relatively uncommon amongst other antebellum reformers. The

---

[102] Margaret M.R. Kellow, "The Oriental Imaginary: Constructions of Female Bondage in Women's Antislavery Discourse," in *The Problem of Evil: Slavery, Race, and the Ambiguities of American Reform*, eds. Steven Mintz and John Stauffer (Amherst: University of Massachusetts Press, 2007), 186.

[103] Caroline Lee Hentz, *Marcus Warland; or, the Long Moss Spring* (Philadelphia: T.B. Peterson & Brothers, 1852), 131–132.

[104] E.C.S., "Why Must Women Vote," *Lily*, May 1850.

[105] Tracey, *Plots and Proposals*, 50–52.

suggestion that marriage was worse than chattel slavery would become far more prominent amongst postbellum reformers. During the antebellum era, however, this claim was far more representative of proslavery and popular literature than it was of reform print culture.

It was at this juncture that African-American women began to consider such questions in the context of antislavery literature. "Reader," Harriet Jacobs famously proclaimed, "my story ends with freedom; not in the usual way, with marriage. I and my children are now free!"[106] Free and self-emancipated African Americans described that which women's rights novels were coming to construct as inherently oppressive and a state of slavery—marriage—as a privilege of freedom. A recently discovered 1850s manuscript, which Henry Louis Gates describes as the first novel by an African-American woman, offers another significant counterpoint to proslavery and antislavery debates about marriage.[107] Hannah Crafts' novel *The Bondwoman's Narrative* directly problematized the analogy between marriage and chattel slavery. The main character questions how marriage could be dignified "in a state of servitude" and concludes that the "responsibilities" of marriage could "only be filled with profit, and honor, and advantage by the free."[108]

Yet, even as Crafts criticized the analogy between marriage and chattel slavery, she pondered whether to refute chattel slavery as an analogy altogether. In the tradition of much other antislavery literature, *The Bondwoman's Narrative* envisioned a mixed-race woman as the embodiment of the legal and social oppressions emanating from race and gender. In doing so, Crafts found enduring points of comparison between the legal and social status of women and enslaved people of African descent. One character, Mr. Trappe, is a lawyer who traffics in the "sexual economy" of chattel slavery.[109] Trappe blackmails his previous employer's daughter by threatening to reveal her mixed-race heritage to her white planter husband. "We are all slaves to something or somebody," he utters,

---

[106] L. Maria Child, ed. *Incidents in the Life of a Slave Girl* (Boston: The Author, 1861), 302.
[107] Hannah Crafts, *The Bondwoman's Narrative*, ed. Henry Louis Gates, Jr. (New York: Warner Books, 2002), xxi.
[108] Crafts, *Bondwoman's Narrative*, 131.
[109] Adrienne Davis, "'Don't Let Nobody Bother Yo' Principle': The Sexual Economy of American Slavery," in *Sister Circle*, 103–127. For the economic value accorded "fancy girls" and "fancy slaves," see: Eugene D. Genovese, *The Political Economy of Slavery: Studies in the Economy and Society of the Slave South*, 2nd ed. (Middletown: Wesleyan University Press, 1989), 16–31; Hartman, *Scenes of Subjection*, 40–41.

attempting to assuage the unnamed woman's panic when he finally acquires her for the purpose of sale. This character further echoed proslavery southerner William Harper, reflecting:

> A man perfectly free would be an anomaly, and a free woman yet more so. Freedom and slavery are only names attached surreptitiously and often improperly to certain conditions and in many cases the slave possesses more. They are mere shadows the very reverse of realities, and being so, if rightly considered, they have only a trifling effect on individual happiness.[110]

The Bondwoman's Narrative set forth the possibility that women's freedom was an anomaly, but ultimately refuted that enslaved people could ever possess more freedoms than the free. Complete with crossed-out passages, the manuscript nature of Crafts' novel reveals how carefully she considered this point. By refusing to attribute such a perspective to a slave-trading character, Crafts rejected an argument that had become central to proslavery thought.

The relegation of free white women to the same category of dependence as enslaved people of African descent constituted enough of a contradiction to influence the worldview of many elite southern women. When proslavery women embraced discourses of slavery to interrogate their ambivalence toward courtship and marriage, they paid little to no attention to the coercion at the root of chattel slavery. Rarely did they consider any direct identification between themselves and their enslaved property, being uninterested in any forms of oppression beyond their own. Complaints about parental or social "tyranny" simply emphasized that white young ladies should not be "bought and sold like a negro slave," as Hentz would have it. Further, popular literature in the tradition of the "stolen slave narrative" concluded by reifying marriage—the very institution that Hentz had, somewhat ironically, described as worse than chattel slavery. Slave narratives such as Jacobs' *Incidents in the Life of a Slave Girl* (1861), however, strove toward freedom. African Americans mobilized discourses of slavery to condemn chattel slavery and begin to query the status of free women. After the Civil War, the manner in which elite southern women had approached the woman-slave analogy became increasingly prevalent amongst northern women reformers.

---

[110] Crafts, *Bondwoman's Narrative*, 97.

From Fugitive Slave to Fugitive Wife

The women's rights movement expanded significantly in the years before the Civil War. Many reformers, from the rank-and-file to famous lecturers, had become ever more convinced of the aptness as well as the reasonableness of the woman-slave analogy. Its rise in popularity anticipated the conceptual shift it would undergo during the 1850s and the aftermath of the Civil War. During the antebellum era, the imperative of most white women's rights reformers had been to re-envision marriage as a state of slavery alongside a variety of other forms of oppression. Yet, at a moment when chattel slavery was gaining unprecedented political and cultural attention, this soon gave way to the belief that white women's own oppression was both ignored and singular. This process was encapsulated in a new literary trope that emerged amongst women's rights reformers and free love advocates following the Fugitive Slave Law of 1850: the "fugitive wife."

The Fugitive Slave Law was part of the Compromise of 1850, an act of Congress that represented one of the most stringent examples of northern complicity in chattel slavery. Abolitionists denounced this controversial new legislation, which legalized the kidnapping of enslaved and free African Americans in the North and their return to chattel slavery in the South, and undermined its implementation by aiding fugitive slaves.[111] First serialized in the *National Era* across 1851–1852, Stowe's *Uncle Tom's Cabin* was an antislavery literary response to the Fugitive Slave Law. Through the character of Eliza, this novel sensationalized and sentimentalized the figure of the fugitive slave. Eliza's escape with her child followed the generic conventions of slave narratives and other antislavery literature, in which the North Star and Canada became a metaphor that symbolized fugitive slaves' hope for personal liberty.[112] As Frederick Douglass had recalled of his own escape from Maryland, he and his compatriots progressed "toward the north star, till we reached a free state."[113] When asked about his wife's whereabouts, Eliza's husband

---

[111] David Brion Davis, *Inhuman Bondage: The Rise and Fall of Slavery in the New World* (Oxford: Oxford University Press, 2006), 265–266.

[112] Frances Smith Foster, *Witnessing Slavery: The Development of Ante-Bellum Slave Narratives* (Westport: Greenwood Press, 1979), 55; Renford Reese, "Canada: The Promised Land for U.S. Slaves," *Western Journal of Black Studies* 35, no. 3 (2011): 208–217.

[113] Frederick Douglass, *My Bondage and My Freedom* (New York: Miller, Orton & Mulligan, 1855), 285.

Fig. 3.2 "Eliza: Uncle Tom's Cabin" (New York: A.S. Seer's Union Square Print, 1886). Library of Congress, Theatrical Poster Collection

replies: "Gone, … with her child in her arms, the Lord only knows where;—gone after the north star; and when we ever meet, or whether we meet at all in this world, no creature can tell."[114] Eliza's escape across the Ohio River gained exceptional fame in antebellum popular culture, featuring in theatrical renditions as well as posters, playbills, and illustrations in various editions of the book (Fig. 3.2).[115]

---

[114] Harriet Beecher Stowe, *Uncle Tom's Cabin; or, Life among the Lowly* (London: George Routledge & Co., 1852), 127.

[115] Jo-Ann Morgan, *Uncle Tom's Cabin as Visual Culture* (Columbia: University of Missouri Press, 2007), 87–88.

Beyond abolitionist responses to the Fugitive Slave Law, print culture had long publicized the possibility that wives sometimes made attempts to escape their husbands. A century earlier, husbands were known to place advertisements about recalcitrant wives in the mainstream press; such epistles appeared alongside notices seeking to retrieve lost animals, fugitive slaves, and escaped servants.[116] This tradition continued in the antebellum era, in both the mainstream and reform press. An 1855 report about failed marriages, for example, described "runaway" husbands and wives.[117] Free love communities were known to sometimes harbor unhappily married women who sought refuge from their matrimonial abode.[118] Early oral histories also reveal personal accounts of such experiences. Married at 14 years old to a man 30 years her senior, Elvina Apperson Fellows was obliged to flee to her mother's domicile to escape her abusive, alcoholic husband. After pursuing and shooting at his wife, thinking he had killed the young Elvina, her husband then killed himself. "Back in 1851," Fellows later recalled of her horrifying ordeal, "we had slavery of Negroes in the South, and we had slavery of wives all over the United States."[119]

Women's rights print culture soon began to embrace such themes, although this was far from wholly original. As Frances Smith Foster suggests, much antebellum literature reflected the slave narrative, a literary genre very clearly defined by its impetus toward either manumission or escape.[120] For example, short stories and novels which depicted girls and women seeking to escape domestic abuse often situated the factories of Lowell, a Massachusetts town that became a famous destination for working women during the 1830s and 1840s, in the guise of the North Star.[121] The literary conventions that reform literature appropriated, especially women's rights literature, is telling nonetheless. More explicit comparisons between the situation of women, particularly married women, and fugitive slaves gradually emerged amongst women's rights reformers. "Her bondage, though it differs from that of the Negro slave, frets and chafes her just the same," Elizabeth Cady Stanton wrote of married women in an 1856 letter to Lucy Stone. "She too sighs and groans in her chains; and lives but in the

---

[116] Yalom, *A History*, 150–151.
[117] "Unhappy Marriages," *Una*, January 1855.
[118] Passett, *Sex Radicals*, 82.
[119] Fred Lockley, *Conversations with Pioneer Women*, ed. Mike Helm (Eugene: Rainy Day Press, 1981), 65.
[120] Foster, *Witnessing Slavery*, 87.
[121] Husband, *Antislavery Discourse*, 91, 96.

hope of better things to come. She looks to heaven; whilst the more philosophical slave sets out for Canada."[122] Together, the North Star and Canada came to symbolize what Stanton perceived as divergent experiences: enslaved people had the opportunity to escape to freedom, she believed, but because divorce was so difficult to obtain, women had limited recourse to ameliorate their own condition.

The fugitive wife trope thrived because abolitionists and women's rights reformers had become so accustomed to describing married women's experiences, including their own, as a state of slavery. But the fugitive wife would offer a far more discrete example of the woman-slave analogy than anything that had preceded it. Previously, reformers had employed discourses of slavery as either a rhetorical flourish or a more elongated comparison in a broader work—be it an address, editorial, article, pamphlet, or novel—but seldom as the rationale for an entire work. The fugitive wife trope fully embodied a concept that reformers had only attempted to theorize previously. Something of a response to the tragic mulatta trope, the fugitive wife drew on a specifically gendered and racialized conceptualization of the fugitive slave. Its potential to create a fully formed character found particular expression in women's rights literature, as epitomized by Laura Curtis Bullard's 1856 novel.

Christine; or, Woman's Trials and Triumphs depicted the inverse trajectories of two characters: the upward mobility of Christine herself, the women's rights career woman who ultimately establishes a companionate marriage; and the downward mobility of Annie Murray, a happy young socialite, who becomes engaged on the whim of the season to the rich Mr. Howard. Only following marriage, however, do the couple discover their inherent incompatibility. "Every day," Bullard states, "the fetters which bound them seemed more galling, and contentions grew more and more frequent." No longer able to bear her husband's "tyranny," Annie eventually entreats assistance from her uncle. But her uncle cannot help his niece and her daughter because coverture entrusted the wife's person, property, and children to the husband. "Do you know what you are dooming me to?" Annie laments; "the life of a slave, who hates and fears her master[!]"[123]

---

[122] Elizabeth Cady Stanton to Lucy Stone, 24 November 1856, in *History of Woman Suffrage*, Vol. I, eds. Elizabeth Cady Stanton, Susan B. Anthony, and Matilda Joslyn Gage (Rochester: Susan B. Anthony, 1881), 860.

[123] Bullard, *Christine*, 198, 273–275.

Later, Annie's uncle berates Howard for refusing to "let your slave escape" through the legal means of divorce.

Fleeing her unhappy marriage, Annie's character exemplified the downward trajectory of the fugitive wife and demonstrated the degree to which the trope drew on popular conceptions of the fugitive slave. Struggling to support herself and her daughter as a seamstress, this character's difficulties reflected the literary pathos associated with working women as much as the idea that, if emancipated, formerly enslaved people would not be able to support themselves adequately. Annie is briefly rescued by a family friend, who then proposes marriage. Although a bigamous union, as she is still married, Annie is convinced it is a "sacred" one nonetheless.[124] But the rogue paramour eventually abandons her, dooming Annie to a life of prostitution and an early death. Such a conclusion echoed the tragic fates suffered by fallen women in popular literature as much as mixed-race characters in antislavery literature, rather than the successful self-emancipation with which Stowe rewarded the character of Eliza.

The fugitive wife trope offered the foundations for a new approach to the woman-slave analogy in women's rights literature. Soon, however, this figure appeared with even greater clarity in free love discourse. Around the beginning of the Civil War, Warren Chase published his free love manifesto, *The Fugitive Wife: A Criticism on Marriage, Adultery, and Divorce* (1861). Chase began his book with little prelude, expecting his readers to be familiar with such concepts:

> In the June of 1859, the scribes of Chicago furnished the daily papers of that city with an interesting item of news, by announcing that a fugitive wife had escaped from one of the villages on Lake Superior, in Michigan, had been legally seized, and returned with the officer ... to her legal and proper owner.

By recounting the style of press reporting long evident in print culture, Chase definitively named the phenomenon of the fugitive wife. Yet, while he articulated knowledge of "a national fugitive-slave law, which was considered by most people in the free States to be very cruel, and by many unjust," Chase expressed ignorance of the "State fugitive-wife laws, by which [wives] could be caught and returned to their owners, as chattel

[124] Ibid., 297.

slaves are, although I knew many wives were as effectually enslaved and controlled as the black chattels of Georgia."[125]

The addresses of Chase, an itinerant free love lecturer, and his compatriots complemented the circulation of free love periodicals and thus "played a vital role in transporting sex radical ideas from community to community."[126] Chase's book may have drawn on the material he used in his free love public addresses, vying for attention with the abolitionist lecturers who had decried the Fugitive Slave Law for the past decade. Yet, by explicitly appropriating the implications of the Fugitive Slave Law, the fugitive wife trope emphasized the oppression of white married women alone. Chase's avowed sympathy toward the self-emancipated African Americans who managed to reach "a free State, or Canada," was tempered somewhat by his greater outrage for the situation of married women. Officers of the law, he related, could "return a woman of their [own] race and color to a tyrant who had treated her so cruelly that it … compelled her to leave even her children, and flee for life, to escape the grave, as I know some have." Some laws did exist "to protect the wife against [the] physical abuse of the husband, with the whip or fist," Chase conceded, yet he highlighted women's lack of protection "against a personal abuse, often worse than a severe whipping." Ultimately, he believed that the situation of the fugitive wife was "not the condition of all wives, but only those who are merely *legal* wives."[127] Free love and the transformation of public opinion was, for Chase, central; but most women's rights reformers, in contrast, focused on legislative change.

Chase's book *The Fugitive Wife* used the Fugitive Slave Law as a vehicle for developing a criticism of marriage, but did not dismiss the experiences of self-emancipated African Americans entirely. Yet, by describing "chattel slavery or marriage slavery," he found the experience of fugitive slaves to be exactly equivalent to that of married women. Chase condemned any institution that enabled the "slavery and ownership of persons" or denied the autonomy and self-ownership of the individual. The joys of motherhood could be enjoyed by all women, he suggested, whether married, unmarried, or enslaved. However, his false equivalence between what he

---

[125] Warren Chase, *The Fugitive Wife: A Criticism on Marriage, Adultery and Divorce* (Boston: Bela Marsh, 1861), 7, 53. This book appears to have been published just after the Civil War began in April 1861, as it referenced an editorial in a weekly spiritualist journal, the *Banner of Light*, published on 13 July that year.
[126] Passett, *Sex Radicals*, 51.
[127] Chase, *The Fugitive Wife*, 7–10.

described as the "slave-mother" and the "wife-mother" found public opinion to be more exacting toward the latter than the former:

> When a slave-mother leaves her children, to escape into a land of freedom and gain her liberty, we approve her act ...; but when a wife-mother is forced to fly from her children, by the brutality of a husband, ... what do we do for her?

Situated as he was within the milieu of northern reformers, Chase conceivably gave too much credence to the prevalence of an antislavery ethos. Perhaps anticipating the social, cultural, and legal shifts about to take place across the decade, he evoked a public sentiment that was more sympathetic to slave emancipation than ameliorating the condition of women. As for so many women's rights reformers, Chase's real sympathies were with the latter. "It seems to me more and more, on reflection," he emphasized, "that a law is more cruel that returns a wife to her master, than that which returns a slave to the owner."[128]

Some historians interpret the Married Women's Property Acts of the 1850s, which Chase cited favorably, and the Emancipation Proclamation of 1863 as comparable. Both, according to Carole Shammas, undermined patriarchal authority and created a new relationship between women and formerly enslaved people and the state.[129] As President Abraham Lincoln pronounced on 1 January 1863:

> [A]ll persons held as slaves ... shall be then, thenceforward, and forever free; and the Executive Government of the United States ... will recognize and maintain the freedom of such persons, and will do no act or acts to repress such persons ... in any efforts they may make for their actual freedom.[130]

The realization that an unprecedented number of women had come to embrace a woman-as-slave worldview by the 1850s reshapes the salience and resonance that women's rights reformers found in this antislavery legislation. For some, the prospect of slave emancipation did not just serve to transform the lives of enslaved people of African descent. In the opinion

---

[128] Chase, *The Fugitive Wife*, 25, 28, 14, 8.

[129] Carole Shammas, "Re-assessing the Married Women's Property Acts," *Journal of Women's History* 6, no. 1 (1994): 9.

[130] The Emancipation Proclamation, 1 January 1863, *National Archives*, https://www.archives.gov/exhibits/featured-documents/emancipation-proclamation.

of women such as Stanton and Anthony, it could equally—and should literally—be applied to that other group of slaves: women. This would have consequences for their interpretation of legislative developments during the Civil War and in its aftermath.

To a certain extent, congressional debates about the meaning of slave emancipation substantiated a woman-as-slave worldview as well as the position of women's rights reformers. The political debates that followed the Civil War enabled the "parallel between the master's right over his slave and the husband's right over his wife" to flourish.[131] Historians describe the process whereby states' rights senators debated whether the tenets of slave emancipation might be extended to women. In 1866, for example, Senator Edgar Cowan asked if the Thirteenth Amendment of 1865 would subvert the "*quasi* servitude[,] which the wife to some extent owes her husband?" This was a question, however, that was posed purely rhetorically. "Certainly not," he proclaimed. "Nobody pretends that it was to … cover [anything but] the relations which existed between the master and his negro African slave."[132] Lawmakers ultimately sought to disassociate slave emancipation from any domestic relation except chattel slavery.[133]

Both women's rights reformers and lawmakers conceded that there were grounds for a comparison between marriage and chattel slavery, however. Differences emerged in terms of what to do with this realization, as a woman-as-slave worldview could be mobilized to differing ends. Lawmakers ultimately refuted that slave emancipation need effect any transformation in the institution of marriage. This attacked and invalidated a Thirteenth Amendment interpretation that could have any implications for the marriage contract or married women.[134] As a result, these lawmakers' analyses had far more in common with that of proslavery commentators who had desired to reform neither institution. This meant that lawmakers ultimately refuted the manner in which northern reformers, particularly women's rights reformers, had come to interpret the woman-slave analogy. Yet, by merely raising the possibility that slave emancipation might somehow extend to wives, lawmakers did validate the concerns of women's rights reformers to a degree.

---

[131] Cott, *Public Vows*, 79.
[132] *Congressional Globe*, 39th Congress, 1st Session (1866), 499.
[133] Stanley, *From Bondage to Contract*, 57–59; Cott, *Public Vows*, 79–81.
[134] Stanley, *From Bondage to Contract*, 57–59.

This political framework encouraged women's rights reformers and the growing movement of suffragists to pursue the fugitive wife trope even more zealously in the aftermath of the Civil War. Following the abolition of chattel slavery, the woman-slave analogy was rendered even more "natural and powerful" at a moment when slavery and freedom "became the ruling paradigm through which liberal feminists conceived and developed their vision of rights within marriage."[135] But it only seemed natural on account of the degree to which antebellum women's rights reformers had normalized the claim that marriage could be a state of slavery for wives. Some white women began to invoke the Thirteenth Amendment of 1865, which had nullified the Fugitive Slave Law. An 1868 woman suffrage plea, for example, asked whether lawmakers would "repeal our fugitive slave laws" and "emancipate all adult female slaves."[136] After the Civil War, the ongoing transformation of this trope contributed to the gradual erasure of the fugitive slave's experience. "Wherever there is a woman loose," Susan B. Anthony maintained, "for we have sometimes women loose, as they had negroes loose, in slavery, & we have fugitive wives as they had fugitive slaves ... she is an interloper, & she is paid but one half or one third the price that men receive." These women needed the ballot, Anthony concluded, as their only options were "marriage or prostitution."[137] The specter of the fugitive wife offered women's rights reformers the foundations for women to be included in the Reconstruction amendments.

Over the next two years, Stanton and Anthony's radical but short-lived suffrage newspaper, the *Revolution*, shared more narratives about fugitive wives. Stanton recounted the story of a friend who had married a dishonest, rapacious, and indebted rake, and whom she had urged to "fly from such a monster and villain" as her violent husband. Appreciative of Stanton's "words of encouragement," this friend confided: "I should never have escaped from that bondage; before I could ... have found courage to break those chains, any heart would have broken in the effort."[138] Tracy A. Thomas suggests that, as Stanton increasingly recognized gender as a legal class, she came to use her legal knowledge to develop narratives about women's experiences of the "law

[135] Clark, "Matrimonial Bonds," 30.
[136] Aurora C. Phelps, "Ballot, Bench and Barricade," *Revolution*, 21 May 1868.
[137] Susan B. Anthony, American Equal Rights Association, 12 May 1869, in *The Selected Papers of Elizabeth Cady Stanton and Susan B. Anthony*, Vol. II, ed. Ann D. Gordon (New Brunswick: Rutgers University Press, 1997), 240.
[138] E.C.S., "Marriage and Divorce," *Revolution*, 22 October 1868.

of domestic relations to collectivize women."[139] In doing so, Stanton continued to pivot what she regarded as the greater freedom of enslaved men against free women. Responding to a critic in 1869, Stanton asserted that while the "black man" had been "fighting his way to Canada, his earthly paradise," women had been attempting to forge their own sphere. But women could not "run off," she reiterated, "for they were fastened with silver chains to their tyrants, and there was no Canada for them on the habitable globe."[140]

The *Revolution* echoed the style of Chase's earlier disclosures by drawing on contemporary press reports, especially through its coverage of the McFarland-Richardson trial. In 1869, Abby Sage McFarland's paramour, the journalist Albert Richardson, was fatally shot by her ex-husband Daniel McFarland. Abby had left her husband in 1867, later claiming that he had been an abusive alcoholic, and moved to the boarding house where Albert lived. The following year, she established residency in Indiana (a state that had become infamous for its liberal divorce laws) to obtain a divorce, which she received by October 1869. After the couple's notice to marry appeared in the *New York Tribune*, McFarland shot and mortally wounded Richardson. The couple married on Richardson's deathbed, in a ceremony officiated by Revs Henry Ward Beecher and Octavius Frothingham. Across the summer of 1870, both the *New York Times* and the *Tribune* sensationalized the subsequent trial. Legally, the case was based on the controversial principle of the "unwritten law," in which husbands who murdered their wives' seducers in the moment of discovery could plead momentary insanity to avoid conviction.[141]

However, the *Revolution* interpreted the case quite differently. As Ellen Carol DuBois observes, when McFarland was acquitted from his murder trial, Stanton described Abby McFarland as if she were a fugitive slave. "I rejoice over every slave that escapes from a discordant marriage," she concluded. Stanton emphasized the degree to which the press had elided the perspective of women throughout the whole affair. "One would really suppose that a man owned his wife as the master the slave, and that this was simply an affair between Richardson and McFarland," she proclaimed.

[139] Tracy A. Thomas, "Elizabeth Cady Stanton and the Notion of a Legal Class of Gender," in *Feminist Legal History: Essays on Women and Law*, eds. Tracey Jean Boisseau and Tracy A. Thomas (New York: New York University Press, 2011), 139.
[140] E.C.S., "What Rev. Theodore Cuyler Says," *Revolution*, 3 June 1869.
[141] Hendrik Hartog, "Lawyering, Husbands' Rights, and 'the Unwritten Law' in Nineteenth-Century America," *Journal of American History* 84, no. 1 (1997): 67–96.

"It is the old story, the slave running to Canada, while the master's statutes and scriptures sent [the biblical slave] Onesimus back, and made his bondage legal and divine."[142] Stanton and Anthony responded to the acquittal by organizing a mass meeting for women to protest the verdict, as well as the decision to grant custody of the McFarlands' son to his father.[143] Abby was a "fugitive wife," Stanton proclaimed.[144] The McFarland decision, she continued, was women's equivalent of the *Dred Scott v. Sanford* Supreme Court decision of 1857, which, in the words of Chief Justice Roger B. Taney, had ruled that African Americans had "no rights which the white man was bound to respect."[145] Only four years after slave emancipation, the figure of the "slave" had, for Stanton, morphed almost wholly into the figure of the fugitive wife.

As the rationale for the fugitive wife trope gained greater complexity, white suffragists came to trivialize chattel slavery and express a near-complete disregard for the situation of freedpeople. Instead, narratives about married women fleeing their husbands emerged more frequently. In her famous 1871 address on marriage and divorce, Stanton again described "wives running to Indiana and Connecticut like slaves to their Canada, from marriages worse than plantation slavery; paramours shot in broad day light," with neither the legal establishment nor the press making any attempt to safeguard victimized women. Undermining the dangers and difficulties of self-emancipation for African Americans in the antebellum era, she used the abolition of chattel slavery merely as an occasion to highlight how marriage remained a largely unreformed institution—despite the Married Women's Property Acts. Stanton considered the postbellum era as "woman's transition period, from slavery to freedom," so she expressed frustration when other reformers—let alone the American public—did not share in this interpretation.[146] But Stanton was not, in fact, alone in embracing such an analysis. "I reflected long

---

[142] E.C.S., "Editorial Correspondence," *Revolution*, 23 December 1869.

[143] Ellen Carol DuBois, "The Nineteenth-Century Woman Suffrage Movement and the Analysis of Women's Oppression," in *Capitalist Patriarchy and the Case for Socialist Feminism*, ed. Zillah Eisenstein (New York: Monthly Review Press, 1979), 145–146; Griffith, *In Her Own Right*, 159–160.

[144] Elizabeth Cady Stanton, Speech to a Mass Meeting of Women in New York, 17 May 1870, in *Selected Papers*, Vol. II, 337.

[145] *Dred Scott v. Sanford*, 1857.

[146] Elizabeth Cady Stanton, "Marriage and Divorce," 1871, in *A History of the National Woman's Rights Movement, for Twenty Years*, ed. Paulina W. Davis (New York: Journeymen Printers' Co-operative Association, 1871), 70, 61.

upon the fact that there was in all America no Canada for that fugitive woman to flee with her little ones," Abigail Scott Duniway similarly contemplated more than a decade later.[147]

Slave emancipation did not transform marriage in the manner advocated by women's rights reformers, but it did expand the institution in other ways. Most crucially, it offered freedpeople the opportunity to formalize their unions. The reconstruction era witnessed the legalization of marriage for African Americans, creating what Stanley describes as "new bonds between freedmen and freedwomen."[148] This did not undermine the institution's patriarchal norms, however. At least some black freedmen, like many free white men, expressed the belief that marriage would entitle them to their wives' bodies and labor. According to Victoria E. Bynum, the Freedmen's Bureau sometimes mediated domestic disputes between freedpeople. One wife's attempt to deny her husband's claims ultimately proved unsuccessful. In response to his wife's intent to divorce him, Alfred Gray maintained: "I consider her my property and thus I have a right to her."[149]

African Americans do not appear to have resorted to the fugitive wife trope. However, some embraced discourses of slavery to acknowledge—if not necessarily to condemn—the patriarchal character of marriage. In the last published version of *Clotel*, entitled *Clotelle; or, The Colored Heroine* (1867), William Wells Brown contemplated a freedman who had "purchased his wife" after the Civil War, "nor had he forgotten the fact":

> The woman, like many of her sex, was an inveterate scold, and Jim had but one way to govern her tongue. "Shet your mouf, madam, an' hole your tongue. ... I bought you, an' paid my money fer you, an' I ain't gwine ter let you sase me in dat way. ... [E]f you don't I'll sell you; 'fore God I will. Shet up, I say, or I'll sell you." This had the desired effect, and settled Dinah for the day.[150]

[147] *New Northwest*, 9 August 1883.
[148] Stanley, *From Bondage to Contract*, 45. See also: Cott, *Public Vows*, Chapter 4.
[149] Alfred Gray to General Sickels, Commander, Military District #2, 12 April 1867, Records of the Bureau of Refugees, Freedmen, and Abandoned Bureau Papers Lands, National Archives, in Victoria E. Bynum, *The Long Shadow of the Civil War: Southern Dissent and Its Legacies* (Chapel Hill: University of North Carolina Press, 2010), 70–71.
[150] William Wells Brown, *Clotelle; or, the Colored Heroine* (Boston: Lee & Shephard, 1867), 114. For the four editions published between 1853 and 1867, see: Geoffrey Sanborn, "'People Will Pay to Hear the Drama': Plagiarism in *Clotel*," *African American Review* 45, no. 1–2 (2012): 65–82.

3 "BOUGHT AND SOLD": ANTISLAVERY, WOMEN'S RIGHTS, AND MARRIAGE   111

According to Ann duCille, Brown was not exhibiting a protofeminist consciousness; rather, he was astutely reading and replicating the representational strategies that had become so common amongst white women writers in the nineteenth-century literary marketplace.[151] Wherever a novelist, reformer, or commentator might position themselves in relation to debates about the woman question, discourses of slavery had gained such prevalence with respect to marriage that such rhetoric continued unabated.

Despite such claims, African-American women were far more aware of marriage's ambiguities for freedwomen. Frances Ellen Watkins Harper reported with sadness about freedmen who "positively beat their wives!" During the five years she spent in service to freedpeople in the South, she reflected:

> Part of the time I am preaching against men ill-treating their wives. The condition of the women is not very enviable in some cases. [Women] had a terribly hard time in Slavery and their subjection has not ceased in freedom. One man said of some women that a man must leave them or whip them.[152]

Such examples of cruelty, domestic, and family violence were extreme manifestations of the entitlement that men could legally claim through the marriage contract, and so felt toward their wives.[153] However, Harper's observations did not rely on sensationalist narratives about fugitive wives. Instead, she spoke to very real concerns about coverture and the subjection of married women, periodically embracing discourses of slavery in her analysis of women's rights. Yet, when Harper did use discourses of slavery, she routinely emphasized the rights of enslaved people and racial minorities over that of women.[154]

As African-American women introduced greater nuance into postbellum debates about marriage and women's rights, some elite young belles began to interpret their own situation in similar terms to that of women's rights reformers. Prior to her 1874 marriage to Albert Janin, Violet Blair of Washington, D.C., became deeply aware of the power she held over men as a belle, but would lose as a wife.[155] Echoing the popular novels of

---

[151] duCille, *Coupling Convention*, 27–28.
[152] Dorothy Sterling, *We are Your Sisters: Black Women in the Nineteenth Century* (New York: W.W. Norton & Company, 1984), 340, 405.
[153] Stanley, *From Bondage to Contract*, 46–57, esp. 48.
[154] Chakkalakal, *Novel Bondage*, 65.
[155] Yalom, *A History*, 281–285.

Caroline Lee Hentz, her diary expressed her deep aversion to the prospect of marriage. In 1868, Violet consoled herself by writing, "I will never love & never marry—no man shall ever be my master—I will never promise to obey."[156] "I do not believe it is possible for me to love any man," she reiterated in 1870, declaring, "I will be no man's slave."[157] As in the antebellum era, individual concerns often correlated with those expressed in women's rights print culture. The "idea of ownership" in courtship and marriage rendered women the "owned and men the owners," an 1871 article in the *Woman's Journal* emphasized; this sense of ownership, this contributor reflected, had become "inseparable from the idea of love."[158] For Violet, however, the prospect of marriage could be made more palatable if women were to feel this same sense of ownership toward men. As she wrote in 1871, her beau Albert possessed one especial point of appeal: "He obeys me."[159]

The reservations Violet Blair Janin expressed privately were equally evident in Lillie Devereux Blake's novel, *Fettered for Life; or, Lord and Master: A Story of To-Day* (1874). An important example of postbellum women's rights literature, this novel explored the conjugal exploitation of women across the social strata. A popular young belle who would later become a suffragist, Blake personally experienced the contradictions of nineteenth-century womanhood and brought these insights to her novels.[160] Her earlier works, *Southwold: A Novel* (1859) and *Rockford; or, Sunshine and Storm* (1863), considered the consequences of an ill-suited marriage, a theme she developed most thoroughly in her later novel. Much like Sarah Grimké's 1830s salutation, "Thine in the bonds of womanhood," biographer Grace Farrell suggests that the title of Blake's *Fettered for Life* had acquired multiple meanings by the 1870s. Antebellum abolitionist women had interpreted being "fettered" in terms of chattel slavery, while "lord and master" referenced women's coercion under chattel slavery as well as in marriage.[161]

Both trajectories are exemplified by Flora Livingstone, a character who wishes to pursue her interest in the law but whose parents force her into

---

[156] Violet Blair Janin Diary, 14 July/1 July/10 October 1868, Janin Family Collection, Henry Huntington Library, in Virginia Jeans Laas, *Love and Power in the Nineteenth Century: The Marriage of Violet Blair* (Fayetteville: University of Arkansas Press, 1998), 19.

[157] Janin Diary, 3 October 1870; 24 September 1870, in Ibid., 24.

[158] Lydia Fuller, "Love versus Ownership," *Woman's Journal*, 15 April 1871.

[159] Janin Diary, 27 October 1871, in Laas, *Love and Power*, 29.

[160] Grace Farrell, *Lillie Devereux Blake: Retracing a Life Erased* (Amherst: University of Massachusetts Press, 2002).

[161] Ibid., 132.

the socially acceptable "career" of a belle. Her mother, Blake wrote, had once "protested against her destiny as bitterly as ... any revolted slave; but having for years past been contented with her chains, she could endure no thought of revolt in others." Soon flattered by Ferdinand Le Roy, the young Flora proudly boasts of his romantic attentions, saying, "I don't care to be his slave for life, though I would like to see him at my feet." After a kiss which shatters her virginal sensibilities, Flora completely loses her sense of personal autonomy. Echoing the character of Annie Murray, she felt as if "she was no longer free, no longer belonged to herself, she had received a master, and been compelled to submit to the symbol of his power." Following her engagement, Flora reflected: "'I have passed under the yoke,' she thought, 'I am a slave.'" Such a lack of self-ownership rendered this character the epitome of the fugitive wife—or more accurately, the fugitive fiancée. Flora eventually succumbs to an engagement that she remembers not with joy but "as a mark of servitude" and comes to envy unmarried women "because they, at least, are free." In one chapter, entitled "Flora Seeks Freedom," this character proves unable to escape her impending marriage to a man she describes as "a born tyrant" and concludes that she would become "a slave bound hand and foot" if she were to marry him. But Le Roy manages to apprehend Flora and "bore the fainting captive away." After the marriage, during which she swore "to love, honor and obey," Flora finds herself living in what she describes as a "prison-house" and eventually succumbs to her husband's stifling expectations. On her deathbed, Flora imparts that "marriage without love, is worse than death."[162]

For many women's rights reformers, suffragists, and free love advocates, the hypocrisies of courtship and the specter of a loveless and potentially violent marriage enabled the fugitive wife trope to flourish. Her plight indeed represented the antithesis of the companionate marriage: the fugitive wife became the victim of the inherently oppressive union that antebellum reformers so feared. As it developed amongst white reformers by the 1870s, however, the fugitive wife trope became almost completely devoid of any explicit reference to antebellum chattel slavery.

[162] Lillie Devereux Blake, *Fettered for Life; or, Lord and Master: A Story of To-Day* (New York: The Feminist Press, 1874/1996), 101–103, 72–73, 129, 146–148, 236–245, 263, 351. For further analysis, see: Farrell, *Lillie Devereux Blake*, 131–142; Ana Stevenson, "The Novel of Purpose and the Power of the Page: Breaking the Chains That Bind in *Fettered for Life*," *Crossroads* 6, no. 2 (2013): 104–114.

Conclusion

Situating the analogy between marriage and chattel slavery in the context of multiple social movements, proslavery thought, and popular culture reveals the many and varied analyses that discourses of slavery provoked. Abolitionists and women's rights reformers rejected the brutality of chattel slavery and the lack of self-ownership that unequal matrimonial unions engendered, for both enslaved and free women. While too great a focus on the situation of white women began to undermine the antislavery movement's tenuous interracial coalitions, this remained quite distinct from the proslavery commentators who embraced discourses of slavery to challenge the subjugation of elite white women and condone chattel slavery. In contradistinction to the increasingly literal manner in which northern reformers had come to use the woman-slave analogy by the 1850s, proslavery commentators and popular culture embraced this rhetoric in a manner that proved to be purely rhetorical. African Americans, however, explored the important differences between marriage and chattel slavery.

Yet, while some commentaries upon marriage continued to place the institution as one of many types of oppression, this became less common amongst white reformers in the postbellum era. Most creative and insidious was the fugitive wife trope, which represented the complete appropriation of abolitionist discourse for the purposes of white women's rights. Increasingly, women's rights reformers and suffragists followed free love advocates to convince themselves that the situation of women was worse than that of enslaved African Americans. Perhaps, some contemplated, it was worse than chattel slavery had ever been. This presented a significant transformation from the position of antebellum abolitionists and women's rights reformers, many of whom had been legitimately concerned with the oppression of enslaved people of African descent as well as white married women. For African Americans, however, using discourses of slavery to interrogate marriage did not entail a negation of chattel slavery and its abuses. Rather, African-American women, in particular, acknowledged the degree to which marriage remained a patriarchal institution and explored its implications for freedpeople of color.

PART II

Between Public and Private

You think there is little of kinship between them?
Perhaps not in blood, yet there's likeness of soul;
And in bondage 'tis patent to all who have seen them
 That both are fast held under iron control.
The simpering girl, with her airs and her graces,
 Is sister at heart to the hard-working drudge;
Two times of to-day, as they stand in their places;
 Whose lot is the sadder I leave you to judge.

One chained to the block is the victim of Fashion;
 Her object in life to be perfectly dressed;
Too silly for reason, too shallow for passion,
 She passes her days 'neath the tyrant's behest.
Thus pinioned and fettered, and warily moving,
 Lest looping should fail her, or band come apart;
What room is there left for her thinking or loving?
 What noble ambition can enter her heart?

And one, the worn wife of a grizzled old farmer;
 She kneads the great loaves for the "men-folk" to eat.
In the wheat-fields the green blades are springing like armor;
 Afar in the forests the flowers are sweet.
She lifts not her eyes. Within kitchen walls narrow
 Her life is pent up. The most hopeless of slaves,
Though weary and jaded in sinew and marrow,
 She never complains. Women *rest* in their graves.

Twin victims, for which have we tenderest pity –
For mother and wife toiling on till she dies,
Or the frivolous butterfly child of the city,
All blind to the glory of earth and of skies?
Is it fate, or ill fortune, hath woven about you
Strong meshes which ye are too helpless to break?
Shall we scornfully wonder, or angrily flout you,
Or strive from their torpor your minds to awake?

Yet, Venus of old, with your queenly derision,
How would you disdain the belle's tawdry array!
Free footsteps untrammeled, cool hand of decision,
Sweet laugh like the bells pealing, were yours in the day
When you reigned over men by the might of your beauty;
No fetters were o'er you in body or brain;
The world would bow down in the gladness of duty
Could you but awake in your splendor again.

And, Pallas and Venus, if now you were holding
A talk over womanhood, what would you say,
The words of wise counsel while you were unfolding,
If some one should show you these pictures to-day?
I dream of your faces: divinest compassion
Would yearn the poor toiler to pity and save;
And your largeness of scorn would descend on the fashion
Which binds, unresisting, the idler a slave.

"Sister Slaves," *Harper's Bazaar*, in
B.O. Flower, *Fashion's Slaves* (Boston: The Arena Publishing Co., 1892)

CHAPTER 4

"Tyrant Chains": Fashion, Antifashion, and Dress Reform

When Amelia Bloomer, editor of the women's rights and temperance newspaper, the *Lily*, embraced an alternative style of dress in 1851, it quickly came to be known as the "bloomer" costume. That year, the new style spread from Seneca Falls, New York, to London and beyond. Women's rights reformers and dress reformers, to a lesser and greater extent, expressed the belief that women's fashion was oppressive and that this fashion alternative could offer women freedom. "Poor, silly, chain-fettered things," the little-known dress reformer Lydia M. Collins said of women who wore fashionable dress. "How in my heart I pity your weakness. Would that I could 'break your chains,' and bid you go free."[1] However, Sojourner Truth, the famous abolitionist and women's rights reformer, did not agree with dress reformers such as Collins. "I had Bloomers enough when I was in bondage," she reflected a few years later.[2] Fostering a comparison that was at once significant and superficial, the woman-slave analogy became central to the perception and analysis of the restrictions associated with fashionable dress.

Fashion is a form of cultural expression that does not have any commonalities with chattel slavery. To understand the connection that so many reformers did perceive, it is necessary to return to Manisha Sinha's

[1] Lydia M. Collins, "Determined and Independent," *Sibyl*, November 1857.
[2] Harriet Beecher Stowe, "Sojourner Truth, The Libyan Sibyl," *Atlantic Monthly* 11 (April 1863): 479.

© The Author(s) 2019
A. Stevenson, *The Woman as Slave in Nineteenth-Century American Social Movements*, Palgrave Studies in the History of Social Movements, https://doi.org/10.1007/978-3-030-24467-5_4

assertion that chattel slavery became the "benchmark of oppression" during the antebellum era.[3] Many commentators and reformers responded to changing fashion trends by embracing discourses of slavery. Some scholars recognize the currency that such rhetoric gained in the public discourse about fashion. As fashion historian Valerie Steele observes, "women have been positioned as the 'slaves' or 'victims' of fashion," yet the "subtext has been that women were 'vain' or 'foolish.'"[4] The analysis of the cultural meanings or psychology of fashion, however, has often meant the historical context that produced the woman-slave analogy has been overlooked. As a result, the use of this rhetoric has been inadequately contextualized in terms of the rise and fall of the institution of chattel slavery. Thus, the implications and significance of the woman-slave analogy in fashion and dress-reform discourse is yet to be fully appreciated.[5]

This chapter charts the cultural contestations surrounding fashionable dress, which led to the emergence of the bloomer costume. The responses to dress reform in antebellum print culture reveals the degree to which fashion could be theorized through discourses of slavery. However, such an analysis was more consistently abstracted from chattel slavery than the other themes addressed in this book, a trend only disrupted in the decade prior to and following the Civil War. Yet Annemarie Strassel stresses the need for scholars to move beyond the bloomer costume and toward an analysis that encompasses the "*principles* and *desires*" of those who promoted the transformation of women's dress.[6] The advocacy of postbellum fashion alternatives, such as underwear and artistic or aesthetic dress, relied not only on discourses of slavery but also on discourses of emancipation. Across the antislavery, women's rights, dress reform, health reform, free love, and suffrage movements, countless reformers embraced the woman-slave analogy to articulate that women expressed either too great

---

[3] Manisha Sinha, *The Slave's Cause: A History of Abolition* (New Haven: Yale University Press, 2016), 347.

[4] Valerie Steele, *The Corset: A Cultural History* (New Haven: Yale University Press, 2001), 2.

[5] For some notable exceptions, see: Gayle V. Fischer, *Pantaloons & Power: A Nineteenth-Century Dress Reform in the United States* (Kent: Kent State University Press, 2001), 123–124; Ana Stevenson, "'Symbols of Our Slavery': Fashion and Dress Reform in the Rhetoric of Nineteenth-Century American Print Culture," *Lilith: A Feminist History Journal* 20 (2014): 5–20.

[6] Annemarie Strassel, "Designing Women: Feminist Methodologies in American Fashion," *WSQ: Women's Studies Quarterly* 41, no. 1 & 2 (2013): 39–40.

a devotion to fashionable dress or a deep dissatisfaction toward its demands. All collectively envisaged the possibility for freedom through the transformation of women's dress.

FASHIONABLE DRESS AND ITS ANTIFASHION CRITICS

Scholars describe fashion as a form of display through which the social and cultural meanings associated with gender, race, and class are constructed. According to sociologist Diana Crane, fashion was defined by a standard of appearance that was both broadly embraced and adopted during the nineteenth century. Since women enjoyed only very tenuous legal and political rights, fashionable dress could also operate as a form of social control. For upper-class women, fashion was highly ornamental and impractical, making many forms of labor difficult or impossible. Middle-class women, in turn, habitually sought to emulate the upper classes, but did not necessarily have the resources to do so. Working-class women, many of whom labored beyond the home, were seen to negate the gendered expectations associated with the fashionable ideal.[7]

The nineteenth century would witness vast transformations in the style and silhouette of women's fashionable dress, one that was a product of technological change as much as shifting attitudes toward masculinity and femininity.[8] The popular style and silhouette both morphed and accentuated the female form, which made women dependent upon undergarments—corsets, petticoats, crinolines, and bustles—to achieve its ever-changing contours.[9] To maintain respectability, women were expected to be appropriately fashionable. The intricacy of clothing design and expense of materials distinguished class affiliation, including enslaved, indentured, and free status.[10] Although some historians argue against the immediate conflation of dress and women's oppression, others emphasize

---

[7] Diana Crane, *Fashion and Its Social Agendas: Class, Gender, and Identity in Clothing* (Chicago: University of Chicago Press, 2000), 6, 5, 16.

[8] Christopher Breward, *The Culture of Fashion: A New History of Fashionable Dress* (Manchester: Manchester University Press, 1995), Chapter 6.

[9] Patricia A. Cunningham, *Reforming Women's Fashion, 1850–1920* (Kent: Kent State University Press, 2003), 1.

[10] Jonathan Prude, "To Look Upon the 'Lower Sort': Runaway Ads and the Appearance of Unfree Laborers in America, 1750–1800," *Journal of American History* 78, no. 1 (1991): 124–159; Leigh Summers, "Yes, They Did Wear Them: Working-Class Women and Corsetry in the Nineteenth Century," *Costume* 36 (2002): 65–74.

the deleterious effects of corsetry, in particular, on women's health, most especially the practice of tight lacing.[11] Elizabeth Cady Stanton asked in 1851: "Is being born a woman so criminal an offence, that we must be doomed to this everlasting bondage?"[12]

The fashionable ideal presented in popular culture contributed to the cult of true womanhood and the cultural ideal of separate spheres. Women's periodicals, including *Godey's Lady's Book*, *Peterson's Magazine*, and *Sartain's Union Magazine of Literature and Art*, later joined by *Ladies' Home Journal*, published detailed and colorful fashion plates. Some women exhibited quite a close attention to fashionable dress and its changing ideals, which caused dismay for many commentators. Popular culture promoted fashionable dress but also expressed a deep uneasiness toward women who used their clothing to gain too much power and influence, as encapsulated in such common phrases as "slaves to fashion" (Fig. 4.1). In 1893, Helen Gilbert Ecob disparaged what she saw as a "slavish following of fashion-plates," further observing: "Those [women] who have emancipated themselves from the bondage of conventional dress have liberty of thought in other directions."[13] According to art historian Julie Wosk, the need to follow fashion's injunctions led critics to satirize "women as foolish slaves to fashion's whims."[14]

These tensions produced a body of literature that embraced discourses of slavery to express vehement objections to the developments in women's fashion. Since fashion defined arbitrary standards of beauty and true womanhood, conservative critics responded by ensuring women did not forsake these expectations. Gayle V. Fischer labels these conservative critics, which included the clergy, medical practitioners, and journalists, as "antifashion."[15] Other scholars define antifashion differently, as any style that resists or rejects current fashion trends. Often found within specific belief systems or subcultures, antifashion has the purpose of "making a political statement, and is meant to communicate a message about the

---

[11] Steele, *The Corset*; Leigh Summers, *Bound to Please: A History of the Victorian Corset* (Oxford: Berg, 2001).
[12] E.C.S., "Our Costume," *Lily*, April 1851.
[13] Helen Gilbert Ecob, *The Well-Dressed Woman: A Study in the Practical Application to Dress of the Laws of Health, Art, and Morals* (New York: Fowler & Wells, 1893), 233.
[14] Julie Wosk, *Women and the Machine: Representations from the Spinning Wheel to the Electronic Age* (Baltimore: Johns Hopkins University Press, 2001), 53.
[15] Fischer, *Pantaloons & Power*, 23–24.

4 "TYRANT CHAINS": FASHION, ANTIFASHION, AND DRESS REFORM 121

A slave to Fashion's tyrant laws,
You court each silly fop's applause;
Did you but know what I can see,
How shocked, I fancy, you would be.
You will, I hope, leave off this style,
Your dress provokes a pitying smile.

Fig. 4.1 Frank Beard, "A slave to Fashion's tyrant laws," c. 1869. Library Company of Philadelphia, Comic Valentine Collection, 10.4

group that embraces it."[16] These two descriptions of antifashion are useful, as they offer an explanation as to why different and ideologically disparate groups might embrace discourses of slavery to develop a criticism of fashionable dress.

---

[16] Patricia Anne Cunningham and Susan Voso Lab, eds. *Dress and Popular Culture* (Bowling Green: Bowling Green State University Press, 1991), 13–14.

Quakers, or the Religious Society of Friends, had resisted the lure of fashionable dress since the movement's origins in seventeenth-century Britain. American Quakers valued "plainness of speech, behavior and apparel."[17] Quaker women espoused a simple, plain, and modest style that had domestic and religious connotations.[18] Early abolitionist women and women's rights reformers included prominent Quakers such as Lucretia Mott, Sarah Grimké, Angelina Grimké Weld, and Abby Kelley Foster. During the late 1820s, after Sarah found a new spiritual home amongst Philadelphia's Orthodox Quakers, she discarded her "superfluities of naughtiness"—the decorative, elaborate clothing of a Charleston belle.[19] Carol Mattingly suggests that abandoning the fashionable dress of the southern slaveholding woman enabled the Grimké sisters to foster a closer association with the enslaved people for whom they agitated.[20] But this seems somewhat superficial, as competing class and religious impulses meant that Quakers often opted for a plain style of outfit made from the best available materials.[21] Southern slave codes ensured that clothing was one of the distinguishing features of chattel slavery; it often instituted a sense of class status among enslaved fieldworkers versus enslaved domestic servants as much as it contributed to the maintenance of white supremacy.[22] The Grimké sisters did not wear the "linsey-woolsey dress" that Harriet Jacobs so distinctly described as "one of the badges of slavery."[23]

Rather, it was through their experiences as southern ladies as well as their controversial reputation as abolitionist orators that the Grimké sisters gained a greater awareness of the social connotations surrounding women's clothing.[24] Under her "lordly master," Sarah believed, "woman's

---

[17] Joan Kendall, "The Development of a Distinctive Form of Quaker Dress," *Costume* 19 (1985): 58; Carol Faulkner, *Lucretia Mott's Heresy: Abolition and Women's Rights in Nineteenth-Century America* (Philadelphia: University of Pennsylvania Press, 2011), 30.

[18] Carol Mattingly, *Appropriate[ing] Dress: Women's Rhetorical Style in Nineteenth-Century America* (Carbondale: Southern Illinois University Press, 2002), 26, 30–36.

[19] Angelina Grimké, Diary, 1 February 1828, Weld-Grimké Family Papers, William L. Clements Library, University of Michigan, in Katharine du Pre Lumpkin, *The Emancipation of Angelina Grimke* (Chapel Hill: University of North Carolina Press, 1974), 31.

[20] Mattingly, *Appropriate[ing] Dress*, 31.

[21] Frederick B. Tolles, "'Of the Best Sort but Plain': The Quaker Aesthetic," *American Quarterly* 11, no. 4 (1959): 484–502.

[22] Helen Bradley Foster, *"New Raiments of Self": African American Clothing in the Antebellum South* (Oxford: Berg, 1997), 134–145.

[23] L. Maria Child, ed., *Incidents in the Life of a Slave Girl* (Boston: The Author, 1861), 20.

[24] Mattingly, *Appropriate[ing] Dress*, 31–32.

elevation" was impeded by "her love of dress."[25] Angelina's husband, the abolitionist Theodore Dwight Weld, questioned whether or not the dictates of Quaker fashion were, in fact, empowering:

> The moment certain shades of color, ... or arrangement of seams and angles, are made the *sine qua non* [essential condition] of religion and principle, ... [you will] become *slaves* instead of *rulers*. I cannot get it out of my mind that these must be a fetter on the spirit[.] ... Think about it, dear sisters.[26]

Weld followed the many other abolitionist men who embraced discourses of slavery to interpret their private lives. Yet, as Mattingly notes, this observation also indicated his "sense of the disciplining power inherent in clothing."[27] In spite of the challenge that Quaker women's fashion posed to fashionable dress, discourses of slavery could also be mobilized to contradict the sense of autonomy that women exhibited in their mode of dress. "If You Would Have Freedom, Strike for It," Sarah Grimké would later write of dress reform in the *Lily*.[28]

Occasionally, the editors of popular women's periodicals advocated for the moderate reform of fashionable dress. Between 1828 and 1877, Sarah Josepha Hale, the famous and typically conservative editor of *Godey's Lady's Book*, presented images of the nineteenth century's woman at "the center of her own culture" through fashion plates celebrating women's friendship and intimacy.[29] Alison Piepmeier describes Hale as "a moderate fashion reformer" because she advocated health and comfort in women's dress rather than fashion alone.[30] Indeed, she expressed indignation at the "tyranny of fashion," both in *Godey's* and in her own book, *Traits of American Life* (1835). This "tyranny" was being imposed by European tailors and milliners, Hale believed, and so encouraged American women to create their own costume.[31] However, since commentators such as Hale offered

---

[25] Sarah M. Grimké, *Letters on the Equality of the Sexes, and the Condition of Woman* (Boston: Isaac Knapp, 1837), 67, 71.
[26] Catherine H. Birney, *The Grimké Sisters: Sarah and Angelina Grimké; the First American Women Advocates of Abolition and Woman's Rights* (Boston: Lee and Shepard, 1885), 217.
[27] Mattingly, *Appropriate[ing] Dress*, 31.
[28] Sarah M. Grimké, "If You Would Have Freedom, Strike for It," *Lily*, 1 April 1852.
[29] Patricia Okker, *Our Sister Editors: Sarah J. Hale and the Tradition of Nineteenth-Century American Women Editors* (Athens: University of Georgia Press, 1995), 1, 63.
[30] Alison Piepmeier, *Out in Public: Configurations of Women's Bodies in Nineteenth-Century America* (Chapel Hill: University of North Carolina Press, 2004), 178–183, esp. 179.
[31] Sarah Josepha Hale, *Traits of American Life* (E.L. Carey & A. Hart, 1835), 273. As one historian notes, Hale "inveighed against 'the tyranny of fashion,' and sought to enlighten

no alternative to fashionable dress, she and her contemporaries revealed the "antifeminism" of those conservative critics who became so occupied with the question of dress reform.[32]

As Gayle V. Fisher reveals, antebellum utopian communities also reimagined women's dress. Nashoba, Frances Wright's failed antislavery community in New Harmony, Indiana, promoted a fashion alternative during the 1820s, as did the 1840s millennial Oneida Community in New York State. These communities made attempts to develop a new social order which redefined gender roles, partially through the transformation of fashion. This was often achieved more in philosophy than through action: challenging fashion could become less about clothing and more about who had the power to determine and maintain women's place in society. While alternative family structures and cooperative housekeeping meant utopian communities afforded women greater freedom, somewhat ironically, women did not necessarily have direct influence over their own dress. Some were even persuaded to wear fashion alternatives as the political statement of the men around them. Henry B. Blackwell later condemned this type of male interference as "an impertinence," maintaining that women's dress should concern women alone.[33] Consequently, early antebellum overtures toward dress reform did not always disrupt power relations in communal and private settings, while modesty still dictated that bifurcated pantaloons were indecent when sported by women. The alternative lifestyles and perceived moral transgressions of utopian communities further influenced public perceptions of dress reform.[34]

Other antebellum reformers began to consider the relationship between fashion and women's health, thus anticipating the apprehensions that health reformers would more fully express. Many believed that individuals

---

women on the 'pernicious effects of tight lacing'." See: Sarah Josepha Hale, "Health and Beauty," *Godey's Lady's Book* 36 (1848): 66–67, in Deborah Jean Warner, "Fashion, Emancipation, Reform, and the Rational Undergarment," *Journal of the American Costume Society* 4 (1978): 25.

[32] David Kunzle, "Dress Reform as Antifeminism: A Response to Helene E. Roberts's 'The Exquisite Slave: The Role of Clothes in the Making of the Victorian Woman'," *Signs: Journal of Women in Culture and Society* 2, no. 3 (1977): 570–579.

[33] Henry B. Blackwell, "Dress Reform Convention," *Woman's Journal*, 20 February 1875.

[34] Fischer, *Pantaloons & Power*, Chapter 2, esp. 17, 38, 53, 49, 77; Suzanne M. Spencer-Wood, "A Feminist Theoretical Approach to the Historical Archaeology of Utopian Communities," *Historical Archaeology* 40, no. 1 (2006): 152–185. Spencer-Wood includes Quakers as a utopian community, focusing on Brook Farm, Oneida, the Koreshans, and Llano Del Rio.

could not act with moral responsibility "unless their bodies were unfettered and uncorrupted."[35] "God created woman to be the companion of man, not his slave, not his menial," Rev. Samuel J. May emphasized in an 1845 sermon. A "frame cheated of half its growth ... by subserviency to fashion, will be less pleasing than a frame made, by wholesome exercise, proper nourishment, and due obedience to the laws of health," he concluded.[36] The health reform movement focused on a "healthful" lifestyle to be achieved through interventions such as homeopathy, hydrotherapy (the water cure), phrenology, and Sylvester Graham's dietary reforms, as well as the fledgling dress-reform movement.[37] The *Water-Cure Journal*, in particular, espoused an especial commitment to dress reform. Long after dress reform fell out of popularity, its vestiges existed largely in enclaves such as hydrotherapist Dr. James C. Jackson's Dansville Water Cure.[38]

Antifashionists, Quakers, and various antebellum reformers did not offer an alternative to what they found wanting in fashionable dress. Prior to the emergence of a committed dress-reform movement, some women's rights reformers followed the Grimké sisters and began to develop a vehement criticism of fashion. According to Julia Ward Howe, women were "very naturally glad" to embrace any opportunity "to throw off their chains with their petticoats, and to assume for a time the right to go where they please, and the power of doing as they please."[39] Although Paulina Wright Davis, like a number of other women's rights reformers, never offered support for dress reform per se, she, too, acknowledged how the "tyrannic law of fashion" compelled women's "[abject] submission."[40] Thus, an embrace of discourses of slavery united the criticisms developed by those who both supported and condemned fashionable dress.

[35] Ronald G. Walters, *American Reformers: 1815–1860* (New York: Hill and Wang, 1978/1997), 147.
[36] Samuel J. May, "The Rights and Condition of Women; A Sermon, Preached in Syracuse, Nov., 1845," *Woman's Rights Tracts* no. 1 (1853): 10.
[37] Susan E. Cayleff, *Wash and Be Healed: The Water-Cure Movement and Women's Health* (Philadelphia: Temple University Press, 1987), 2; Fischer, *Pantaloons & Power*, 12.
[38] Cayleff, *Wash and Be Healed*, 130. For the workingwomen and frontierswomen who continued to wear bifurcated garments after the Civil War, see: Brenda M. Brandt, "Arizona Clothing: A Frontier Perspective," *Dress* 15, no. 1 (1989): 71; Sally Helvenston, "Fashion on the Frontier," *Dress* 17, no. 1 (1990): 141–155; Crane, *Fashion and Its Social Agendas*, 120–121.
[39] Julia Ward Howe, *The Hermaphrodite* (Lincoln: University of Nebraska Press, 2004), 29. For further discussion of Howe's novel, see: Stevenson, "'Symbols of Our Slavery'," 8–9.
[40] "Dress, Taste, and Fashion," *Una*, April 1854.

The Bloomer Costume

Women reformers soon began to develop a new costume, one they claimed would offer new and unprecedented freedoms. These early dress-reform efforts, as much as the transformation of fashionable dress itself, were a product of the era's new technologies.[41] But the bloomer costume was equally a product of the widespread press attention it garnered, in both reform and mainstream print culture. At each crucial moment in its circulation, women's rights and dress reformers as well as journalists embraced the woman-slave analogy to describe fashion's constraints and advocate this fashion alternative. This rhetoric characterized the reform advocacy as much as the press satirization of the bloomer costume, to such a degree that it amounted to an early attempt to theorize women's dress.

Between 1850 and 1851, Elizabeth Smith Miller became one of the first women known to have publicly donned an alternative style of dress. To describe her personal experiences of fashionable dress, she made constant recourse to discourses of slavery. It was because her skirts "clung in fettering folds about her feet," Miller expressed, that she had first resolved to adopt an alternative style.[42] Describing her journey toward becoming an antebellum innovator and fashion pioneer, Miller recalled how years of "dissatisfaction … suddenly ripened into the decision that this shackle should no longer be endured."[43] But Miller's experiences may also have reflected the undue influence of male reformers; scholars question the degree to which her prominent father, the abolitionist and philanthropist Gerrit Smith, encouraged her interest in dress reform.[44] In 1853, Smith would write to his cousin, Elizabeth Cady Stanton, to express his hope that women's rights conventions would produce "women whose dress would indicate their translation … from slavery to freedom"—a perspective that could not have been lost on his daughter.[45]

---

[41] Catherine Mas, "She Wears the Pants: The Reform Dress as Technology in Nineteenth-Century America," *Technology and Culture* 58, no. 1 (2017): 35–66.

[42] Elizabeth Smith Miller, n.d., Smith Family Papers, New York Public Library, in Amy Kesselman, "The 'Freedom Suit': Feminism and Dress Reform in the United States, 1848–1875," *Gender and Society* 5, no. 4 (1991): 498.

[43] "Symposium on Women's Dress, Part I," *Arena* 6 (October 1892): 490.

[44] Roberta J. Park, "'All the Freedom of the Boy': Elizabeth Cady Stanton, Nineteenth-Century Architect of Women's Rights," *International Journal of the History of Sport* 18, no. 1 (2001): 16–17.

[45] Gerrit Smith to Elizabeth Cady Stanton, 1 December 1853, in *History of Woman Suffrage* [hereafter *HWS*], Vol. I, eds. Elizabeth Cady Stanton, Susan B. Anthony, and Matilda Joslyn Gage (Rochester: Susan B. Anthony, 1881), 838.

Miller nonetheless experienced what she perceived as a newfound freedom of movement on account of her new outfit. When she visited her cousin in Seneca Falls, New York, she and Stanton found that they both lamented the rigors of fashionable dress.[46] In an 1852 letter to Lucretia Mott, Stanton went on to describe woman as "a slave to her rags" who could "never develop in her present drapery."[47] Impressed with Miller's new ensemble, she quickly adopted similar attire and expressed delight in the physical freedom it offered. These women could directly compare the restrictions of fashionable dress with the mobility of their new outfit, a change they viewed as a transition from slavery to freedom. In her 1898 memoir, Stanton again recalled how the new outfit had made her feel like "a captive set free from his ball and chain," further exulting: "What incredible freedom I enjoyed for two years!"[48]

What was this new outfit? Amelia Jenks Bloomer, Stanton's friend and neighbor in Seneca Falls, would soon promote it in her newspaper. As editor of the *Lily*, she became the new costume's main proponent. Bloomer advocated that its bodice should not be "constraining to the motions of the arms" and its skirt should cover bifurcated pantaloons:

> Leaving the portion above the waist to the taste of the wearer, ... we would have a skirt reaching down to nearly half way between the knee and ankle, and not made quite so full as is the present fashion. ... Underneath this skirt, trowsers [sic] moderately full, ... and there gathered in with an elastic band.[49]

Other prominent abolitionists and women's rights reformers would soon adopt the bloomer costume. When Lucy Stone first did so, she became "a fashion rage" and particularly captured the attention of the press.[50] Not all reformers, however, were convinced of the need to reform women's dress. One of the *Lily*'s readers directed Bloomer's husband to "exercise his

---

[46] Kesselman, "The 'Freedom Suit'," 498–500.

[47] Elizabeth Cady Stanton to Lucretia Mott, 22 October 1852, in *Elizabeth Cady Stanton as Revealed in her Letters, Diary and Reminiscences*, Vol. II, eds. Theodore Stanton and Harriot Stanton Blatch (New York: Harper & Brothers, 1922), 44–45.

[48] Elizabeth Cady Stanton, *Eighty Years and More: Reminiscences 1815–1897* (New York: T. Fisher Unwin, 1898), 201.

[49] The New Dress, "The New Costume for the Ladies," *Lily*, September 1851. See also: E. "Short Dresses," *Lily*, April 1851; E.C.S., "Our Costume," *Lily*, 1 April 1851; "Our Dress," *Lily*, April 1851; "Our Fashion Plate," *Lily*, January 1852.

[50] Joelle Million, *Woman's Voice, Woman's Place: Lucy Stone and the Birth of the Woman's Rights Movement* (Westport: Praeger, 2003), 113–114.

authority" and prohibit his wife from wearing the outfit. Bloomer responded by rejecting such matrimonial "dictation and tyranny," concluding: "A silken cord is sometimes stronger than an iron chain, and a respectful entreaty has more power than the tyrant's command."[51] Quickly becoming a dress-reform "icon," the bloomer costume provoked controversy because it "implied a radical sartorial reworking of clothing in form and function based on a desire for bodily liberation, utility, and sexual equality."[52]

Alongside the new costume, antebellum reformers established a binary between the restrictions of fashionable dress and the freedom that women experienced wearing the bloomer costume. As Stanton wrote in the *Lily*, "'the drapery' is quite too much—one might as well work with a ball and chain."[53] These reformers thus characterized fashionable dress not merely as a whim, as had antifashionists, but as a central form of women's oppression. Health reformers also offered support for the new outfit, especially in the *Water-Cure Journal*. "I rejoice in all new freedom for woman," wrote Mary Gove Nichols, believing fashionable dress to be both "enthralling and expensive" as well as rendering women the "pretty slave of man." As Nichols concluded: "The day of woman's freedom has dawned; God speed its meridian!"[54] This reveals the degree to which discourses of slavery flourished beyond the nucleus of the women's rights movement and its analysis of fashionable dress. Anticipating "a day of 'universal emancipation' of the sex," Rachel Brooks Gleason, for example, promoted the new outfit and exulted at how "glorious would it be to see every woman free from *every* fetter that fashion has imposed!"[55]

Carol Mattingly describes the process whereby print culture exchanges between the reform and mainstream press established the prominence—and then rapid notoriety—of the bloomer costume. The outfit was initially well-accepted by the press and public alike. The *New York Tribune* and other publications circulated excerpts from the *Lily*, as well as exchanges between Bloomer and the Seneca County *Courier*. Editors of mainstream newspapers often commented positively and took pride in their local women rejecting Parisian fashions. But fashion periodicals expressed

[51] "Our Dress," *Lily*, April 1851.
[52] Strassel, "Designing Women," 40.
[53] E.C.S., "Our Costume," *Lily*, 1 April 1851.
[54] Mary S. Gove Nichols, "The New Costume, and Some Other Matters," *Water-Cure Journal*, August 1851.
[55] Mrs. R.B. Gleason, "Woman's Dress," *Water-Cure Journal*, February 1851.

their opinion largely through silence. *Sartain's Magazine*, for example, originally referred to all the hype merely as a news item.[56] During September 1851, however, *Sartain's* did call attention to American women's attempt to "break the thraldom in which they have been so long held ... by the *artistes* of Paris and London."[57] Its coverage of the new outfit was a significant moment in the magazine's history, as it marked a turning point in *Sartain's* support for the advancement of women.[58] Yet, like antifashionists, *Sartain's* acknowledged the "thraldom of fashion" without endorsing any of the potential benefits of dress reform or providing any fashion alternative.

A growing body of fashion criticism witnessed commentators on all sides of the debate embrace these abstracted discourses of slavery to structure their responses to the bloomer costume. One prominent critic was Jane Grey Swisshelm, an antislavery advocate and Pittsburgh-based newspaper editor who, in 1850, had expressed reservations about the efficacy of analyzing questions relating to antislavery and women's rights in conjunction. Swisshelm satirically described the bloomer controversy as the "campaign against the bondage of petticoats."[59] In spite of Rev. Henry Ward Beecher's similar ambivalence toward dress reform, he, too, admitted that "our eye is yet in bondage to the old forms" and conceded to "let every woman have a bloomer dress, for the sake of foot excursions."[60] Despite such reservations, women continued to embrace the new costume. Later in 1851, some began to sport the bloomer costume in London and across the British Isles.[61] For at least the next two years, it continued to captivate both spectators and the press as far afield as Australia and New Zealand.[62]

[56] Mattingly, *Appropriate[ing] Dress*, 40–42, 62–66, 76–77.
[57] "The Bloomer Costume," *Sartain's Union Magazine of Literature and Art*, September 1853.
[58] Heidi L. Nichols, *The Fashioning of Middle-Class America: Sartain's Union Magazine of Literature and Art and Antebellum Culture* (New York: Peter Lang, 2004), 23, 78.
[59] Jane Grey Swisshelm, "The Bloomer Costume," *Saturday Visiter*, 26 July 1851, in Mattingly, *Appropriate[ing] Dress*, 54.
[60] Henry Ward Beecher, *Star Papers; or, Experiences of Art and Nature* (Boston: Phillips, Sampson & Co., 1855), 175. For further discussion of these points, see: Mattingly, *Appropriate[ing] Dress*, 38.
[61] Julia Petrov, "'A Strong-Minded American Lady': Bloomerism in Texts and Images, 1851," *Fashion Theory: The Journal of Dress, Body & Culture* 20, no. 4 (2016): 381–413; Tiffany Urwin, "Dexter, Dextra, Dextrum: The Bloomer Costume on the British Stage in 1851," *Nineteenth Century Theatre* 28, no. 2 (2000): 91–113.
[62] Ana Stevenson, "'Bloomers' and the British World: Dress Reform in Transatlantic and Antipodean Print Culture, 1851–1950," *Cultural & Social History* 14, no. 5 (2017): 621–646.

Fig. 4.2 "Amelia Bloomer, Originator of the New Dress," *Illustrated London News* (27 September 1851): 396. The Victorian Web, http://www.victorianweb.org/art/costume/bloomer.html

AMELIA BLOOMER, ORIGINATOR OF THE NEW DRESS—FROM A DAGUERREOTYPE BY T. W. BROWN.—(SEE PRECEDING PAGE.)

The appellation, "bloomers," came to dominate public discourse, at least partially due to the word's potential association with self-display and immodesty.[63] Bloomer attempted to disassociate herself from the name, yet this became increasingly unlikely. An engraving of Bloomer wearing the outfit appeared in the *Illustrated London News*, captioned "Amelia Bloomer, Originator of the New Dress" (Fig. 4.2). At least some of the alternative appellations, especially in reform print culture, encapsulated

[63] Mattingly, *Appropriate[ing] Dress*, 70.

the prominence that discourses of slavery had gained within the debate. While the Lowell Bloomer Institute supported "Costumal Reform," others adopted the term "freedom suit" because of the degree to which the new outfit offered "freedom of both mind and body" to its wearer.[64] Health and dress reformers alike made reference to the "reform dress," as well as the "short dress," the "Turkish dress" or "Turkish trowsers," and the "Camille costume."[65] A November 1851 fashion plate in the *Water-Cure Journal* featured the now-famous image of Bloomer, labelled "The American Costume," alongside a woman in a highly ornamental full crinoline, labelled "The French Costume."[66] An 1853 contributor recalled how she had "thrown off the bonds of fashionable slavery" to adopt "the full 'American costume,'" a trend in nomenclature that emphasized the outfit's republican virtues.[67]

The public's relatively positive reception of the bloomer costume soon began to transform, however. This was facilitated by what Bonnie Anderson describes as the "titillation caused by crossing the boundary between the sexes," something that satirists and humorists would increasingly deride.[68] London's *Punch* published some of the most prominent satirical cartoons. Two key 1851 examples were "Bloomerism—An American Custom" and "Woman's Emancipation" (Fig. 4.3). Both depicted bloomer-wearing women who command the cityscape and contravene expectations about femininity by promenading or standing in masculine poses, smoking, and chatting freely. Since respectability placed middle- and upper-class women and girls within the confines of the home, idling in the city associated these figures with the poor and working-class women predominantly found on the streets—in both the antebellum United States and Victorian Britain.[69] Journalists and satirists soon came to connect the bloomer cos-

---

[64] "The Lowell Bloomer Institute," *Lily*, December 1851; H., "Value of the Reform Dress," *Sibyl*, 15 August 1858.

[65] Kesselman, "The 'Freedom Suit'," 497–498; Gayle V. Fischer, "'Pantalets' and 'Turkish Trowsers': Designing Freedom in the Mid-Nineteenth-Century United States," *Feminist Studies* 23, no. 1 (1997): 110–140.

[66] "The American and French Fashions Contrasted," *Water-Cure Journal*, November 1851.

[67] Sarah K. Selby, "Dress Reform. A Bloomer to Her Sisters," *Water-Cure Journal*, June 1853.

[68] Bonnie S. Anderson, *Joyous Greetings: The First International Women's Movement, 1830–1860* (Oxford: Oxford University Press, 2000), 197; Kesselman, "The 'Freedom Suit'," 496.

[69] Sharon E. Wood, *The Freedom of the Streets: Work, Citizenship, and Sexuality in a Gilded Age City* (Chapel Hill: University of North Carolina Press, 2005), 28.

Fig. 4.3 "Woman's Emancipation," *Harper's New Monthly Magazine* 3 (August 1851)

tume with existing anxieties about bifurcated garments and transgressive womanhood. Mainstream print culture routinely denounced the bloomer costume as an example of women wearing the "breeches," envisaging the outfit as the nucleus of a dangerous and unsettling form of gender inversion.[70] By transforming the bloomer costume into a symbol that transgressed gender, class, and racial boundaries, satire rearticulated the catastrophic consequences of women embracing bifurcated garments.

The apprehensions expressed alongside the bloomer costume, however, were far from new. A decade before the emergence of the bloomer costume, a social panic had manifested in Britain when it emerged that women were being employed in the mining industry. Anne McClintock suggests that these

[70] Kesselman, "The 'Freedom Suit'," 508; Gayle Veronica Fischer, "A Matter of Wardrobe? Mary Edwards Walker, a Nineteenth-Century American Cross-Dresser," *Fashion Theory: The Journal of Dress, Body & Culture* 2, no. 3 (1998): 259–261; Fisher, *Pantaloons & Power*, 42.

4 "TYRANT CHAINS": FASHION, ANTIFASHION, AND DRESS REFORM   133

working women, who sported "breeches" or skirts flounced into trousers, caused deep anxieties about gender. Commentators perceived these women as "embodying a regression to an earlier moment of racial development." When depicted in visual culture, the cross-dressing, white, female miner was often imbued with African or simian features. This figure, McClintock argues, evoked the "transition from an industrialism based on imperial slavery to industrial imperialism based on waged labor."[71] Similar apprehensions were equally evident in the *Punch* cartoons. "Bloomerism" juxtaposed the bloomer-wearing women with middle-class women and street children, who look on disparagingly.[72] If cartoonist John Leech's central figures were haggard working-class women, then "Woman's Emancipation" portrayed women with the aquiline facial features associated with racial progress. However, the bulldog in its foreground offered class-based overtones. Described as a "fighting dog," the bulldog was closely associated with working-class leisure activities until it was reclaimed as a fashionable pedigree animal during the 1880s.[73]

The text that accompanied "Woman's Emancipation" satirized the woman-slave analogy even more explicitly, reflecting the degree to which such rhetoric had come to be perceived as a definitive feature of reform discourse in the United States. In its title as much as its text, this cartoon illustrated how women's rights reformers mobilized discourses of slavery alongside discourses of emancipation to denounce fashionable dress and promote dress reform. Framed as an excerpt from a fictional periodical, the "*Free Woman's Banner*," the article was authored by an equally fictional "strong-minded American Woman" by the name of "Theodosia E. Bang, M.A.":

> We are emancipating ourselves, among other badges of the slavery of feudalism, from the inconvenient dress of the European female. With man's functions, we have asserted our right to his garb, and especially to that part of it which invests the lower extremities. ... [I]t is generally calculated that the

[71] Anne McClintock, *Imperial Leather: Race, Gender, and Sexuality in the Colonial Contest* (New York: Routledge, 1995), 104–118, esp. 112.
[72] John Leech, "Bloomerism—An American Custom," *Punch* 21 (1851): 141. The same year, this cartoon was issued in the United States as a lithograph, under the title "Two of the Fe'He Males," where each figure had a speech bubble, see: Gary L. Bunker, "Antebellum Caricature and Woman's Sphere," *Journal of Women's History* 3, no. 3 (1992): 25–27.
[73] "Woman's Emancipation," *Punch* 21 (July 1851): 3. Harriet Ritvo, "Pride and Pedigree: The Evolution of the Victorian Dog Fancy," *Victorian Studies* 29, no 2 (1986): 227–253.

dress of the Emancipated American female is quite pretty—as becoming in all points as it is manly and independent.[74]

Not only did this establish the woman-slave analogy as central to transatlantic interpretations of contemporary social movements, but the ridicule aimed toward the "Emancipated American female" reflected its perceived significance amongst antebellum women reformers. Months later, when this cartoon was reprinted in New York's *Harper's New Monthly Magazine*, it again reflected the ongoing process of transatlantic circulation that was being undertaken by a woman-as-slave worldview itself.

However, the amount of ridicule the outfit generated led many women's rights reformers to abandon the bloomer costume by the mid-1850s.[75] Those women who experienced personal controversy justified their choices—both to themselves and others—through discourses of slavery. As Bloomer herself observed, "the blessings of freedom" should ensure that women would not have to "rivet the chains upon ourself again," even "to avoid the frowns of slavish conservatives."[76] Many women's rights reformers continued to support the abstract ideals of dress reform. All too aware that the spectators who witnessed bloomer-wearing women tended to fixate on their clothing rather than what they said, some became increasingly cautious of how this was shaping the public's perception of their movement.[77] "When I heard of the cold looks you had to encounter, my bruised heart did pity you," Stanton wrote to Miller in 1851. "Well, we have lived through it[.] ... But had I counted the cost of the short dress, I would never have put it on; however, I'll never take it off, for now it involves a principle of freedom."[78] Despite her proclamations, Stanton no longer saw the bloomer costume as a source of women's freedom and abandoned it by 1854.

Women's rights reformers would dedicate themselves to legal, social, and political reform across the coming decades. Stone, together with Miller and Anthony, remained steadfast in her support for the bloomer costume for much longer than other women's rights reformers. When she finally abandoned the bloomer costume, Stone agonized over the inherent

---

[74] "Woman's Emancipation," *Harper's New Monthly Magazine* 3 (August 1851).
[75] Fischer, *Pantaloons & Power*, 106.
[76] "Our Fashion Plate," *Lily*, January 1852.
[77] Fischer, *Pantaloons & Power*, 105.
[78] Elizabeth Cady Stanton to Elizabeth Smith Miller, 4 June 1851, in *Elizabeth Cady Stanton as Revealed in her Letters*, Vol. II, 30.

principle in a letter to Anthony. "Women are in bondage," she proclaimed; Stone asked whether reformers "should give an example by which woman may more easily work out her own emancipation?" Anthony, too, was conflicted about returning to what many commentators, including Stanton, described as the "tyranny of fashion," so Stanton consoled them both: "We put it on for greater freedom, but what is physical freedom compared with mental bondage?"[79] By embracing discourses of slavery to envisage the relationship between womanhood and fashionable dress, women's rights reformers began to theorize the meaning of fashion and understand how it operated alongside other forms of women's oppression.

DRESS REFORM AND THE CIVIL WAR

As support for the bloomer costume declined following the hype of 1851, a small subset of the women and men who remained steadfast went on to establish the National Dress Reform Association (NDRA) in 1856. Organized dress reform was more than a movement dedicated toward fashion change; it aimed to empower women to abandon the constraints of fashion and thus attacked how fashion acted as a signifier of gender and class.[80] Dress reformers, however, increasingly embraced the woman-slave analogy to situate fashion as more deleterious than other sites of women's oppression. In 1860, for example, the NDRA promoted a resolution stating that women could never expect "to be recognized [as] the equal of man, until she emancipates herself from a dress which is both [the] cause and the sign of her vassalage."[81] Although antifashionists and earlier dress-reform advocates had long embraced abstracted discourses of slavery, the Civil War era witnessed the dress-reform movement gradually reimagine its criticism of fashionable dress.[82] This shift was not absolute, as some continued to embrace abstracted discourses of slavery in much the same vein as other women's rights and health reformers. However, when establishing this new and sudden connection

---

[79] Ida Husted Harper, *The Life and Work of Susan B. Anthony: Including Public Addresses, Her Own Letters and Many from Her Contemporaries During Fifty Years*, Vol. I (Indianapolis: Bowen-Merrill Company, 1898), 115–116.

[80] Kathleen M. Torrens, "All Dressed Up with No Place to Go: Rhetorical Dimensions of the Nineteenth Century Dress Reform Movement," *Women's Studies in Communication* 20, no. 2 (1997): 189–190.

[81] "National Dress Reform Association," *Sibyl*, 15 June 1860, in Fischer, *Pantaloons & Power*, 122.

[82] Stevenson, "'Symbols of Our Slavery'," 14–15.

between fashionable dress and chattel slavery, dress reformers effectively envisaged fashion to be an evil comparable to—or worse than—chattel slavery. The NDRA embraced Lydia Sayer Hasbrouck's the *Sibyl: A Review of the Tastes, Errors, and Fashions of Society* as its official newsletter. But dress reform itself had not remained popular, nor had it ever gained the mainstream embrace beyond communities of antebellum reformers that its proponents had desired. The *Sibyl* listed 403 women who, in 1858, continued to wear the bloomer costume.[83] Hasbrouck herself was particularly scathing of the women's rights reformers who had abandoned the bloomer outfit in previous years.[84] Perhaps ironically, she ensured the comparative longevity of her periodical by "clubbing" it, at a reduced subscription rate, with more popular fashion magazines such as *Godey's Lady's Book* and *Peterson's Magazine*, thus exposing a new readership to the benefits of the bloomer costume and dress reform.[85] This was a tactic that also introduced her new readers to dress-reform discourse, specifically the relatively distinctive manner in which dress reformers used the woman-slave analogy.

Hasbrouck published letters in which rank-and-file dress reformers could interact with celebrated reformers. This placed her, as editor of the *Sibyl*, at the center of a conversation with her community of readers. As Karin Wahl-Jorgensen argues of late-twentieth-century newspapers, editors select letters to the editor that express what is "considered 'good' for the community": usually, large newspapers only publish between 5 percent and 50 percent of their correspondence, whereas small newspapers might publish nearly all the letters that are received. Although practical considerations about circulation and advertising revenue influence these decisions, editors ultimately construct public debate by choosing which letters to publish.[86] How might this dynamic have played out in the women's rights and dress-reform periodicals of the 1850s? As a small, radical periodical dedicated to a comparatively marginal cause in the "Sisterhood of Reforms," the *Sibyl* may well have published nearly all its correspondence. If this was indeed the case, discourses of slavery held a privileged position in the perspectives its readership expressed. This suggests that Hasbrouck believed her periodical's embrace

---

[83] Kesselman, "The 'Freedom Suit'," 502–508.

[84] "Lucy Stone's Position," *Sibyl*, 15 April 1859; "The Reform Dress: Lucy Stone, Miss Anthony and Mrs. Stanton," *Sibyl*, 1 January 1857.

[85] Mattingly, *Appropriate[ing] Dress*, 58.

[86] Karin Wahl-Jorgensen, "Letters to the Editor as a Forum for Public Deliberation: Modes of Publicity and Democratic Debate," *Critical Studies in Media Communication* 18, no. 3 (2001): 309–310.

of a woman-as-slave worldview had become normalized enough to gain traction—not only in the *Sibyl*, but also amongst the wider readership that was facilitated through clubbing.

As a result, the woman-slave analogy began to play a central role in interactions between rank-and-file dress reformers. Hasbrouck may even have perceived its potential to facilitate a community ethos, as she repeatedly published correspondence that was predicated on discourses of slavery. "E.B.," for example, expressed her readiness and willingness to "throw off the shackles of fashion, and be at least OUTWARDLY free." In response, Hasbrouck reminded her "DEAR SISTER[S]" that they were not alone in their continued embrace of the bloomer costume. This choice, she emphasized, enabled each woman to be "both *outwardly and inwardly free*, for none are free save those who can break the shackles of both soul and body."[87] This interplay between Hasbrouck, as editor, and her readership heightened the manner in which rank-and-file correspondents were willing to describe their personal experiences of fashion. Those who described fashion as a "badge of servility and degradation" evoked highly personal, embodied experiences which were common to so many women.[88]

Dress reformers, in contrast to antifashionists, used discourses of slavery to describe the need for a viable fashion alternative. But these reformers did not always take themselves seriously. If satire is defined by ridicule and criticism, parody is most often sympathetic to its subject.[89] An 1857 poem, entitled "Parody," encouraged women to reform their dresses. "Ladies who in hoops are bound," it began:

> Now's the day, and now's the hour,
> Would you crush the Tyrant's power,
> And be free forevermore,
> From chains and slavery?
> Still may those who dare to be
> From all hoops and fetters free,
> Let the tyrant Fashion see
> That they dare her frown.
> Sisters, if you wish to find,

---

[87] "Extracts from Correspondence," *Sibyl*, 1 November 1856.
[88] S.H., "Thoughts on Mrs. Weld's Letter," *Sibyl*, 1 November 1857.
[89] For more on parody and satire, see: Margaret A. Rose, *Parody: Ancient, Modern and Post-modern* (Cambridge: Cambridge University Press, 1993).

> Health and joy, and peace of mind,
> Bow no more at Fashion's shrine –
> Nature's laws obey.
> By your weak and suffering frames,
> By your children's woes and pains,
> Swear you'll break the tyrant's chains,
> That you will be free.[90]

This approach was in contradistinction to the vicious satire in London's *Punch*. Indeed, the poems published in the *Sibyl* were in deep sympathy with the aims of dress reformers.

Like other antebellum antislavery, women's rights, and health reform newspapers, the *Sibyl* existed as a site of constant rhetorical exchange. Hasbrouck published another poem, entitled "Parody on 'The Farmer's Life's the Life for Me,'" the following year:

> The "Bloomer" dress's the dress for me –
> I own I love it dearly;
> And every season, light and free,
> I'll wear it all so cheerily.
>
> 'T is good for work, 't is good for play,
> 'T is good to walk the street, sir,
> It gives us comfort, grace and speed,
> For it fetters not our feet, sir. ...
>
> Now, sisters, daughters, mothers too,
> Who crouch beneath this tyrant,
> Shake off the fetters from your feet –
> Come forth free—triumphant.[91]

Although the bloomer costume's potential to "fetter not our feet" may have been lighthearted, the poem's intent was quite serious. For celebrated reformers and rank-and-file correspondents, developing an understanding of how to apply the woman-slave analogy shaped contributors' perspectives toward how to conceive of different types of oppression.

---

[90] "Parody," *Sibyl*, March 1857.
[91] "Parody on 'The Farmer's Life's the Life for Me'," *Sibyl*, 1 June 1858. See: Fisher, *Pantaloons & Power*, 132.

However, Amy Kessleman suggests that a growing ideological divide emerged between the politically oriented women's rights movement and the fashion-centered dress reformers. While the former envisaged social, economic, and political concerns as the foundations of women's oppression, the latter advocated the reform of the individual and cast the transformation of fashionable dress in these terms.[92] Each, however, mobilized discourses of slavery to debate as well as to theorize their differing perspectives toward the relative significance of fashion. Lucy Stone, the abolitionist and women's rights reformer who had reluctantly abandoned the bloomer costume, suggested that "[woman's] miserable style of dress is a consequence of her present vassalage[,] not its cause." Only the achievement of women's rights, she believed, would enable woman to "dictate the style of her dress."[93] One correspondent took exception to these comments about women's "loathsome long skirts," asking: "Would Lucy Stone think this the most reasonable and common-sense way to hasten the slaves' emancipation? We trow not."[94] At an 1857 dress-reform convention, dress reformer Louisa Humphrey similarly expressed the belief that fashion was the "real cause of her bondage," although she did acknowledge women's "servile and dependent position" in the family.[95]

The use of the woman-slave analogy amongst dress reformers could inspire women to experience the freedom that the bloomer costume could offer. However, it could also imply that they were wholly controlled by fashion. Should their personal discipline fail, women could be seen as responsible for their own oppression. The *Sibyl* not only criticized "men for oppressing women," but also condemned "women for consenting to be oppressed."[96] Passing culpability for enslavement was not a new phenomenon, however. The revolutionary era's focus on individualism implied that those unable to maintain their freedom were deserving of slavery—a particularly insidious ideology, given the reality of chattel slavery and the growing influence of scientific thought that justified racial hierarchy.[97] Even non-violent abolitionists sometimes praised slave insurrections

---

[92] Kesselman, "The 'Freedom Suit'," 502–508.

[93] Lucy Stone, *Sibyl*, 1 July 1857.

[94] L.H., "True Position of Dress Reform," *Sibyl*, 1 September 1857.

[95] Louisa Humphrey, "Letters Read at the Convention," *Sibyl*, 1 July 1857.

[96] *Sibyl*, 1 September 1856, in Kesselman, "The 'Freedom Suit'," 503–504.

[97] François Furstenberg, "Beyond Freedom and Slavery: Autonomy, Virtue, and Resistance in Early American Political Discourse," *Journal of American History* 89, no. 4 (2003): 1302–1303, 1310–1311.

because they supposedly proved that enslaved people did resist their condition. Blaming women for the rigors of fashionable dress contributed to gendered power differentials in dress reform as a social movement.

Despite its principal commitment to dress reform, the *Sibyl* also revealed an allegiance with other antebellum reforms. In the heightened climate of the 1850s, political debate became dominated by questions of chattel slavery and free soil, a political ideology in opposition to the institution's extension alongside westward expansion. The specifics of these antebellum political debates soon influenced dress-reform discourse. This represented something of a departure for dress reformers and antifashionists alike, as their rhetoric had remained far more abstracted from chattel slavery than that of many of their reform contemporaries. An 1854 contributor to the *Lily*, for example, had viewed "the petty despotism in which society holds woman" as most "ridiculously apparent" in the opposition to any change in fashion, saying, "it would be difficult to say in what particular her condition differs, either legally or socially, from the Southern slave!"[98] By decade's end, reports about the abolitionist John Brown's October 1859 raid on Harper's Ferry, which aimed to trigger an armed slave revolt across the South, impelled the *Sibyl* toward rhetoric that was at once more militant and more inspired by abolitionist discourse.[99]

It was because Hasbrouck considered dress reform and abolitionism to be of equal importance that the *Sibyl* increasingly positioned women's oppression as literally and ideologically analogous to that of enslaved people of African descent. However, the subsequent intensification of an explicit comparison between fashion and chattel slavery created ambiguity in the dress-reform movement. Not all direct analogies between women's rights and chattel slavery were wholly oblivious to the exploitation of enslaved people, but the dress-reform movement nonetheless became increasingly devoid of any sense of perspective by the late 1850s. The allusions to chattel slavery in dress-reform discourse, Fisher argues, occasioned greater "insensitivity to the plight of enslaved African Americans in the South, as the NDRA opportunistically compared the 'negro slavery crisis' to women's 'slavery' to fashion."[100]

Some dress reformers evoked what David Roediger describes as a "'Down with all slavery!' position," the byproduct of which could be the

[98] S.L. Brown, "Dress," *Lily*, August 1854.
[99] For a broader discussion, see: Stevenson, "'Symbols of Our Slavery'," 16.
[100] Fischer, *Pantaloons & Power*, 123.

conclusion that chattel slavery was not the most egregious form of oppression.[101] When Hasbrouck discussed the situation of chattel slaves in comparison to "*Northern White Slaves*," for example, she declared:

> [W]e hate slavery—hate it in all its forms—hate it when it enslaves man or woman, or when they enslave themselves to passions, appetite, fashion, or aught that degrades their highest man or womanhood.[102]

Others came very close to expressing the opinion that fashionable dress was actually worse than chattel slavery. "Slavery to fashion is one of the meanest, most grinding and debasing of bonds," one contributor protested, decrying dress reformers' struggles in comparison to the relative success of the antislavery and temperance movements.[103] This reflects what scholars describe as "a level playing field," another metaphor developed to describe the myth of colorblindness shared among white Americans in contrast to the sense of social inequality that black Americans continue to perceive.[104] Accordingly, dress reformers disregarded the differential implications of the social death that chattel slavery inflicted upon enslaved people of African descent.[105]

These tendencies were perhaps most apparent in a letter to the *Sibyl* entitled "The Wanderer Returned," which featured as the cover story of a January 1859 edition. It was prefaced by an epigraph: "The fetters have fallen, *the woman is free*." Although stylistically similar to the epigraphs so many women's rights reformers in the United States and Britain had embraced to legitimate a woman-as-slave worldview, the origins of this particular quotation appear to be untraceable. It is possible that Dr F.R. Harris wrote her own epigraph to preface what would be the central theme of her letter. Claiming to "[detest] slavery in all its forms, whether moral, social, or physical," this letter took a "'Down with all slavery!' posi-

---

[101] David R. Roediger, *The Wages of Whiteness: Race and the Making of the American Working Class* (London: Verso, 1991/2007), 82.

[102] Lydia Sayer Hasbrouck, "Revolvers—Gov. Wise—Northern White Slaves," *Sibyl*, 15 December 1859.

[103] X., "Thoughts on Dress Reform," *Sibyl*, 15 May 1858.

[104] Charles A. Gallagher, "Color-Blind Privilege: The Social and Political Functions of Erasing the Color Line in Post Race America," *Race, Gender & Class* 10, no. 4 (2003): 22–37.

[105] See: Orlando Patterson, *Slavery and Social Death* (Cambridge: Harvard University Press, 1982).

tion" to its logical extremes. Dr Harris chronicled how she had "struggled long" and "chafed under that last galling fetter that bound me to Fashion's arbitrary rule!" When the "last fetter" was "broken," she finally felt "free and happy" in the bloomer costume. Dr Harris described this experience through three analogies: an eagle; a prisoner; and an enslaved person of African descent. To express her joy, she told of how dress reform made her feel as if she were "the caged eagle ... [that] burst the bars of his unnatural prison ... for freedom's flight"; "the prisoner just released from ... the captive's cell"; or "the ransomed slave just ... breathing freedom's atmosphere." Yet, concerned that she would again succumb to the demands of fashion, Dr Harris then inverted these analogies. Would "the caged eagle ... break the bars of his prison in his strong struggles for freedom, and soar away ... [only to] voluntarily return ... [to] his cage again?" Would "the prisoner walk proudly among the free earth; but ... crave an asylum again within the prison walls?" Finally, Dr. Harris asked: "Has not the southern slave, ... after having ... escaped from slavery, ... been known to turn back and seek a master's protection and release from care and responsibility, in slavery again?"[106]

The dress-reform discourse of the Civil War era reflected the heightened national consciousness surrounding the sectional issue of chattel slavery. However, at a moment when dress reformers were beginning to use discourses of slavery in a manner much more directly connected to chattel slavery, African-American women began to espouse a wholly different approach to the question of fashionable dress. Slaveowners often provided enslaved people with only inadequate clothing and sometimes even used dress as a punitive measure, forcing enslaved women to wear trousers and enslaved men dresses in order to effect a sense of humiliation, punishment, and degradation.[107] Frances Ellen Watkins Harper and Sojourner Truth both distanced themselves from the bloomer costume because they were more interested in the positive image that fashionable dress could convey, especially during their public addresses.[108] Having had "Bloomers enough ... in bondage," as Truth told Harriet Beecher Stowe and the readership of the

---

[106] Dr. F.R. Harris, "The Wanderer Returned," *Sibyl*, 15 January 1859.
[107] Foster, "*New Raiments of Self*," 159–172.
[108] Mattingly, *Appropriate[ing] Dress*, 110–111; Pamela E. Klassen, "The Robes of Womanhood: Dress and Authenticity among African American Methodist Women in the Nineteenth Century," *Religion and American Culture* 14, no. 1 (2004): 45.

Atlantic Monthly, she rejected the imperatives of dress reform.[109] For Truth, fashion's ability to inscribe social control was far more problematic for enslaved people than it was for free northern women. Thus, African-American women periodically pivoted discourses of slavery against their analysis of fashionable dress so as to question the premise of the dress-reform movement.

Harriet Tubman, in contrast, approached fashion more from the perspective of practicality, which meant she contemplated dress reform quite differently. The context in which she meditated upon the nature of women's clothing, however, was specific, being limited to the experiences of only a few African Americans. During the Civil War, the missions Tubman undertook beyond Union lines enabled her to lead many enslaved people to freedom. "General Tubman," as she was sometimes known by her abolitionist admirers, found fashionable dress to be too inconvenient and dangerous during these missions. "I want ... a *bloomer* dress, made of some coarse, strong material, to wear on *expeditions*," she dictated in a June 1863 letter from Beaufort, South Carolina, to the educator, abolitionist, and free-soil advocate Franklin B. Sanborn:

> In our late expedition ... I started to run, stepped on my dress, it being rather long, and fell and tore it almost off[.] ... I made up my mind then that I would never wear a long dress on another expedition of the kind, but would have a *bloomer* as soon as I could get it.[110]

As Jean M. Humez observes, Tubman's request evoked "how thoroughly comfortable she was with the claims made on behalf of women's rights in the elite Garrisonian antislavery circles in which she had become a 'heroine' in the 1850s and 1860s."[111] While Tubman certainly echoed the claims of women's rights and dress reformers in her praise of the bloomer costume's utility and mobility, her analysis also differed because she believed its benefits should not necessarily be enjoyed in public.[112]

---

[109] Stowe, "Sojourner Truth," 479. For an analysis of this article, which suggests that "Stowe's Truth disdains feminism," see: Nell Irvin Painter, *Sojourner Truth: A Life, a Symbol* (New York: W.W. Norton, 1996), Chapter 17, esp. 154.

[110] Sarah H. Bradford, *Scenes in the Life of Harriet Tubman* (Auburn: W.J. Moses, 1869), 5, 85–86.

[111] Jean M. Humez, *Harriet Tubman: The Life and the Life Stories* (Madison: University of Wisconsin Press, 2006), 154, 60–61.

[112] See: Mattingly, *Appropriate[ing] Dress*, 110–111.

The antebellum dress-reform movement receded following the NDRA's demise in 1864. However, the tendency to place the onus on women to change their own dress sometimes continued after the Civil War. "Woman's 'subjection' in dress is very galling and degrading," one woman lamented to the *Woman's Journal* in 1873. Her dubious analogy between the "happy slaves in the South" and women of "easy circumstances" who could "dress in fashion or not, just as suits their fancy," concluded that women themselves were "the tyrants who hold ourselves (individually) in subjection."[113] This reflected a broader transformation that would take place amongst so many postbellum women's rights reformers and suffragists, who collectively came to embrace ever more explicit references to chattel slavery to effect a more complete focus on white women's oppression. For the vestiges of the dress-reform movement, however, the specific comparisons that some had pursued between fashion and chattel slavery became far less frequent as the urgency of the Civil War dissipated. Among the remnants of the dress-reform movement, those who advocated the transformation of fashionable dress again returned to more abstracted discourses of slavery.

From Emancipatory Undergarments to Fashion's Slaves

The analysis of fashionable dress was soon dominated by the abstracted discourses of slavery that had defined the early antebellum era. In the absence of any sustained dress-reform movement, this rhetoric reflected that of early-nineteenth-century antifashionists more than that of the reformers of the previous two decades. However, it was also unlike the limited vision of antifashionists in that it was coupled with a growing focus on how fashion existed as one among many forms of women's oppression. This demonstrated the connections between postbellum reform movements, as well as a certain continuity in how reformers approached the woman-slave analogy. Postbellum dress reformers, who largely operated as individuals within other social reform movements, increasingly developed a more nuanced understanding of women's oppression in the context of fashion, yet this seldom extended to any of the pressing questions surrounding race or class.

One major outlier to these rhetorical trends emerged alongside the new undergarments developed in the late 1860s. Few dress-reform philosophies had been embraced beyond reform circles, however the use of light-

[113] Faith Rochester, "The Dress Question," *Woman's Journal*, 28 June 1873.

weight textiles gained some popularity and a willingness amongst some women to reject constrictive underwear created rich marketing opportunities.[114] Some women's rights reformers had realized as early as the 1850s that reforming women's dress completely was proving unrealistic. This gradually led to what fashion historians describe as a subtle shift toward women's undergarments. The success of this new "rational" fashion was that it could help alleviate the restrictions and weight of fashionable dress in a concealed, and thus more conservative, manner. One of the first new lightweight reform undergarments, the Emancipation Union Under-Flannel, was patented in 1868. Susan Taylor Converse then designed an improved version, the Emancipation Suit, and another corset alternative known as the Emancipation Waist, by 1875. Patented that year, Converse's new designs could be adapted to various patterns and eliminated the heavy material (cashmere and merino wool) used for the original in favor of cotton or linen. These undergarments were endorsed and promoted by the Dress Reform Committee of the New England Women's Club (NEWC), founded in 1868 by Boston suffragist Julia Ward Howe and affiliated with the American Woman Suffrage Association (AWSA). When the Emancipation Waist was displayed at the 1876 Centennial Exhibition in Philadelphia, it appeared alongside the commercial exhibits rather than as part of the Women's Pavilion.[115] As early as the 1870s, advertisements for reform-related underwear appeared in both mainstream and reform periodicals, from the *Ladies Home Journal* to AWSA's *Woman's Journal*.

These new undergarments created none of the public outcry that had surrounded the bloomer costume. However, the appellations chosen to describe them are seldom contextualized in terms of the era in which they emerged. For antebellum reformers, the possibility of slave emancipation had seemed a hopeful, if unlikely, prospect. Although neither slavery nor emancipation are static concepts, discourses of emancipation had long figured as the opposite of discourses of slavery. The bloomer costume's advocates had used both to describe the outfit's capacity to offer women freedom. However, at a moment when dress reformers began to retreat from direct allusions to chattel slavery, their descriptions for these new

---

[114] Breward, *Culture of Fashion*, 156.

[115] Warner, "Fashion, Emancipation, Reform," 24–29; Cunningham, *Reforming Women's Fashion*, Chapter 3, esp. 75–76, 78–81; Autumn Stanley, *Mothers and Daughters of Invention: Notes for a Revised History of Technology* (New Brunswick: Rutgers University Press, 1995), 170.

undergarments were equally a product of the era of slave emancipation. The Emancipation Proclamation of January 1863 was, as Ira Berlin observes, "an enigma from the first." Many enslaved people secured their own freedom by fleeing beyond Union lines and offering their invaluable services as laborers. The Emancipation Proclamation itself did not proclaim universal liberty, but rather, he argues, the "compromised and piecemeal arrival of an undefined freedom."[116] How does this relate to dress reform, a social movement that had effectively become unorganized after the demise of the NDRA in 1864? The reformers who embraced discourses of emancipation to describe the new undergarments may have been aware that this surreptitious fashion transformation was a partial solution only. This subtle rhetorical shift, from discourses of slavery toward a tempered embrace of discourses of emancipation, suggests a certain resignation to the limited potential for the reform of women's outergarments.

The lack of a sustained dress-reform movement meant that the analysis of fashionable dress was fragmented across many postbellum social movements. Those who did discuss dress reform as an ideal nonetheless maintained a degree of rhetorical continuity through their continued recourse to the woman-slave analogy. Jennifer Ladd Nelson suggests that the rise and fall of the antebellum era's bloomer costume meant that dress reform and its ethos were no longer considered radical.[117] Those postbellum reformers who continued to express an interest in dress reform often operated within the broader women's movement rather than as a movement unto themselves. But if dress reform had become less radical, the woman-slave analogy's prevalence had simultaneously become normalized. This enabled a style of hyperbolic, embodied fashion criticism that was grounded in discourses of slavery to flourish. More reformers than ever before had come to accept the possibility that fashion, to varying degrees, might result in woman becoming "voluntarily bound hand and foot, soul and body, with her galling chains."[118]

During the late 1860s, Elizabeth Cady Stanton and Susan B. Anthony's newspaper, the *Revolution*, which was the organ of the National Woman Suffrage Association (NWSA), expressed only a tangential concern toward

---

[116] Ira Berlin, "Who Freed the Slaves? Emancipation and Its Meaning," in *Union and Emancipation: Essays on Politics and Race in the Civil War Era*, eds. David W. Blight and Brooks D. Simpson (Kent: Kent State University Press, 1997), 105, 109–112.

[117] Jennifer Ladd Nelson, "Dress Reform and the Bloomer," *Journal of American and Comparative Cultures* 23, no. 1 (2000): 24.

[118] Mrs. M. Stephenson Organ, "Grace Greenwood and Dress Reform," *Revolution*, 11 March 1869.

questions relating to fashionable dress. Its financial proprietor, the controversial proslavery white supremacist and woman suffragist George Francis Train, encouraged women to "break the bondage of fashion," yet he also blamed women for their own oppression. "Did woman, in order to debase woman, invent the badge of slavery which she takes pride in wearing?" he asked.[119] Train suggested that an intrinsic enmity existed between women, thus evoking the myth of women hating other women which, according to Alana Piper, achieved transnational circulation across the nineteenth century.[120] While critical of fashionable dress, the *Revolution* did not necessarily offer outright acceptance toward any style of dress reform. In 1869, when the editor of the *Tribune* asked the *Revolution* to respond to what might have been considered quite a valid question, its reply both expressed annoyance and denigrated dress reform.[121] The *Tribune* had even posed its question—"What is to be the costume of the emancipated woman?"—in terms of the rhetoric to which so many suffragists had become accustomed.[122]

Some considered the degree to which political equality, sexual purity, and practicality might be achieved through a change in fashion, a possibility that had briefly been considered during the antebellum era.[123] If everyone could "dress as nearly alike as possible," Stanton suggested in 1869, the "concealment of sex" would enable equal wages for equal work at the same time as protecting girls and women from various kinds of oppression and exploitation.[124] However, surprise and outrage were expressed when individual women embraced these measures, as physicians and sexologists viewed cross-dressing as a symbol of "sexual inversion or impurity."[125] Stanton professed that cross-dressing was illegal; although her legal knowledge ensured she knew otherwise, women who wore men's clothing were frequently detained in spite of the lack of official statutory prohibitions.[126]

---

[119] "Letter from George Francis Train," *Revolution*, 19 November 1868.

[120] Alana Jayne Piper, "'Woman's Special Enemy': Female Enmity in Criminal Discourse During the Long Nineteenth Century," *Journal of Social History* 49, no. 3 (2016): 671–692.

[121] Mattingly, *Appropriate[ing] Dress*, 120; Lana F. Rakow and Cheris Kramarae, eds. *The Revolution in Words: Righting Women, 1868–1871* (London: Routledge, 1990), 140, 155.

[122] W., "Costume," *Revolution*, 18 November 1869.

[123] For example, see: "Mrs. Kemble and Her New Costume," *Lily*, 1 December 1849.

[124] Elizabeth Cady Stanton, "Woman's Dress," *Revolution*, 22 July 1869.

[125] Caroline Field Levander, *Voices of the Nation: Women and Public Speech in Nineteenth-Century American Literature and Culture* (New York: Cambridge University Press, 1998), 117–118.

[126] See: Mattingly, *Appropriate[ing] Dress*, 119.

Only a certain degree of male attire was considered acceptable in a woman's wardrobe. Some women engaged in what Diana Crane describes as "nonverbal resistance" through "alternative dress," which incorporated elements of men's fashion—hats, ties, suit jackets, waistcoats, and shirts— into an otherwise feminine wardrobe.[127] The suit jacket, for example, became what Xavier Chaumette describes as the "symbol of the emancipated woman in the nineteenth century."[128]

The AWSA continued to express ongoing concerns about fashionable dress. In Boston, the AWSA-affiliated NEWC invited novelist and reformer Elizabeth Stuart Phelps to address the subject of "What to Wear?" in 1873.[129] Her approach to dress reform might be seen as non-radical, emanating as it did from her Christianity and moderate commitment to women's rights.[130] Yet Phelps, too, predicated her dress-reform rhetoric on abstracted discourses of slavery. Women were robust, she argued, perhaps even more so than men, "or we should have sunk in our shackles long ago." Phelps denounced the popular corset silhouette known as the "wasp waist," as it "[im]prisoned [the] vital organs ... it binds," and proclaimed "Off with the corsets!":

> No, don't give them to Biddy. Never fasten about another woman, in the sacred name of charity, the chains from which you have yourself escaped. ... Make a bonfire of the cruel steel that has lorded it over [your body] ... [for] so many thoughtless years, and heave a sigh of relief; for your "emancipation" ... has from this moment begun.[131]

Despite the underlying nativism and elitism characteristic of the broader women's rights movement, Phelps effectively proclaimed a tentative sisterhood between women when it came to combatting the oppression engendered by fashion. Indeed, working-class women, like middle-class women, did wear corsets—sometimes acquired as cast offs from their employers.[132]

[127] Crane, *Fashion and its Social Agendas*, 101.
[128] Xavier Chaumette, *Le Costume tailleur: La culture vestimentaire en France au XIXème siècle* (Paris: Esmond Edition, 1995), 9. See: Crane, *Fashion and Its Social Agendas*, 104.
[129] Warner, "Fashion, Emancipation, Reform," 26.
[130] Roxanne Harde, "'One-Hundred-Hours': Elizabeth Stuart Phelps' Dress Reform Writing," in *Styling Texts: Dress and Fashion in Literature*, eds. Cynthia Kuhn and Cindy Carlson (New York: Cambria Press, 2007), 168–169.
[131] Elizabeth Stuart Phelps, *What to Wear?* (Boston: James R. Osgood and Company, 1873), 18–19, 66, 78–79.
[132] Summers, "Yes, They Did," 65, 67.

4 "TYRANT CHAINS": FASHION, ANTIFASHION, AND DRESS REFORM   149

But fashionable dress also evoked respectability. White women reformers often hailed from the middle classes; their social position enabled them to reject corsetry as unnecessary without such a decision necessarily affecting their economic mobility.

Postbellum dress reformers increasingly mobilized abstract discourses of slavery in a manner that framed fashion not as the main source of women's oppression, but as one of many oppressions. Soon after Phelps' address, the NEWC's Dress Reform Committee hosted a lecture series, later compiled in *Dress-Reform* (1874). This event was organized by Abba Gould Woolson, who was joined by four female physicians.[133] Fashion held women "in immovable bondage," said Mary J. Safford-Blake, M.D., who believed that the "thumb-screws of the inquisition" were less harmful than the corset's "firm plates of metal" between which women were "cruelly pressed ... so snugly that an impression of her fetters is indented into the flesh." Women's dress was "a terrible tyrant" that subjected body and mind to its "tormenting control," Mercy B. Jackson, M.D. concluded. If men and women were to exchange their dress for a day, Woolson suggested, men would celebrate "their escape from the strange bondage ... [and] the wailing of the women at their return to the old fetters would be heart-rending to hear."[134] These reformers and physicians used discourses of slavery to emphasize the degree to which a woman's health and physical mobility, if impeded by fashionable dress, was synonymous with her oppression and inhibited her potential for self-ownership.

Historians suggest that AWSA and its leadership were less radical than the NWSA, often describing the former in terms of its commitment to suffrage alone.[135] However, the analyses of dress reform circulated by AWSA and the *Woman's Journal* challenge assertions about its conservatism, the extent of its suffrage-only reform platform, and the degree to which its ethos differed from the imperatives espoused by Stanton and Anthony. For example, the *Woman's Journal* periodically featured reports from the American Free Dress League and the National Dress Reform Association.[136]

[133] Warner, "Fashion, Emancipation, Reform," 26.
[134] Abba Gould Woolson, *Dress-Reform; a Series of Lectures Delivered in Boston, on Dress as It Affects the Health of Women* (Boston: Roberts Brothers, 1874), 20, 23, 70–71, 171–172.
[135] For example, see: Aileen S. Kraditor, *The Ideas of the Woman Suffrage Movement, 1890–1920* (New York: Anchor Books, 1965, 1971), 69–70; Suzanne M. Marilley, *Woman Suffrage and the Origins of Liberal Feminism in the United States, 1820–1920* (Cambridge, MA: Harvard University Press, 1996), 159.
[136] Mattingly, *Appropriate[ing] Dress*, 123.

It also fostered a rhetorical interplay that recalled the exchanges between celebrated reformers and the rank-and-file contributors to the *Sibyl*. The concept of "slavery to custom," for example, emerged as an explanation for the interaction between different forms of oppression in the *Woman's Journal*. One contributor praised the newspaper for creating a "fellowship" to enable women to collectively combat "slavery to the demands of fashion," although she still despaired the "extent of [women's] slavery to fashion."[137] The "tyranny of fashion over women," another argued, represented a broader problem because society placed both sexes "under a kind of thralldom."[138] A decade later, Stanton herself affirmed something similar in an 1880s lyceum circuit lecture. "Custom," she noted, "has made the girl the slave, and subject womanhood perpetuates the custom."[139] Many women remained reluctant to don any type of reformed dress in public, but the *Woman's Journal* also suggested that some experimented with what became known as "hygienic dress," a full-body outfit with a torso design reminiscent of the Emancipation Suit.[140]

Despite its evident interest in the imperatives of dress reform, women's enfranchisement nonetheless remained AWSA's central concern. As a result, the *Woman's Journal* routinely connected the rigors of fashionable dress to women's disenfranchisement. This was epitomized across 1873 in articles such as "Suffrage or Servitude" and "Resistance to Tyrants," respectively penned by former abolitionists Henry B. Blackwell and Stephen S. Foster.[141] In 1884, the suffragist Celia B. Whitehead similarly asked: "Are Women Enslaved to Dress?"[142] The answer was quite clearly in the affirmative. It was often implied that if one form of oppression could be rectified, then others would soon follow and women would experience freedom. This

[137] C.M.S., "Dress Reform and Moral Reform," *Woman's Journal*, 31 May 1873.
[138] Martha Perry Lowe, "The Power of Fashion," *Woman's Journal*, 4 March 1871.
[139] Elizabeth Cady Stanton, "Our Girls," 1880, in *Voices of Democracy: The U.S. Oratory Project*, 2009, http://voicesofdemocracy.umd.edu/stanton-our-girls-speech-text/. For Stanton's perspectives on dress reform, see: Park, "'All the Freedom of the Boy'," 7–26; Lisa S. Strange, "Dress Reform and the Feminine Ideal: Elizabeth Cady Stanton and the 'Coming Girl'," *Southern Communication Journal* 68, no. 1 (2002): 1–13.
[140] "Hygienic Under Garments," *Woman's Journal*, 20 October 1877. For examples of women's reluctance, see: Lucia E. Bloust, "Dress Reform," *Woman's Journal*, 22 February 1873; M.H. McKee, "A Comfortable Dress Reformer," *Woman's Journal*, 22 March 1873; Sophia L.O. Allen, "The Significance of Dress Reform," *Woman's Journal*, 6 February 1875.
[141] Henry B. Blackwell, "Suffrage or Servitude," *Woman's Journal*, 16 August 1873; S.S. Foster, "Resistance to Tyrants," *Woman's Journal*, 21 June 1873.
[142] Celia B. Whitehead, "Are Women Enslaved to Dress?" *Woman's Journal*, 24 May 1884.

pattern continued over the next 20 years. An 1893 article entitled "Dress Emancipation," for example, offered readers an exchange between dress reformers Alida C. Avery and Frances E. Russell.[143]

Other postbellum reform newspapers similarly used discourses of slavery to connect concerns about fashionable dress to broader reform imperatives. Victoria Woodhull's radical free love and suffrage newspaper, *Woodhull and Claflin's Weekly*, strongly aligned itself with the principles of dress reform. At the height of her popularity in the early 1870s, Woodhull often donned masculine dress. However, she managed to avoid what Cari M. Carpenter describes as "a debilitating sexualization" by negotiating an "adequately feminine" appearance.[144] Her newspaper illustrated its commitment to many reforms, describing how fashionable dress inhibited women's economic independence and featuring reports from the Anti-Fashion Convention.[145] One contributor saw fashion as "the badge of her servitude": a "natural outgrowth of the harem, of social and political inequality, of marriage, customs, and laws, which give woman to man," and only upon woman's "release from that servitude" would she be able to create "a costume which shall fitly express her free womanhood."[146] Abigail Scott Duniway, who had worked in millinery and dressmaking prior to becoming a leading suffragist in Portland, Oregon, also condemned fashionable dress.[147] "A trailing dress is an emblem of degradation," she asserted in the *New Northwest*, her Portland-based suffrage newspaper; it demonstrated both "dependence and incompetence" as well as women's "frailty and subjugation."[148]

Despite the homage that Stanton had paid to the benefits of men's clothing during the late 1860s, women's rights reformers often expressed dismay when faced with women who actually embraced these ideals. Those who did appropriate masculine dress, such as Dr Mary E. Walker, often

---

[143] Alida C. Avery, reply by Frances E. Russell, "Dress Emancipation," *Woman's Journal*, 21 October 1893.
[144] Cari M. Carpenter, ed. *Selected Writings of Victoria Woodhull: Suffrage, Free Love, and Eugenics* (Lincoln: University of Nebraska Press, 2010), xx.
[145] "Fashion vs. Freedom," *Woodhull and Claflin's Weekly*, 17 January 1874; "Miscellaneous: The Anti-fashion Convention," *Woodhull and Claflin's Weekly*, 14 February 1874.
[146] Olive Frelove Shepard, "Woman's Dress," *Woodhull and Claflin's Weekly*, 24 February 1872.
[147] Jean M. Ward and Elaine A. Maveety, eds. *"Yours for Liberty": Selections from Abigail Scott Duniway's Suffrage Newspaper* (Corvallis: Oregon State University Press, 2000), 7, 11.
[148] "Trained Dresses," *New Northwest*, 12 April 1872, in Ibid., 66.

already existed on the fringe of social movements. Walker's experience, however, was quite different to that of Woodhull. When she was 16, the young Mary's father encouraged her to abandon corsets.[149] Walker experimented further with dress as a medical student and Civil War surgeon, but never sought to conceal her gender identity. Although she worked within a traditionally feminine nurturing capacity, her clothing caused a mounting controversy. After Walker assumed the masculine role of doctor and surgeon, she also elected to wear the accompanying male uniform.[150] Some women, such as Grace Greenwood (the *nom-de-plume* for journalist Sarah Jane Lippincott), praised "Dr. Walker in her emancipated garments" at an 1869 suffrage convention.[151] However, the majority of her fellow reformers were infuriated by her mounting preference for trousers.[152]

Regardless, Walker dedicated her first book *Hit* (1871) to her parents, the "PRACTICAL DRESS REFORMERS," her "PROFESSIONAL SISTERS," and, finally:

> TO THAT
> GREAT SISTERHOOD,
> Which embraces women with their thousand unwritten trails and sorrows, … I dedicate this work, in hope that it will contribute to right your wrongs, lighten your burdens and increase your self-respect and self-reliance, and place in your hands that power which shall emancipate you from the bondage of all that is oppressive.[153]

Walker's dedication to women's emancipation "from the bondage of all that is oppressive" again illustrated the degree to which her own commitment to dress reform existed in terms of a broader understanding of women's oppression. However, as she aged and lost the long feminine ringlets of a younger woman, Fisher suggests that Walker "came to be seen as merely eccentric."[154] The few women who actually acted on dress reform's rhetorical injunctions experienced many difficulties because their

---

[149] Fischer, "A Matter of Wardrobe?" 248.
[150] Mattingly, *Appropriate[ing] Dress*, 93; Fischer, "A Matter of Wardrobe?" 246–247.
[151] Grace Greenwood, "Grace Greenwood on the Washington Suffrage Convention," *Revolution*, 4 February 1869.
[152] Cunningham, *Reforming Women's Fashion*, 79.
[153] Mary E. Walker, *Hit* (New York: The American News Company, 1871), 4–6.
[154] Mattingly, *Appropriate[ing] Dress*, 97. For nineteenth-century cross-dressing, see: Clare Sears, *Arresting Dress: Cross-Dressing, Law, and Fascination in Nineteenth-Century San Francisco* (Durham: Duke University Press, 2015).

contemporaries found it challenging to come to terms with the consequences of the practices they theoretically advocated.

The dress and health reformers of the Gilded Age persisted with criticisms of fashionable dress that were grounded in abstracted discourses of slavery. This era witnessed the emergence of artistic or aesthetic dress, a fashion defined by its loose-fitting form, its lack of corset, and its idealization of comfort and grace.[155] The *Arena*, a magazine edited by B.O. Flower, was an "intellectually respectable" publication known for championing causes such as dress reform, health reform, and artistic dress.[156] In 1891, Flower published an article entitled "Fashion's Slaves," which denounced the deleterious nature of fashionable dress. The article was accompanied by rich illustrations of the outfits of the fashionable woman.[157] Soon after, the magazine received a wealth of positive responses. This reception, Flower noted, "leads me to believe that the day for woman's emancipation from cruel, deforming, and inartistic dress is at hand." Of the nine responses he later published, the majority echoed the premise of the original article, in that readers responded by embracing discourses of slavery to describe fashionable dress. Sometimes, this could result in women blaming themselves for succumbing to fashion's demands. In a representative response, Elizabeth Askew wrote: "'Fashion's Slaves' you have rightly called us; and wear they their bonds smilingly or scornfully, all women are conscious of their slavery and many are eager to free themselves from their bondage."[158]

The following year, Flower republished this popular article as a short pamphlet, also entitled *Fashion's Slaves* (1892). It is revealing to observe that, despite these titles, neither the book nor the original article upon which it was based relied very heavily on discourses of slavery or discourses of emancipation; only at important junctures throughout each did he embrace this rhetoric. For example, Flower began his commentary by emphasizing his belief that fashion constituted a "problem upon which the last word will not be spoken until woman is emancipated." Flower then went on to chronicle women reformers who had "boldly denounc[ed] the bondage of fashion," including Gould, Russell, and temperance leader Frances E. Willard. Finally, he concluded by asserting his belief that "morality,

---

[155] Cunningham, *Reforming Women's Fashion*, 146–162.

[156] Ruth Clifford Engs, *The Progressive Era's Health Reform Movement: A Historical Dictionary* (Westport: Greenwood Publishing, 2003), 34–35.

[157] B.O. Flower, "Fashion's Slaves," *Arena* 4 (September 1891): 401–430.

[158] B.O. Flower, ed. *Arena*, Vol. 4 (Boston: The Arena Publishing Co., 1891), xlix–lii.

education, practical reform, and enduring progress wait upon her [woman's] complete emancipation from the bondage of fashion, prejudice, superstition, and conservatism."[159] Framing his discourse on dress reform in this manner helped reiterate the woman-as-slave worldview that each publication embraced.

In both works, Flower republished in its entirety an anonymous poem, entitled "Sister Slaves," which he believed originally appeared in *Harper's Bazaar*.[160] Fashion historian Patricia A. Cunningham uncovered what she believed to be an 1880s proof etching illustrated for *Harper's Weekly* by the caricaturist Thomas Nast, although remains unsure whether it ever appeared in print.[161] Both of Flower's works alluded to a very similar image having appeared alongside this poem, suggesting that this etching may, indeed, have been published, although perhaps not in *Harper's Weekly*:

> *Harper's Bazaar* published two striking cartoons illustrating the poem given below. One represented a poor man's wife, "The slave of toil," and was pathetically powerful in its fidelity to truth; the other, drawn by the powerful Nast, represented a society lady of the day. ... This slave was chained to fashion's column.[162]

In fact, both the poem and the accompanying illustration (Fig. 4.4) had been published in *Harper's Bazaar* in April 1878. Nast's illustration, moreover, reflected the posture of Hiram Powers' antebellum ideal sculpture, *The Greek Slave*, in that the woman, with her shackled wrists, stands alongside a column dedicated to "FASHION." Both figures stand to the same side of the column, their heads turned away in the same direction; and both have a single hand on the column. Yet, while *The Greek Slave* appears resigned to her fate, the coquettish gaze of "The Slave of Fashion" addresses the spectator directly.[163]

It is notable that the wrists of the woman in Nast's illustration were bound by manacles rather than chains. Jean Fagan Yellin describes how, during the 1850s, Powers had made attempts to distinguish between

---

[159] B.O. Flower, *Fashion's Slaves* (Boston: The Arena Publishing Co., 1892), 3–6, 32.
[160] Ibid., 10–11. This poem also appeared, in part, in other newspapers, see: Huldah T. Gunn, "The Martyrdom of Woman," *Medical Tribune: A Monthly Magazine* 7, no. 7 (15 July 1892): 359.
[161] Cunningham, *Reforming Women's Fashion*, 2.
[162] Flower, *Fashion's Slaves*, 10.
[163] "Sister Slaves," *Harper's Bazaar* XI, no. 16 (April 1878): 256–258.

4 "TYRANT CHAINS": FASHION, ANTIFASHION, AND DRESS REFORM   155

Fig. 4.4 "The Slave of Fashion," *Harper's Bazaar* XI, no. 16 (April 1878): 256. Home Economics Archive, Research, Tradition and History, Cornell University

chains and manacles. Broken chains, he argued, represented tyranny, whereas broken manacles represented the emancipation of Africans from chattel slavery. All five versions of *The Greek Slave* wrought during the 1840s and 1850s, before slave emancipation, had been adorned with chains. Knowing this to be historically inaccurate for his sculpture, in that no chains had been forced upon Greek women in Turkish slave markets, Powers still found chains to be aesthetically legitimate. But for a sixth version, completed in the aftermath of the Civil War, Powers insisted on replacing the chains with manacles. In so doing, Yellin suggests, Powers conformed to his spectators' perception that chains signified chattel slavery.[164] Symbolically, however, given his own earlier interpretation of the different meanings associated with each, Powers' final version of *The Greek Slave* extended what he himself construed as representative of chattel slavery and slave emancipation—manacles—to a white woman. That this particular alteration occurred during the late 1860s mirrored the reform discourse of white reformers across multiple social movements. As the fugitive wife trope itself suggested, white reformers gradually began to use discourses of slavery to theorize and condemn the oppression of white women at the expense of formerly enslaved people of African descent.

Frances E. Russell, a relatively active figure within a still largely disorganized dress-reform movement, chronicled the earlier successes and failures of individual dress reformers at century's end. The *Arena* published her collation, "A Brief Survey of the American Dress Reform Movements of the Past, with Views of Representative Women," in 1892. It featured many of the prominent white women who had either worn the bloomer costume or somehow advocated for dress reform since the antebellum era, including such celebrated reformers as Amelia Bloomer, Elizabeth Cady Stanton, Lucy Stone, Angelina Grimké Weld, Harriet Martineau, Elizabeth Stuart Phelps, Abba Gould Woolson, Celia B. Whitehead, Alice Stone Blackwell, and Frances B. Willard.[165] Bloomer herself had reflected on her "wish that every woman would throw off the burden of clothes that was dragging her life out."[166] In bringing together all these voices, both Flower and Russell inadvertently revealed how the woman-slave analogy had emerged as a central rhetorical device and reform strategy through which both antebellum and postbellum reformers had theorized fashion.

---

[164] Jean Fagan Yellin, *Women and Sisters: The Antislavery Feminists in American Culture* (New Haven: Yale University Press, 1989), 117–118, 122–123.
[165] Frances E. Russell, "A Brief Survey of the American Dress Reform Movements of the Past, with Views of Representative Women," *Arena* 6 (August 1892): 325–340.
[166] Ibid., 327. For Bloomer's letter, which Russell reprinted in the *Arena*, see: "'The Bloomer Costume': A Letter from Amelia Bloomer," *Ladies Home Journal* 7, no. 2 (January 1890): 8.

Conclusion

The nineteenth century witnessed antifashionists, cultural commentators, and reformers across multiple social movements embrace the woman-slave analogy to develop their analyses of fashionable dress. Each came to different conclusions about how—and even whether—to reform women's clothing, yet concerns about women's dress also diverged from marriage and other aspects of the woman question. The embodied nature of fashion enabled a more immediately tangible form of "emancipation" to transpire, first through the bloomer costume and then through the far more subtle reform of women's undergarments. Dress-reform discourse also remained quite distinct from other analyses of women's oppression as it was largely dominated by abstracted discourses of slavery. However, when a direct comparison between fashion and chattel slavery did transpire during the 1850s and 1860s, dress reformers expressed the particularly dubious opinion that fashionable dress had the potential to be a source of greater oppression than chattel slavery. Since at least some of the individuals who made these claims were abolitionists or antislavery sympathizers, this emerges as one of the most egregious misapplications of the woman-slave analogy.

The exchanges between the rank-and-file, celebrated reformers, and the editors of women's rights and dress-reform periodicals, newspapers, and magazines reveal the degree to which discourses of slavery gained both prominence and influence amongst dress reformers. This process had been evident in the National Dress Reform Association's antebellum periodical, the *Sibyl*, and persisted well into the 1890s in the works of B.O. Flower. These editors embraced the voices of celebrated reformers and penned reflections of a similar nature themselves. Their readership responded by accepting the woman-slave analogy as a rationale for dress reform. In contrast, while African-American women periodically questioned the demands of fashionable dress, most demonstrated some ambivalence toward considering fashion itself as a site of oppression at all. If Flower himself did not reiterate this rhetoric obsessively, then his readership certainly did in their own rejoinders. The rank-and-file's tendency to focus their responses around such an interpretation of fashionable dress thus suggests that they found particular salience in abstracted discourses of slavery. It also suggests that many white dress reformers had conveniently forgotten about the realities of chattel slavery by century's end.

CHAPTER 5

"Degrading Servitude": Free Labor, Chattel Slavery, and the Politics of Domesticity

Across the nineteenth century, labor reformers routinely embraced discourses of slavery to criticize industrial capitalism and its pernicious effects. Women became increasingly central to labor protest, especially after unprecedented numbers gained employment in New England's antebellum textile industry. Those who participated in the 1836 mill strikes in Lowell, Massachusetts, sang:

> Oh! isn't it a pity, such a pretty girl as I
> Should be sent to the factory to pine away and die?
> Oh! I cannot be a slave;
> I will not be a slave,
> For I'm so fond of liberty,
> That I cannot be a slave.[1]

These white working-class women embraced discourses of slavery in a manner that was both abstracted from and connected to chattel slavery. For African-American women, however, the reality of chattel slavery dominated analyses of labor. Collectively, women reformers strove to reveal the multifaceted nature of women's labor beyond the home, by both enslaved

[1] To the tune of "I Won't Be a Nun," *National Laborer*, 29 October 1836, in Philip S. Foner, *American Labor Songs of the Nineteenth Century* (Urbana: University of Illinois Press, 1975), 44–45.

and free workers; within the home, as wives, daughters, and productive workers; and as reformers across social movements, from the rank-and-file to the podium, as lecturers, essayists, and novelists.

Deep cultural anxieties manifested as women began to contribute more clearly to the market economy during the 1830s. Marriage remained central to women's lives, as it provided the basis for the sexual division of labor predicated upon women's unpaid housework. Although more working-class women were becoming engaged in wage labor, domesticity and separate spheres ideology confined many middle-class women to the home. Women's rights reformers sought to illustrate the contribution and fundamental worth of women's household labor, yet the domestic ideal existed uneasily alongside their insistence that women should have the opportunity to establish their own economic self-sufficiency. These contradictions both challenged and reified the connections labor reformers and women's rights reformers established between women's labor, capitalist exploitation, and domestic tyranny.

This chapter considers how women reformers embraced the woman-slave analogy to illuminate the many facets of women's labor. As Eric Foner observes, "many Americans experienced the expansion of capitalism not as an enhancement of the power to shape their world, but as a loss of control over their own lives."[2] Women reformers drew on discourses of slavery to highlight the exploitation of wage-earning women, the confines of domesticity, and the contested nature of women's public presence in social reform and the literary marketplace. But this did not exist in isolation; it was part of the broader antebellum trend amongst the antislavery, women's rights, and dress reformers who mobilized discourses of slavery to expose the subjugation women experienced. Some proved reticent to posit too close a connection between labor and chattel slavery. Others, especially African Americans, saw a clear connection between chattel slavery and other forms of labor exploitation under colonialist capitalism. The experiences of white working-class women, however, often emerged as a central concern for the labor and women's rights movements following slave emancipation.

---

[2] Eric Foner, "Free Labor and Nineteenth-Century Political Ideology," in *The Market Revolution in America: Social, Political, and Religious Expressions, 1800–1880*, eds. Melvyn Stokes and Stephen Conway (Charlottesville: University Press of Virginia, 1996), 104.

I Cannot Be a Slave

Between the 1820s and 1840s, the Massachusetts mills pioneered a system of textile industrialization in the United States. This era also witnessed the development of the market economy, which led to the expansion of wage labor and a low-skill workforce. A contradiction soon emerged, however, between the Jeffersonian ideal of a nation of yeoman farmers and an industrial economy that was reliant on wage labor. Charles Sellers describes how work was redirected from the home and toward the needs of the market in a subsistence economy, a shift which emphasized the connections between economic growth, railroads and territorial expansion, and religious revivalism. Initially experienced in the context of the local markets that surrounded New England's manufacturing cities, these transformations would also fundamentally reshape the meaning of women's labor and the ideal of domesticity.[3]

According to David Roediger, the "white worker" emerged as a discrete figure across the early republic and antebellum eras. The colonial era was characterized by many degrees of unfreedom; indeed, "[i]ndentured servitude, impressment, apprenticeship, convict labor, farm tenancy, wage labor and combinations of wage labor and free farming made for a continuum of oppression among whites." This meant that it could be difficult to make any clear distinctions between free and enslaved workers. For a time at least, Roediger argues, "a large body of whites could imagine themselves as slaves—and on socioeconomic, as well as political, grounds." Over the course of the nineteenth century, however, the unfree white workers of the eighteenth century were gradually absorbed into a free community of wage earners, with many even having the opportunity to become artisanal masters. Their trajectory was therefore quite distinct from that of enslaved people of African descent.[4] Ideologically, free labor and slave labor existed in opposition. However, the sense of unity that free labor generated between working-class men also obscured essential differences: the degree of dependence engendered

---

[3] Charles Sellers, *The Market Revolution, Jacksonian America: 1815–1846* (New York: Oxford University Press, 1991).

[4] David R. Roediger, *The Wages of Whiteness: Race and the Making of the American Working Class* (London: Verso, 1991/2007), 25, 31–33. See also: Carol Wilson and Calvin D. Wilson, "White Slavery: An American Paradox," *Slavery & Abolition: A Journal of Slave and Post-Slave Studies* 19, no. 1 (1998): 1–23.

by wage work, for example, was quite different from the landowning small producer's independent proprietorship.[5]

The manner in which male labor reformers mobilized discourses of slavery reflected these contradictions. Roediger suggests that the antebellum labor movement might be regarded as the "world leader in militant criticisms of wage work as slavery." These concepts—wage slavery and white slavery—encouraged workers to consider whether such a great distance did, in fact, exist between free labor and chattel slavery, offering workers a terminology through which to articulate their understanding of their own labor exploitation. Many remained reticent, however, to entertain direct comparisons with either enslaved people or free blacks, while at least some commentators actually used this rhetoric to evoke proslavery sentiments. Labor reformers who did embrace discourses of slavery often did so with caution, sometimes by implying that labor exploitation anticipated, rather than constituted, their enslavement. Only for a minority of committed reformers did either term, especially white slavery, evoke a true sense of interracial solidarity. Many commentators, in turn, believed that people of African descent were naturally suited to enslavement, to the extent that the terminology of white slavery suggested that "it was the 'slavery' of *whites* that deserved censure."[6] As Stephen Simpson's 1831 book of political economy expressed, "bondage degrades, cramps and degenerates man; labor shares the same disgrace because it is part of the slave."[7]

It was in the context of the labor movement that such men most frequently used discourses of slavery to describe that which was not chattel slavery. However, the relationship between the antislavery movement and free labor ideology remains a point of historiographical contention. Roediger suggests that abolitionism appealed only to "a minority of white workers," yet Paul Goodman argues that its "heterogeneous appeal" engaged both the working and middle classes.[8] According to Julie Husband, the deteriorating conditions of wage work meant the

[5] Foner, "Free Labor," 100–101.
[6] Roediger, *Wages of Whiteness*, 67–69, 73–74; Foner, "Free Labor," 104–105.
[7] Stephen Simpson, *The Working Man's Manual: A New Theory of Political Economy, on the Principle of Production the Source of Wealth* (Philadelphia: Thomas L. Bonsal, 1831), 16.
[8] Roediger, *Wages of Whiteness*, 67; Paul Goodman, *Of One Blood: Abolitionism and the Origins of Racial Equality* (Berkeley: University of California Press, 1998), xvii.

working classes did feel an ontological sense of identification with enslaved people of African descent, even while some were inclined to differentiate their own situation from chattel slavery. Although contradictory, these impulses meant that antislavery iconography gained significance in white working-class social movements.[9] Abolitionists, in turn, extended their condemnation of chattel slavery to its violation of the principles of free labor, sometimes querying the claims of northern workers who described their own situation as wage slavery.[10] As Harriet Beecher Stowe's antislavery novel *Uncle Tom's Cabin; or, Life among the Lowly* (1852) revealed, anti-abolitionist and proslavery commentators believed that the conditions of wage laborers, in Britain as in the North, were worse than that of enslaved people in the South. An 1850s cartoon (Fig. 5.1) visualized such an opinion, portraying joviality amongst enslaved people in the American South in contradiction to the unhealthful and poverty-stricken wage laborers—or wage "slaves"—of Britain.

However, the terminology of wage slavery also encouraged antebellum labor reformers to consider the degree to which wage labor engendered economic dependence.[11] Amy Dru Stanley suggests that the domestic relations of marriage and chattel slavery offered a legal parallel for the relations of wage labor as it was defined between employer and employee. From this perspective, the dependent position of the wage-earning hireling, in contrast to the independence of the yeoman farmer, was rendered equivalent to either wifely subordination or even enslavement. On account of such a threat to the gender identity of free white men, capitalists sought to redefine the hireling's independence in the context of the free labor system. This, Stanley emphasizes, "sharply distinguished women's dependent household labor from men's independent wage labor."[12] After industrial capitalism touched the lives of antebellum women, working women were expected not only to labor for their employers, but also to continue the full extent of their domestic labors.[13]

---

[9] Julie Husband, *Antislavery Discourse and Nineteenth-Century American Literature: Incendiary Pictures* (New York: Palgrave Macmillan, 2010), 3.

[10] Evelyn Nakano Glenn, *Unequal Freedom: How Race and Gender Shaped American Citizenship and Labor* (Cambridge: Harvard University Press, 2002), 65–66.

[11] Foner, "Free Labor," 105.

[12] Amy Dru Stanley, "Home Life and the Morality of the Market," in *The Market Revolution in America*, 74–75, 82–86; Glenn, *Unequal Freedom*, 58.

[13] Susan Thistle, *From Marriage to the Market: The Transformation of Women's Lives and Work* (Berkeley: University of California Press, 2006), 23–26.

164 A. STEVENSON

Fig. 5.1 *Slavery as it exists in America: Slavery as it exists in England* (Boston: J. Haven, c. 1850). Library Company of Philadelphia, Print Department, Political Cartoons, P.9675

Women came to constitute a primary source of labor for the emerging textile industry during the 1830s. Very few labor reformers, however, were convinced that women should even be working beyond the home. To advocate hierarchy within the family, these men routinely embraced discourses of slavery to describe the exploitation of women and children as workers.[14] Seth Luther, a labor organizer in Providence, Rhode Island, described what he perceived as an important class distinction, noting how "the *wives* and *daughters* of the *rich* manufacturers would no more associate with a '*factory girl*,' than they would with a *negro slave*. So much for equality in a *republican* country."[15] Another labor reformer looked wistfully toward a time "when our wives [are] no longer doomed to servile labor," so they could instead become the domestic companions of husbands and educators of children.[16] By connecting working women to enslaved people, labor reformers evoked visions of a corrupted South; this signaled the "compromised whiteness of wage-earning women while revealing a wish to police racial boundaries through fantasies of domestic rescue."[17] Some women would come to envision the market economy as an opportunity to acquire independence; men, however, seldom supported such measures.

Other labor reformers went so far as to romanticize middle-class wives' housework, also criticizing the domestic struggles that less privileged women experienced. In 1843, as part of his communitarian labor ideal, Albert Brisbane condemned working-class women's subjection to their "unremitting and slavish domestic duties" within the home:

> The wives of the poor are complete domestic drudges, whose whole time is absorbed in complicated household cares and occupations, and the women of the more favored classes who escape the burthen of toil of the isolated household, do so only at the expense of a class of their fellow-creatures who

---

[14] Roediger, *Wages of Whiteness*, 70–71.

[15] Seth Luther, *An Address to the Working Men of New England, on The State of Education, and on the Condition of the Producing Classes in Europe and America* (New York: George H. Evans, 1833), 19.

[16] William English, Fourth of July Address, Philadelphia Trades' Union, 1 August 1835, in Helen L. Sumner, *Report on the Condition of Women and Child Wage Earners in the United States*, Vol. 9: History of Women in Industry in the United States (Washington: Government Printing Office, 1910), 14.

[17] Lori Merish, *Archives of Labor: Working-Class Women and Literary Culture in the Antebellum United States* (Durham: Duke University Press, 2017), 40–46.

are reduced to the most menial Servitude, to a degrading bondage and dependence.

Brisbane's condemnation of what he described as the "servile system of domestic Servitude" did acknowledge the importance of women's labor; his repeated use of discourses of slavery was suggestive of the degree of his concern. It also reflected how working-class women's domestic labor was often more tangible than that of more privileged women, whose household labors could be far less obvious.[18] Brisbane, like so many other antebellum reformers, hoped to see "this and all other species of servitude" abolished.[19]

The mills of Lowell, Massachusetts, became famous not only for pioneering textile industrialization, but also for employing many women as textile workers. Often described as female operatives, these women experienced conflicts between the ideal of true womanhood, their position as working-class wage earners, and the benevolent paternalism of factory owners.[20] As Alice Kessler-Harris emphasizes, communities across New England not only expressed skepticism about women's entrance into wage work, but also toward the factories themselves. To combat the assumption that women had a moral imperative to labor within the home and address this broader community opposition, Francis Cabot Lowell advocated that farmers' daughters could fulfill their family obligations by pursuing work beyond the home.[21] The Waltham-Lowell system instituted what one historian describes as "corporate paternalism," as it offered boarding-house accommodation for young women and sometimes for married workers. Many of these women initially envisaged themselves as only working in the factories for a few years prior to marriage.[22] However, although some had defied the factory system since its beginnings, the 1840s witnessed an increased proportion of

[18] Jeanne Boydston, *Home and Work: Housework, Wages, and the Ideology of Labor in the Early Republic* (Oxford: Oxford University Press, 1990), 128.

[19] Albert Brisbane, "Exposition of Views and Principles," *Phalanx*, 5 October 1843, in *Antebellum American Culture: An Interpretative Anthology*, ed. David Brion Davis (University Park: Pennsylvania State University Press, 1979), 452.

[20] Anne F. Mattina, "'Corporation Tools and Time-Serving Slaves': Class and Gender in the Rhetoric of Antebellum Labor Reform," *Howard Journal of Communications* 7, no. 2 (1996): 154–155.

[21] Alice Kessler-Harris, *Out to Work: A History of Wage-Earning Women in the United States* (Oxford: Oxford University Press, 1982/2003), Chapter 2, esp. 33.

[22] Thomas Dublin, *Women at Work: The Transformation of Work and Community in Lowell, Massachusetts, 1826–1860*, 2nd ed. (New York: Columbia University Press, 1979/1981), Chapter 5.

female operatives become more permanent workers (and sometimes even their family's primary wage earner) after the economic crisis of 1837. Many women soon became more committed to improving their working conditions, coming to envisage themselves in long-term rather than temporary employment.[23] In an attempt to manage these contradictions, New England mill corporations even embraced an idealized "mill girl" as a propaganda tool.[24]

The women who did organize around the labor question seem to have embraced the woman-slave analogy more insistently than many of their male counterparts. If, as Roediger suggests, antebellum workers were somewhat reticent to evoke any direct comparison between wage work and chattel slavery, then the degree to which working-class women did embrace this rhetoric is all the more remarkable. Their gradual entrance into the market economy challenged the assumption that the workplace was a male environment, meaning that women constantly had to validate their contribution as workers.[25] The need to emphasize their entitlement to work beyond the home, as well as to demonstrate their ability to undertake such work, may have impelled these working women toward direct comparisons with chattel slavery. In her analysis of these women's literary self-representation, Lori Merish observes the degree to which their writings evoked "an explicit locus of cultural contest, anchoring both gender subjection and class privilege." The very term *mill girl*, she argues, like its late-nineteenth-century counterpart *working girl*, evoked a certain liminality. Both essentially envisaged women's labor as "a transitory state; obviously serving the logic of capitalist exploitation, this construction cheapened female labor by severing it from adulthood, making the female breadwinner a conceptual impossibility." It was far from insignificant, Merish suggests, and perhaps even inevitable, that working women's self-representation would find inspiration in "a vocabulary of race and slavery."[26]

---

[23] Philip S. Foner, *Women and the American Labor Movement: From Colonial Times to the Eve of World War I* (New York: The Free Press, 1979), 28–37, 55–56.

[24] Amal Amireh, *The Factory Girl and the Seamstress: Imagining Gender and Class in Nineteenth-Century American Fiction* (New York: Garland Publishing, 2000), Chapter 1.

[25] Jeanne Boydston, "The Woman Who Wasn't There: Women's Market Labor and the Transition to Capitalism in the United States," *Journal of the Early Republic* 16, no. 2 (1996): 205–206.

[26] Merish, *Archives of Labor*, 9, 25, 60.

The *Lowell Offering* was a famous monthly literary magazine featuring the writings of Lowell's women textile workers. Edited by Harriet Farley and Harriot Curtis and published across 1840–1845, this magazine was a genteel literary outlet that contributed, at least in part, to the literary idealization of the mill girl.[27] Although the *Lowell Offering* regularly confronted the assumption that factory work was too degrading or exploitative for women, its contributors also experienced tensions between the ideal of femininity and the reality of women's labor.[28] Editors and contributors alike mobilized discourses of slavery with at least some ambivalence. Farley, for example, expressed concern about the "gross injustice done to the character of the factory girl." The factory overseer, she observed, merely saw her as "a brute, or a slave, to be beaten ... or pushed about."[29] Many were aware of how the rhetoric of white slavery might associate workers not only with degradation, but also the implication of sexual exploitation.[30] While the *Lowell Offering* mobilized what Husband describes as "metaphors of slavery and seduction," it also sought to present wage labor as a positive alternative for young women—one that offered possibilities beyond the familial dependence that defined the rural lives of many wives and daughters. Consequently, its contributors resisted any "simple conflation" or "too frantic denial" of the similarities and differences between factory work and chattel slavery.[31]

The print culture of these female operatives, together with that of their supporters and detractors, reveals how working-class women embraced discourses of slavery to focus on the differing experiences that emanated from enslaved or free status, race, and class. Female operatives both acknowledged and disavowed what Merish describes as the "racial intimacies of the cotton trade," as they experienced ontological connections between their own work and chattel slavery exactly because southern plantations often produced the raw materials with which they worked.[32] Importantly, however, their analyses did not always find female operatives to be the poorer. In fact, the *Lowell Offering* often denied that

---

[27] Amireh, *The Factory Girl*, Chapter 1.
[28] Elizabeth Freeman, "'What Factory Girls Had Power to Do': The Techno-Logic of Working-Class Feminine Publicity in *The Lowell Offering*," *Arizona Quarterly: A Journal of American Literature, Culture, and Theory* 50, no. 2 (1994): 109–128.
[29] H.F., "Editorial," *The Lowell Offering* (Lowell: Misses Curtis and Farley, 1845), 239.
[30] Roediger, *Wages of Whiteness*, 85.
[31] Husband, *Antislavery Discourse*, 86–87, 90, 96–97.
[32] Merish, *Archives of Labor*, 60.

any similarity existed between wage work and the experiences of enslaved people, especially enslaved women.[33] A desire to disassociate Lowell from chattel slavery led at least some contributors to acknowledge that enslaved people of African descent faced a situation that was far worse than that of any factory worker. One contributor, for example, disputed the "myths" in which the mill girl appeared as "a mere servile drudge, chained to her labor by almost as strong a power as that which holds a bondsman in his fetters; ... some have already given her the title of '*the white slave of the North.*'" The "real situation" of these female operatives, she emphasized, did not approach any such "extremes."[34]

Some working-class women, however, did invoke more direct references to chattel slavery. This often occurred amongst female operatives and labor reformers who espoused more radical perspectives. One contributor to the *Factory Girl*, for example, developed "New Definitions":

> Overseer. – A servile tool in the hands of an Agent; who will resort to the lowest, meanest and most grovelling measures, to please his Master, and to fill the coffers of a soulless Corporation.
> Operative. – A person who is employed in a Factory, and who generally earns three times as much as he or she receives. ...
> Oppressive. – To make two men do the work of three, without making any addition to their wages.[35]

Each redefinition had the capacity to summon the figure of the factory overseer as much as the overseer on southern plantations. However, the female operatives who were most interested in the exploitation of white workers sometimes sensed hypocrisy amidst the antislavery movement. "A Ten Hour Woman," for example, was "greatly disappointed in men who have heretofore advocated the cause of humanity" and who "dole out pity for the souther[n] slave, but would crush with an iron hand the white laborer of the north."[36] Two competing impulses thus emerged in the comparison between factory work and chattel slavery: first, many women

---

[33] Husband, *Antislavery Discourse*, 88.
[34] "A Week in the Mill," *The Lowell Offering* (Lowell: Misses Curtis and Farley, 1845), 217.
[35] "New Definitions," *Factory Girl*, 15 January 1845, in *The Factory Girls*, ed. Philip S. Foner (Urbana: University of Illinois Press, 1977), 76–77.
[36] A Ten Hour Woman, "Slavery, North and South," *Mechanic*, 5 October 1844, in Ibid., 276.

situated the exploitation of male and female operatives as indefensible, like chattel slavery; and second, they sometimes implied that such worker exploitation was worse than chattel slavery.

To reflect upon and criticize their own working conditions, Lowell's more radical female operatives contributed to other reform platforms. The Female Labor Reform Association (FLRA), for example, actively questioned the legitimacy of the perspectives championed by the *Lowell Offering*.[37] The FLRA's class consciousness and gender awareness introduced what Anne F. Mattina describes as "a unique public voice" into public debate, one which was representative of working-class women.[38] Alongside its dedication to causes such as the 10-hour day, one of the causes to which it dedicated itself was the antislavery movement.[39] Initially appearing under the auspices of the New England Workingmen's Association, the *Voice of Industry* was published across 1845–1848. Soon after it moved to Lowell, Sarah G. Bagley and the FLRA embraced the newspaper. Some of its poetry, such as the 1846 poem "North and South," evoked an antislavery ethos.[40] More frequently, however, the *Voice of Industry* published articles and poetry that pivoted around what Merish describes as the "rhetoric of enslavement," or discourses of slavery. These analyses offered differing degrees of nuance as well as varying levels of actual engagement with chattel slavery.[41] Only after "slavery and oppression, mental, physical and religious," had been eliminated, the newspaper reported in 1846, would the FLRA's labors cease.[42]

The FLRA's *Factory Tracts* series, in particular, developed far more emphatic references to chattel slavery than *Lowell Offering* ever did. Modeled on British parliamentary reports dedicated to the condition of working-class laborers, these tracts also reflected antislavery trends in print culture.[43] For example, each of the three subsections of an 1845 tract invoked antislavery discourse. The first installment, "Factory Life as It Is: By an Operative," had a strikingly similar title to Theodore D. Weld's abolitionist compendium published only a few years earlier. Co-edited

[37] Amireh, *The Factory Girl*, 19.
[38] Mattina, "'Corporation Tools'," 151.
[39] Foner, *The Factory Girls*, 275; Husband, *Antislavery Discourse*, 102.
[40] Mary, "North and South," *Voice of Industry*, 13 February 1846.
[41] Merish, *Archives of Labor*, 62.
[42] Hannah Tarlton, "Report of the Lowell Female Labor Reform Association," *Voice of Industry*, 23 January 1846.
[43] Husband, *Antislavery Discourse*, 102.

with Angelina Grimké Weld and Sarah Grimké, *American Slavery as It Is: Testimony of a Thousand Witnesses* (1839) amassed excerpts from southern newspapers to collate eye-witness accounts of chattel slavery and its horrors. Through the testimony of "An Operative," the FLRA's tract recast discourses of slavery for the cause of working-class women. Should "tyranny and cruel oppression be allowed to rivet ... chains" on those who were "the *real* producers of all its improvements and wealth[?]" they asked. The "*real* producers," they clarified, were "the female operatives of New England," and while "no colored slave" could exist in the ostensibly "*free* states," mill women were rendered "slaves in every sense of the word!" "An Operative" regarded a large proportion of women workers as being "destined to a servitude as degrading, as unceasing toil can make it."[44] A strong sense of regional and class awareness could thus undermine an understanding of the oppression that resulted from chattel slavery and race. The next installment also condemned the aristocratic bearing of factory owners—the "Nobility of America"—in its anticipation of how "the yoke of tyranny" would lead to a future wherein the nation was "one great hospital, filled with worn out operatives and colored slaves!"[45]

Another installment in the *Factory Tracts* series, "Some of the Beauties of our Factory System—Otherwise, Lowell Slavery," pointedly stated that it had initially been "written for the Lowell Offering, and rejected by the Editress," according to its author, Amelia. Too radical for the *Lowell Offering*, this tract reported on the "tyrannous and oppressive rules" faced by female operatives, which rendered them "a slave, a very slave to the caprices of him for whom she labors." Amelia offered multiple points of comparison between female operatives in New England and the "poor peasant of Ireland, or the Russian serf," and further asked when they would be "reduced to the servile condition" of operatives in English factories. While this rhetoric distanced white working women from enslaved people of African descent, it developed what amounted to a transnational vision of labor exploitation. Amelia found the mill girl's long hours and cloistered boarding house to be incongruous with American ideals and illustrative of the "petty tyranny of the employer." The "*drivelling* cotton

---

[44] An Operative, "Factory Life as It Is: By an Operative," *Factory Tracts* no. 1 (Lowell: Female Labor Reform Association, 1845), in Lise Vogel, "Their Own Work: Two Documents from the Nineteenth-Century Labor Movement," *Signs: Journal of Women in Culture and Society* 1, no. 3 (1976): 794–802.

[45] Julianna, "The Evils of Factory Life," in Ibid.

lords," whom she described as the "aristocracy of New England," needed to be made to realize that the workers' "rights cannot be trampled." "We call on you to deliver/Us, from the tyrants [*sic*] chain," she concluded.[46] Amelia would continue to embrace revolutionary ideals to develop more explicit connections between working-class women, female operatives, and chattel slavery. In an 1845 poem, "The Summons," she encouraged the "children of New England" to "perish or be free."[47] Some of the women of the FLRA situated factory work as one of many forms of oppression, in the United States and around the world, thus implicitly contrasting the exploitation of industrial workers and chattel slaves with the Jeffersonian ideal.

Despite these parallels between the "cotton lords" of the North and South, the working-class women of Lowell and other New England textile factories did not necessarily develop a sense of solidarity with either enslaved people of African descent or immigrant workers.[48] Being primarily concerned with the industrial exploitation of women, these labor reformers had more discrete interests than many of their antislavery and women's rights contemporaries. Even so, at least some women in the antebellum labor movement embraced discourses of slavery to discuss the nature of women's oppression more broadly. The literary connections between wage work and chattel slavery hinged upon the issue of bodily ownership and the embodied nature of labor, an analysis which had obvious implications for the analysis of marriage.[49]

The *Voice of Industry* soon followed the *Liberator*'s "Ladies' Department" and established its own "Female Department." Hereafter, the newspaper began to pursue more discussions about women's rights. Women could only experience "true liberty and freedom" when they assumed their "proper place ... as a rational intelligent being—a fit *companion* and *friend* of man, not a *slave*," one contributor emphasized.[50] Another believed that it was inconceivable for "one soul" to be "subservient to another" in a true marriage. Since the "same lie which reveals itself

---

[46] Amelia, "Some of the Beauties of our Factory System—Otherwise, Lowell Slavery," in Ibid.

[47] Amelia, "The Summons," *Voice of Industry*, 7 November 1845.

[48] Teresa Amott and Julie Matthaei, *Race, Gender, and Work: A Multicultural Economic History of Women in the United States* (Boston: South End Press, 1991), 102.

[49] Cindy Weinstein, *The Literature of Labor and the Labors of Literature: Allegory in Nineteenth-Century American Fiction* (Cambridge: Cambridge University Press, 1995), 20–21.

[50] "Female Department," *Voice of Industry*, 6 March 1846.

in slavery is at the bottom of our marriage institution," they rationalized, mutual "elevation" was needed in marriage.[51] Huldah J. Stone was similarly critical of middle-class men who considered themselves "Lord and Master," saying an "*equal* she must not be."[52] Although the antebellum labor movement emerged in tandem with the women's rights movement, working-class women such as Sarah Bagley, Huldah Stone, and Mehitable Eastman often found it difficult to gain respect from middle-class women.[53] The rhetorical similarities between the discussion of women's rights across the antislavery, women's rights, dress reform, and women's labor movements suggests that a woman-as-slave worldview could transcend class and race in a way that so many reformers themselves could not.

In 1898, when Harriet H. Robinson reminisced about her labors as an antebellum female operative, she refuted the possibility that "Southern slaves are better off than Northern operatives."[54] Women labor reformers markedly expanded the rhetoric of their male predecessors and, in their use of the woman-slave analogy, developed creative parallels between chattel slavery and women's industrial labor. Many of these women, especially in Lowell, Massachusetts, did not condone the oppression that resulted from either institution. A sense of class consciousness impelled at least some female operatives to view themselves as fortunate, in comparison with enslaved people of African descent, yet this same class consciousness incited others to emphasize that they could "never be a slave." The analyses that female operatives developed actually became most radical, however, when coupled with direct allusions to chattel slavery. Many women in the antebellum labor movement nonetheless evoked a belief that white northern women should be treated in a manner quite distinct from the exploitation engendered by chattel slavery.

Public, Private, and Literary Labors

Frederick Douglass duly credited women's pivotal contribution to the antebellum antislavery movement. "When the true history of the antislavery cause shall be written," he wrote in his final 1892 autobiography,

---

[51] "Rights of Married Women," *Voice of Industry*, 14 August 1847.
[52] H.J.S., *Voice of Industry*, 9 July 1847.
[53] Foner, *Women and the American Labor Movement*, 56, 72.
[54] Harriet H. Robinson, *Loom and Spindle: Or, Life Among the Early Mill Girls* (Boston: Thomas Y. Crowell & Company, 1898), 196.

"women will occupy a large space in its pages; for the cause of the slave has been peculiarly woman's cause."[55] However, neither these women nor their contemporaries always considered their social reform endeavors to be a form of labor. Many women reformers, as much as their critics, in fact envisioned their reform labors as an extension of women's duty to benevolence.[56] After the Civil War, however, women's rights reformers and suffragists made attempts to reconceptualize their efforts, from the antebellum era to the present, as a form of labor. In 1867, Sojourner Truth conveyed the sense of self-worth as well as disappointment that many women found in lives dedicated to laboring for reform. "I suppose I am here because something remains for me to do," she said. "I suppose I am yet to help break the chain."[57]

Questions relating to women's labor preoccupied some abolitionists and women's rights reformers. Working-class women had played a significant role in the industrialization of New England, yet women's exclusion from notions of free labor often made marriage a necessity. Although free labor remained precarious alongside capitalist industrialization and the expansion of chattel slavery, male independence entailed the control and ownership of the labor of wives and children.[58] At the same time, escalating distinctions between the home and work led to questions about the gainful nature of domestic labor. While working-class women continued to labor beyond the home, many commentators deemed industrial work unsuitable for more privileged women. The moral elevation and idealization of the domestic realm, Nancy Folbre emphasizes, existed alongside the "economic devaluation of the work performed there."[59] As household labor was redefined as leisure, women were left to the "reproductive"

---

[55] Frederick Douglass, *Life and Times of Frederick Douglass* (Boston: De Wolfe & Fiske Co., 1892), 570.

[56] Lori D. Ginzberg, *Women and the Work of Benevolence: Morality, Politics, and Class in the Nineteenth-Century United States* (New Haven: Yale University Press, 1990); Susan M. Ryan, *The Grammar of Good Intentions: Race and the Antebellum Culture of Benevolence* (Ithaca: Cornell University Press, 2003).

[57] Sojourner Truth, American Equal Rights Association, 9 May 1867, in *History of Woman Suffrage* [hereafter *HWS*], Vol. II, eds. Elizabeth Cady Stanton, Susan B. Anthony, and Matilda Joslyn Gage (Rochester: Susan B. Anthony, 1881), 193–194.

[58] Glenn, *Unequal Freedom*, 56–57.

[59] Nancy Folbre, "The Unproductive Housewife: Her Evolution in Nineteenth-Century Economic Thought," *Signs: Journal of Women in Culture and Society* 16, no. 3 (1991): 465.

tasks associated with the social unit, a process Jeanne Boydston describes as "the pastoralization of housework."[60]

These cultural contestations were so pervasive that the controversies that emerged during the 1830s about women's role in the antislavery movement were never truly resolved. As a result, the efforts of women reformers remained contentious throughout the nineteenth century. Although those who labored for immediate abolition often considered it "a sacred vocation," abolitionist women had to negotiate additional social and cultural obstacles—what Julie Roy Jeffrey describes as the "permeable boundaries" of separate spheres ideology.[61] Indeed, benevolent organizations had routinely required that women would express "subserviency to men, who guide our labors," Sarah Grimké recognized.[62] In the midst of the 1837 controversy that engulfed the Grimké sisters, their friend and fellow abolitionist Henry C. Wright had issued reports about their speaking tour of New England to the *Liberator* and its readership. His column, "Labors of the Misses Grimké," clearly framed their abolitionism as just that: labors. Writing from Salem, Massachusetts, one of Wright's letters proclaimed that it was "affecting to hear the sisters plead the cause of the slave."[63] Not all of his fellow abolitionists were convinced, however, as these columns caused consternation. James Birney, for example, wrote of the incident: "What a blunder and that of a most ridiculous kind he has fallen into ... the 'labors'? of the Miss Grimkés!! ... Can he not be stopped?"[64]

Some women reformers embraced the ideology of separate spheres to offer a rationale for their political involvement, defining social reform as an extension of women's morality; others, however, criticized domestic-

---

[60] Boydston, *Home and Work*, Chapter 7, esp. 155.
[61] Donald M. Scott, "Abolition as a Sacred Vocation," in *Antislavery Reconsidered: New Perspectives on the Abolitionists*, eds. Lewis Perry and Michael Fellman (Baton Rouge: Louisiana State University Press, 1979), 51; Julie Roy Jeffrey, "Permeable Boundaries: Abolitionist Women and Separate Spheres," *Journal of the Early Republic* 21, no. 1 (2001): 79–93.
[62] Sarah M. Grimké, *Letters on the Equality of the Sexes, and the Condition of Woman: Addressed to Mary S. Parker* (Boston: Isaac Knapp, 1837/1838), 73, 75.
[63] H.C. Wright, "Labors of the Misses Grimké," *Liberator*, 7 July 1837.
[64] Dwight L. Dumond, ed. *Letters of James Gillespie Birney*, Vol. I (New York: D. Appleton-Century Co., 1938), 418. See: Gerda Lerner, *The Grimké Sisters from South Carolina: Pioneers for Women's Rights and Abolition* (Chapel Hill: University of North Carolina Press, 1967/2004), Chapter 11, esp. 126.

ity as a social ideal and experienced the full force of its constraints.[65] Antebellum women's rights reformers advocated for the reform of marital property laws and, alongside many women in the labor movement, emphasized women's need for financial independence. In contrast to many labor reformers, however, few antislavery or women's rights reformers seemed to object to developing overt rhetorical connections between themselves and enslaved people of African descent. While women's rights reformers certainly suggested that the labors of free women should not be degrading, many asserted that neither should that of enslaved people. In fact, women's rights reformers embraced the woman-slave analogy to the degree that it began to shape their conceptualization of their own labors as reformers as well as women's labor more broadly.

Angelina Grimké was assured that her abolitionist addresses were, indeed, labors. Historians suggest that these very labors spurred the Grimké sisters toward a greater awareness of their own rights, as women.[66] Writing to Weld and John Greenleaf Whittier in 1837, Angelina defended the sisters' right to continue their abolitionist addresses and speaking tour. Women's "*right* to labor ... *must* be firmly established," she emphasized:

> If we surrender the right to *speak* to the public this year, we must surrender the right to petition next year and the right to *write* the year after and so on. What *then* can *woman* do for the slave when she is herself under the feet of man and shamed into *silence*?

If the Grimké sisters and other women were to be silenced, Angelina suggested, their situation would be rendered even more analogous to the enforced silence of chattel slavery. As she concluded, "can you not see that women *could* do, and *would* do a hundred times more for the slave if she were not fettered?"[67]

---

[65] Lora Romero, *Home Fronts: Domesticity and Its Critics in the Antebellum United States* (Durham: Duke University Press, 1997); Julie Roy Jeffrey, *The Great Silent Army of Abolition: Ordinary Women in the Antislavery Movement* (Chapel Hill: University of North Carolina Press, 1998).

[66] Anna M. Speicher, *The Religious World of Antislavery Women: Spirituality in the Lives of Five Abolitionist Lecturers* (New York: Syracuse University Press, 2000), Chapter 6.

[67] Angelina Grimké to J.G. Whittier and Theodore Weld, 20 August 1837, in *Letters of Theodore Dwight Weld, Angelina Grimke Weld, and Sarah Grimke, 1822–1844*, Vol. II, eds. G.H. Barnes and D.L. Dumond (Gloucester: Peter Smith, 1965), 40.

Thus, abolitionist women routinely developed a sense of self-worth by laboring on behalf of enslaved people of African descent. Although "women may labor to produce a correct public opinion at the North," Angelina Grimké reflected in her *Appeal to the Christian Women of the South* (1836), southern attitudes could not change without the efforts of southern women. Despite the labors of abolitionists, she asked, "are the rights of female slaves in the South ... secured?"[68] Among abolitionist women, their own conceptualization of labor and their own reform efforts were ever more closely informed by the realities of chattel slavery. "We have good cause to be grateful to the slave," Abby Kelley reflected in 1838. "In striving to strike his irons off, we found most surely that *we* were manacled *ourselves*."[69] This approach, however, like metempsychosis, only really worked to strengthen the self-identification that many abolitionist women were already developing between themselves and enslaved people of African descent.

Many women reformers remained acutely aware that they operated in a political culture that devalued their contributions. Some even perceived that "there exists in the minds of men a tone of feeling towards women as towards slaves," Margaret Fuller reflected in 1845.[70] Their labors in social movements nonetheless offered a meaningful life, for the rank-and-file as much as for celebrated reformers. When Stone became an abolitionist lecturer in the late 1840s, she similarly concluded: "I expect to plead not for the slave only[,] ... but for suffering humanity everywhere. ESPECIALLY DO I MEAN TO LABOR FOR THE ELEVATION OF MY SEX."[71] The process of finding self-worth in the labors of social reform continued even following the abolition of chattel slavery. When Sojourner Truth hoped that she could "break the chain," she inadvertently expressed the fulfillment that she and so many other women found in their reform endeavors.[72]

[68] Angelina E. Grimké, *Appeal to the Christian Women of the South* (New York: American Anti-Slavery Society, 1836), 24, 9.

[69] Abby Kelley, 1838 Album, Western Anti-Slavery Society Papers, Library of Congress, in Blanche Glassman Hersh, *The Slavery of Sex: Feminist-Abolitionists in America* (Urbana: University of Illinois Press, 1978), 34. For antebellum antislavery albums, see: Jasmine Nichole Cobb, *Picture Freedom: Remaking Black Visuality in the Early Nineteenth Century* (New York: New York University Press, 2015).

[70] Margaret Fuller, *Woman in the Nineteenth Century* (New York: W.W. Norton, 1845/1997), 112.

[71] Alice Stone Blackwell, *Lucy Stone: Pioneer of Women's Rights* (Charlottesville: University Press of Virginia, 1930), 67.

[72] Sojourner Truth, *HWS*, Vol. II, 193–194.

But personal fulfillment did not necessarily mean financial security. Whether single or married, living with family or in a worker's boarding house, all free women were assumed to have access to the support of male relatives who, in turn, would reap the benefits of their domestic labors. This also meant that employers could justify lower wages for their female employees.[73] Susan B. Anthony and Lucy Stone resented the connection that some labor reformers established between chattel slavery and wage slavery, finding it to be too great a diversion from the objectives of the antislavery movement.[74] Yet, as an abolitionist herself, Anthony continued to pursue metempsychosis well into the 1850s. This was also the period during which, as a burgeoning women's rights reformer, she began to embrace the woman-slave analogy. "Not being free," Anthony stated in the late 1840s, woman was taught that "the fruits of her industry belonged to others":

> [Woman is] the uncomplaining drudge of the household, condemned to the severest labor, ... systematically robbed of her earnings, which have gone to build up her master's power, and she has found herself in the condition of the slave, deprived of the results of her own labor.[75]

This analysis linked discourses of slavery with other colonialist imaginings. Envisioning women laboring as "drudges" evoked the treatment thought to be accorded to colonized women—those women believed to exist beyond the bounds of civilization.[76]

It was in this context that antebellum women's rights reformers began to position the factory as a parallel to the home, as both were sites where wealth was transferred from the female body to the capitalist or the husband. At this juncture, Lori Merish argues, women reformers "theorized a gendered relation of class." More thorough analyses of these questions would develop across the 1850s in periodicals such as the *Lily* and the *Una*. What women's rights reformers came to perceive as the different "forms of servitude in the factory and in the household" emerged concurrently, Merish continues, with factory women often at the center of the discourse; indeed, "the very

---

[73] Thistle, *From Marriage to the Market*, 16.

[74] Ellen Carol DuBois, "The Nineteenth-Century Woman Suffrage Movement and the Analysis of Women's Oppression," in *Capitalist Patriarchy and the Case for Socialist Feminism*, ed. Zillah Eisenstein (New York: Monthly Review Press, 1979), 139; Foner, "Free Labor," 108.

[75] Susan B. Anthony, "WOMAN: The Great Unpaid Laborer of the World," c. 1848, in *Voices from Women's Liberation*, ed. Leslie B. Tanner (New York: Mentor, 1970), 42.

[76] Merish, *Archives of Labor*, 49.

public image of the mill girl helped advertise the ways emerging capitalist class relations were constitutively gendered and racialized."[77] Women's rights reformers also directly addressed the limited earning power of working-class women. As the abolitionist and women's rights reformer Rev. Samuel J. May asked, could the men who make women "drudges" and "pay them ... miserable pittances" respect their workers? "Yes, *about as much as the slaveholders feel for their slaves.*"[78]

In response, women's rights reformers emphasized the economic value of women's domestic labors. Many sought to reconceptualize household labor as real and valuable work that was equivalent to that performed beyond the home.[79] "The wife owes service and labor to her husband as much and as absolutely as the slave does to his master," Rev. Antoinette Brown observed at an 1853 women's rights convention. For Brown, women could not and should not be contented with little to no remuneration for their labors: "[I]f we are to be satisfied with things as they are, so should the slave. He should be grateful for the care of his master, for according to the established price paid for labor, he does not earn enough to take care of himself."[80] But Brown did not end there; neither women nor enslaved people of African descent, she implied, should be contented with their situation.

"Poverty is essentially slavery, if not legal, yet actual," Paulina Wright Davis insisted that same year. To achieve their "emancipation," it would have to be through work, that women "*must* purchase themselves out of bondage."[81] This suggestion—that women should "purchase themselves"— reflected a genuine, although controversial, antislavery strategy. Some abolitionists, believing in the sanctity and self-ownership of each individual, did not, on principle, support enslaved people purchasing their freedom or being purchased by others from slaveowners. However, such high-minded principles were not always practical, especially following the Fugitive Slave Law of 1850. Indeed, national and transatlantic antislavery networks mobilized to raise funds to purchase the freedom of famous

---

[77] Ibid., 49–51.

[78] Samuel J. May, "The Rights and Condition of Women; A Sermon, Preached in Syracuse, Nov., 1845," *Woman's Rights Tracts*, no. 1 (1853): 11–12.

[79] Glenn, *Unequal Freedom*, 67.

[80] Antoinette Brown Blackwell, Woman's Rights State Convention, 30 November–1 December 1853, in *HWS*, Vol. I, eds. Elizabeth Cady Stanton, Susan B. Anthony, and Matilda Joslyn Gage (Rochester: Susan B. Anthony, 1881), 580, 586–587.

[81] Paulina Wright Davis, "Remarks at the Convention," *Una*, September 1853.

abolitionists such as Frederick Douglass and Harriet Jacobs. In contrast, Davis implied that women did not have access to such benevolence in order to achieve their own emancipation. This could only be achieved through greater access to labor and its economic benefits. "Pecuniary independence first and political freedom will come as a necessity," Davis wrote in a letter to Caroline Wells Healey Dall, echoing many of her claims in the *Una*. As its editor, Davis purposefully had this periodical printed by women. Women apprentices were more expensive to employ, she confided to Dall, but this was inconsequential; wage-earning women would have the capacity to "resist taxation without representation," that form of political subjugation so often understood to be yet another class of slavery.[82]

Other women's rights reformers came to the realization that women's dependence was imposed not only through the marriage contract but through the minutiae of marital property law. In 1855, Frances Dana Gage observed how the "husband and master" was legally given "entire control of the person and the earnings" of both "woman and the slave," maintaining that women should assert their "rights to be free" to escape the "prison-house of law." Gage further addressed how the ideology of true womanhood influenced how male reformers perceived women's labor. When she debated this question with abolitionist and philanthropist Gerrit Smith, Gage criticized the myopic view that many men held toward women, perhaps even obliquely deriding Smith's wealth:

> Mr. Smith says, "That women are helpless, is no wonder, so long as they are paupers"; he might add, no wonder that the slaves of the cotton plantation are helpless, so long as they are paupers.[83]

Gage, much like Blackwell, condoned neither those ideologies that implied the helplessness of women or enslaved people, or the broader perception that either were "property." Many women's rights reformers believed that women's oppression could be remedied through demands for joint marital property laws. To a degree, the Married Women's Property Acts that passed from midcentury onward alleviated some of the restrictions surrounding property ownership.[84]

[82] Paulina Wright Davis to Caroline Wells Healey Dall, 13 October 1853, Caroline Wells Healey Dall Papers, Microfilm: Reel 2, Box 2, Folder 7, Massachusetts Historical Society.
[83] Frances Dana Gage to Gerrit Smith, 24 December 1855, *HWS:* I, 843.
[84] Tracey Jean Boisseau and Tracy A. Thomas, eds. *Feminist Legal History: Essays on Women and Law* (New York: New York University Press, 2011), 4–5.

Although Brown, Davis, and Gage condemned the subordination of women as well as chattel slavery, other reformers implicitly suggested that enslaved people of African descent chose their own situation—either actively or passively. François Furstenberg describes the process whereby political discourse in the early republic routinely positioned chattel slavery as "an act of individual choice," rendering slavery the opposite of freedom in a manner that suggested individuals could fall from the latter into the former. The continued enslavement of Africans seemed to suggest that, in some way, enslaved people had submitted to their condition.[85] Some reformers perpetuated these racist rationales to justify their own causes, antislavery and otherwise. As an 1854 poem in the *Lily* entitled "Woman's Sphere," possibly even penned by Stone's husband and Brown's future brother-in-law Henry B. Blackwell, commanded:

> An equal be to lordly man;
> Be not a slave, like the African!
> *Plead, plead* thy cause, 'tis woman's sphere,
> Till man shall yield thy rights so dear.[86]

Although neither women nor enslaved people were thought to possess full autonomy, not all reformers definitively advocated the self-ownership of enslaved people even while claiming it for women.

Some women began to achieve a degree of economic self-sufficiency through their success in the literary marketplace, especially by the 1850s. Famous journalists, novelists, and reformers such as Fanny Fern (the *nom-de-plume* for Sara Willis), Harriet Beecher Stowe, E.D.E.N. Southworth, Grace Greenwood (the *nom-de-plume* for Sarah Jane Lippincott), and Lillie Devereux Blake began their literary careers in order to support themselves and their families.[87] Their interrogation of women's labor contravened the fallacy that women did not work, while the simple fact that their writings appeared in the nineteenth-century literary marketplace implicitly challenged the ideal of domesticity.[88] Antebellum reform culture relied on

---

[85] François Furstenberg, "Beyond Freedom and Slavery: Autonomy, Virtue, and Resistance in Early American Political Discourse," *Journal of American History* 89, no. 4 (2003): 1295–1330.

[86] H** B**, "Woman's Sphere," *Lily*, 15 February 1854.

[87] Husband, *Antislavery Discourse*, 57.

[88] Bonnie S. Anderson, *Joyous Greetings: The First International Women's Movement, 1830–1860* (Oxford: Oxford University Press, 2000), 101.

print culture to circulate its demands; reformers were keenly aware of the need to develop cultural representations of social problems and so embraced the "novel of purpose" as a platform for advocating the reform of society.[89] Some of the journalism and many of the novels authored by these women and their contemporaries were concerned with these reform themes, especially the labors of seamstresses and housewives.

Women often found literary inspiration in the economic exploitation of seamstresses. Writing about this particular form of labor regularly served as a preface for broader discussions of the political, economic, and social questions surrounding women's rights.[90] The expanding market for ready-made clothing in the wholesale trade meant needlewomen, like female operatives, became wage workers. However, these women routinely faced miserable working conditions—at home or in "slop shops," for long hours and at low "piece rate" pay—which, Merish notes, generated discussions of class victimization and women's oppression. The sentimentality of the antebellum antislavery movement became central to descriptions of class and poverty, rendering the "sentimental seamstress" yet another literary trope in reform literature. Seamstresses, who had fewer opportunities than female operatives "to engage in acts of literary self-definition," were often depicted as the "deserving poor" because their economic dependence was thought to be dictated by capitalism and its whims. Thus, the sentimental seamstress presupposed the feminine nature of economic dependence, a process which underscored cultural anxieties about working women's economic and sexual autonomy.[91]

Whether concerned with characters who were seamstresses, domestic servants, or social reformers, much women's rights literature sought to esteem women's labors. This was epitomized in Laura Curtis Bullard's *Christine; or, Woman's Trials and Triumphs* (1856), a novel which Denise M. Kohn describes as presenting one of the antebellum era's "most radical heroines: a woman's rights leader."[92] After the character of Annie Howard flees her marriage and becomes a fugitive wife, the trade to which she

---

[89] Amanda Claybaugh, *The Novel of Purpose: Literature and Social Reform in the Anglo-American World* (Ithaca: Cornell University Press, 2007).

[90] Jacqueline M. Chambers, "'Thinking and Stitching, Stitching and Thinking': Needlework, American Women Writers, and Professionalism," in *Famine and Fashion: Needlewomen in the Nineteenth Century*, ed. Beth Harris (Hampshire: Ashgate, 2005), 172.

[91] Merish, *Archives of Labor*, 116–117.

[92] Denise M. Kohn, ed. *Christine; or, Woman's Trials and Triumphs* (Lincoln: University of Nebraska Press, 1856/2010), ix.

turns is the arduous and poorly remunerated occupation of needlework. Despite being sexually harassed by the foreman when she seeks her wages, Annie is determined to continue "her never-ending drudgery, her never-resting needle," in order to support her sick child.[93] Such sentimental representations of this figure eroticized dependency by anchoring poverty to feminine weakness and delicacy. The seamstress' feminine modesty and "tragic fatalism" result in "economic ineptitude"—which Edith Wharton later epitomized in *The House of Mirth* (1905) through Lily Bart's social descent and failure as a milliner—because of the degree to which economic agency, which could lead to success, was viewed as a masculine characteristic.[94] Annie, a fugitive wife who is unable to prevail economically, also dies a fallen woman. This leads Christine, the novel's title character, to argue that women should be employed in any profession in which they excel, and should "be paid for her labor as much as a man would be, for the same amount."[95]

Many women's rights reformers also analyzed the sense of confinement that could be the consequence of women's restriction to the domestic sphere, most famously encapsulated at century's end in Charlotte Perkins Gilman's 1892 short story "The Yellow Wallpaper." This same sense of confinement also extended to more personal experiences. When Rosetta Douglass, the eldest child of Frederick Douglass, was boarding with family friends in Philadelphia, for example, she expressed her frustrations to her father. Free African Americans enjoyed only a precarious freedom in antebellum Philadelphia despite the city's thriving free black community.[96] In 1854, the 15-year-old Rosetta had attended the Oberlin College Preparatory Department, but only for one year. As Leigh Fought notes, when Rosetta later sought to pursue a career as an educator, she encountered professional difficulties in securing a position, as well as an experience defined by the "perils of being a young, single, and independent black woman." In her early twenties, Douglass decided to seek new professional opportunities in a world beyond Rochester, New York. Her time lodging in Philadelphia with the family of Thomas and Louisa Dorsey, however, was most trying; she found being immersed in an unfamiliar family situation particularly challenging, especially on account of the con-

[93] Laura Curtis Bullard, *Christine; or, Woman's Trials and Triumphs* (New York: De Witt & Davenport, 1856), 282–284.
[94] Merish, *Archives of Labor*, 123.
[95] Bullard, *Christine*, 184.
[96] Erica Armstrong Dunbar, *A Fragile Freedom: African American Women and Emancipation in the Antebellum City* (New Haven: Yale University Press, 2008).

flict and judgment she felt from the mistress of the house.[97] "All the time I am here I feel in bondage," Rosetta despairingly told her father in 1862, "for I must not even go out which is necessary to get or at least to try and negotiate for a school."[98] Rosetta may have mobilized discourses of slavery, which had become so common in reform circles, either to express the depth of her anxiety or perhaps even to pique the attention of her formerly enslaved abolitionist father. The emotional and spatial challenges of domesticity, of living in close quarters, provoked Rosetta Douglass toward similar reflections as those expressed in so much women's rights literature.

On the eve of the Civil War, some women's rights reformers articulated frustration with their movement's lack of success. In 1860, Caroline Wells Healey Dall proclaimed that "'Woman's Rights' [is] ... a phrase which we all hate," as it was spoken "with such unction, as a slave might clank his chains!"[99] Despite the passage of the Married Women's Property Acts, few women had been able to realize the pecuniary independence that women's rights reformers had envisaged as key to their self-ownership. This 1860 address was republished seven years later in *The College, the Market, and the Court: Or, Woman's Relation to Education, Labor and Law* (1867), Dall's paean to women's capacities beyond the domestic sphere. Dall believed that women's rights reformers needed to follow in the footsteps of Mary Astell and Mary Wollstonecraft and reassert women's "Right to Labor."[100]

CHATTEL SLAVERY AND FREE LABOR

Concerns about women's labor were by no means limited to white reformers in the labor, antislavery, and women's rights movements, as African Americans expressed still more perspectives. Frederick Douglass' second autobiography, *My Bondage and My Freedom* (1855), emphasized that wage labor was, in fact, neither wage slavery nor chattel slavery. In fact, wage labor had offered him the opportunity to be his "own master ... [in] a state of

[97] Leigh Fought, *Women in the World of Frederick Douglass* (Oxford: Oxford University Press, 2017), 160–161, 179–181.
[98] Rosetta Douglass to Frederick Douglass, 4 April 1862, Frederick Douglass Papers, Library of Congress, in Ibid., 181.
[99] "Progress of the Cause" (Fraternity Lecture), 23 October 1860, 3–4, Caroline Wells Healey Dall Papers, Schlesinger Library, Harvard University.
[100] Caroline Wells Healey Dall, *The College, the Market, and the Court: Or, Woman's Relation to Education, Labor and Law* (Boston: Lee and Shepard, 1867), 360, 367.

independence, beyond seeking [the] friendship or support of any man."[101] African Americans also examined the incongruities that shaped these divergent experiences. Sometimes their discussions directly described chattel slavery and the labors of enslaved women and men. At other times, however, African Americans employed discourses of slavery in a manner that was reasonably abstracted from chattel slavery.

North and South, enslaved or free, as well as before and after slave emancipation, work was a necessity for the majority of African-American women. During the early 1830s, Maria Stewart became the first American woman, black or white, to publicly address a promiscuous audience on political themes.[102] Widowed a few short years after her marriage, Stewart found herself in the same precarious circumstances that Frances Ellen Watkins Harper would later experience following her own brief marriage in the 1860s. These realities were central to Stewart's analyses of work amongst free African-American women. Although she, like many fellow antislavery women, envisioned reform as an appropriate extension of domesticity, Stewart did not believe that women should be confined to the home.[103] Her analyses were particularly attentive to oppressions derived from race, gender, and class.[104] As early as 1831, Stewart observed that, while men had "practiced nothing but head-work these 200 years," it had been African Americans, and particularly women, who were confined to doing their "drudgery." "How long shall the fair daughters of Africa," she asked, "be compelled to bury their minds and talents beneath a load of iron pots and kettles?"[105]

Across 1832 and 1833, Stewart presented a series of addresses to Boston's Afric-American Female Intelligence Society as well as in Franklin Hall and the African Masonic Hall. Soon after, Garrison published these lectures in

[101] Frederick Douglass, *My Bondage and My Freedom* (New York: Miller, Orton & Mulligan, 1855), 349.
[102] Carla L. Peterson, *"Doers of the Word": African-American Women Speakers and Writers in the North* (New Brunswick: Rutgers University Press, 1995), 58, 67.
[103] Christina Henderson, "Sympathetic Violence: Maria Stewart's Antebellum Vision of African American Resistance," *MELUS* 38, no. 4 (2013): 61.
[104] Kathryn T. Gines, "Race Women, Race Men, and Early Expressions of Protointersectionality, 1830s–1930s," in *Why Race and Gender Still Matter: An Intersectional Approach*, eds. Namita Goswami, Maeve O'Donovan, and Lisa Yount (London: Pickering & Chatto, 2014); Jean Fagan Yellin, *Women and Sisters: The Antislavery Feminists in American Culture* (New Haven: Yale University Press, 1989), 46–48.
[105] *Meditations from the Pen of Mrs. Maria W. Stewart* (Washington: Enterprise Publishing Company, 1879), 32.

the *Liberator*. Addressing herself directly to African Americans, although some white spectators were in attendance, Stewart positioned the necessary cultural work of black women as existing between that of black men and white women.[106] "O, ye daughters of Africa, awake! awake! arise!" she demanded in 1832. Stewart went on to use discourses of slavery to describe the situation of working-class African Americans in the North. With "few exceptions," she considered "our condition but little better" than the "horrors of slavery ... of Southern slavery." However, instead of asserting outright that the condition of free African Americans was analogous to chattel slavery, Stewart instead conceded the possibility that "I may be very erroneous in my opinion."[107] This anticipated the style of analysis to later emerge in 1837 when Sarah Grimké qualified her statement by asserting that women were "much in the situation of the slave."[108]

But Stewart did not believe that the condition of free blacks was little better than chattel slavery on account of racism or racial subjugation alone. Believing that there were "no chains as galling as the chains of ignorance— no fetters so binding as those that bind the soul," her conclusions echoed the expansive manner in which so many other antebellum reformers and commentators embraced discourses of slavery. Stewart dictated that her "fairer sisters" should attempt to appreciate the "disadvantages under which we labor," also insisting that African Americans "make some mighty efforts to raise your sons and daughters from the horrible state of servitude and degradation in which they are placed."[109] Through their efforts as reformers, African-American women sought to challenge the prevailing racist assumptions about their own inferiority.[110] Sometimes, the method whereby women such as Stewart pursued this analysis was, in fact, through discourses of slavery.

However, a clear disparity existed between the situation of enslaved black women and free white women. Jacqueline Jones argues that enslaved women's labor took place in three distinct yet interconnected spheres on antebellum southern plantations: the domestic sphere of their own households; their communities of enslaved people; and the slave economy, which included both domestic and manual labor. While enslaved women's

[106] Peterson, "*Doers of the Word*," 66–68.
[107] *Meditations*, 55.
[108] Grimké, *Letters*, 33.
[109] *Meditations*, 57–58.
[110] Shirley J. Yee, *Black Women Abolitionists: A Study in Activism, 1828–1860* (Knoxville: University of Tennessee Press, 1992), 112.

labor was valued in the first two spheres, it was devalued in the latter.[111] Besides laboring for plantation owners, enslaved women also carried out the majority of the essential household tasks for their own families.[112] This challenged northern white reformers' pronouncements that women were inherently oppressed by household labors, as many enslaved women took pride in the artisanal aspects of domestic tasks.[113] However, enslaved women as much as working-class women were expected to labor for their masters as well as to continue their domestic labors; as Susan Thistle suggests, "[slave] emancipation initially meant freedom from the additional work forcibly imposed on them by [chattel] slavery, allowing them to focus on the care of their own families."[114] After slave emancipation, however, many African-American women found themselves at the mercy of a penal system that promoted and relied on convict labor. As Talitha L. LeFlouria argues, these women found themselves "stranded between a free labor market that refused to admit [them] as a skilled worker and an open system of prison labor that would only allow [them] to work in chains." In these "carceral polities," many African Americans remained in a penitentiary system that scholars describe as involuntary servitude long after slave emancipation.[115]

African-American women, therefore, brought a wholly different perspective to the question of free labor. The free produce movement was one of the antislavery causes to which the young Frances Ellen Watkins dedicated herself across the 1850s.[116] As an abolitionist lecturer who toured the northern states, she often shared her poetry with spectators. One 1850s poem, entitled "Free Labor," emphasized that free labor was not just wage labor performed by people who were not enslaved. Rather, it also entailed boycotting the merchandise—in this case, clothing—produced by the labors of enslaved people. "This fabric is too light to bear/The weight of

[111] Jacqueline Jones, *Labor of Love, Labor of Sorrow: Black Women, Work, and the Family, from Slavery to the Present* (New York: Basic Books, 1985).
[112] Thistle, *From Marriage to the Market*, 21–26.
[113] Susan Strasser, *Never Done: A History of American Housework* (New York: Pantheon Books, 1982, 2000), 47, 226.
[114] Thistle, *From Marriage to the Market*, 21–22.
[115] Talitha L. LeFlouria, *Chained in Silence: Black Women and Convict Labor in the New South* (Chapel Hill: University of North Carolina Press, 2015), 4–6.
[116] Many antislavery women boycotted slave-made goods in the hope of undermining the market for such southern produce while also instilling and enacting antislavery morals, see: Jeffrey, *Great Silent Army of Abolition*, 20–21; Peterson, *"Doers of the Word"*, 120.

bondsmen's tears," she wrote; neither did it "bear a smother'd sigh,/From some lorn woman's heart." Thus, she implicitly questioned the manner in which so many labor reformers alluded to chattel slavery to analyze the exploitation of those workers employed under circumstances of free labor. In boycotting slave produce, she concluded, "I have nerv'd Oppression's hand,/For deeds of guilt and wrong."[117] Since African Americans could be accused of failing to embody republican virtues, their free labor rhetoric differed from that of many other labor reformers in that it sought to hold the state accountable.[118] Collectively, Frances Ellen Watkins Harper's poetry as well as her later novels were concerned with a variety of reforms, from abolitionism and temperance to marriage. The theme that united her poetic oeuvre, however, was a criticism of the "perversion of power relations between strong and weak, whether between master and slave, man and woman, or rich and poor," yet, as Carla L. Peterson emphasizes, her "sweeping moral vision of universal freedom" was undergirded by the understanding that chattel slavery remained the most egregious perversion of this power.[119] As a result, Watkins Harper emphasized what many other antebellum reformers had effectively obscured: that chattel slavery was the most severe form of oppression and exploitation.

However, although white women could hope to gain a sense of authorial autonomy through their literary endeavors, this was not always true for African Americans. On account of the prevalence of illiteracy and poor literacy during the antebellum era, Jacqueline Jones Royster argues that many African Americans understood "literacy as emanating from lived experience."[120] Some formerly enslaved women published slave narratives, often in conjunction with white abolitionist women who acted as everything from ghostwriters to amanuenses. Sojourner Truth's lack of formal literacy meant that her publications were the product of collaborations with Olive Gilbert and Frances W. Titus, while Harriet Jacobs worked alongside Lydia Maria Child. As Xiomara Santamarina observes of the way scholars have interpreted these relationships, "either the illiterate

---

[117] "Free Labor," in *A Brighter Coming Day: A Frances Ellen Watkins Harper Reader*, ed. Frances Smith Foster (New York: The Feminist Press, 1990), 81.
[118] Michael Stancliff, *Frances Ellen Watkins Harper: African American Reform Rhetoric and the Rise of a Modern Nation State* (New York: Routledge, 2011), 52–53.
[119] Peterson, *"Doers of the Word"*, 120–135.
[120] Jacqueline Jones Royster, *Traces of a Stream: Literacy and Social Change among African American Women* (Pittsburgh: University of Pittsburgh Press, 2000), 45.

Truth was irredeemably susceptible to her interlocutors' agendas, or she was all-powerful."[121]

But Truth also shared with labor reformers and other African Americans the challenge of discussing the nature of labor and freedom at a moment when both were becoming increasingly commodified, amongst enslaved as well as free laborers.[122] Born during the late 1790s not in the South but in New York State, Isabella Van Wagenen was of the generation of enslaved people of African descent to experience gradual abolition in 1827. Reinventing herself in 1843 as Sojourner Truth, she became an itinerant preacher. However, as Nell Irvin Painter observes, Truth's personal history and experience of chattel slavery "automatically migrated into a vague, composite antebellum South," on account of the degree to which southern chattel slavery symbolized chattel slavery in the antebellum United States. If the geographic location of Truth's enslavement was unclear, many of her contemporaries definitively interpreted it as having been lived out below the Mason-Dixon line. In the coming decades, she published works such as the *Narrative of Sojourner Truth; A Northern Slave* (1850) and advocated for abolitionism, women's rights, and universal suffrage at significant antebellum and postbellum reform conventions.[123] Her addresses, which were the product of oral traditions in both African and African-American cultures, focused far more frequently on abolitionism than women's rights.[124]

Truth's address at the 1851 women's rights convention in Akron, Ohio, has become a site of both historiographical contention and intrigue amongst feminist scholars. Described as her "A'n't I a woman?" speech, some argue that later generations of white feminists effectively undermined Truth's original statement by misappropriating this famous quote, which evokes black women's hardiness and strength, for their own purposes.[125] Other historians focus on the manner in which this address came down to posterity—through the mediated transcriptions of white journal-

---

[121] Xiomara Santamarina, *Belabored Professions: Narratives of African American Working Womanhood* (Chapel Hill: University of North Carolina Press, 2006), 35.
[122] Ibid., 37.
[123] Nell Irvin Painter, *Sojourner Truth: A Life, a Symbol* (New York: W.W. Norton, 1996), 8.
[124] Peterson, *"Doers of the Word"*, 48; Carleton Mabee, *Sojourner Truth: Slave, Prophet, Legend* (New York: New York University Press, 1993), 182.
[125] Phyllis Marynick Palmer, "White Women/Black Women: The Dualism of Female Identity and Experience in the United States," *Feminist Studies* 9, no. 1 (1983): 152.

ists or the remembrances of white reformers—to the degree that they question its veracity at all.[126] In 1851, the *Anti-Slavery Bugle*, the *Liberator*, the *New-York Daily Tribune*, and Pittsburgh's *Saturday Visiter* first reported Truth's address. More than a decade later, in 1863, New York's *Independent* and the *National Anti-Slavery Standard* published Frances Dana Gage's "Reminiscences" of Truth's 1851 address. Painter goes so far as to suggest that Gage—potentially inspired by Harriet Beecher Stowe's 1863 article, "Sojourner Truth, the Libyan Sibyl," which had appeared in the *Atlantic Monthly* only months earlier—may have wholly invented what would become Truth's most famous quotation.[127] Gage's remarks were then republished in the *Narrative of Sojourner Truth; A Bondswoman of Olden Time* (1875) and Volume I of Elizabeth Cady Stanton, Susan B. Anthony, and Matilda Joslyn Gage's *History of Woman Suffrage* (1881). If the truth of what she said may always remain elusive, Theresa C. Zackodnik argues that it is still possible to "know something of Truth's politics … by attending to a wider body of her work and listening for more than that single refrain 'A'n't I a woman?'"[128]

The address that Truth presented in 1851 clearly articulated the many labors performed by enslaved women of African descent. Describing the orator as "Sojourner Truth, an emancipated slave," Marius Robinson of the *Anti-Slavery Bugle* recalled that Truth opened her address by asserting "I am a woman's rights." To be both an "emancipated slave" and "a woman's rights" was to encapsulate the ethos of the woman-slave analogy—not through metempsychosis, as abolitionist women and so many other antebellum reformers had envisaged it, but rather through lived experience. Thus, the symbolic linking of these two causes through both the person and the words of Sojourner Truth occurred in 1851 as much as it would in 1863 and again in 1881. This address went on to chronicle the labors Truth had performed as an enslaved woman. "Why children," she concluded, "if you have woman's rights give it to her and you will feel better."[129] This evoked a sense of what many reformers, from Frederick Douglass to Susan B. Anthony, perceived to be the self-evident nature of women's rights in a culture

---

[126] Painter, *Sojourner Truth*; Deborah Gray White, *Ar'n't I a Woman? Female Slaves in the Plantation South*, Revised Edition (New York: W.W. Norton, 1985, 1999), 5, 11.

[127] Painter, *Sojourner Truth*, Chapter 18. See also: Mabee, *Sojourner Truth*.

[128] Teresa C. Zackodnik, *Press, Platform, Pulpit: Black Feminist Publics in the Era of Reform* (Knoxville: University of Tennessee Press, 2011), Chapter 3, 268, 94–95.

[129] "Women's Rights Convention: Sojourner Truth," *Anti-Slavery Bugle*, 21 June 1851.

5 "DEGRADING SERVITUDE": FREE LABOR, CHATTEL SLAVERY... 191

convinced that neither women nor enslaved people of African descent should be accorded the same rights as free white men.

The *Anti-Slavery Bugle* introduced themes and imagery that would be absent from Gage's later account. It concluded with Truth's observation that "man is in a tight place, the poor slave is on him, woman is coming on him, and he is surely between a hawk and a buzzard."[130] As Peterson emphasizes, "'hawk' and 'buzzard' are also figures from an African-American folktale in which the two vultures are seen as oppositional and come into conflict in a struggle for survival, [with] the buzzard, a descendant of the powerful African 'King Buzzard,' always gaining ascendancy." To African-American spectators, this may have suggested not a sense of symmetry between the rights of enslaved people and the rights of women, but rather a divergence—and possibly even hostility. Zackodnik suggests that Truth used a double-voiced strategy to highlight the degree to which the women's rights movement sidelined the interests of African Americans; and, as with countless other antebellum women's rights conventions, the white women at this event again mobilized the woman-slave analogy with little nuance in their own addresses. But if Truth's 1851 address had "suggested the oppositionality of slave and woman," one of her other antebellum addresses instead conflated these figures more closely.[131]

In her 1853 address at the Broadway Tabernacle in New York City, for example, Truth would "come forth to speak 'bout Woman's Rights" after representing herself as having been "a slave in the State of New York; and now ... a good citizen of this state." In these dual capacities, Truth observed that both enslaved people and women had "all been thrown down so low that nobody thought we'd ever get up again; but we have been long enough trodden down; we will come up again, and now I am here."[132] Truth offered strong declarations of presence through such statements, particularly emphasizing the importance of her own presence as an African-American woman and formerly enslaved person. Her 1853 proclamation "I am here"—as with her 1851 assertion, "I am a woman's rights"—perhaps acknowledged the erasure of race from so many interpretations of the woman question, while also speaking to the ongoing

---
[130] Ibid.
[131] Peterson, *"Doers of the Word"*, 54; Zackodnik, *Press, Platform, Pulpit*, 103–104.
[132] Sojourner Truth, Mob Convention in New York, 6–7 September 1853, *HWS*: I, 567–568.

contestations about gender within abolitionism. Again, Truth reiterated her sense of the importance of a formerly enslaved woman having arrived on the reform platform, for the antislavery as much as the women's rights movement.

Gage had presided over the 1851 women's rights convention in Akron, Ohio. A temperance advocate, abolitionist, and women's rights reformer, Gage was unlike many of her white reform contemporaries in that she was also a working-class woman.[133] Her 1863 recollections of this convention began by describing the spectators' racism prior to Truth's address: "A buzz of disapprobation was heard all over the house, and there fell on the listening ear, 'An abolition affair!' 'Woman's rights and niggers!'"[134] The convention, however, had been advertised as a reform affair that would discuss topics such as chattel slavery and women's rights, which raises uncertainty about the degree to which Gage's recollections of such raucousness could, in fact, be accurate.[135] Moreover, while Truth often addressed African-American spectators in other contexts, this particular setting was very likely dominated by white women.[136] Despite these discrepancies, and the 20 years that had elapsed since Stewart's first addresses as well as the 15 years since the controversy surrounding the Grimké sisters, black abolitionist women continued to experience the full weight of public opposition to both women and African Americans speaking in public. Gage also evoked the sense of censure that Jane Grey Swisshelm (also present) had feared should the antislavery and women's rights causes be brought together, in her 1850 exchange with Parker Pillsbury in the *Saturday Visiter* and *North Star*.[137] Gage recalled that "few women in those days ... dared to 'speak in meeting';" and although such prejudices may have weakened in the years since, spectators had been "hugely enjoying" what she recalled as the "discomfiture" of Sojourner Truth, "of the 'strong-minded.'"[138] This uneasiness was derived from the disorderliness attributed to women's

---

[133] Painter, *Sojourner Truth*, 175–177; Jeffrey E. Smith, "'Turning the World Upside Down': The Life and Words of Frances Dana Gage," in *Feminist Frontiers: Women Who Shaped the Midwest*, ed. Yvonne Johnson (Kirksville: Truman State University Press, 2010).

[134] "Reminiscences by Frances D. Gage: Sojourner Truth," *HWS*: I, 115.

[135] Zackodnik, *Press, Platform, Pulpit*, 98; Painter, *Sojourner Truth*, 129, 169–175.

[136] Peterson, *"Doers of the Word"*, 50.

[137] Since 1849, Frances Dana Gage's writings had appeared with regularity in Pittsburgh's *Saturday Visiter*, ed. Jane Grey Swisshelm. Painter, *Sojourner Truth*, 121–124.

[138] "Reminiscences by Frances D. Gage: Sojourner Truth," *HWS*: I, 115.

bodies as much as to the embodied representativeness spectators observed in black bodies.[139]

Gage's "Recollections," however, did not directly align with accounts of Truth's address from the early 1850s. Yet, while the *Anti-Slavery Bugle* made no report of the famous "A'n't I a woman?" refrain, it did reflect Gage's 1863 account in other ways.[140] In Gage's estimation, Truth began not by asserting "I am a woman's rights" but by pursuing a comparison between the "rights" for which the abolitionist and women's rights movements advocated. Between southern blacks and northern women "all talkin' 'bout rights," she observed, white men were going to "be in a fix pretty soon. But what's all dis here talkin' 'bout?" In this account, Truth went on to stress the different treatment bestowed upon white women, who were always accorded the "best place," while black women always had to labor:

> I have ploughed, and planted, and gathered into barns, and no man could head me! And a'n't I a woman? I could work as much and eat as much as a man—when I could get it—and bear de lash as well! And a'n't I a woman? I have borne thirteen children, ... all sold off to slavery, and when I cried out with my mother's grief, none but Jesus heard me! And a'n't I a woman?[141]

Gage recalled Truth's descriptions of women's labor, as well as other aspects of the 1851 address, in a manner that was quite similar to that of the *Anti-Slavery Bugle*. Through wry wit and pointed analysis, she suggested, Truth had transformed a crowd of racist skeptics into appreciative and thoughtful reform spectators. What was new in Gage's account was Truth's principle rhetorical flourish: "A'n't I a woman?" This question, Painter emphasizes, famously "linked two causes—of women (presumed to be white) and of blacks (presumed to be men)—through one black female body."[142]

In Peterson's analysis, Gage's account of Truth's address rewrote its subject "not only as a 'darkey' but also as a masculine body seeking feminization implied in the repeated question 'a'n't I a woman?'"[143] By seizing

---

[139] Zackodnik, *Press, Platform, Pulpit*, 96–97; Caroline Field Levander, *Voices of the Nation: Women and Public Speech in Nineteenth-Century American Literature and Culture* (New York: Cambridge University Press, 1998).

[140] Peterson, "*Doers of the Word*," 52–55.

[141] "Reminiscences," 115–117.

[142] Painter, *Sojourner Truth*, 171.

[143] Peterson, "*Doers of the Word*," 53.

on Truth's own experiences as a working woman deserving of her rights, Painter suggests that Gage developed a more radical revisioning of Stowe's analysis of Truth in the *Atlantic Monthly*.[144] According to Zackodnik, this was the product of Gage's own need to displace the embodied concerns about women's labor onto the body of a formerly enslaved black woman. At the particular moment of penning her "Remembrances," then, Gage developed a sensationalized account of the 1851 women's rights convention by creating "an exceptional 'slave' who symbolically linked the forgotten cause of woman's rights to one much more visible in 1863, the emancipation of enslaved blacks."[145] The focus on women's labors under chattel slavery as well as its violence thus emerges, for these scholars, as the product of Gage as well as Truth. If this is the case, not only did Gage emphasize that Truth had the strength and willpower to "bear de lash" as an enslaved woman, but her account also paralleled the manner in which discourses of slavery flourished amongst the antebellum era's female operatives in Lowell, Massachusetts, as well as her own earlier embrace of discourses of slavery with reference to marital property law.

These concerns persisted during the Civil War and its aftermath, when some African-American men expressed patriarchal interests when the prospect of marriage became a legal possibility. Asked in 1863 about what had encouraged him to marry, one freedman testified to the American Freedman's Inquiry Commission:

> My idea was to have a wife to prevent me running around—to have somebody to do for me and to keep me. The colored men in taking wives always do so with reference to the service the women will render.[146]

This reflected how the Freedmen's Bureau sought to replicate social structures which imbued freedmen, as husbands, with authority over the "persons and labor of his wife and children" as a "reward" of his freedom and evidence of his citizenship.[147] Some African-American women perceived the need to challenge such perspectives. This offers context for the manner in which Truth and Harper responded to the Reconstruction era's

[144] Painter, *Sojourner Truth*, 177.
[145] Zackodnik, *Press, Platform, Pulpit*, 100–102.
[146] Robert Smalls, American Freedman's Inquiry Commission Interviews, South Carolina, 1863, in *Slave Testimony: Two Centuries of Letters, Speeches, Interviews, and Autobiographies*, ed. John W. Blassingame (Baton Rouge: Louisiana State University Press, 1977), 374–375.
[147] Nancy F. Cott, *Public Vows: A History of Marriage and the Nation* (Cambridge, MA: Harvard University Press, 2000), 93.

debates, supporting the rights and enfranchisement of freedmen yet also insisting on the same rights for freedwomen.

Despite the questions surrounding the authorship of her 1851 address, Truth's embrace of the woman-slave analogy persisted well into the 1860s. In fact, Truth emerged as an important figure in the American Equal Rights Association (AERA), established in 1866 to advocate universal suffrage for African-American men and all women. Her 1867 address at an AERA meeting in New York City emphasized that black women's labors rendered them deserving of their enfranchisement as well as entitled to their rights and their earnings:

> I come from another field—the country of the slave. They have got their liberty—so much good luck to have slavery partly destroyed; not entirely. I want it root and branch destroyed. Then we will all be free indeed. I feel that if I have to answer for the deeds done in my body just as much as a man, I have a right to have just as much as a man.

Reminding many former abolitionists that chattel slavery was only "partly destroyed" was particularly significant, given the degree to which white reformers were beginning to abandon the cause of freedpeople following the Civil War. Men, Truth suggested, were neither sufficiently appreciative of women's labors nor realized how little women were paid. "You have been having our rights so long," she concluded, "you think, like a slaveholder, that you own us."[148] By the end of her address, Truth had made it clear that women's rights to their earnings was of greater importance than their right to suffrage.[149]

Ultimately, the manner in which Sojourner Truth mobilized discourses of slavery both reflected and transcended the rhetorical paradigm of many white women reformers. As a formerly enslaved woman, she offered her contemporaries proof of their own rhetoric—what Zackodnik describes as "that rather abstract trope of white woman's condition, 'woman as slave.'" Yet, unlike her white reform contemporaries, Truth focused this analogy around the particular condition of formerly enslaved people, especially black women.[150] Maria Stewart had used discourses of slavery to describe the subjugation that free African Americans experienced in the North; so,

---

[148] Truth, American Equal Rights Association, 9 May 1867, *HWS*: II, 193–194.
[149] Zackodnik, *Press, Platform, Pulpit*, 119.
[150] Ibid., 110, 116–121.

too, would Truth mobilize discourses of slavery at the moments when she most fully theorized oppressions derived from race, class, and gender. Together, these African-American women embraced the legacy of chattel slavery to develop overarching conclusions about black women's historical and enduring exploitation. These reformers mobilized discourses of slavery in the hope of revealing the coercion of chattel slavery as well as the ongoing connections between different forms of oppression. The conclusions they reached at once identified the issues common to many women's experiences of labor and those specific to enslaved and self-emancipated African Americans, North and South.

SUFFRAGISTS AND WORKING-CLASS WOMEN AFTER THE CIVIL WAR

The years immediately following the Civil War were dominated by the prospect of the enfranchisement of African-American men. At least some of the tensions between reformers can be attributed to what women's rights reformers and suffragists increasingly perceived as a lack of gratitude toward their earlier reform efforts. Elizabeth Cady Stanton and Susan B. Anthony, for example, had spearheaded the petitioning campaign of nearly 400,000 signatures that contributed to the passage of the Thirteenth Amendment of 1865. This created the impression that women had quite literally labored for the abolition of chattel slavery. "What an insult to the women who have labored thirty years for the emancipation of the slave," Stanton and Anthony declared in 1868, "now when he [the freedman] is their political equal, to propose to lift him above their heads."[151] This umbridge was particularly acute amongst those who had been committed to the antislavery movement. Women had been compelled to remain "silent" during the Civil War and instead "labor for the emancipation of the slave," Stanton would again recall in 1898, even though women and formerly enslaved people had both desired their enfranchisement.[152]

Historians suggest that, after the Civil War, Stanton and Anthony would increasingly sacrifice principle for the sake of expediency.[153] Prior to the

---

[151] "Who Are Our Friends?" *Revolution*, 15 January 1868.
[152] Elizabeth Cady Stanton, *Eighty Years and More: Reminiscences, 1815–1897* (New York: T. Fisher Unwin, 1898), 254, 240–241.
[153] Rosalyn Terborg-Penn, *African American Women in the Struggle for the Vote, 1850–1920* (Bloomington: Indiana University Press, 1998), 110–111; Faye E. Dudden, *Fighting*

ratification of the Fourteenth Amendment in 1868, both women compromised their antislavery principles to gain support from the wealthy, racist Democrat and copperhead George Francis Train. His platform, which included his own presidential campaign as well as the endorsement of woman suffrage, was in direct opposition to Stanton and Anthony's erstwhile support for universal suffrage. During the 1867 Kansas referendum over manhood suffrage and woman suffrage, for example, Train suggested:

> White women work to free the blacks from slavery,
> Black men to enslave the whites with political knavery,
> Woman votes the black to save,
> The black he votes to make the woman slave,
> Hence when blacks and "Rads" unite to enslave the whites,
> 'Tis time the Democrats championed woman's rights.[154]

Train mobilized discourses of slavery so as to explicitly evoke white supremacy. This deeply racist approach appealed to at least some former antislavery women. Indeed, racial prejudice continued amongst many reformers despite their avowed abhorrence toward chattel slavery. However, very similar sentiments could also be uttered without such deep vitriol. "Were I a colored man," Parker Pillsbury reflected at the AERA's 1867 meeting, "and had reason to believe that should woman obtain her rights she would use them to the prejudice of mine, how could I labor very zealously in her behalf?"[155]

Many postbellum whites expressed the belief that African Americans should be grateful for the bloody sacrifices of the Civil War.[156] Among white suffragists, an acute sense of resentment came to be coupled with their own continuing disenfranchisement, which propelled some to become more attuned to the situation of another oppressed class of women. At this junc-

Chance: The Struggle over Woman Suffrage and Black Suffrage in Reconstruction America (Oxford: Oxford University Press, 2011), 45.

[154] George Francis Train, *The Great Epigram Campaign in Kansas: Championship of Women* (Leavenworth: Prescott & Hume, 1867), 32. See: Ellen Carol DuBois, *Feminism and Suffrage: The Emergence of an Independent Women's Movement in America, 1848–1869* (Ithaca: Cornell University Press, 1978), 93–101. "Rads" refers to the Radical Republicans who were sympathetic to antislavery principles and African American men's enfranchisement.

[155] Parker Pillsbury, American Equal Rights Association, 10 May 1867, HWS: II, 220.

[156] Saidiya V. Hartman, *Scenes of Subjection: Terror, Slavery, and Self-Making in Nineteenth-Century America* (New York: Oxford University Press, 1997), Chapter 5.

ture, some white suffragists began to turn their efforts toward the exploitative conditions, low remuneration, and economic vulnerability of working-class women. Ellen Carol DuBois describes how, during the late 1860s, Stanton and Anthony's exposure to the National Labor Union introduced these suffragists to the manner in which male labor reformers used discourses of slavery. This, DuBois contends, convinced them of the veracity of a comparison between wage slavery and chattel slavery. As much as the figure of the suffering postbellum worker began to replace that of the suffering antebellum slave, the more specific gendered figure of the degraded woman worker also began to supplant that of the degraded enslaved woman "as a staple of popular imagery and superficial social criticism." Stanton and Anthony's newfound interest in the labor movement seemed to pique their interest in the situation of working women. Unlike many men in the labor movement, however, these suffragists did not see working-class women as aberrant figures in need of a return to the domestic sphere. Instead, they championed women's labors and advocated for economic independence as well as enfranchisement.[157]

The Working Women's Association (WWA) was established in 1868, after Stanton and Anthony's newspaper, the *Revolution*, offered its support to the New York City women who had become involved in a labor dispute between the National Typographical Union and the women typesetters of the *New York World*. Led by Anna Tobbitt alongside Susie Johns, Augusta Lewis, and Emily Peers, the WWA was ostensibly open to all women workers, not only typesetters. While these working-class women differed from Stanton and Anthony in their perspectives toward the primacy of woman suffrage, all continued to work together for both causes— if to differing degrees. The WWA offered critical support to Hester Vaughn, a domestic servant charged for infanticide after becoming pregnant by her employer, which ultimately proved instrumental in achieving her pardon. This was a case that encapsulated the *Revolution*'s many concerns, from the situation of women workers to the sexual double standard. Stanton did not blame infanticide on unwed mothers, but rather, on the "degradation of woman." As she wrote in 1868: "Strike the chains from your women; for as long as they are slaves to man's lust, man will be the slave of his own passions."[158] However, by 1869, the WWA's constituency

---

[157] DuBois, *Feminism and Suffrage*, 118, 136; DuBois, "The Nineteenth-Century Woman," 141–143.

[158] E.C.S., "Infanticide and Prostitution," *Revolution*, 5 February 1868.

of working-class wage earners began to shift more toward a middle-class membership, a shift that frustrated many of its former members. After the Women's Typographical Union was established as a parallel organization and coadjutor with the support of a local men's labor union, the women typesetters' tendency to ally with fellow labor reformers and the suffragists' propensity to side with employers became increasingly apparent. These class antagonisms gradually contributed to the WWA's demise later that year.[159]

Despite these conflicts, the white suffragists of the postbellum era continued to express varying degrees of exception to the reality that their antislavery efforts had not led to their own enfranchisement. Some merely aimed to commemorate the earlier efforts of antislavery women in both verse and music. "Today we women labor still for Liberty and Right," one suffrage song reflected in 1876:

> We boast our land of freedom, the unshackling of the slaves;
> We point with proud, though bleeding hearts, to myriads of graves;
> They tell the story of a war that ended slavery's night,
> And still we women struggle for our Liberty, our Right.[160]

Nearly a decade after the ratification of the Fifteenth Amendment in 1870, which had enfranchised African-American men, other white suffragists continued to express a strong sense of resentment. "I feel that now if ever is the time to strike for woman's emancipation," Emily Parmely Collins wrote to Anthony in 1879. A New England native who resided in Louisiana, Collins believed that, given the opportunity, she would make a strong constitutional convention candidate based on the support of "colored people," because "I have ever been their steadfast friend, and they themselves owe their emancipation chiefly to women."[161]

Some suffragists remained more attentive to the problems that arose on account of the limited employment opportunities available to women. Louisa May Alcott's novel *Work: A Story of Experience* (1873) expressed conflict about whether wage work could be fulfilling for women. Its nar-

---

[159] This account draws on: DuBois, *Feminism and Suffrage*, Chapter 5; DuBois, "The Nineteenth-Century Woman," 139–144.
[160] Marie Le Baron, "The Yellow Ribbon," 1876, to the tune of "Wearing of the Green," in Danny O. Crew, *Suffragist Sheet Music* (Jefferson: McFarland & Company 2002).
[161] Emily Parmley Collins to Susan B. Anthony, 1879, HWS: III, 807.

rative negotiated the differing expectations that derived from gender, race, and class. The main character, Christie, alludes to the undesirability of needlework and resolves to take up this occupation only if all other employments failed. Instead, she becomes a domestic servant. Although Christie expresses that she never believed that housework was degrading, the narrator nonetheless notes that she had "assumed her badge of servitude" upon donning her white servant's apron. One "degradation" to which she "won't submit," however, is a request to clean her employer's wellingtons. Hepsey, the self-emancipated African-American cook with whom Christie labors, responds to the situation differently, saying: "[D]is ain't no deggydation to me now; I's a free woman." Only upon learning that Hepsey had been enslaved does Christie apologize and do the job herself.[162] Alcott thus invoked chattel slavery strategically, to encourage her central character—and therefore her largely white readership—to gain humility. By emphasizing that enslaved labor and the employment opportunities afforded free white women were not comparable, *Work* promoted a greater awareness of differing degrees of oppression. Yet, by simultaneously implying that domestic service was particularly appropriate for African-American women, this novel also suggested that formerly enslaved women should be grateful to be the beneficiaries of freedom and, as a result, should not question their employers.

More often, however, postbellum women's rights literature employed abstracted discourses of slavery rather than direct references to chattel slavery to analyze white women's labor. Alcott's *Work* reflected Bullard's 1856 novel, *Christine,* in that its central character eventually became something of a reformer. As Tara Fitzpatrick observes, this character "finds her true calling acting as a conduit between affluent female philanthropists and laboring women in a working women's association."[163] Speaking after the Civil War, Christie proclaims:

> Others have finished the emancipation work and done it splendidly, even at the cost of all this blood and sorrow. ... This new task seems to offer me the chance of being among the pioneers, to do the hard work, share the perse-

---

[162] Louisa May Alcott, *Work: A Story of Experience* (New York: Schocken Books, 1873/1977), 16, 21–24.

[163] Tara Fitzpatrick, "Love's Labor's Reward: The Sentimental Economy of Louisa May Alcott's 'Work'," *NWSA Journal* 5, no. 1 (1993): 36.

cution, and help lay the foundation of a new emancipation whose happy success I may never see.[164]

Again, Alcott contributed to assumptions about slave emancipation being an undertaking that, by the 1870s, was complete. The "new emancipation," for the character of Christie as much as for Alcott herself, was neither chattel slavery nor racial equality but the amelioration of women's subjugation and exploitation in the labor market.

In the last decades of the nineteenth century, other women reformers continued to pursue the question of women's economic self-sufficiency. In 1871, Martha Coffin Wright reflected on how her experiences amongst women's rights reformers in Salt Lake City, Utah, strengthened her resolution to "work to [for] womans' [sic] entire freedom from man's power over her subsistence," which helped her appreciate the extent to which women remained "in slavery to man's dominion."[165] The suffragist and free love advocate Victoria Woodhull similarly observed, in 1873, that the married woman was driven to serve "a drunken tyrant to whom the law has made her slave [sic], both sexually and industrially."[166] Suffragist Abigail Scott Duniway also condemned the fact that "woman's lot" constituted what she perceived as "a lifetime of unpaid servitude and personal sacrifice."[167]

Although postbellum reformers continued to advocate for working-class women and, to a lesser extent, formerly enslaved women, popular culture was defined by quite a different approach. Rather than using discourses of slavery to condemn the subjugation of women, as was the case amongst women reformers, or to accept and rationalize it, as did proslavery advocates, other commentators instead satirized women's labors. One comic valentine (Fig. 5.2), produced between 1840 and 1880, unsympathetically depicted women who worked in domestic service as being constantly at the mercy of their mistress' bell:

---

[164] Alcott, *Work*, 430–431.

[165] Martha Coffin Wright to Ellen Wright Garrison, 14 July 1871, Garrison Family Papers, Series IX: Wright Family—correspondence, Box 301, Sophia Smith Collection.

[166] "The Scare-Crows of Sexual Slavery," American Society of Spiritualists, August 1873, in *Selected Writings of Victoria Woodhull: Suffrage, Free Love, and Eugenics*, ed. Cari M. Carpenter (Lincoln: University of Nebraska Press, 2010), 204.

[167] Abigail Scott Duniway, "Personal Reminiscences," in *"Yours for Liberty": Selections from Abigail Scott Duniway's Suffrage Newspaper*, eds. Jean M. Ward and Elaine A. Maveety (Corvallis: Oregon State University Press, 2000), 11.

Fig. 5.2 William H. Helfand, "You think no doubt you're quite the style," c. 1840–1880. Library Company of Philadelphia, Comic Valentine Collection, 17.16

> You think no doubt you're quite the style
> When you put on that silly smile,
> But no one likes such affectation
> From one in a servants [*sic*] situation
> You give yourself to many airs
> Your proper place should be down stairs
> To skim the pot and make the gravy
> For after all you're but a slavey.

This cartoon expressed no sense of solidarity for those women it deemed to be the "Slave of the Ring!" let alone for formerly enslaved women. But it did recall the criticisms of some female operatives, whose working day and meal breaks were equally shaped by the ring of a bell; this regimentation, they sometimes complained, evoked a comparison with chattel slavery.[168] Neither did an 1878 *Harper's Bazaar* poem, entitled "Sister Slaves" and republished by B.O. Flowers in *Fashion's Slaves* (1892), evoke solidarity with enslaved women. Although not satirical, this poem instead aroused a sense of sentimental pathos and resignation alone. Describing the privileged "victim of Fashion" and the "worn wife" of a farmer as "twin victims," it conceptualized of their experiences as inherently comparable. Further, this poem suggested that working-class married women, the "most hopeless of slaves," had absolutely no capacity to transcend their situation.[169]

Reflecting upon nearly 50 years of the women's rights movement at century's end, Anthony reiterated many of the same concerns that antebellum women reformers had identified. Women could maintain respectability only if they worked like "galley slaves" for their families, she emphasized; many continued to experience social condemnation should they secure "pecuniary independence" through wage work beyond the home.[170] Even as the woman-slave analogy remained central to deconstructing the paradoxes and prejudices surrounding women's labor, white reformers continued to embrace discourses of slavery to describe the labors of white women. But they also drew attention to the importance of social reform as well as the value of women's labor, from the domestic sphere to the market economy. In affirming their own reform endeavors, women reformers articulated the personal fulfillment women gained in working for social reform.

CONCLUSION

Historians contend that the devaluation of women's domestic labor continued well into the twentieth century. The persistent recourse to the woman-slave analogy a century earlier suggests that women reformers' criticisms were unsuccessful, either in drawing attention to the existence

---

[168] Husband, *Antislavery Discourse*, 107.

[169] "Sister Slaves," *Harper's Bazaar* XI, no. 16 (1878): 256–258; B.O. Flower, *Fashion's Slaves* (Boston: The Arena Publishing Co., 1892), 10–11.

[170] Susan B. Anthony, "Status of Woman, Past, Present, and Future," *Arena* 17 (May 1897): 902. For the history of galley slaves, see: Seymour Drescher, *Abolition: A History of Slavery and Antislavery* (Cambridge: Cambridge University Press, 2009), Chapter 2.

or the importance of women's labor. Among reformers, at least, this rhetoric engendered a greater sense of the variety of women's labors and the deprivations that women experienced as a result. Both working-class women and more privileged women embraced discourses of slavery to develop analyses that articulated the tensions surrounding the ideal of domesticity. Some of the antebellum female operatives who embraced discourses of slavery to reclaim their sense of dignity and worth as women workers came to an understanding of capitalist exploitation that encouraged greater reflection on the abuses of chattel slavery. Women's rights reformers looked not only to the possibilities of wage work, but also toward the inequalities of the domestic sphere. African-American reformers most thoroughly explored the connections between the labors of chattel slavery and other forms of wage exploitation.

Both black and white women found a sense of self-worth through their own reform endeavors across myriad social movements. These women reformers, however, often evoked greater concern for women of their own race and class. This was amplified further in the era of slave emancipation, after which many white reformers erroneously believed that the rights of African Americans had been successfully and adequately secured. In the era of slave emancipation, the idea that African Americans could and should become responsible for their own rights fundamentally overlooked the persistence of racism. By contrast, throughout the nineteenth century, African-American reformers expressed greater awareness of the existence of interdependent forms of oppression, a fact demonstrated in their own use of the woman-slave analogy.

PART III

The Politics of Slavery and Emancipation

O, glorious day! O, happy hour!
When woman, conscious of her power,
Shall make her selfish tyrants cower.

From slavery's long and cheerless night
She ushers forth in freedom's light
To preach and plead for truth and right.

Inspired by spirits from above,
As well as her own faith and love,
Man's full compeer she'll surely prove.

Prof. J.H. Cook, "Woman's Coming Power,"
Woodhull and Claflin's Weekly, 27 February 1875

CHAPTER 6

"Political Slaves": Suffrage, Anti-suffrage, and Tyranny

When Susan B. Anthony addressed the Territorial Legislature of Washington, DC, in October 1871, she described a perspective that had recently gained currency amongst suffragists. In the Fourteenth Amendment's "clause [about] 'involuntary servitude,' a special allusion is made to woman. By all men's definitions of the term," she continued, "the withholding of the ballot and representation while taxes are imposed, is the most abject of servitude."[1] Echoing one of the foremost complaints of the revolutionary generation, of the injustice of taxes being imposed without representation, Anthony explicitly implicated women in its parameters. However, as Reconstruction-era debates about the proposed amendments to the US Constitution demonstrated, lawmakers had no desire to interpret any new legislation relating to slave emancipation as potentially inclusive of women. Women's rights reformers and suffragists, in contrast, still aspired that the vast political changes taking place would indeed encompass women. By explicitly inscribing themselves as an enslaved class, white reformers attempted to write women into the purview of the Reconstruction amendments. As Matilda Joslyn Gage concluded in the centennial year of 1876: "The men alone of this country live

---

[1] Susan B. Anthony, Speech to the Territorial Legislature of Washington, 19 October 1871, in *The Selected Papers of Elizabeth Cady Stanton and Susan B. Anthony*, Vol. II, ed. Ann Gordon (New Brunswick: Rutgers University Press, 1997), 458.

© The Author(s) 2019
A. Stevenson, *The Woman as Slave in Nineteenth-Century American Social Movements*, Palgrave Studies in the History of Social Movements, https://doi.org/10.1007/978-3-030-24467-5_6

in a republic, the women enter the second hundred years of national life as political slaves."[2]

Evelyn Nakano Glenn describes citizenship as representing the individual's full membership in the political community, as well as the symbolic and material rights and privileges that ensue. An ever more inclusive ideal of male citizenship expanded alongside Jacksonian democracy. However, this citizen was defined against the noncitizen—aliens, enslaved people, and women. Civil citizenship entailed "equality before the law, freedom of contract, and protection of person and property," yet political citizenship—the franchise—was considered "a privilege reserved for those who were qualified to exercise it."[3] The institution of marriage also transformed the legal and civil status of women. As Nancy F. Cott demonstrates, this institution rendered the married couple one in the eyes of the law and the husband became the "one *full* citizen in the household."[4]

Historians emphasize that the majority of white suffragists, whether consciously or not, pursued the vote for themselves alone after the Civil War of 1861 to 1865.[5] However, the degree to which this occurred in the context of the transformation of the woman-slave analogy has not been adequately explored. To fully understand the range of responses to the Reconstruction amendments, it is necessary to consider how and why women's rights reformers sought to redefine who could be considered a disenfranchised "slave" in the aftermath of slave emancipation. This new legislation transformed the relationship between the state and formerly enslaved people of African descent from enslaved to legally free; noncitizen to citizen; and disenfranchisement to African-American manhood suffrage. Women's rights reformers and suffragists responded by proclaiming that women, too, were an "enslaved"

[2] Matilda Joslyn Gage, "Call for the May Anniversary," 1876, *History of Woman Suffrage* (hereafter *HWS*), Vol. III, eds. Elizabeth Cady Stanton, Susan B. Anthony and Matilda Joslyn Gage (Rochester: Susan B. Anthony, 1886), 18.

[3] Evelyn Nakano Glenn, *Unequal Freedom: How Race and Gender Shaped American Citizenship and Labor* (Cambridge: Harvard University Press, 2002), 19, 20, 26.

[4] Nancy F. Cott, *Public Vows: A History of Marriage and the Nation* (Cambridge: Harvard University Press, 2000), 11–12, 95–96.

[5] Marjorie Spruill Wheeler, ed. *One Woman, One Vote: Rediscovering the Woman Suffrage Movement* (Troutdale: NewSage Press, 1995); Rosalyn Terborg-Penn, *African American Women in the Struggle for the Vote, 1850–1920* (Bloomington: Indiana University Press, 1998), esp. 166. Other historians emphasize the degree to which the women's rights and suffrage movements progressed toward an ever-greater focus on white women's rights by century's end, see: Louise Michele Newman, *White Women's Rights: The Racial Origins of Feminism in the United States* (New York: Oxford University Press, 1999).

class—often literally rather than figuratively. Some argued that, since women had been one of the antebellum era's classes of enslaved people, they should also be the beneficiaries of Reconstruction. As a result, a subtle transformation took place in their use of the woman-slave analogy. While the embrace of discourses of slavery did not disappear, the success of slave emancipation inspired the earlier focus on women and slaves to become a more emphatic comparison based on the categories of sex and race. This was a particularly dangerous rhetorical transformation, given the precarious freedom enjoyed by African Americans in the postbellum era. Many white suffragists believed that, if women failed to be considered in the radical transformations taking place in their midst, then women would be the only enslaved class that remained.

Revolutionary Beginnings

During the revolutionary era, the slavery analogy had been central to anti-colonial political rebellion and nascent expressions of citizenship.[6] The jurist and founding father James Wilson understood all free people—including women—to be citizens, though he also understood that not all citizens would be imbued with voting rights. This meant that women's participation in civil society, Jan Lewis suggests, would come to be "defined in relationship to that of free blacks." It was a connection derived from the assumption that, while both had the potential to be citizens and members of civil society, both classes would remain disenfranchised.[7]

In 1776, Abigail Adams articulated her concerns about women's lack of political status to her husband, the founding father John Adams. Historians suggest that Abigail was a woman of vast contradictions. In spite of her outspoken support of the American Revolution of 1765 to 1783, she was politically conservative. Still, she detested injustice, from Britain's control of the American colonies to women's disempowerment and the enslavement of Africans.[8] Deeply influenced by the era's patriotic rhetoric and actively involved in her husband's political career, Abigail advocated on behalf of women

[6] Bernard Bailyn, *The Ideological Origins of the American Revolution* (Cambridge: Belknap Press, 1967); François Furstenberg, "Beyond Freedom and Slavery: Autonomy, Virtue, and Resistance in Early American Political Discourse," *Journal of American History* 89, no. 4 (2003): 1300–1301.

[7] Jan Lewis, "'Of Every Age Sex & Condition': The Representation of Women in the Constitution," *Journal of the Early Republic* 15, no. 3 (1995): 382.

[8] Lynne Withey, *Dearest Friend: A Life of Abigail Adams* (New York: Free Press, 1981), x.

during the drafting of the Declaration of Independence.[9] Men were "Naturally Tyrannical," she believed; happiness could only be found by those who "willingly give up the harsh title of Master for the more tender and endearing one of Friend." Abigail rebuked men who treat women "only as the vassals of your Sex" and emphasized the importance of women's political voice:

> I can not say that I think you very generous to the Ladies, for whilst you are proclaiming peace and good will to Men, Emancipating all Nations, you insist upon retaining an absolute power over Wives. ... [W]e have it in our power not only to free ourselves but to subdue our Masters, and without violence throw both your natural and legal authority at our feet –
>
> Charm by accepting, by submitting sway
> Yet have our Humor most when we obey.[10]

John Adams, who aspired to create unity among the colonies, was unlikely to introduce the potentially divisive issues of chattel slavery or women's rights into political debate.[11] That Abigail Adams interpreted women's disenfranchisement as a form of political oppression that warranted criticism situates her as something of a predecessor to nineteenth-century reformers—not only in terms of her ethos, but also her rhetoric.

Petitioning soon became a means through which disenfranchised groups could hope to influence politics. The First Amendment of 1791 encouraged freedom of speech and guaranteed the right of the disenfranchised to petition for a redress of grievances. The capacity to act on these rights, however, remained highly contested. After the American Anti-Slavery Society (AASS) prioritized petitioning campaigns, women began to engage in antislavery petitioning early in the 1830s. Increasingly emboldened, female antislavery societies produced what Susan Zaeske describes as a "major outpouring of discourse aimed at encouraging female activism and articulating in greater detail an emerging ideology of female citizenship."[12] As these campaigns gathered force, the US Congress passed

---

[9] Edith B. Gelles, *First Thoughts: Life and Letters of Abigail Adams* (New York: Twayne Publishers, 1998), 14.

[10] Abigail Adams to John Adams, 31 March 1776 and 7 May 1776, Adams Family Papers, Massachusetts Historical Society.

[11] Gelles, *First Thoughts*, 16–17.

[12] Susan Zaeske, *Signatures of Citizenship: Petitioning, Antislavery, and Women's Political Identity* (Chapel Hill: University of North Carolina Press, 2003), 72.

a series of gag rules between 1836 and 1840—only to be repealed in 1844. The gag rules, which resulted in the tabling of all antislavery petitions, reconfigured what it meant to be a disenfranchised citizen. When southern congressmen attempted to inhibit the abundance of petitions that continued to be submitted, largely from female antislavery societies, Congressman John Quincy Adams spearheaded a free speech campaign. This rendered him something of an antislavery hero. As Sarah Grimké reflected: "Woman has been placed by John Quincy Adams, side by side with the slave, whilst he was contending for the right side of petition."[13] One unintended consequence was that the controversy broadened the public's antislavery awareness, especially in the North. Between the 1830s and 1860s, women dominated antislavery petitioning in their collective attempts to influence the government against chattel slavery, developing an increasingly political identity in the process.[14]

The petitioning of female antislavery societies, in conjunction with the practice of metempsychosis, further advanced the relationship that abolitionist women envisaged between themselves and enslaved people of African descent. Some viewed the gag rule as silencing women in a manner that was comparable to how chattel slavery silenced enslaved people.[15] The Grimké sisters believed that women had the right to influence politics and legislative reform because, enfranchised or not, women were citizens who had a duty to be politically engaged.[16] Angelina Grimké became the first woman to address the Massachusetts State Legislature in 1837. Her unprecedented address accompanied petitions that contained the names of thousands of women.[17] "I stand before you as a citizen, on behalf of the 20,000 women of Massachusetts, whose names are enrolled on petitions

---

[13] Sarah M. Grimké, *Letters on the Equality of the Sexes, and the Condition of Woman: Addressed to Mary S. Parker* (Boston: Isaac Knapp, 1837/1838), 12.

[14] See: Zaeske, *Signatures of Citizenship*; Gerda Lerner, *The Grimké Sisters from South Carolina: Pioneers for Women's Rights and Abolition* (Chapel Hill: University of North Carolina Press, 2004), 193–194.

[15] Gerda Lerner, *The Feminist Thought of Sarah Grimké*, ed. Gerda Lerner (New York: Oxford University Press, 1979/1998), 177; Anna M. Speicher, *The Religious World of Antislavery Women: Spirituality in the Lives of Five Abolitionist Lecturers* (New York: Syracuse University Press, 2000), 109.

[16] Alison M. Parker, *Articulating Rights: Nineteenth-Century American Women on Race, Reform, and the State* (DeKalb: Northern Illinois University Press, 2010), 73, 77.

[17] Katharine du Pre Lumpkin, *The Emancipation of Angelina Grimké* (Chapel Hill: University of North Carolina Press, 1974), 130–131; Jean Fagan Yellin, *Women and Sisters: The Antislavery Feminists in American Culture* (New Haven: Yale University Press, 1989), 40–42.

which have been submitted to the Legislature," she testified. A repentant slaveholder, Angelina Grimké characterized herself as a southerner and a "moral being" who had been unwillingly exiled from her birthplace because of chattel slavery. Expressing her personal identification with the enslaved women for whom she pled, she stated: "I feel that I owe it to the suffering slave ... to do all that I can to overturn a system of complicated crimes, ... cemented by the blood and sweat and tears of my sisters in bonds."[18] Similarly, Sarah Grimké examined the "Legal Disabilities of Women" in her *Letters on the Equality of the Sexes, and the Condition of Woman* (1837). Women had "no political existence," she argued, and were merely "counted, like the slaves of the South," to proportionally increase the number of legislators.[19] Acknowledging how the legal disabilities and disenfranchisement of free and enslaved women differed, Grimké considered the specific points at which the rights of free versus enslaved women both did and did not coalesce.

The ministers, educators, and lawmakers who challenged women's constitutional right to petition against chattel slavery found it unbecoming for women to be involved in politics. Some abolitionist men continued to express their reservations about women's antislavery efforts. According to Allison M. Parker, these men sought to reframe petitioning as "an ineffective tool that was used as a last resort by white women and slaves who could not participate directly at the polls."[20] Some women also remained conflicted about the increasing prominence of abolitionist women. Catharine Beecher's *An Essay on Slavery and Abolitionism, with reference to the Duty of American Females* (1837) argued that women should refrain from petitioning and should not have a vocal role in abolitionism. Since petitioning was the "only political right that women have," Angelina Grimké responded, "why not let them exercise it whenever they are aggrieved?"[21] The controversy that the Grimké sisters were generating led the General Association of Congregationalist Clergy of Massachusetts, in July 1837, to issue a Pastoral Letter that directly condemned their endeavours. The *Liberator* responded by publishing a satirical poem by John Greenleaf Whittier:

[18] "Angelina E. Grimke," *Liberator*, 2 March 1838.
[19] Grimké, *Letters*, 46.
[20] Parker, *Articulating Rights*, 71.
[21] Angelina E. Grimké, *Letters to Catherine E. Beecher, in Reply to an Essay on Slavery and Abolitionism, Addressed to A.E. Grimké* (Boston: Isaac Knapp, 1837), 112.

> So, this is all—the utmost reach
> Of priestly power the mind to fetter!
> When laymen think—when women preach –
> A war of words—a "Pastoral Letter!" ...
>
> What marvel, if the people learn
> To claim the right of free opinion?
> What marvel, if at times they spurn
> The ancient yoke of your dominion?[22]

However, rather than inhibiting women's antislavery efforts, this only worked to inspire other budding women reformers. As Lucy Stone later recalled: "If I had felt bound to silence before by interpretation of Scriptures, or believed that equal rights did not belong to woman, that pastoral letter broke my bonds."[23] Women's rights reformers would not forget the significance of this episode, as later evinced in Volume I of the *History of Woman Suffrage*.[24]

The following decade witnessed the emergence of a fledgling movement dedicated to women's rights. At the first women's rights convention, held in 1848 in Seneca Falls, New York, Elizabeth Cady Stanton and her co-authors penned a Declaration of Sentiments, which was signed by a third of all attendees.[25] Modeling their statement on the 1776 Declaration of Independence enabled women's rights reformers to immediately elicit the public's attention.[26] The 1848 statement, however, was inspired not only by the Declaration of Independence but also by a far more recent antislavery statement: the AASS's own 1833 Declaration of Sentiments.[27] As the 1848 Declaration of Sentiments professed fifteen years later:

> The history of mankind is a history of repeated injuries and usurpations on the part of man toward woman, having in direct object the establishment of an absolute tyranny over her.

---

[22] "Lines," *Liberator*, 20 October 1837. See: Lerner, *Grimké Sisters*, 133.

[23] Lucy Stone, "Workers for the Cause," c. 1888, Blackwell Family Papers, Library of Congress, in Blanche Glassman Hersh, *The Slavery of Sex: Feminist-Abolitionists in America* (Urbana: University of Illinois Press, 1978), 23.

[24] Elizabeth Cady Stanton, Susan B. Anthony, and Matilda Joslyn Gage, eds. *HWS*, Vol. I (Rochester: Susan B. Anthony, 1881), 81–87.

[25] Lisa Tetrault, *The Myth of Seneca Falls: Memory and the Women's Suffrage Movement, 1848–1898* (Chapel Hill: University of North Carolina Press, 2014), 12.

[26] Judith Wellman, "The Seneca Falls Women's Rights Convention: A Study of Social Networks," *Journal of Women's History* 3, no. 1 (1991): 9.

[27] Zaeske, *Signatures of Citizenship*, 178.

Its ninth resolution emphasized that such "tyranny" was achieved because man "has never permitted her to exercise her inalienable right to the elective franchise."[28] However, woman suffrage held only marginal significance as yet. Although some delegates were reluctant to foreground this demand for fear of ridicule, Frederick Douglass encouraged Stanton not to yield in advocating for woman suffrage.[29] From its very beginnings, discourses of slavery and tyranny were at the center of how the women's rights movement conceived of its imperatives.[30]

So, too, were discourses of emancipation. What Ellen Carol DuBois describes as the "generation of 1848" discussed human freedom and equality as ideals alongside specific calls for citizenship and enfranchisement in both Europe and the United States. A belief in "freedom" and "emancipation" constituted the ideal toward which the critics of many forms of oppression were striving.[31] The revolutionary ferment across Europe resulted in many "emancipatory initiatives" in this single year, during which political discussions encouraged reconsiderations of women's enfranchisement—of which the first women's rights convention in Seneca Falls, New York, was a part.[32] Only two weeks later, another women's rights convention was held in Rochester, New York. It was here, the *History of Woman Suffrage* editorialized, that Douglass and fellow abolitionists William C. Nell and William C. Bloss "advocated the emancipation of women from all the artificial disabilities, imposed by false custom, creeds, and codes."[33] As women's rights reformers began to conceptualize suffrage as an essential element of women's citizenship, reformers routinely turned to discourses of slavery, tyranny, and emancipation to frame this demand.

The abolition of chattel slavery remained a central concern for these antebellum reformers, however. At an 1850 women's rights convention in

---

[28] Declaration of Sentiments and Resolutions, 19–20 July 1848, Elizabeth Cady Stanton and Susan B. Anthony Papers Project, Rutgers University.

[29] Elisabeth Griffith, *In Her Own Right: The Life of Elizabeth Cady Stanton* (New York: Oxford University Press, 1984), 54–57.

[30] David Brion Davis, "Declaring Equality: Sisterhood and Slavery," in *Women's Rights and Transatlantic Antislavery in the Era of Emancipation*, eds. Kathryn Kish Sklar and James Brewer Stewart (New Haven: Yale University Press, 2007), 5.

[31] Ellen Carol DuBois, "Ernestine Rose's Jewish Origins and the Varieties of Euro-American Emancipation in 1848," in *Women's Rights and Transatlantic Antislavery*, 280.

[32] Karen Offen, "Women and the Question of 'Universal' Suffrage in 1848: A Transatlantic Comparison of Suffragist Rhetoric," *NWSA Journal* 11, no. 1 (1999): 155.

[33] "The Rochester Convention, August 2, 1848," *HWS*, Vol. I, 76.

Worcester, Massachusetts, a unanimous resolution encouraged an inclusive advancement of women's rights, regardless of race or free status:

> [T]he cause we have met to advocate,—the claim for woman of all her natural and civil rights,—bids us remember the two millions of slave women at the South, the most grossly wronged and foully outraged of all women; ... we will [remember] ... the trampled womanhood of the plantation, and omit no effort to raise it to a share in the rights we claim for ourselves.[34]

Such an explicit recognition of the rights of all women, including that of enslaved women, was sometimes evident at other women's rights conventions and in reform newspapers before the Civil War. One contributor to the *Una*, for example, suggested that women's enfranchisement would "ennoble and elevate [woman] as a moral and intellectual being," proposing that disenfranchisement was "always debasing" and had the same result as African slavery.[35] Ernestine Rose, the first woman to lobby for married women's property rights, invoked what amounted to a personal refrain at both abolitionist and women's rights conventions: "I go for the recognition of human rights, without distinction of sect, party, sex, or color."[36]

In the process, women's rights reformers began to reimagine the meaning of "universal suffrage," arguing that reformers should advocate the enfranchisement of all people—women and men, black and white. As Carole Pateman emphasizes, the phrase's original intent was to advocate the universal enfranchisement of men; that "universal" actually signifies "fraternal," she argues, has been a distinction almost exclusively realized by feminists.[37] This realization interacted with women reformers' embrace of the woman-slave analogy. At the 1853 women's rights convention in Cleveland, Ohio, Rose expressed her belief that the "republican principle of universal suffrage" should either include women or admit that it promoted "'Freedom and Power to one half of society, and submission and slavery to the other.' Give woman the elective franchise."[38] Even as women's rights

---

[34] *Proceedings of the Woman's Rights Convention, Held at Worcester, October 23rd & 24th, 1850* (Boston: Prentiss & Sawyer, 1851), 17.

[35] Mrs. S.T. Martyn, "The Right of Woman to the Elective Franchise," *Una*, February 1854.

[36] "West India Emancipation: Mrs. Rose's Speech," *National Anti-Slavery Standard*, 13 August 1853.

[37] Carol Pateman, *The Sexual Contract* (Stanford: Stanford University Press, 1988), 78.

[38] Ernestine L. Rose, "The Second National Woman's Rights Convention in Worcester," 15 October 1851, *HWS*, Vol. I, 240.

reformers were beginning to describe women as an enslaved class, this occurred in the context of enslaved people of African descent remaining what most antebellum reformers would have envisioned as the primary enslaved class. At the same time, however, white women reformers were increasingly beginning to consider themselves as experiencing an actual state of slavery. Some of the women's rights movement's imperatives, especially the Married Women's Property Acts, gained a measure of success prior to the Civil War—a moment at which, Elizabeth B. Clark suggests, discourses of slavery began to acquire "new value as a language of political opposition."[39]

From Woman and Slave to Sex and Race

The decades surrounding the Civil War witnessed a transformation in the use of the woman-slave analogy. Historians scrutinize the degree to which women's rights reformers became preoccupied with the race-versus-gender politics of the 1860s.[40] However, this is not often contextualized in terms of their earlier mobilization of the woman-slave analogy or its changing implications in the era of slave emancipation. Across the 1850s, the rhetoric of prominent white women's rights reformers had created some tensions. Although African-American reformers did not necessarily refute the woman-slave analogy, some began to repudiate its racist tendencies. After the Civil War, women's rights reformers and suffragists began to approach the meaning and implications of one's "enslaved" status more emphatically.[41] Many white suffragists simultaneously responded to the political climate by pursuing a comparison that was less between woman and slave and more between sex and race.

The intensifying focus on sex and race was deeply embroiled in reformers' abiding recourse to the woman-slave analogy, together with perceived

---

[39] Elizabeth B. Clark, "Matrimonial Bonds: Slavery and Divorce in Nineteenth-Century America," *Law & History Review* 8, no. 1 (1990): 31.

[40] For example, see: Ellen Carol DuBois, *Feminism and Suffrage: The Emergence of an Independent Women's Movement in America, 1848–1869* (Ithaca: Cornell University Press, 1978); Paula J. Giddings, *When and Where I Enter* (New York: HarperCollins, 1984/2009), esp. 60–70; Ann D. Gordon, "Stanton on the Right to Vote: On Account of Race or Sex," in *Elizabeth Cady Stanton, Feminist as Thinker: A Reader in Documents and Essays*, eds. Ellen Carol Dubois and Richard Cándida Smith (New York: New York University Press, 2007); Jen McDaneld, "Harper, Historiography, and the Race/Gender Opposition in Feminism," *Signs: Journal of Women in Culture and Society* 40, no. 2 (2015): 393–415.

[41] See: Kathleen Barry, *Susan B. Anthony: A Biography of a Singular Feminist* (New York: New York University Press, 1988), Chapter 6.

distinctions between enslaved people of African descent and free people of color. As Paulina Wright Davis, for example, declared in 1853:

> Women and negroes, in marriage and singleness, in slavery, and in nominal freedom, stand on the same platform and hold the *same* position in the laws, customs, and conduct of business in the freest government on earth!

These proclamations were founded on the sense of analogical sameness that Carla L. Peterson so astutely observes.[42] But they also cultivated an important sense of difference. Indeed, Davis also observed what she perceived as important distinctions: women experienced the "slavery" of marriage or the "nominal freedom" of spinsterhood; and "negroes," in turn, experienced either chattel slavery or a version of freedom that could only ever be partial. Widows and maidens, she continued, even if "released from the bondage of domestic masterdom," still suffered "like the free negro" on account of "all the disqualifications and oppressions of caste." Davis perceived that "sex, as absolutely as color, denie[d] … all the political rights of citizenship."[43] Women's rights reformers increasingly conceived of a continuum of freedom and unfreedom upon which women and African Americans could hold both similar and different positions.

In 1854, Elizabeth Cady Stanton addressed the New York State Legislature to describe the legal disabilities of women. Although she, too, recognized the differing status between women and free people of color, Stanton also expressed resentment toward the rights accorded free black men. Offering little support for their enfranchisement, she censured the "superior position" that black men supposedly held over the "wives and mothers" of New York State. To challenge lawmakers unable to comprehend "the idea that men and women are alike," Stanton used the example of chattel slavery:

> It is impossible to make the southern planter believe that his slave feels and reasons …—that injustice and subjection are as galling as to him—that the degradation of living by the will of another, … is as keenly felt by him as his master. … He says, the slave does not feel this as I would.

[42] Carla L. Peterson, "'And We Claim Our Rights': The Rights Rhetoric of Black and White Women Activists before the Civil War," in *Sister Circle: Black Women and Work*, ed. Sharon Harley and the Black Women and Work Collective (New Brunswick: Rutgers University Press, 2002).
[43] "Pecuniary Independence of Woman," *Una*, December 1853.

Stanton neither misunderstood nor condoned the exploitation engendered by chattel slavery. However, her condemnation of the laws that classed disenfranchised women "with idiots, lunatics, and negroes," but which offered some political rights to free black men, expressed none of the sympathy Stanton sometimes reserved for enslaved people of African descent.[44]

This was the moment at which Stanton began to provoke the ire of her fellow reformers more frequently, to the point where some started to dispute her rhetoric. Frederick Douglass endorsed the pamphlet version of Stanton's 1854 speech and, significantly, did not refute her analysis of women's oppression per se. What Douglass did criticize was her erstwhile focus on "*white women*" and her "seeming assumption" of women's "superiority over negroes." While he viewed women as having "as good a right" to enfranchisement as African Americans, Douglass could not "grant even as a matter of rhetoric or argument, that she has a better." Finding this to be a "slight blemish" on what he considered an otherwise "eloquent" analysis of "woman's wrongs," Douglass reiterated that "we don't like now-a-days to be classed with 'idiots or lunatics' more than do our fair sisters."[45] As Faye E. Dudden emphasizes, Douglass realized that Stanton's rhetoric could arise not necessarily from personal conviction, but from a sense of pragmatism or the perspective of argumentation. However, he also understood that this political strategy had the potential to incite racism.[46] This suggests that Douglass did not necessarily consider the woman-slave analogy to be inherently racist; he and other African Americans had periodically used similar rhetoric to describe women's oppression and disenfranchisement themselves. What Douglass rejected was Stanton's lack of rhetorical judiciousness, which could so easily sustain ideas about white supremacy.

Despite burgeoning criticisms from fellow reformers, Stanton persisted with this approach during her 1860 address to the New York State Legislature. This address, which supported married women's property rights, echoed Sarah Grimké's earlier conclusions about the legal status of

---

[44] Elizabeth Cady Stanton, Address to the Legislature of New York, 14/20 February, 1854, in *The Selected Papers of Elizabeth Cady Stanton and Susan B. Anthony*, Vol. I, ed. Ann D. Gordon (New Brunswick: Rutgers University Press, 1997), 240.

[45] "Address to the Legislature of the State of New York," *Frederick Douglass' Paper*, 3 March 1854.

[46] Faye E. Dudden, *Fighting Chance: The Struggle over Woman Suffrage and Black Suffrage in Reconstruction America* (Oxford: Oxford University Press, 2011), 43.

women and enslaved people. Grimké, however, had observed legal similarities as well as differences and understood chattel slavery to be the more egregious institution. Stanton, by contrast, found the legal status of women to be less favorable than that of free men of color. Her address was grounded in a sex-race analogy as much as the woman-slave analogy. "The prejudice against color," Stanton suggested, "is no stronger than that against sex." Both, she continued, were "produced by the same cause, and manifested very much in the same way":

> The negro's skin and the woman's sex are both *prima facie* evidence that they were intended to be in subjection to the white Saxon man. The few social privileges which the man gives the woman, he makes up to the negro in civil rights. ... Now, with the black man's right to suffrage, ... the prejudice against sex is more deeply rooted and more unreasonably maintained than that against color. As citizens of a republic, which should we most highly prize, social privileges or civil rights? The latter, most certainly.[47]

This address, which Stanton called "A Slave's Appeal," directly contributed to the passage of the Married Women's Property Act by the New York Assembly.[48] The "slave" in her appeal was not an enslaved person, but a free white woman.

The Civil War and its aftermath changed the rhetorical framework that undergirded the manner in which women's rights reformers used discourses of slavery. Many antebellum reformers had advocated for the rights of both free women and enslaved people of African descent, while also appreciating the distinctions between civil and political rights. When the Civil War united reformers dedicated to the abolition of chattel slavery, woman suffrage temporarily became only a latent goal. Yet, while women's rights reformers believed that abolitionism was morally right, some anticipated that slave emancipation would inspire a reconsideration of the rights of all free people, a process from which they believed women should benefit.[49] "I want to be identified with the negro," Angelina Grimké Weld reflected in May 1863. "[U]ntil he gets his rights, we shall never have ours."[50] Only

---

[47] Elizabeth Cady Stanton, New York State Legislature, 18 February 1860, *HWS*, Vol. I, 681.

[48] Griffith, *In Her Own Right*, 100–101.

[49] Dudden, *Fighting Chance*, 48–49, 50–51.

[50] Angelina Grimké Weld, Woman's National Loyal League, 14 May 1863, *HWS*, Vol. II, eds. Elizabeth Cady Stanton, Susan B. Anthony, and Matilda Joslyn Gage (Rochester: Susan B. Anthony, 1881), 61.

months after President Abraham Lincoln issued the Emancipation Proclamation in January 1863 did Grimké Weld articulate this desire. Abolitionists and women's rights reformers became increasingly influenced not only by chattel slavery but also by the prospect of slave emancipation, embracing both references to enslaved people and "negroes" to construct an analogy for the situation of women.

Many women reformers joined the Woman's National Loyal League (WNLL), a new organization aligned with the Radical Republicans, to spearhead a petitioning campaign in support of a Thirteenth Amendment.[51] Founded by Anthony and Stanton, the WNLL equated women and enslaved people in its emphasis on "political equality," as epitomized in its fifth resolution:

> [T]he property, the liberty and the lives of all slaves, all citizens of African descent, and all women are placed at the mercy of a legislation in which they are not represented. ... There never can be a true peace in this Republic until the civil and political equality of every subject of the Government shall be practically established.

Most of the addresses heard at the WNLL's first convention were dedicated to antislavery themes, although some extended their analysis to women. As Ernestine Rose stated, "it is a painful fact that woman under the law, until very recently, has been entirely in the same category with the slave."[52] The WNLL interpreted "freedom" as the universal extension of equal rights and enfranchisement, for black and white men together with all women. As Dudden explains, this organization "defined loyalty to encompass emancipation, defined emancipation to imply equal rights, and defined equal rights as extending across race *and* gender lines."[53]

The ratification of the Thirteenth Amendment in 1865 abolished chattel slavery throughout the United States. This did not lead to racial equality, however; the subsequent years instead witnessed racial violence and

---

[51] Wendy F. Hamand, "The Woman's National Loyal League: Feminist Abolitionists and the Civil War," *Civil War History* 35, no. 1 (1989): 39–58; Zaeske, *Signatures of Citizenship*, 168–172; Dudden, *Fighting Chance*, esp. 51–58.

[52] *Proceedings of the Meeting of the Loyal Women of the Republic, held in New York, May 14, 1863* (New York: Phair & Co., 1863), 15, 21.

[53] Not all delegates explicitly supported equal rights, however. A Mrs. Hoyt from Wisconsin viewed "women's rights as an unpopular 'ism'" that would draw attention away from the sectional conflict. Dudden, *Fighting Chance*, 51.

draconian black codes become institutionalized across the South. But it certainly transformed the rhetorical framework that undergirded the woman-slave analogy, as the Thirteenth Amendment decreed that chattel slavery was, technically, no longer in existence. Evelyn Brooks Higginbotham argues that prior to the Civil War, the "social context for the construction of race as a tool for black oppression" had been chattel slavery. One of the results of slave emancipation, however, was that race alone would become the distinctive category of otherness as well as the antithesis to whiteness.[54] As debates about extending the franchise to African-American men ensued, abolitionists and women's rights reformers highlighted the degree to which these political developments facilitated a new focus on race rather than chattel slavery alone.

The Radical Republicans advocated African-American manhood suffrage, but quickly withdrew their support for woman suffrage, believing that it would impede the likelihood of success for freedmen's enfranchisement. A month after Lincoln's April 1865 assassination, abolitionist Wendell Phillips declared in his first address as president of the AASS: "As Abraham Lincoln said, 'One war at a time'; so I say, One question at a time. This hour belongs to the negro."[55] Although he had been a longtime supporter of women's rights, Phillips sought to compel reformers to defer to manhood suffrage so as to maximize its chance for success.[56] Biographer James Brewer Stewart observes that Phillips took what might be described as the "correct historical position," for abolitionism had never demanded affiliation with "extraneous issues"—temperance, pacifism, or even women's rights—as a measure of allegiance.[57] The "unprovoked" nature of Phillips' divisive outburst, DuBois suggests, is indicative of the "obvious and compelling" connection between woman suffrage and African-American manhood suffrage during the early Reconstruction era.[58]

Perhaps, however, Phillips' outburst was not wholly unprovoked. African-American manhood suffrage remained a controversial platform

---

[54] Evelyn Brooks Higginbotham, "African-American Women's History and the Metalanguage of Race," *Signs: Journal of Women in Culture and Society* 17, no. 2 (1992): 256.

[55] "Thirty Second Anniversary of the American Antislavery Society: Speech of Wendell Phillips, Esq.," *National AntiSlavery Standard*, 13 May 1865.

[56] Dudden, *Fighting Chance*, 8; Gordon, *Selected Papers*, Vol. I, 565.

[57] James Brewer Stewart, *Wendell Phillips: Liberty's Hero* (Baton Rouge: Louisiana State University Press, 1986), 283.

[58] DuBois, *Feminism and Suffrage*, 60.

Fig. 6.1 "The Two Platforms," 1866. Library Company of Philadelphia Print Department, Political Cartoons: 1866–1868, 9387.F

that faced much resistance—amongst lawmakers as much as in popular culture (Fig. 6.1). Moreover, beyond the nucleus of antebellum reform culture, neither African Americans nor women were widely believed to have the capacity for enfranchisement. Some of the lawmakers who sought to prove that citizenship did not necessarily include political rights or enfranchisement also looked toward the legal and political status of other disenfranchised groups. When Republican Congressmen John Bingham and Lyman Trumbull tried to justify freedmen's continued disenfranchisement in 1866, for example, they cited the fact that half of the white adult population who were considered to be citizens—women—were not, in fact, voters.[59] Lawmakers, much like women's rights reformers, sensed the potency of a comparison between race and sex, but pursued it to distinctly oppositional ends.

[59] Cott, *Public Vows*, 95–97.

The rhetorical substance of the women's rights movement, in contrast, had been predicated on the woman-slave analogy for decades. Increasingly coming to regard the characteristics associated with sex and race as merely incidental, an accident of birth, women reformers emphasized the individual's natural right to enfranchisement.[60] Since the Reconstruction amendments resulted in freedmen's enfranchisement, women's rights reformers found the idea of *women*'s "emancipation" and enfranchisement highly compelling. Yet, when the opportunity to demand universal suffrage arose, Phillips and other abolitionists demurred. This suggests that those abolitionists and women's rights reformers who did embrace a woman-as-slave worldview were becoming equally convinced of the sex-race analogy, which would imply that manhood suffrage should demand woman suffrage. While working to secure the Thirteenth Amendment, women's rights reformers had believed that the "principle of unconditional emancipation led directly to that of universal enfranchisement."[61] Other reformers, however, had always expressed varying levels of acceptance toward the rights of women being synonymous with the antislavery movement. The earlier prominence of the woman-slave analogy offers further context for Phillips' comments, informs the general impetus amongst former abolitionists and Radical Republicans to prioritize manhood suffrage, and illustrates why so many white women's rights reformers were so disappointed by their fellow reformers.

In direct contrast to Phillips, Stanton and Anthony believed that woman suffrage was a timely issue that would not impede, but may even assist, African-American manhood suffrage. As Stanton mockingly challenged:

"This is the negro's hour." ... Have not "black male citizens" been heard to say they doubted the wisdom of extending the right of suffrage to women? Why should the African prove more just and generous than his Saxon compeers?

If the two millions [*sic*] of Southern black women are not to be secured in their rights of person, property, wages, and children, their emancipation is but another form of slavery. In fact, it is better to be the slave of an educated white man, than of a degraded, ignorant black one.

---

[60] Ellen Carol DuBois, "Outgrowing the Compact of the Fathers: Equal Rights, Woman Suffrage, and the United States Constitution, 1820–1878," *Journal of American History* 74, no. 3 (1987): 845–846.
[61] Ibid., 845.

Stanton thus resorted to her antebellum claims about marriage and labor, as well as to racism, to suggest that freedwomen of color had, following slave emancipation, merely graduated to the enslaved status accorded to free white women. As Stanton concluded, "the disfranchised all make the same demand, and the same logic and justice that secures Suffrage to one class gives it to all."[62] While her political approach signaled the racism that would become increasingly common among white suffragists, Stanton was not alone in questioning Phillips' claim. "When has she ever claimed that 'this is woman's hour?' When has she ever asked the negro to wait one moment for her?" Parker Pillsbury asked in 1869. "Never! Nowhere! Side by side with the negro is all she asks."[63]

Some former abolitionists and women's rights reformers united to commit themselves to the goal of universal suffrage. The American Equal Rights Association (AERA) was established in May 1866 at the Eleventh National Woman's Rights Convention in New York City, under the leadership of Stanton, Anthony, and Lucretia Mott. Since "our most professed friends forgot us [women]," Lucy Stone reflected of the AERA's formation, "we resolved to make common cause with the colored class—the only other disfranchised class—and strike for equal rights for all."[64] To advocate universal suffrage, many of the reformers involved with the AERA emphasized the commonalities between the status of women and freedpeople of color. Stanton expressed her hope "to see the Anti-Slavery and Woman's Rights organizations merged into an Equal Rights association, as the two questions were now one and the same." All that African-American men and women—regardless of race—sought, she claimed, was "the right of suffrage."[65] Stanton and Anthony were equally desirous of merging the antislavery and women's rights movements, both as social movements and theoretical approaches. The AERA presented a timely opportunity to pursue "*universal suffrage*" as the "Woman's Rights platform," according to Anthony. These social movements, she believed, needed to transform "in *name*—what it ever has been in *spirit*—a Human

[62] E. Cady Stanton, "*This is the Negro's Hour*," National Anti-Slavery Standard, 30 December 1865.
[63] P.P., "Fifteenth Amendment," Revolution, 1 July 1869.
[64] "Equal Rights," New York World, 21 November 1866, in DuBois, Feminism and Suffrage, 62.
[65] Elizabeth Cady Stanton, Eleventh National Woman's Rights Convention: Constitution of the American Equal Rights Association: Preamble, 10 May 1866, Selected Papers, Vol. I, 587.

Rights platform." Anthony proposed, in the resolution for the AERA's formation:

> By the act of Emancipation and the Civil Rights bill, the negro and woman now hold the same civil and political *status*, alike only needing the ballot; and ... the same arguments apply equally to both classes, proving all partial legislation fatal to republican institutions.[66]

Both women trusted that the AERA could reconcile the question surrounding civil and political status, unifying these goals as well as the impetus to combine social movements through the rhetoric of human rights.[67]

Sojourner Truth, a formerly enslaved woman who advocated universal suffrage, became central to these debates.[68] Dudden suggests that Truth symbolized the AERA's "deep need for a heroic black woman who could resolve race and gender differences and speak truth to power in both directions."[69] Her postbellum universal suffrage addresses recalled her antebellum women's rights addresses insofar as Truth continued to embrace discourses of slavery in a manner that both echoed and inverted the claims of her fellow reformers. At the AERA's first annual meeting in 1867, Truth emphasized the experiences of enslaved women whilst claiming equal rights for all. Acknowledging that chattel slavery had been "partly destroyed," she emphasized her desire to see "it root and branch destroyed." For Truth, this meant universal suffrage as much as equal pay for equal work:

> There is a great stir about colored men getting their rights, but not a word about colored women; and if colored men get their rights, and not colored women theirs, you see the colored men will be masters over the women, and it will be just as bad as before.[70]

---

[66] Susan B. Anthony, Eleventh National Woman's Rights Convention, 10 May 1866, *Selected Papers*, Vol. I, 584.

[67] Ana Stevenson, "The 'Great Doctrine of Human Rights': Articulation and Authentication in the Nineteenth-Century US Antislavery and Women's Rights Movements," *Humanity: An International Journal of Human Rights, Humanitarianism, and Development* 8, no. 3 (2017): 413–439.

[68] Nell Irvin Painter, *Sojourner Truth: A Life, a Symbol* (New York: W.W. Norton, 1996), 221–223.

[69] Dudden, *Fighting Chance*, 19.

[70] Sojourner Truth, American Equal Rights Association, 9 May 1867, *HWS*, Vol. II, 193–194.

At a moment when the rhetoric of so many white reformers was becoming ever more opportunistic, Truth specifically embraced discourses of slavery to highlight the situation of African-American women. Her address, however, also reflected the conclusions that Stanton had espoused when challenging Phillips' emphasis on the "Negro's Hour."

Why did Truth's addresses later feature so prominently in the *History of Woman Suffrage*, when these volumes sidelined the efforts of so many other African Americans? Rosalyn Terborg-Penn speculates that it could be because her perspective aligned with—or, perhaps, was revised to align with—that of its editors.[71] However, "Truth refused any systematic alliance with her 'sex' over her 'race,'" Peterson argues; instead, she pursued "a series of complex ideological negotiations between the categories of race, sex, and class." For Truth, these negotiations were repeatedly grounded in her embrace of the woman-slave analogy. "In constructing her argument against the mastery of black men," Peterson continues, "Truth sought to forge a rhetorical alliance with white women." Unlike so many white suffragists, however, Truth articulated a sense of difference as well as of sameness.[72] Given the degree to which other African-American reformers would embrace such rhetoric in the subsequent decades, Truth might be positioned more as a pioneer in using the woman-slave analogy to nuanced and inclusive, rather than racist, ends.

Historians observe that the emphasis on African-American women's rights was one of the strengths of these Reconstruction debates. Frances Dana Gage, for example, particularly centered her analysis around the rights of African-American women. This was not mere opportunism, DuBois suggests, but it was certainly strategic. The acquisition of African-American manhood suffrage in 1870 would leave African-American women disenfranchised, and emphasizing this hypocrisy brought women's rights into a political discourse focused on race. But universal suffrage ultimately lacked urgency, as those in favor of manhood suffrage could speak of a "historically specific need" for freedmen's enfranchisement.[73] Deep inconsistencies emerged, however, when white women foregrounded the rights of freedwomen. One white suffragist, for example, emphasized that "the

---

[71] Terborg-Penn, *African American Women*, 31, 35.

[72] Carla L. Peterson, *"Doers of the Word": African-American Women Speakers and Writers in the North* (New Brunswick: Rutgers University Press, 1995), 225–228.

[73] DuBois, "Outgrowing the Compact," 846–847. See also: DuBois, *Feminism and Suffrage*, 68–71.

claims of, and justice to, the black *woman* are of paramount importance, and should not be ... ignored and overlooked."[74] The remainder of her 1869 address was predicated upon racist and nativist rhetoric. The *Revolution*, too, often positioned African-American women merely as figures through which to negotiate their own "contradictory identity" as women who were the beneficiaries of race and often class privilege, but nonetheless remained subjugated on account of gender.[75] Without the vote, Stanton suggested, freedwomen would merely "change their form of slavery from white to black masters, under the same code of laws we have been repudiating for ourselves for the last twenty years."[76]

These claims suggest that it is therefore worth reflecting on the degree to which women's rights reformers envisaged black and white women, both enslaved and free, as an enslaved class. During the antebellum era, white reformers mostly conceded that the class of women who had most clearly experienced enslavement were, of course, enslaved women of African descent. This analysis was predicated on many forms of oppression, including disenfranchisement. By the late 1860s, however, white women's rights reformers increasingly suggested that women, black and white, could only be truly emancipated by acquiring full citizenship and voting rights. Some African-American reformers shared in these very concerns, as Truth's own AERA addresses revealed. But white reformers tended to approach the situation of freedwomen with far less delicacy and more sensationalism than Truth. During an 1867 debate over whether pursuing manhood suffrage was the duty of abolitionists, Stephen S. Foster asked: "Who is going to save the black *woman* from slavery?" One spectator retorted, "Her Husband!" "God pity her, then!" Parker Pillsbury responded. "The right of suffrage, if it came from God, came for woman as well as man."[77] Thus, even when white reformers attempted to use the woman-slave analogy to emphasize the subjugation of all women, many failed to express an unwavering insistence on the connections between oppressions derived from gender, race, and class. In the absence of chattel slavery, suffrage discourse was at odds with white reformers' waning interest in the needs of freedpeople.

[74] "Speech of Phœbe Couzins: Before the National Woman Suffrage Association," *Revolution*, 8 July 1869.
[75] Jen McDaniel, "White Suffragist Dis/Entitlement: The *Revolution* and the Rhetoric of Racism," *Legacy: A Journal of American Women Writers* 30, no. 2 (2013): 244–245.
[76] E.C.S., "The Fifteenth Amendment," *Revolution*, 20 May 1869.
[77] "Proceedings of the New England Anti-Slavery Convention," *National Anti-Slavery Standard*, 15 June 1867. See: DuBois, *Feminism and Suffrage*, 72.

This very disconnect shaped the changing meaning and implications of the woman-slave analogy, a process epitomized by Stanton herself. Biographer Elisabeth Griffith emphasizes that Stanton's postbellum defense of woman suffrage was grounded in an "antiblack, antimale, pro-female argument" that was so racist and nativist that it alienated even her supporters.[78] Stanton expressed this racism in many ways, from wielding the specter of the black male rapist to describing the unworthiness of black and immigrant men; however, many such remarks were grounded in either the woman-slave analogy or the sex-race analogy. Her opportunistic use of this rhetoric is all the more egregious, given her (admittedly, only periodic) ability to use these comparisons in a more measured manner. For example, Stanton invariably emphasized the need "to bury the black man and the woman in the citizen," thus using analogy strategically to undermine the significance of both categories.[79] In an unpublished address, Stanton even reflected that the disenfranchised "black woman was doomed 'to triple bondage that man never knows.'"[80] Her sincerity in advocating for freedwomen's enfranchisement during the Reconstruction era remains questionable, given the degree to which she would abandon cross-racial reform imperatives across the coming decades.

The Reconstruction amendments ultimately extended civil and political rights to African-American men alone. The Fourteenth Amendment of 1868 overturned the *Dred Scott v. Sanford* decision of 1857, which had ruled that African Americans could not be citizens of the United States; it also signaled that "male citizens" would become the benchmark for congressional representation.[81] The failure of universal suffrage together with the introduction of this sex-based qualification left many white women reformers both devastated and angry.[82] The passage of the Fifteenth Amendment in February 1869, which was then ratified the following year,

---

[78] Griffith, *In Her Own Right*, 124. For Stanton's racism, see: DuBois, *Feminism and Suffrage*, 95–96, 174–179; Terborg-Penn, *African American Women*, 22–23; Newman, *White Women's Rights*, 128–142; McDaneld, "White Suffragist Dis/Entitlement," 243–264.

[79] Stanton, Eleventh National Woman's Rights Convention; Constitution of the AERA: Preamble, 10 May 1866, *Selected Papers*, Vol. I, 587.

[80] Elizabeth Cady Stanton, "Reconstruction," unpublished manuscript speech, Elizabeth Cady Stanton Papers, Library of Congress, in DuBois, *Feminism and Suffrage*, 69.

[81] DuBois, "Outgrowing the Compact," 847–848.

[82] Newman, *White Women's Rights*, 60–62.

intensified the differences in perspective that were already looming between suffragists.[83] The *Revolution* had emphasized in 1869: "Women of America; ye into whose souls has entered this iron of caste legislation! Has our slavery been so sweet that we can calmly contemplate the further riveting of its chains?"[84]

The sensationalistic comparisons between women and slaves or sex and race certainly contributed to these tensions, but did not necessarily cause the most consternation. Across 1869, amid the prospect of the Fifteenth Amendment's ratification, the *Revolution* came under particular scrutiny because Douglass was so disconcerted by its frequent use of "Sambo" imagery.[85] It was this racism, rather than the woman-slave analogy per se, that most incensed Douglass. At the AERA convention that year, he reiterated and expanded upon the position he had first expressed, in response to Stanton, as early as 1854. "When women, because they are women, are hunted down through the cities of New York and New Orleans," he proclaimed, "then they will have an urgency to obtain the ballot equal to our own." A spectator replied, asking: "Is that not all true about black women?" Responding in the affirmative, Douglass emphasized that this was not on account of gender, but rather, on account of race. Alternately, Paulina Wright Davis could not condone the passage of the Fifteenth Amendment without the prospect of a Sixteenth Amendment, "for woman would have a race of tyrants raised above her in the South," a situation, she conceded, that would disproportionately impact freedwomen.[86] According to Stanton, the Fifteenth Amendment would render men the "rightful owners and masters of all womankind."[87]

Collectively, these conflicts were central to the events which galvanized the fragmentation of the suffrage movement in 1869. The demise of the AERA later that year precipitated the emergence of two new and competing suffrage organizations. Each was differentiated by its approach to the Reconstruction amendments. Stanton and Anthony led the breakaway

---

[83] DuBois, *Feminism and Suffrage*, 172.
[84] R.C.M., "Ingratitude of Colored Men," *Revolution*, 7 January 1869.
[85] Andrea Moore Kerr, "White Women's Rights, Black Men's Wrongs, Free Love, Blackmail, and the Formation of the American Woman Suffrage Association," in *One Woman, One Vote*, 69–70.
[86] "The May Anniversaries in New York and Brooklyn," *HWS*, Vol. II, 379–398.
[87] E.C.S., "Anniversary of the American Equal Rights Association," *Revolution*, 13 May 1869.

National Woman Suffrage Association (NWSA), which boycotted the Fifteenth Amendment and championed controversial women's rights imperatives such as divorce and labor reform. The majority of reformers, however, viewed Stanton and Anthony's campaign against the Fifteenth Amendment as "politically unwise" and "morally repugnant."[88] Led by Lucy Stone, Henry Blackwell, Thomas Wentworth Higginson, and Julia Ward Howe, the American Woman Suffrage Association (AWSA) did support the ratification of the Fifteenth Amendment. Many hoped that women would soon be enfranchised by another congressional amendment, an expectation that did not ultimately transpire.

Historians emphasize the ideological and organizational differences between NWSA and AWSA, especially the racism and elitism espoused by the former and the state-by-state suffrage agenda of the latter. Despite these differences, both organizations' newspapers exposed a certain rhetorical continuity at the center of the suffrage debate. While continuing to mobilize the woman-slave analogy to advocate for women's enfranchisement, both the *Revolution* and the *Woman's Journal* reflected upon antebellum chattel slavery. To refute the anti-suffrage argument that women did not desire the ballot, the *Revolution* suggested that the "emancipation of our millions of slaves did not first come from the bondmen."[89] This was a claim that questioned the severity of chattel slavery and elided a long history of slave resistance, implying that enslaved people of African descent had accepted their own subjugation in a way that women did not—or at least, should not. The "subjection of woman," the *Woman's Journal* similarly maintained, "is by far more subtle, more profound, more complex, than any chattel slavery." Higginson, however, did observe how the postbellum era attested to freedmen's "unanimous love of freedom." "In this particular work of emancipation," he continued, in reference to women, "the chief labor ... [lies] in convincing the oppressed class that they are oppressed."[90] Although he found himself allied with Stone and Blackwell after 1869, this 1871 article, entitled "Slaves and Women," actually reflected the realizations he had shared with Stanton five years earlier. His 1866 letter revealed his newly acquired awareness of women's "political rights" by acknowledging "the impossibility of a race of <u>contented</u> slaves," saying: "I had always taken the ground that the acquiescence of the vast majority of women was like that of slaves, but observation has taught me that no such phenomenon is to be found among slaves."[91] The postbellum rheto-

---

[88] Kerr, "White Women's Rights," 77.
[89] "The True Question," *Revolution*, 22 September 1870.
[90] T.W.H., "Slaves and Women," *Woman's Journal*, 3 June 1871.
[91] Thomas W. Higginson to Elizabeth Cady Stanton, 2 May 1866, *Selected Papers*, Vol. I, 578.

ric of suffragists transcended their new allegiances to NWSA or AWSA insofar as both organizations found lessons, albeit divergent ones, in the history of antebellum chattel slavery that they went on to apply to the condition of women.

After this organizational schism, woman suffrage continued to enjoy support amongst many African Americans. Some black women periodically resorted to discourses of slavery to describe women's disenfranchisement. Often, however, they engaged with this rhetoric in a far more roundabout or obfuscated manner than did their white contemporaries. When Naomi Talbert addressed an 1869 NWSA convention in Chicago, she emphasized:

> Woman has a power within herself, and the God that reigns above, who commanded Moses to lead the children of Israel from out the land of Egypt, from out the house of bondage, ... who furnished Abraham Lincoln with knowledge to write the emancipation proclamation, whereby four millions of blacks were free—that God, ... will hear the call of woman, and her rights will be granted, and she shall be permitted to vote.[92]

Talbert situated women's enfranchisement in the context of slave emancipation, using the biblical imagery of bondage to contextualize Lincoln's Emancipation Proclamation of 1863. In making these connections, her address broadly situated women's disenfranchisement in terms of discourses of slavery.

At this juncture, other African Americans evoked what might be understood as a greater willingness to embrace comparisons between sex and race than between woman and slave. Frances Ellen Watkins Harper, for example, expressed a particular sense of conflict toward the question of manhood versus universal suffrage. Her recent experiences as a widow offered insight into the hardship that accompanied women's lack of property rights, yet she still found the needs of the African-American community to be more immediate than that of women.[93] By decade's end, Harper became increasingly convinced of white and black women's failure to unite even on fundamental issues.[94] Her novella *Minnie's Sacrifice* (1869)

---

[92] "A Colored Woman's Voice," *Revolution*, 4 March 1869. Rosalyn Terborg-Penn identifies this as a speech by Naomi Talbert (Anderson). For African Americans' criticism of Talbert, given Stanton and Anthony's stance toward the Fifteenth Amendment, see: Terborg-Penn, *African American Women*, 49–50.

[93] Shirley Wilson Logan, *"We Are Coming": The Persuasive Discourse of Nineteenth-Century Black Women* (Carbondale: Southern Illinois University Press, 1999), 44, 69.

[94] Parker, *Articulating Rights*, 119–120, 112.

attempted to resolve some of these conflicts. After Minnie, a mixed-race character raised by Quaker abolitionists, discovers and embraces her African heritage, she works to strengthen the Reconstruction South as a young woman. But, to the surprise of her new husband, Minnie also supports women's enfranchisement:

> "Louis" said Minnie very seriously, "I think the nation makes one great mistake in settling this question of suffrage. It seems to me that everything gets settled on a partial basis. When they are reconstructing the government why not lay the whole foundation anew, and base the right of suffrage not on the claims of service or sex, but on the broader basis of our common humanity."
>
> "Because, Minnie, we are not prepared for it. This hour belongs to the negro."

To respond to a claim that echoed Wendell Phillips, Minnie herself evoked the words of Parker Pillsbury, asking: "[I]s it not the negro woman's hour also? Has she not as many rights and claims as the negro man?" Minnie, much like Harper herself, recognized that the claims of "the negro man" were not in isolation; enfranchisement would enable woman to "have some power to defend herself from oppression, and equal laws as if she were a man."[95]

Minnie's Sacrifice thus encapsulated the dilemma that many African Americans experienced. Terborg-Penn emphasizes that black men did support universal suffrage, all without resorting to sexist remarks; and although Douglass had bowed to expediency, many remained committed to combatting "both racism and sexism simultaneously."[96] Robert Purvis, for example, was particularly conflicted about the implications of the Reconstruction amendments. As he revealed in an 1870 letter to the *Revolution*:

> As a colored man, and a victim to the terrible tyranny inflicted by the injustice and prejudice of the Nation, I ask no right that I will not give to every other human being, without regard to sex or color. I cannot ask white women to give their efforts and influence in behalf of my race, and then

---

[95] Frances E.W. Harper, *Minnie's Sacrifice, Sowing and Reaping, Trial and Triumph: Three Rediscovered Novels*, ed. Frances Smith Foster (Boston: Beacon Press, 2000), 78.
[96] Terborg-Penn, *African American Women*, 24–35, 4.

meanly and selfishly withhold countenance of a movement tending to their enfranchisement.[97]

His stance was unusual, as most African Americans supported the Reconstruction amendments as an important step toward racial equality.[98] In his analysis of the Fifteenth Amendment, Purvis embraced the sex-race analogy almost as wholeheartedly as many white women reformers, yet he saw both categories as equal and interlinked in a way that many of these contemporaries were increasingly willing to sacrifice.

Beginning to develop new strategies in the wake of the Fifteenth Amendment, suffragists would focus even more emphatically on the comparison between sex and race. As early as 1869, Wyoming and a few other western states and territories began to extend the franchise to women. That year, at the first convention of the Missouri Woman Suffrage Association, Virginia Minor and her husband, Francis Minor, shared a new approach to enfranchising women. Grounded in the Fourteenth Amendment and the US Constitution, it reflected what Stanton had long maintained: that manhood suffrage would open the "constitutional door" for women.[99] Inspired by the success of the Reconstruction amendments, the Minors relied on the assumption that citizenship entailed voting rights, a connection most legislators and jurists denied.[100] In her 1869 address, Virginia Minor envisaged enfranchisement as dependent "merely on the acknowledgment of [women's] right as citizens." While denouncing that it had taken so long for African-American citizenship to be acknowledged, she suggested that its recent "discovery" by powerful judiciary men meant that any arguments for woman suffrage were not imagined by "illogical, unreasoning women, totally incapable of understanding politics."[101] As Francis Minor, an attorney, stated: "We no longer beat the air—no longer

---

[97] Robert Purvis, *Revolution*, 6 January 1870.
[98] Newman, *White Women's Rights*, 3–4.
[99] Stanton, "This is the Negro's Hour"; Elizabeth Cady Stanton to Martha C. Wright, 20 December 1865, in *Elizabeth Cady Stanton as Revealed in Her Letters, Diary and Reminiscences*, eds. Theodore Stanton and Harriot Stanton Blatch (New York: Harper & Brothers, 1922), 108–109. See: DuBois, "Outgrowing the Compact," 845.
[100] Angela G. Ray and Cindy Koenig Richards, "Inventing Citizens, Imagining Gender Justice: The Suffrage Rhetoric of Virginia and Francis Minor," *Quarterly Journal of Speech* 93, no. 4 (2007): 378.
[101] "Mrs. Francis Minor," *Revolution*, 28 October 1869.

assume merely the attitude of petitioners. We claim a right, based upon citizenship."[102]

After Virginia Minor undertook an unsuccessful attempt to vote in St Louis, Missouri, the Minors developed what became known as the "New Departure" strategy. *Minor v. Happersett* was then heard in the St Louis Circuit Court in 1872; in the Missouri State Supreme Court in 1873; and in the US Supreme Court across 1874–1875. As Angela G. Ray and Cindy Koenig Richards explain, the Minors' argument symbolically reformulated the federal citizen as a person who "possessed no characteristics of race, sex, regional or national origin, socioeconomic status, or religion that were relevant to the government." Accordingly, their arguments "offered the potential to reject the framing of race versus sex ... and instead provided a legal foundation for universal suffrage." At the same time, however, the Minors also highlighted these very categories because of their everyday political and cultural salience. This paradoxical trend followed the rhetorical trajectory and imperatives of many other suffragists, including Stanton. The Minors embraced what Ray and Richards describe as "explicit analogies" between sex and race, their reliance upon which actually increased as they proceeded through the courts. The analogy—between black men and women, with the racial casting of gender remaining unclear—offered the "simple equivalence" that women, like African Americans, had always been citizens of the United States.[103]

The New Departure soon gained support from suffragists such as Stanton and Victoria Woodhull. Ann D. Gordon suggests that this was a moment at which Stanton was "*aligned* with, though hardly *allied* with, the pressing needs of African Americans."[104] Since the US Constitution no longer allowed "any distinction between its citizens in their rights and privileges," the Minors argued, it had become a point of discrimination "that the negro has a right which is denied to the woman." Citing Roger B. Taney's 1857 opinion from the *Dred Scott v. Sanford* decision, which had stated that "persons of the African race" would only be entitled to "privileges and immunities" if they were citizens, the Minors pursued an explicit analogy between sex and race: "Now, substitute in [*Dred Scott v. Sanford*], for 'persons of the African race,' *women*, who are 'citizens of the State and of the United States,' and you have the key to the whole

---

[102] Francis Minor, "Make the Trial," *Revolution*, 21 October 1869.
[103] Ray and Richards, "Inventing Citizens," 379–381, 387–389.
[104] Gordon, "Stanton on the Right to Vote," 117.

position."[105] By arguing that voting rights were a privilege of citizenship, Ray and Richards observe, the Minors assumed an analogy between black men—enfranchised through the Fifteenth Amendment—and women—whose citizenship had been ensured by the Fourteenth Amendment.[106]

These rationales enabled an ever more discernable shift to comparisons grounded in sex and race, rather than woman and slave, to formulate during the postbellum era. However, the arguments that undergirded the New Departure were not benign; in fact, it was deeply informed by the logic of white supremacy. It also envisaged the rights of African-American men as being fully secured—if only recently. This was a highly idealistic position to take, given the circumscription of African-American rights by the late 1860s and across the next decades. At a moment when some lawmakers sought to refute African-American men's citizenship or voting rights, the Minors advocated that women should also have these rights. But it proved more difficult to convince the judiciary of the Minors' argument. In the *Minor v. Happersett* decision of 1875, the US Supreme Court acknowledged that women were citizens, but followed earlier judicial conclusions by denying that this must include enfranchisement.[107] This again suggests that the majority of Americans did not see analogies between either woman and slave, or even sex and race, as relevant or evocative for the purposes of women's rights or enfranchisement. For white suffragists, its judicial failure emphasized that unequal citizenship could be constructed through sex, but no longer on the basis of race.

In the wake of this ruling, white suffragists largely abandoned the New Departure strategy.[108] However, they continued to believe that woman suffrage could be achieved by invoking other aspects of the Reconstruction amendments, especially its specific allusions to chattel slavery. According to the Minors, women's disenfranchisement was "a badge of servitude" in breach of the Thirteenth Amendment.[109] Anthony's 1871 address to the Territorial Legislature of Washington also recalled that the Fourteenth Amendment overturned the *Dred Scott v. Sandford* decision, by suggesting that citizenship did include "civil and political" rights. Had the Fifteenth Amendment been extended to women on account of the clause that guar-

---

[105] "Virginia L. Minor's Petition," *HWS*, Vol. II, 726, 728, 719, 723.
[106] Ray and Richards, "Inventing Citizens," 390–391.
[107] Ibid., 390–391, 376.
[108] Parker, *Articulating Rights*, 85–86; Griffith, *In Her Own Right*, 168.
[109] "Virginia L. Minor's Petition," 730.

anteed enfranchisement regardless of "race, color, or previous condition of servitude," Anthony implied, NWSA likely would have supported its ratification. Through the reference to "'involuntary servitude,' a special allusion is made to woman," she maintained. It was from this perspective that the Fourteenth and Fifteenth Amendments had already determined "who are citizens and who are entitled to vote."[110]

Other more radical reformers were equally captivated by this same clause in the Fifteenth Amendment. Its explicit reference to chattel slavery offered the perfect opportunity to persist with the woman-slave analogy as a rationale for women's enfranchisement. "Women, white and black, have from time immemorial groaned under what is properly termed in the Constitution [a] 'previous condition of servitude'," Woodhull claimed.[111] This was equally evident amongst those who advocated for a Sixteenth Amendment dedicated to woman suffrage. "Negro slavery involved a few millions of individuals," the free love periodical *Woodhull and Claflin's Weekly* asserted; the "woman question involves hundreds of millions scattered all over the face of the earth."[112] In its overview of the events of 1869, the *History of Woman Suffrage* related the many imperatives toward this goal.[113] By directly invoking the wording of the Reconstruction amendments, suffragists began to suggest that women were the only oppressed group that remained in the United States.

At least some women responded to their continued disenfranchisement by enacting voting-based civil disobedience. Across 1868–1869, hundreds of rank-and-file women, especially in the radical, spiritualist community of Vineland, New Jersey, engaged in performative acts of voting; many such efforts took place in groups, as women believed suffrage to be "an individual right that would be achieved and experienced collectively."[114] The Grimké sisters also voted alongside a group of women in an 1870 Massachusetts town election.[115] Some African-American women had partaken in the earlier 1868–1869 actions, while Truth, Mary Ann Shadd Cary, and

[110] Anthony, "Women Already Voters," 1871, *Selected Papers*, Vol. II, 458–459.

[111] "Constitutional Equality," 1871, in *Selected Writings of Victoria Woodhull: Suffrage, Free Love, and Eugenics*, ed. Cari M. Carpenter (Lincoln: University of Nebraska Press, 2010), 25.

[112] "The Sixteenth Amendment," *Woodhull and Claflin's Weekly*, 4 October 1870.

[113] "The Sixteenth Amendment," *HWS*, Vol. II, 333–337.

[114] Ellen Carol DuBois, "Taking the Law into Our Own Hands: *Bradwell*, *Minor*, and Suffrage Militance in the 1870s," in *One Woman, One Vote*, 86–87.

[115] Parker, *Articulating Rights*, 85–86.

others made unsuccessful attempts to register to vote across 1871–1872.[116] Renowned suffragists, including Gage, Stone, and Anthony, either registered as voters, attempted to vote, or successfully cast their ballot.[117] While these grassroots efforts were certainly localized, the explanation for such behavior indicates the broader influence of more prominent suffragists.

Some of these women were inspired to try and cast a ballot on account of the Reconstruction amendments. Mary Olney Brown, when recalling her 1869 attempt to vote in Washington territory, described to polling booth election officials how she interpreted the suffrage question in relation to the situation of freedmen:

> I went on to show them that the original constitution recognized women as citizens, and that the word citizen includes both sexes[;] ... the emancipation of the Southern slaves threw upon the country a class of people, who, like the women of the nation, owed allegiance to the government, but whose citizenship was not recognized. To settle this question, the fourteenth amendment was adopted.[118]

Following the 1872 presidential election, Anthony herself was arrested for casting her illegal ballot. Her 1873 defense similarly rested on the fact that "the slaves who got their freedom must take it over ... the unjust forms of law, precisely so, now, must women, to get their right to a voice in this government, take it; and I have taken mine, and mean to take it at every possible opportunity."[119]

After the Civil War, many reformers hoped and believed that chattel slavery had been confined to the annals of history. As this institution became ever more distant, women's rights reformers and suffragists persisted with the woman-slave analogy, but also exhibited a new willingness to respond to the Reconstruction era's debates by embracing the sex-race analogy. Some African-American reformers exhibited a greater affinity toward the latter than the former, understanding that the comparison between sex and race was necessarily flawed, but sometimes also politically useful. However, as white suffragists exhibited less and less interest in the cause of

---

[116] Terborg-Penn, *African American Women*, 37, 40–41.
[117] DuBois, "Taking the Law," 86–87, 98.
[118] Mary Olney Brown, 1881, *HWS*, Vol. III, 783.
[119] Susan B. Anthony, Circuit Court of the United States for the Northern District of New York, 19 June 1873, *Selected Papers*, Vol. II, 615. See: Barry, *Susan B. Anthony*, Chapter 10.

free people of color, some would return to more abstracted discourses of slavery. This allowed them to focus their attention more squarely on the situation of white women alone, a tactic which later influenced their approach to the national centenary in 1876.

Anti-suffragists in the North and South

The antebellum abolitionists who embraced a woman-as-slave worldview often articulated a deep and abiding concern for the rights of enslaved women as well as free women, a concern which began to evaporate following the Civil War. However, those who opposed woman suffrage and even supported chattel slavery periodically employed discourses of slavery to describe the situation of women. Many proslavery southerners viewed the domestic institutions of marriage and chattel slavery as analogous, both in terms of women's relationship to their husbands and to the state.[120] The prospect of slave emancipation and women's enfranchisement caused consternation for those desirous of maintaining systems of dependence grounded in racial and gender hierarchies. Anti-suffragists appear to have embraced the woman-slave analogy in mocking imitation of the northern reformers they sought to oppose, using discourses of slavery to denounce rather than support the prospect of women's enfranchisement.

Louisa S. McCord is described as one of the antebellum era's foremost conservative political essayists and commentators.[121] Much like the Grimké sisters, McCord was born and raised in South Carolina and then moved briefly to Philadelphia. Elite white southern women overwhelmingly endorsed chattel slavery as necessary for maintaining their own societal position.[122] Unlike the Grimké sisters, however, McCord neither remained in the North nor experienced an antislavery awakening. However, she periodically approached questions relating to gender in race in a manner that was remarkably similar, though oppositional, to the Grimké sisters. That McCord could share with these abolitionist women a belief that "women suffered from a kind of slavery," David Brion Davis observes, is something of a paradox; it can only be accounted

---

[120] Cott, *Public Vows*, 60.
[121] Richard C. Lounsbury, ed. *Louisa S. McCord: Political and Social Essays* (Charlottesville: University Press of Virginia, 1995).
[122] Elizabeth Fox-Genovese, *Within the Plantation Household: Black and White Women of the Old South* (Chapel Hill: University of North Carolina Press, 1988), 242.

for, he suggests, because of the "specificity and generality of the concept 'slavery,' a word that signifies the ultimate in the loss of freedom and independence."[123]

Across the 1850s, McCord's essays appeared in proslavery periodicals, including the *Southern Quarterly Review*. In an 1854 review essay about the slave trade, she elaborated on the existence of hierarchical relationships between husband and wife, master and slave, parent and child, and suggested that the legal and political status of women was analogous to chattel slavery:

> In every government, ... woman has been placed in a position of slavery—actual, legal slavery. Not perfect slavery, we grant—not under as perfect a system of slavery even, as are our negroes; but still in a very decided state of bondage, inasmuch as she is deprived of many rights which men enjoy, and legally subjected to the supremacy of man.[124]

In her analysis of the condition of women, McCord agreed with the conclusions of many women's rights reformers. Where her analysis differed, quite distinctly, was in terms of what to do about this conclusion. As a southern proslavery apologist, McCord accepted that domination and subordination were inevitable, whereas northern reformers did not.[125]

Her flirtation with such rhetoric was admittedly far more transitory than the Grimké sisters and their abolitionist coadjutors. But McCord also appears to have used the comparison between women and people of African descent as something of a response to northern reformers.[126] This response was both pointed and even mocking. An 1852 review essay partially responded to the proceedings of the 1851 women's rights convention in Worcester, Massachusetts: "Follow close, ladies. The door of privilege is open pretty wide for the admission of Cuffee. Should *he* get in, surely *you* might follow." For McCord, the prospect of woman suffrage was just as unlikely and undesirable as slave emancipation or the enfranchisement of African Americans. "Woman's condition certainly admits of improvement," she conceded, yet her belief that woman suffrage contravened the "Almighty laws of Nature" meant women's condition could not

---

[123] Davis, "Declaring Equality," 13–14.
[124] "Carey on the Slave Trade," *Southern Quarterly Review* 9, no. 17 (January 1854): 168.
[125] Davis, "Declaring Equality," 13–14.
[126] Ibid.

be ameliorated through enfranchisement.[127] McCord preferred only the marginal amelioration of women's status, even if this meant that elite women would continue to share with enslaved people of African descent a hierarchical category of dependence. At the same time, she made no real distinction between enslaved people and free people of color, merely conceptualizing the existence of all people of African descent in terms of chattel slavery.

Other anti-suffragists and woman suffrage skeptics returned to similar themes during the late 1860s, a moment at which northern reformers were debating the degree of women's enslaved status. Gail Hamilton (the *nom-de-plume* for Mary Abigail Dodge) embraced the Reconstruction amendments and the enfranchisement of African-American men, but did not support the prospect of woman suffrage. As a literary humorist, the degree to which readers embraced Hamilton's "combative and irreverent sketches" suggests that "the opinionated female wit was not [necessarily] a radical figure in the nineteenth century."[128] This is significant, especially given that, in her book, *Woman's Wrongs: A Counter-Irritant* (1868), Hamilton evoked the conservative sentiments of McCord as well as the radical reform rhetoric of northern suffragists:

> The vote in the hands of the freedman marks a real change. He was a slave; he is a man, and the ballot is at once the sign and the staff of his freedom. But women are free-born. ... Those women who are wise and thoughtful, who understand politics, ... are too high to be degraded by the absence of the ballot.[129]

Hamilton made important distinctions between the experiences of formerly enslaved people of African descent and free white women. However, she also overlooked the situation of freedwomen as completely as some of her suffragist contemporaries. Hamilton did not share their belief that women faced a form of enslavement, yet her analysis of enfranchisement was nonetheless grounded in a comparison of sex and race. Further, while this passage was

---

[127] "Enfranchisement of Women," *Southern Quarterly Review* no. 5 (April 1852): 323–324.

[128] Erika M. Kreger, "The Nineteenth-Century Female Humorist as 'Iconoclast in the Temple': Gail Hamilton and the Myth of Reviewers' Disapproval of Women's Comic-Ironic Writings," *Studies in American Humor* no. 11 (2004): 6.

[129] Gail Hamilton, *Woman's Wrongs: A Counter-Irritant* (Boston: Ticknor and Fields, 1868), 110–111. See: Newman, *White Women's Rights*, 79–85.

not itself humorous, readers may have been used to interpreting the writings of Gail Hamilton in this mode, thus finding amusement in some women's desire for their own enfranchisement.

A decade later, the *North American Review* published a series of anti-suffrage articles by the prominent historian Francis Parkman. Much like many suffragists themselves, Parkman began to use the memory of chattel slavery as an analogy by drawing a latent comparison between woman suffrage and the antislavery movement:

> Some half a century ago, a few devoted men began what seemed a desperate crusade against a tremendous national evil. American slavery has now passed into history. It died a death of violence, to our shame be it said; for the nation had not ... wisdom enough, to abolish it peacefully and harmlessly; but it is dead.[130]

Following McCord, however, Parkman also mobilized reform discourse mockingly to condemn the suffragists' demands. Well aware of the divisions that existed among northern reformers, he used this as a point of ridicule: "While one thinks that women are 'omnipotent,' and wants to lessen their power by requiring them to vote, others cry with emotion that they are slaves, whose shackles the ballot must strike off."[131] According to biographer Wilbur R. Jacobs, Parkman directed a "tone of cool rage" toward the reformers who publicly challenged his assertions, including such influential white suffragists as Elizabeth Cady Stanton, Lucy Stone, and Julia Ward Howe. However, he reserved his most incensed reactions for his male opponents, including Wendell Phillips and Thomas Wentworth Higginson, ostensibly because they were men.[132]

The influence that both the woman-slave analogy and the sex-race analogy had gained amongst northern reformers might be gleaned by the degree to which it defined this early anti-suffrage discourse. These commentators differed as to whether they viewed women as literally or metaphorically enslaved, as well as whether their supposed enslaved status was even worthy of consideration or amelioration. Yet, collectively, anti-

---

[130] Francis Parkman, "The Failure of Universal Suffrage," *North American Review* 127, no. 263 (1878): 19.

[131] Francis Parkman, "The Woman Question Again," *North American Review* 130, no. 278 (1880): 18.

[132] Wilbur R. Jacobs, *Francis Parkman, Historian as Hero: The Formative Years* (Austin: University of Texas Press, 1991), 146.

suffragists and other woman suffrage skeptics responded to the claims of northern reformers by embracing their own rhetoric, whether in earnest or in jest.

TAXATION, REPRESENTATION, AND THE SOUTHERN STRATEGY

The 1876 centenary of the United States witnessed the woman suffrage movement promote what amounted to a new conclusion. Women, many suffragists came to believe in the wake of slave emancipation, were the only oppressed class left in the Republic. This analysis continued to be predicated on the woman-slave analogy. However, it was also indebted to earlier analyses of political oppression, abstractions that had been grounded in discourses of slavery during the American Revolution. African-American suffragists, in contrast, progressively espoused a preference for the sex-race analogy.

The national centenary encouraged reformers to return to the ideals of the revolutionary era. The NWSA viewed the centennial anniversary of 1876 as an opportunity to use a patriotic setting to present "a new Declaration of Women's Rights."[133] Many Bostonian organizations laid claim to the American Revolution during the centennial celebrations between 1870 and 1876. Prominent suffragists, many of whom had Yankee lineage, alluded to taxation without representation to connect their own cause to the revolutionary era.[134] Such claims were not wholly new, however. Women's rights reformers had protested women's taxation without representation as early as the 1850s, celebrating the efforts of women such as Lucy Stone and Lydia Sayer Hasbrouck, who refused to pay their taxes—either periodically or annually. When, in 1872, Abby Kelley Foster and her husband Stephen also refused to pay taxes on their farm, their coadjutors responded by assuring the Fosters of the rightness of their cause.[135] "These sales of property are to the Woman Suffrage movement what the Fugitive Slave cases were to the Anti-Slavery movement," Thomas Wentworth Higginson assured them. "They are the nearest we can come to 'the blood of martyrs.'"[136] In 1873, Virginia Minor herself

[133] Griffith, *In Her Own Right*, 166.
[134] Craig Bruce Smith, "Claiming the Centennial: The American Revolution's Blood and Spirit in Boston, 1870–1876," *Massachusetts Historical Review* 15 (2013): 7–53.
[135] Dorothy Sterling, *Ahead of Her Time: Abby Kelley and the Politics of Antislavery* (New York: W.W. Norton & Company, 1991), 367–373.
[136] Thomas Wentworth Higginson to Abby Kelley Foster, 15 February 1874, Kelley-Foster Papers, Worcester Historical Museum, in Ibid., 369.

similarly claimed that taxation without representation was the "sum of all tyranny."[137]

The centennial celebrations reshaped the process whereby some suffragists approached discourses of slavery. Matilda Joslyn Gage and Susan B. Anthony called for unity to demonstrate that the "women of 1876 know and feel their political degradation no less than did the men of 1776":

> On July Fourth, while the men of this nation and the world are rejoicing that "All men are free and equal" in the United States, a declaration of rights for women will be issued ... [along with] a protest against calling this centennial a celebration of the independence of the people, while one-half are still political slaves.[138]

The most "fitting contributions" that women could make to the centennial exposition, Volume III of the *History of Woman Suffrage* proclaimed in 1881, were "these protests, laws and decisions which show her political slavery."[139] These allusions to the American Revolution exemplified a shift that was already underway, wherein white suffragists reimagined women's disenfranchisement as the only form of oppression that yet remained. The rhetoric surrounding woman suffrage increasingly positioned white women's rights as more important than a genuinely universal vision of enfranchisement.

Suffrage songs also featured the centennial celebrations prominently. Antebellum reform culture had been imbued with music. The "soul-stirring" Hutchinson Family Singers were the most famous antislavery and women's rights ensemble. Scott Gac argues that their "musical metamorphosis" derived from integrating popular blackface minstrelsy melodies with church hymns. This forged what Gac describes as "a native American identity" through "a new kind of 'sacred' music."[140] The Hutchinson Family Singers adapted the song "One Hundred Years Hence" for both antislavery and women's rights gatherings. In an 1876 centennial reiteration, new lyrics by Frances Dana Gage and John Hutchinson embraced the recent success of the antislavery movement. "Oppression and war shall

---

[137] "A Woman Refuses to be Taxed," *Woman's Journal*, 25 October 1873.
[138] Matilda Joslyn Gage and Susan B. Anthony, *HWS*, Vol. III, 21–22.
[139] Stanton, Anthony, and Gage, eds. *HWS*, Vol. III, 56.
[140] Scott Gac, *Singing for Freedom: The Hutchinson Family Singers and the Nineteenth-Century Culture of Reform* (New Haven: Yale University Press, 2007), 4–5.

be heard of no more,/Nor the foot of a slave, leave its print on our shore," the lyrics proclaimed, speciously equating slave emancipation with full civil and political rights. For oppression to truly be eliminated, the song continued:

> Woman, man's partner, man's equal shall stand,
> While beauty and harmony govern the land,
> To think for one's self shall not be an offence,
> For the world will be thinking, a hundred years hence.[141]

The transformation of "One Hundred Years Hence" reflected a growing belief that the rights of African Americans had been secured and women's oppression alone was still in need of amelioration. Since women were not enfranchised upon the national centenary, white suffragists continued to develop criticisms of the limits of citizenship that made fewer allusions to the ongoing project of African Americans' rights.

Despite these intensifying tendencies, some African-American reformers continued to embrace analogical reasoning in their continued advocacy of woman suffrage. After the passage of the Reconstruction amendments, Frederick Douglass firmly re-established his unqualified support for women's enfranchisement. Some of his endorsements appeared in the *New National Era*, a new African-American newspaper based in Washington, DC, in which he invested financially. In 1870, he became its editor-in-chief.[142] In October that year, Douglass lamented that the Fifteenth Amendment had left women "absolutely in the hands of her political masters: and though these may be kind and tender hearted," he admitted, this was the same excuse that had been used to pardon "individual slave masters" and thus went against the woman suffrage movement's principles.[143] Douglass expressed constant tensions between his awareness that free women had never experienced chattel slavery, his advocacy of woman suffrage, and his own long-held sympathy for a woman-as-slave worldview. "Woman herself loses in her own estimation by her enforced exclusion from the elective franchise," Douglass continued, "just as slaves doubted their own fitness for freedom, from the fact of being looked upon as only

---

[141] Frances Dana Gage and John Hutchinson, "One Hundred Years Hence," 1876, in Danny O. Crew, *Suffragist Sheet Music* (Jefferson: McFarland & Company, 2002), 66.
[142] Leigh Fought, *Women in the World of Frederick Douglass* (Oxford: Oxford University Press, 2017), 211–212.
[143] "Woman Suffrage Movement," *New National Era*, 20 October 1870.

fit for slaves." Given free women's educational advantages, as well as their connections to the "ruling power," Douglass averred that women had "not fallen so low as the slave in the scale of being," yet he also believed that enfranchised womanhood would be even more empowered: "She has power now—mental and moral power—but they are fettered."[144]

Douglass may have accepted the rationale behind the woman-slave analogy, yet across the 1870s, he again found himself denouncing the racism espoused by white suffragists.[145] His patience with certain suffrage leaders—namely, "Mrs. Stanton, Miss Anthony, and their colaborers"—diminished as early as 1873. These women's "flings at the negro and their constant parading him before their conventions as an ignorant monster possessing the ballot, while they are denied it," he claimed, "are of no real benefit to their cause."[146] This again suggests that it was not necessarily the fact that white women embraced discourses of slavery to advocate for women's rights or enfranchisement that drew the ire of African-American reformers. Indeed, such rhetoric was not only common, but had been used to condemn all manner of oppression and to advocate myriad social movements. It was the racism which increasingly underpinned suffrage discourse that was of far greater concern to Douglass than a woman-as-slave worldview.

Suffragists also routinely responded to the claims of anti-suffragists. Aware of Francis Parkman's series in the *North American Review*, Caroline Wells Healey Dall penned a response in which she questioned her fellow reformers' use of the woman-slave analogy. Echoing Parkman's strategic remembrance of chattel slavery, Dall pondered why so many of her fellow reformers interpreted women's historical experience as one of slavery. Suffragists, she observed, tended to "declaim against past & present generations of men, as if they had been conscious tyrants or women unwilling slaves." But men did need to realize that "their attitude is tyrannical," Dall emphasized, and women that "theirs is slavish."[147] If she saw women's attitude as "slavish," did this extend to all women? Dall's increasing interest in qualified suffrage diverged from the universal ideal of a decade earlier, anticipating an approach that would gain greater influence by the 1890s: the introduction of educational and property qualifications that

---

[144] "Woman and the Ballot," *New National Era*, 27 October 1870.
[145] Terborg-Penn, *African American Women*, 109–110.
[146] "The Woman's Rights Convention," *New National Era*, 23 January 1873.
[147] "Mr. Parkman on Woman Suffrage in the North American Review," 5 December 1879, Caroline Wells Healey Dall Papers, Schlesinger Library, Harvard University.

would effectively enfranchise privileged white women and more acutely elide the interests of working-class women and women of color.[148]

Across the 1870s and 1880s, the woman suffrage movement began to gain new adherents from the southern states. A generation behind its northeastern counterpart, the southern suffrage movement was similarly influenced by factors such as a growing middle class, women's education, industrialization, and increasingly poverty-stricken urban populations. Postbellum political debate deeply influenced white suffragists across the South, who embraced the idea that white women's votes could counterbalance that of black men.[149] In the tradition of southern popular novelists such as Caroline Lee Hentz and proslavery commentators such as Louisa S. McCord, white southern suffragists became equally willing to embrace discourses of slavery to describe the condition of women. However, their analyses departed from that of Hentz and McCord in that it did advocate women's enfranchisement. When reflecting on the antebellum antislavery movement, for example, Emily Parmely Collins expressed surprise that "all Abolitionists did not see the similarity in the condition of the two classes"—between women and enslaved people of African descent. For Collins, a New England native but long-time resident of Louisiana, the "denunciation of the wrongs of the Southern slave" was, in the postbellum era, "equally applicable to the wrongs of my own sex."[150] Thus, white suffragists in the South espoused not only an implicit assumption but also a certain resentment that the rights of African Americans had been secured while their own had not.

Elizabeth Avery Meriwether, an elite southerner reputed to have had associations with the Ku Klux Klan in Memphis, Tennessee, was one of the white women who became dedicated to such causes as temperance, women's rights, and woman suffrage.[151] In one 1889 account, Meriwether told of her invitation to a servant—whom she describes as "a coal-black woman,"—to participate in a suffrage petitioning campaign she was organizing with her friends:

---

[148] For racism, nativism, and educational qualifications for woman suffrage, see: Suzanne M. Marilley, *Woman Suffrage and the Origins of Liberal Feminism in the United States, 1820–1920* (Cambridge, MA: Harvard University Press, 1996), Chapter 6.

[149] Elna C. Green, *Southern Strategies: Southern Women and the Woman Suffrage Question* (Chapel Hill: University of North Carolina Press, 1997).

[150] Emily Parmley Collins, "Reminiscences," *HWS*, Vol. I, 89.

[151] Kathleen Christine Berkeley, "Elizabeth Avery Meriwether, 'An Advocate for Her Sex': Feminism and Conservatism in the Post-Civil War South," *Tennessee Historical Quarterly* 43, no. 4 (1984): 390–407.

[I]f I would give her a paper she could get a thousand names among the black women, [as] many ... felt that they were as much slaves to their husbands as ever they had been to their white masters. I gave her a petition, and said to her, "Tell the women this is to have a law passed that will not allow the men to *whip their wives*, and will put down drinking saloons." "Every black woman will go for that law!"

In the process of procuring "110 signatures," Meriwether reported this woman's fear of the "strong opposition of black men who in some cases threatened to whip their wives if they signed." Given that former abolitionists and suffragists such as Frances Dana Gage are believed to have mediated or purposefully misremembered the addresses of Sojourner Truth, it seems highly probable that, in her recollection of this incident, Meriwether did the same. Indeed, the editorial comment in the *History of Woman Suffrage* expressed that this event was "both novel and amusing." This makes it unclear as to whether servant or mistress embraced the woman-slave analogy to advocate women's enfranchisement, although Meriwether certainly invoked threats of violence to spur political action. The petitions, which garnered 130 signatures from "*white* women" and "110 names of black women," were also racially segregated.[152]

In claiming discourses of slavery for themselves, white suffragists all too easily sidelined the interests of African Americans, both substantively and rhetorically. The famous novelist and AWSA suffragist Louisa May Alcott, for example, proclaimed herself "a traitor" if she did not support the "emancipation of the white slaves of America."[153] Not only did Alcott seem to assume that the rights of African Americans had been fully realized; she also overlooked the continued disenfranchisement of black women. In contrast, African-American women increasingly emphasized that, on account of the discrimination that their communities continued to suffer, their own need for enfranchisement was greater than that of white women.[154] Some even began to mobilize the woman-slave analogy to highlight this very analysis. Meeting white women on their own rhetorical terrain, black women sought to illuminate their own experiences grounded in an analysis of oppressions derived from race, gender,

---

[152] Elizabeth Avery Meriweather, 11 December 1889, *HWS*, Vol. III, 154.

[153] Louisa May Alcott, American Woman Suffrage Association, 1885, *HWS*, eds. Susan B. Anthony and Ida Husted Harper, Vol. IV (Indianapolis: The Hollenbeck Press, 1902), 412.

[154] Terborg-Penn, *African American Women*, 55.

and class. An 1885 poem by Frances Harper, for example, entitled "John and Jacob—A Dialogue on Woman's Rights," appeared in the *New York Freeman*. One character complains of how his wife says "women are not free," only to have his friend reply:

> The masters thought before the war
> That slavery was right;
> But we who felt the heavy yoke
> Didn't see it in that light.
> Some thought that it would never do
> For us in Southern lands,
> To change the fetters on our wrists
> For the ballot in our hands.
> Now if you don't believe 'twas right
> To crowd us from the track
> How can you push your wife aside
> And try to hold her back?[155]

Harper specifically embraced discourses of slavery—"freedom" versus "fetters"—to advocate woman suffrage and condemn African-American women's disenfranchisement. Both white and black suffragists mobilized discourses of slavery in order to make claims about which women faced a greater degree of oppression.

In his later years, Douglass reflected on his lifelong career as a reformer, including his advocacy of woman suffrage, with a note of nostalgia. Although he remained immersed in racial uplift organizations, the woman suffrage movement continued to invigorate Douglass. In 1885, for example, he wrote to a friend to express how "he found the woman's rights meetings 'a substitute for the old time anti-slavery meetings.'"[156] This sentiment could have been borne of the movement's ethos as much as its rhetoric. At the twentieth anniversary of the New England Woman Suffrage Association in 1888, Douglass expressed a wistful note in his address, entitled "Emancipation of Women" and published in the *Woman's Journal*. His own "special mission in the world," Douglass believed, had been the abolition of chattel slavery and freedmen's enfranchisement. Yet, somewhat surprisingly, he reflected that woman suffrage was "a much

---

[155] "John and Jacob—A Dialogue on Woman's Rights," *New York Freeman*, 28 November 1885, in Sterling, *We are Your Sisters*, 416–417.

[156] Philip S. Foner, ed. *Frederick Douglass on Women's Rights* (New York: Da Capo Press, 1976/1992), 40.

greater cause": a movement that was, in fact, "a continuance of the old anti-slavery movement."[157] Douglass, like Parkman, could use the memory of chattel slavery to discuss the need for woman suffrage. Parkman, however, invoked this memory for the purpose of ridicule. Douglass, in contrast, referenced the antislavery movement in order to underscore the many forms of oppression that had collectively characterized the concerns of nineteenth-century reformers.

Most white suffragists, however, had effectively abandoned the goal of universal suffrage by century's end. When NWSA and AWSA reunited in 1890, the National American Woman Suffrage Association (NAWSA) began to appease white southern leaders such as Kate Gordon of Louisiana and Laura Clay of Kentucky. NAWSA's new "Southern Strategy" embraced racist, classist, and nativist approaches for achieving women's enfranchisement, including an increased acceptance for qualified or educated suffrage.[158] Some of the northern suffragists who had supported the Fifteenth Amendment in the late 1860s openly embraced these exclusionary measures. Henry B. Blackwell's 1890 pamphlet, "A Solution of the Southern Question," for example, advocated qualified suffrage by arousing the South's fear of African-American voters. "[I]f educated Southern women were enfranchised, there would no longer be a negro majority of voters in any State," he reasoned.[159] The southern suffrage movement was ultimately unsuccessful in generating more support amongst white southerners; instead, it aggravated racial tensions because of its potential to further alienate those who remained fearful of woman suffrage, especially those located in areas with large black populations.[160]

In this hostile political and cultural climate, Evelyn Brooks Higginbotham argues, African Americans continued to refute common assumptions about their political incapacity. One of the contradictory outcomes of the systematic disenfranchisement of black men from the 1890s onward was that it enabled black women to express greater support for

---

[157] Frederick Douglass, "Emancipation of Women: Speech at the Twentieth Annual Meeting of the New England Woman Suffrage Association," *Woman's Journal*, 2 June 1888.

[158] Marjorie Spruill Wheeler, *New Women of the New South: The Leaders of the Woman Suffrage Movement in the Southern States* (Oxford: Oxford University Press, 1993), 117–121; Terborg-Penn, *African American Women*, 68–69, 115–135.

[159] Henry B. Blackwell, "A Solution of the Southern Question," *Woman Suffrage Leaflet* 3, no. 2 (October 1890): 2, Suffrage Collection, Sophia Smith Collection. See also: C.L. James, "Intelligent Suffrage," *Revolution*, 6 January 1870.

[160] Green, *Southern Strategies*, 39.

their own enfranchisement.[161] A younger generation of African-American women continued to pursue the goal of women's enfranchisement, largely within black community and religious organizations as well as the black club movement, North and South. The National Association of Colored Women (NACW), established in 1896, promoted woman suffrage as one of its main goals and became the largest federation of black women's clubs by century's end.[162] As African Americans emerged in public debates about suffrage and anti-lynching, black women periodically embraced the sex-race analogy and sometimes even discourses of slavery to describe the situation of black women, past and present, as well as their need for enfranchisement.

Mary Church Terrell, an educated, middle-class woman who had been a professional educator in Washington, DC, was one of the few African Americans whose woman suffrage advocacy NAWSA continued to recognize.[163] In her capacity as the NACW's first president, Terrell addressed the 1898 NAWSA convention and its commemoration of the 1848 women's rights convention in Seneca Falls, New York, celebrating the "prospective enfranchisement of my sex" as well as the "emancipation of my race." Terrell acknowledged the earlier reform efforts of women such as Rose, Mott, Stanton, Stone, and Anthony. However, she also emphasized that these women had advocated for the rights of free women at a moment when "their sisters who groaned in bondage" could "possess no property, ... even their bodies were not their own." Only since slave emancipation could African-American women "stand erect in the dignity of womanhood, no longer bond but free." Terrell astutely accentuated exactly who had been enslaved during the antebellum era. In a turn of phrase to which she would constantly return, she observed, "not only are colored women with ambition and aspiration handicapped on account of their sex, but they are everywhere baffled and mocked on account of their race."[164]

[161] Evelyn Brooks Higginbotham, *Righteous Discontent: The Women's Movement in the Black Baptist Church, 1880–1920* (Cambridge, MA: Harvard University Press, 1993), 12.

[162] Terborg-Penn, *African American Women*, Chapter 5.

[163] Adella Hunt Logan and Georgia Stewart are said to have secretly attended white suffrage meetings in the South, and perhaps even the 35th Annual Convention of the NAWSA in New Orleans in 1903, by passing as "white spies" and sharing their findings with the Tuskegee Woman's Club. Terborg-Penn, *African American Women*, 69–70, 59–60, 91–92.

[164] Mary Church Terrell, *The Progress of Colored Women* (Washington, DC: Smith Brothers Printers, 1898), 7–8.

Terrell had not been mentioned in the *History of Woman Suffrage* prior to this occasion, "twenty years after Mary Ann Shadd Cary and Charlotte E. Ray became the last Black female participants noted in national woman suffrage convention proceedings."[165]

At the beginning of the twentieth century, W.E.B. DuBois and the National Association for the Advancement of Colored People (NAACP) continued to advocate for woman suffrage. The *Crisis*, founded in 1910 as the NAACP's magazine, revealed the degree to which African Americans mobilized both the woman-slave analogy and the sex-race analogy in their suffrage discourse. The September 1912 edition of the *Crisis*, the "Woman Suffrage Number," featured articles from "A Woman Suffrage Symposium." These articles were penned by black and white suffragists, including Fanny Garrison Villard, co-founder of the NAACP and William Lloyd Garrison's daughter, Adella Hunt Logan, and Terrell, who compared disenfranchisement based on sex to disenfranchisement based on race.

One example of this political writing was Rosalie Jonas' 1912 poem, entitled "Brother Baptis on Woman Suffrage": "When hit come ter de question er de female vote,/De ladies an' de cullud folks is in de same boat."[166] Jonas expressed her sense of the intrinsic connections between sexism, racism, and politics, Terborg-Penn observes. In its realization of both the social and economic implications of this connection, this poem revealed both a "sophisticated level of political analysis" as well as an ability to capture popular culture by using "slave dialect as a literary form."[167] Jonas also echoed Harper, whose 1888 poem "John and Jacob" had developed a dialogue between two men, in that she offered an African-American man's perspective for advocating women's enfranchisement. This reflected one of DuBois' broader imperatives for the NAACP's magazine, as he aimed to encourage more men to support women's enfranchisement.[168]

Some African-American women might therefore be said to have collectively and gradually expressed a greater preference for the sex-race analogy over the woman-slave analogy. In the August 1915 "Votes for Women" edition, however, Coralie Franklin Cook embraced both types of analogy:

---

[165] Terborg-Penn, *African American Women*, 65–66.
[166] Rosalie Jonas, "Brother Baptis on Woman Suffrage," *Crisis* 4 (September 1912): 247.
[167] Terborg-Penn, *African American Women*, 78.
[168] Ibid., 102.

If men could choose their own mothers, would they choose free women or bond-women? Disfranchisement because of sex is curiously like disfranchisement because of color. It cripples the individual, it handicaps progress, it sets a limitation upon mental and spiritual development.[169]

Cook's predecessors, including Douglass, Truth, and Harper, had articulated these very concerns through comparable language as early as the 1860s. As the passage of the Nineteenth Amendment became increasingly likely, black women's suffrage organizations reiterated their commitment to the enfranchisement of all women.[170] The same could not be said of white women's suffrage organizations.

At the turn of the twentieth century, both black and white suffragists began to invoke the memory of President Abraham Lincoln. Historians largely interpret the era of slave emancipation through two lenses, focusing either on the agency of enslaved people of African descent, who struggled primarily to liberate themselves, or on the decisive role of the Lincoln, the "Great Emancipator." Ira Berlin stresses that the efforts of both were, ultimately, not only necessary but essential.[171] Early-twentieth-century suffrage visual culture, however, embraced the latter worldview in its veneration of Lincoln. Both black and white suffragists found themselves inspired to use his reflections about universal suffrage and slave emancipation to advocate for women's enfranchisement. But "emancipation" meant something quite different in each context. For freedpeople, the Emancipation Proclamation of 1863 had represented the first steps toward the abolition of chattel slavery and the possibility of freedom. For white women, in contrast, it simply represented the possibility of enfranchisement.

This can be observed in the visual culture of three quite different organizations: NAWSA; the National Woman's Party (NWP); and the NAACP. Around 1910, NAWSA produced a postcard (Fig. 6.2) that quoted Lincoln's reflections about universal suffrage to advocate for women's enfranchisement. His statue appeared alone on this postcard, letting his acceptance of universal suffrage speak for itself. Other suffragists believed that Lincoln's pivotal role in the Emancipation Proclamation offered an

---

[169] Coralie Franklin Cook, "Votes for Mothers," *Crisis* 10, no. 4 (August 1915): 185. See: Terborg-Penn, *African American Women*, 118.

[170] Terborg-Penn, *African American Women*, 97.

[171] Ira Berlin, "Who Freed the Slaves? Emancipation and Its Meaning," in *Union and Emancipation: Essays on Politics and Race in the Civil War Era*, eds. David W. Blight and Brooks D. Simpson (Kent: Kent State University Press, 1997), 107, 120.

6 "POLITICAL SLAVES": SUFFRAGE, ANTI-SUFFRAGE, AND TYRANNY   253

Fig. 6.2 National American Woman Suffrage Association, "Abraham Lincoln" (Grand Rapids: The Cargill Co., 1910). Catherine H. Palczewski, Postcard Archive, University of Northern Iowa, Cedar Falls, IA

even more compelling and concrete basis for the rhetoric they had so long pursued. A cartoon by Nina Allender, entitled "Great Statues of History" (Fig. 6.3), appeared in the January 1915 edition of NWP's newspaper, the *Suffragist*. Allender represented Lincoln at the moment of slave

Fig. 6.3 Nina Allender, "Great Statues of History," *Suffragist*, January 1915. Wikimedia Commons

emancipation, his proclamation offering precedent for the enfranchisement of women by President Woodrow Wilson. The effect was to visualize the woman-slave analogy. If Lincoln could emancipate enslaved people of African descent, Allender reasoned, then the current president could enfranchise women. As much as the NWP's visual culture anticipated suffragists picketing the White House on the eve of the nation's entrance into World War I, it also began to visualize nineteenth-century suffrage discourse.

Fig. 6.4 National Association for the Advancement of Colored People, *Crisis: A Record of the Darker Races* 10, no. 4 (August 1915). Brown University, The Modernist Journals Project

The August 1915 "Votes for Women" edition of the *Crisis* (Fig. 6.4) morphed the analogy yet again. This time, Lincoln stood not with a white woman but alongside Sojourner Truth, whose iconic status had intensified by the end of the nineteenth century. Lincoln had, in fact, met Truth in October 1864; the magazine reproduced Frank Courter's 1893 painting of this encounter, which, according to Nell Irvin Painter, depicted "a highly unlikely arrangement, given their relative status."[172] In the context of the NAACP, however, the *Crisis* placed a black woman—rather than a white woman—at the center of what amounted to an elaborate sex-race analogy.

When Susan B. Anthony addressed the National Negro Race Conference of 1900, she insisted that African Americans should work toward "political equality for all the race, and not for the male half alone." Following slave emancipation, she maintained, the "colored wife owed service to a husband instead of to a slave-owner, so that legally she simply exchanged a

[172] Painter, *Sojourner Truth*, 203–207, 260–262.

white master for a colored one who controlled her earnings, her children, and her person."[173] At the turn of the twentieth century, Anthony did not find herself impelled to reconsider how nineteenth-century women's rights and suffrage discourse might be interpreted amongst spectators who had been, or who had close ties to those who had been, formerly enslaved. Her insistence that marriage was fundamentally a patriarchal institution failed to account for how it might constitute a relationship within a community also resisting racism. For white suffragists, perhaps this was exactly the point—it would be shocking to suggest that African-American men, now free, continued to enslave African-American women.

Conclusion

The woman suffrage movement collectively transitioned the woman-slave analogy into a sex-race analogy to evoke a common experience of political disenfranchisement between white women and all formerly enslaved people of African descent. After the Civil War, white suffragists attempted to expand the notion of who could be considered one of the antebellum era's enslaved classes, at the same time as yielding to the era's preoccupation with the categories of sex and race. This was particularly true of NWSA, yet it was a strategy that was also evident in AWSA and, later, the reunited NAWSA. Anti-suffragists, in turn, realized the significance of this rhetoric for northern reformers and so embraced it to ridicule their efforts. While the use of the woman-slave analogy persisted amongst white as well as black suffragists, African-American suffragists gradually exhibited a greater willingness to embrace the sex-race analogy.

Later generations of feminists and women's liberationists would again return to the sex-race analogy and sometimes even the woman-slave analogy. This rhetoric would come to define everything from feminist literature to legal strategy.[174] Tracing this important rhetorical transformation from woman and slave to sex and race, as far back as the Reconstruction era, reveals its long and contested history, competing meanings, and unfinished legacy.

[173] Susan B. Anthony, National Negro Race Conference, 12 July 1900, Rochester Public Library, in Barry, *Susan B. Anthony*, 319.
[174] For example, see: Lisa M. Hogeland, "*Invisible Man* and Invisible Women: The Sex/Race Analogy of the 1970s," *Women's History Review* 5, no. 1 (1996): 31–53; Serena Mayeri, *Reasoning from Race: Feminism, Law, and the Civil Rights Revolution* (Cambridge, MA: Harvard University Press, 2011).

CHAPTER 7

"*Slavery Redivivus*": Free Love, Racial Uplift, and Remembering Chattel Slavery

The "real emancipation of the sex," Lillie Devereux Blake remarked in May 1863, just months after President Abraham Lincoln issued the Emancipation Proclamation, "is still far from being accomplished."[1] Twenty years later, after having gained greater fame and influence as both a women's rights novelist and a suffragist, Blake returned to the substance of these comments. The "champions of liberty" had gradually claimed "personal freedom" and extended it "to the laborer, to the slave, and last of all to woman, who is still held in bondage by the teachings of the past," she claimed, in a series of 1883 addresses.[2] Frances Ellen Watkins Harper concurred, remarking a decade later upon the many monumental shifts "toward [a] broader freedom, an increase of knowledge, [and] the emancipation of thought" that had taken place across the nineteenth century. The next step, she implied, was for all such developments to include women.[3]

The woman-slave analogy provided countless nineteenth-century reformers a paradigm through which to conceptualize women's oppression

---

[1] "The Social Condition of Woman," *Knickerbocker*, May 1863. Biographer Grace Farrell attributes this to Lillie Devereux Blake. Grace Farrell, *Lillie Devereux Blake: Retracing a Life Erased* (Amherst: University of Massachusetts Press, 2002), 101.

[2] Lillie Devereux Blake, *Woman's Place To-Day* (New York: John W. Lovell Company, 1883), 168.

[3] Frances E.W. Harper, "Woman's Political Future," in *World's Congress of Representative Women*, ed. May Wright Sewell (Chicago: Rand, McNally & Company, 1894), 433.

in chattel slavery, marriage, fashion, labor, and politics. One of the greatest failures amongst white women reformers was their inability to articulate a political position that could encompass the heterogeneous experiences of all women. But white women had been far from alone in mobilizing the woman-slave analogy, as African Americans periodically used discourses of slavery as well as the sex-race analogy to condemn women's subjugation. During the century's last decades, however, the legal abolition of chattel slavery left a representational lacuna upon which a variety of reformers began to capitalize. In its place emerged a collective memory of chattel slavery, the Civil War, and slave emancipation. Collective memory provokes an emotive response to discussions about social transformation or political upheaval, leading to what psychologist James W. Pennebaker describes as "a shared sense of anxiety and fear." But collective memory can also be influenced by the political demands of the present, having the potential to distort the meaning of collective histories.[4] This was especially true in the aftermath of the Civil War, an era that witnessed substantial social, political, economic, and cultural transformations alongside rapid urbanization and increased immigration. New legal codes emerged to refashion labor regimes and race relations as much as to respond to changing gender norms.

Many white reformers mobilized collective memory in their attempts to establish the subjugation of women as the only extant form of oppression. The abolition of chattel slavery has long dominated the collective memory of activists, Sharon Crozier-De Rosa and Vera Mackie observe, as each new generation seek their predecessors' successes as models to inspire and emulate in future campaigns.[5] But postbellum reformers, in contrast to later social movements, were not so far removed from an era when chattel slavery had reigned supreme. Over the next few decades, the meanings associated with chattel slavery, the Civil War, and slave emancipation held different implications for different reformers. As the desire to eliminate women's oppression increased, many white reformers came to marginalize women of color. At the heart of this process was either a belief that the Reconstruction amendments had achieved racial equality, or a complete disregard for African Americans. In contrast, African-American women

---

[4] James W. Pennebaker, Dario Paez, and Bernard Rimé, eds. *Collective Memory of Political Events: Social Psychological Perspectives* (Mahwah: Lawrence Erlbaum Associates, 1997), vii–x.
[5] Sharon Crozier-De Rosa and Vera Mackie, *Remembering Women's Activism* (Oxon: Routledge, 2019), 5.

focused on the continued subjugation and victimization of freedwomen. The white supremacist politics of the Jim Crow era facilitated systemic rape, lynching, and disenfranchisement, as well as the convict leasing system and intergenerational poverty.[6] Remembering chattel slavery meant African-American women analyzed sexual violence in terms of a continuance of its specific legacy. White reformers, however, often conceived of the exploitation of white women and girls as a wholly new social phenomenon. These tensions influenced the ongoing transformation of the woman-slave analogy, which itself structured the commemoration of nineteenth-century reformers' lives as celebrated individuals began to pass on.

A Woman, and Therefore a Slave

Women's oppression was sometimes described as "Slavery Redivivus"—slavery relived, slavery come again—as early as the 1870s. One contemporary lexicographical work, *A Latin Dictionary* (1879), defined *redivivus* as "That lives again."[7] For the antebellum reformers who had considered chattel slavery to be just one among many forms of oppression, slavery had perhaps never really disappeared. The fugitive wife trope had represented a gradual shift toward the claim that the subjugation of women, especially married women, was worse than chattel slavery. This perspective became ever more prevalent amongst white reformers during the postbellum era. For many white suffragists, free lovers, and anti-vice crusaders, slavery was indeed *redivivus*. This new generation would express the belief that this one particular state of slavery—women's slavery, in its many interconnected forms—was worse than any other yet. "The horrors of African slavery scarcely exceeded the tortures endured by the white slaves of New York," the radical free love newspaper *Woodhull and Claflin's Weekly* claimed in 1870. "[T]he most casual observer must notice the cruel exactions made upon female labor by capital."[8]

The last decades of the nineteenth century witnessed a transformation in how former abolitionists and their fellow reformers approached the

---

[6] See: Crystal N. Feimster, *Southern Horrors: Women and the Politics of Rape and Lynching* (Cambridge, MA: Harvard University Press, 2009); Estelle B. Freedman, *Redefining Rape: Sexual Violence in the Era of Suffrage and Segregation* (Cambridge, MA: Harvard University Press, 2013).

[7] Charlton T. Lewis and Charles Short, *A Latin Dictionary; Founded on Andrews' Edition of Freund's Latin Dictionary* (Oxford: Clarendon Press, 1879/1984), 1542.

[8] "Slavery Redivivus," *Woodhull and Claflin's Weekly*, 16 July 1870.

woman-slave analogy. This occurred in the context of the changing meaning of white slavery across both social movements and popular culture. Antebellum abolitionists had long condemned chattel slavery for transforming human beings into merchandise, seeing the slave auction and especially the auction block as symbolic of market corruption.[9] Their appeals contributed to the development of the tragic mulatta trope that black and white abolitionists mobilized in antislavery literature. These narratives revealed the intergenerational consequences of the rape and exploitation of enslaved women. William Wells Brown's novel *Clotel; or, The President's Daughter* (1853), for example, had forced antebellum northerners to the realization that light-skinned, mixed-race people could be subject to chattel slavery.

By the 1850s, stories about the individuals designated real-life "white slaves" gained immense circulation in print and visual culture. Mary Niall Mitchell examines an example of this phenomenon, exploring the case of a formerly enslaved child who became popularly known as "Ida May." Her self-emancipated father, the fugitive Seth Botts (pseudonym Henry Williams), enlisted antislavery senator Charles Sumner to assist his family in fleeing their enslavement in Prince William County, Virginia. Sumner nicknamed the young Mary Botts, a very pale-skinned child, after a character from Mary Langdon's recent antislavery novel, *Ida May: A Story of Things Actual and Possible* (1854). Published soon after Harriet Beecher Stowe's *Uncle Tom's Cabin; or, Life Among the Lowly* (1852), *Ida May* envisaged the passage of the Fugitive Slave Law of 1850 as revealing the national reach of chattel slavery. Far more than abolitionists or even antislavery literature had been able to achieve, the Fugitive Slave Law had exposed how "whites as well as blacks could be captured and enslaved." Both in person and through a widely circulated 1855 daguerreotype, the young Mary Botts seemed to confirm this possibility. During the 1850s and 1860s, other light-skinned, self-emancipated fugitives such as Ellen Craft and Harriet Jacobs also gained immense fame and notoriety.[10]

Issued in January 1863, President Abraham Lincoln's Emancipation Proclamation became a pivotal moment in the Civil War. Many, however,

---

[9] Amy Dru Stanley, "Home Life and the Morality of the Market," in *The Market Revolution in America: Social, Political, and Religious Expressions, 1800–1880*, eds. Melvyn Stokes and Stephen Conway (Charlottesville: University Press of Virginia, 1996), 88.

[10] Mary Niall Mitchell, "The Real Ida May: A Fugitive Tale in the Archives," *Massachusetts Historical Review* 15 (2013): 54–88.

remained unconvinced that slave emancipation was, in fact, the correct course for the nation. A phenomenon Linda Frost describes as "emancipation anxiety" dominated popular culture across 1863. This evoked a fear that the United States would witness something akin to the slave uprisings that had taken place in the French colonies of Saint-Domingue during the Haitian Revolution of 1791 to 1804. Despite all the cultural panic, however, the violence that did transpire came not from enslaved or freedpeople of African descent but from the New York City draft riots, which culminated in more than 100 deaths as well as the brutalization and lynching of African Americans. At a moment when a national social order that condoned chattel slavery was beginning to fray, Frost argues, the public became increasingly fascinated by and expressed a longing for chattel slavery. This was an interest that popular culture could satiate. Prior to the Civil War, blackface minstrelsy and antislavery lectures had gained immense popularity in the northern states. Both entertainments naturalized the "slave-as-spectacle," although the latter in particular attracted spectators whose interests ranged from the moral to the prurient.[11]

In this decade of political and cultural disarray, the enterprising showman P.T. Barnum harnessed the shifting discourses about chattel slavery and white slavery, specifically, to promote what came to be described as the "Circassian Beauty" (Fig. 7.1). As Nell Irvin Painter explains, European scientists concluded that the Circassian, Georgian, and Caucasian peoples of the Black Sea represented the epitome of human beauty between the seventeenth and nineteenth centuries. Circassian women, like the woman depicted in Hiram Powers' ideal sculpture of the 1840s, were also believed to be particularly vulnerable to enslavement in Turkish slave markets. The term *odalisque*—a young, white enslaved women—became an erotic figure that represented what was thought to be a regional phenomenon. The term was imbued with an "aura of physical attractiveness, submission, and

---

[11] Linda Frost, *Never One Nation: Freaks, Savages, and Whiteness in U.S. Popular Culture, 1850–1877* (Minneapolis: University of Minnesota Press, 2005), Chapter 2. For the New York City draft riots, see: Adrian Cook, *The Armies of the Streets: The New York City Draft Riots of 1863* (Lexington: University Press of Kentucky, 1974). For blackface minstrelsy, see: Saidiya V. Hartman, *Scenes of Subjection: Terror, Slavery, and Self-making in Nineteenth-Century America* (New York: Oxford University Press, 1997), 25–32; Sarah Meer, *Uncle Tom Mania: Slavery, Minstrelsy, and Transatlantic Culture in the 1850s* (Atlanta: University of Georgia Press, 2005).

Fig. 7.1 "Circassian Beauty," c. 1865. Wisconsin Historical Society, Image ID: 109430

sexual availability—in a word, femininity."[12] In 1864, Barnum hired a young woman to portray a Circassian Beauty at Barnum's American Museum in New York City. However, Frost suggests that the regional and ethnic origins of the Circassian Beauties exhibited between the 1860s and the 1880s remain ambiguous: it is more likely that women known as Zalumma Agra and Zoe Meleke, for example, were not from the Caucasus, but rather, from New York City. The woman Barnum first hired in 1864 had little to recommend her apart from an unusual hairstyle; as Frost suggests, the showman reinvented the Circassian Beauty to render her "a kind of minstrel figure, a bushy-haired slave with heightened sexuality in white face (and body)."[13] By creating a figure that channeled the appearance of a light-skinned African American, Barnum "reconciled conflicting

---

[12] Nell Irvin Painter, *The History of White People* (New York: W.W. Norton and Company, 2010), 43–50, 53–54.
[13] Frost, *Never One Nation*, Chapter 3; Robert Bogdan, *Freak Show: Presenting Human Oddities for Amusement and Profit* (Chicago: University of Chicago Press, 1988), 235–241.

American notions of beauty (that is, whiteness) and slavery (that is, Negro)."[14] For spectators, the Circassian Beauty was equally a Circassian slave; her life testimony, as told by Barnum and his ilk, suggested that she could enjoy freedom only in the United States. Thus, while the Civil War still raged, Barnum introduced a new slave-type into the popular imagination: one whose racial ambiguity contributed to the fiction that her life in a Turkish harem would have been determined by an enslavement borne of her womanhood rather than her race.[15]

The US Congress proclaimed the ratification of the Thirteenth Amendment in December 1865, a moment that abolitionist William Lloyd Garrison declared as "The Death of Slavery."[16] Garrison soon stepped down as president of the American Anti-Slavery Society (AASS), though not without contention. The last issue of the *Liberator* appeared in December 1865, although the *National Anti-Slavery Standard* continued until April 1870. Abolitionists and Radical Republicans supported the Reconstruction amendments, as did suffragists, in principle—although many women reformers remained deeply vexed by their own exclusion therefrom. With antislavery societies disbanding by 1870, the former abolitionists were not successful in defining the historical memory of chattel slavery and the Civil War.[17] The mobilization of women, which had been unprecedented and therefore quite noteworthy during the conflict itself, was equally forgotten by century's end.[18] As David W. Blight argues, three different memories of the Civil War developed between 1865 and 1915: a "reconciliationist vision," grounded in the postwar realities of the battlefield dead; a "white supremacist vision," which led to the terrorization of and violence toward African Americans; and an "emancipationist vision," in which freedpeople constructed remembrances about freedom in the political and social context of new possibilities for civil rights.[19]

Many white commentators were convinced that the Emancipation Proclamation and the subsequent Reconstruction amendments had not

---

[14] Painter, *History of White People*, 51–52.

[15] Frost, *Never One Nation*, 62–73.

[16] "The Death of Slavery," *Liberator*, 10 February 1865.

[17] Julie Roy Jeffrey, *Abolitionists Remember: Antislavery Autobiographies and the Unfinished Work of Emancipation* (Chapel Hill: University of North Carolina Press, 2008).

[18] Frances M. Clarke, "Forgetting the Women: Debates over Female Patriotism in the Aftermath of America's Civil War," *Journal of Women's History* 23, no. 2 (2011): 64–86.

[19] David W. Blight, *Race and Reunion: The Civil War in American Memory* (Cambridge: Belknap Press, 2001), 2.

only abolished chattel slavery but successfully eliminated all its ills. These assumptions shaped the manner in which reformers began to conceive of the legacy of abolitionism, influencing their continued investment in discourses of slavery. In the legal absence of chattel slavery, more reformers than ever before realized that discourses of slavery could offer a sense of immediacy to that which was not chattel slavery. Many white reformers, and most especially women, began to appropriate discourses of slavery for the sole purpose of promoting women's rights. In their commitment to women's enfranchisement, this new generation believed that freedpeople's citizenship and the rights of African-American men, at least, had been secured; for too many white reformers, this was enough. But African Americans, as well as a small minority of white reformers, were all too aware that slave emancipation did not constitute the end of racism; nor did it represent an end to labor practices that reflected chattel slavery or a society that was predicated on white supremacy. Indeed, the most enduring characteristics of the institution's legacy were the "travestied liberation, castigated agency, and blameworthiness" which Saidiya V. Hartman describes as being routinely attributed to freedpeople across the postbellum era.[20]

Many of the reformers who began to appropriate the collective memory of chattel slavery, the Civil War, and slave emancipation had formerly been active abolitionists or antislavery sympathizers, at the very least. The manner in which they began to embrace collective memory correlated less with their antislavery sentiments and more with the white supremacist visions quickly taking root. These ideas were not only gaining wide cultural acceptance, but also becoming theoretically institutionalized amongst the intellectual elite. The Dunning School emerged to represent a wide consensus of opinion, concluding that Reconstruction had been a failure. Led by historian William A. Dunning, its proponents believed that the enfranchisement of African-American men had been an error with immense unforeseen social and political ramifications. The Dunning School focused not on military history but political history, justifying policies of disenfranchisement during the Jim Crow era.[21]

It was in this context that more expansive analyses of women's oppression came to be predicated on the woman-slave analogy. Although reform

[20] Hartman, *Scenes of Subjection*, 6–7, Chapter 5.
[21] John David Smith and J. Vincent Lowery, eds. *The Dunning School: Historians, Race, and the Meaning of Reconstruction* (Lexington: University Press of Kentucky, 2013).

print culture and women's rights conventions had produced extended analyses of women's oppression as early as the 1850s, the tendency to apply discourses of slavery as a rhetorical flourish in a larger work began to recede.[22] Increasingly, entire poems, addresses, articles, pamphlets, and sometimes even books began to theorize women's subjugation through the premise of a woman-as-slave worldview. Warren Chase's free love manifesto, *The Fugitive Wife: A Criticism on Marriage, Adultery and Divorce* (1861), had extemporized on this concept at length, particularly the section entitled "Part First. Marriage." Chase expressed the belief that enslaved people could be either black or white. Some wives "try to run away," he observed, only to find that "society has hedged up the road to freedom for wives almost, or quite, as effectually as it has for slaves of a darker color."[23] Quite apart from earlier analyses of marriage, fashion, labor, or disenfranchisement, these white reformers would come to envisage the female experience as a new, but also enduring, state of slavery.

This tendency was perhaps most prevalent in women's rights and suffragist print culture, yet it was by no means limited to social movement discourse or even to the United States. The legal implications of chattel slavery's abolition in the American South reverberated all around the world. Originally published in London's *Examiner*, Charles Weatherby Reynell's 1872 pamphlet, "Black and White Slaves," is a prime example of this phenomenon. Reynell directly considered the connections between women's oppression and the now-abolished enslavement of people of African descent. To establish that the prospect of "female emancipation" was not hopeless, this pamphlet pursued an extended analysis of proslavery arguments. Establishing three major points of analogy, it analyzed the extent to which each argument applied to the subjugation of women. Reynell criticized the idea that enslaved people were contented with their lot; that the slaveholder's limitless power was curbed by one's own personal property interests; and finally, that enslaved people were constitutionally unfit for freedom. Since these proslavery arguments had effectively been nullified by the abolition of chattel slavery across the British Empire and the United States, he implied, they must equally be questioned when

---

[22] Some antebellum analyses had theorized the woman-slave analogy at length, see: "Pecuniary Independence of Woman," *Una*, December 1853.

[23] "Soon we shall have the right of suffrage secured to women, and all our colleges and professions open to them," Chase had also hopefully proclaimed. Warren Chase, *The Fugitive Wife: A Criticism on Marriage, Adultery and Divorce* (Boston: Bela Marsh, 1861), 13, 31.

applied to women. Although Reynell used this reasoning to refute both chattel slavery and women's subjugation, his pamphlet accepted other assumptions about formerly enslaved Africans as well as women:

> The slave, powerless to help himself, [was] too completely crushed even to seek deliverance ...: woman is not so helpless or so ignorant, but she must yet lean for help and support in a struggle which still promises to be severe, on the men who ... have not hesitated to cast in their lot with those who have no claim but that of necessity on their generous assistance.[24]

Most significantly, the "black" and "white" of the pamphlet's title—as well as the pronouns Reynell used throughout—neatly demarcated formerly enslaved men of African descent from women. If enslaved people were only black and male then women alone were white, as later scholars so compellingly emphasize.[25]

It was because so many reformers continued to acknowledge the immorality of antebellum chattel slavery that slave emancipation inspired something of a paradox. Not only did the legal, social, and political subjugation of women persist, but some white reformers believed that this was a far more egregious and insidious social ill. In this context, direct allusions to chattel slavery flourished because more abstracted discourses of slavery did not capture the depth of irony that these reformers, including the rank-and-file, were seeking:

> Man cannot progress until woman's free
> To use her talents just as well as he.
> The sable moor, and every other race,
> In freedom's land have found a welcome place:
> But patient woman, to this hour despoiled,
> Her inspirations and her genius foiled.
> But how unjust and perfectly absurd –
> Her voice in Legislature never heard!
> Our pure Republicans should be ashamed
> To have so plain a contradiction named.
> America, indeed! is "Freedom's land?"

---

[24] Charles Weatherby Reynell, *Black and White Slaves* (London: Office of "The Examiner," 1872).

[25] See: Gloria T. Hull, Patricia Bell Scott, and Barbara Smith, eds. *All the Women are White, All the Blacks are Men, but Some of Us are Brave: Black Women's Studies* (New York: The Feminist Press, 1982).

> Where half the people can't approach the stand. ...
> Give her companions virtuous and dear,
> Instead of uncongenial masters here.
> Give her true partners and assistant pure,
> For bloated tyrants she cannot endure.
> Her right is suffrage, and 'tis very plain.
> She'll be elected in the next campaign.[26]

In consequence, chattel slavery and slave emancipation came to be considered ever more legitimate analogies for describing all manner of women's wrongs.

Woodhull and Claflin's Weekly, a newspaper committed to free love, women's rights, and other political questions, became stridently dedicated to the idea that the subjugation of women was the only form of oppression that still remained. According to Joanne E. Passett, this newspaper purposefully sought to "challenge, provoke, and excite" its readers through its analyses of marriage, divorce, and prostitution, among other controversial topics. The unconventional lifestyles of its editors, Victoria Woodhull and her sister Tennessee Claflin, were well-known and widely publicized.[27] Those who advocated free love routinely used the example of chattel slavery and prostitution to criticize women's lack of self-ownership and sexual autonomy. In what amounted to a relentless embrace of the woman-slave analogy, *Woodhull and Claflin's Weekly* published poetry, letters, and articles that mobilized the figure of the "white slave." The 1871 poem "Lament of a White Slave" began: "I was a woman, and therefore a slave, / In homeliest duties my songs found a grave." It went on to elaborate upon a woman-as-slave worldview to describe the breadth of women's experiences:

> I am a woman lone and desolate,
> Striving for freedom, O dark is my fate!
> Ever from childhood I've pined in my chains,
> Fettered and bleeding and worn down with pains; ...
> It all is the same, a woman's a slave,
> With small hope of freedom, except in the grave.[28]

---

[26] E.N.K., "Woman's Suffrage," *Woodhull and Claflin's Weekly*, 14 August 1873.

[27] Joanne E. Passett, *Sex Radicals and the Quest for Women's Equality* (Chicago: University of Illinois Press, 2003), 44.

[28] M. Merton, "Lament of a White Slave," *Woodhull and Claflin's Weekly*, 23 September 1871.

Repeatedly referring to husbands as the "owners" of their wives, another contributor asked: "Is there any analogy between the late system of American slavery and conventional marriage?" This letter unequivocally answered in the affirmative. Since antebellum abolitionists had found that "*any* system which rendered outrageous cruelties possible must be bad *per se*," so too should postbellum reformers, its author concluded.[29] Months later, when *Woodhull and Claflin's Weekly* published an article entitled "Bought and Sold," it returned again to a concept embraced by both northern women's rights reformer Elizabeth Cady Stanton and southern proslavery novelist Caroline Hentz between 1850 and 1852.[30]

Other free love advocates explored these ideas in more detail during the 1870s. One such example was Ezra Heywood's *Cupid's Yokes; or, the Binding Forces of Conjugal Life* (1877), a pamphlet most famous for having run afoul of the Comstock Act of 1873. Heywood had been active amongst an antebellum reform milieu dedicated to antislavery, women's rights, temperance, labor, and other causes, although he also held anarchist and free love beliefs. In 1872, he founded *The Word: A Monthly Journal of Reform* and then established the New England Free Love League with his wife, Angela Heywood, the following year. This periodical encapsulated the variety of interests, as well as the rhetoric, embraced by so many antebellum social movements. Indeed, *The Word* advocated for the "abolition of speculative income, of woman's slavery and war government," an advertisement on the back cover of *Cupid's Yoke* read.[31] Heywood pursued these concerns further in his 1877 pamphlet, in which he examined the anarchist and individualist possibilities of free love in the context of abolitionism and labor reform.[32]

Cupid's Yoke actually used discourses of slavery only periodically and pursued comparatively few direct comparisons with chattel slavery—far less, for example, than pamphlets by Warren Chase and other free love newspapers. The manner in which Heywood did employ the woman-slave analogy was nonetheless pivotal. Describing marriage as the "creation of men's laws," Heywood saw it as an institution which constituted both

---

[29] Lyon, *Woodhull and Claflin's Weekly*, 4 July 1874.
[30] "Bought and Sold," *Woodhull and Claflin's Weekly*, 28 November 1874.
[31] E.H. Heywood, *Cupid's Yokes: Or, the Binding Forces of Conjugal Life* (Princeton: Co-Operative Publishing Co., 1877).
[32] David M. Rabban, *Free Speech in Its Forgotten Years, 1870–1920* (Cambridge: Cambridge University Press, 1997), 32–41.

"sexual slavery" and the "legalized slavery of women therein."[33] To endorse the latter claim, he cited an influential contemporary work by John Stuart Mill in a footnote: "Marriage is the only actual bondage known to our law." Should Heywood have gone on to quote the subsequent sentence, it would have read: "There remain no legal slaves, except the mistress of every house."[34] A British Member of Parliament and advocate of women's enfranchisement, Mill was an early member of the London National Society for Women's Suffrage alongside such influential figures as his wife, Helen Taylor, Frances Power Cobbe, and Millicent Garrett Fawcett.[35] His classic work, *The Subjection of Women* (1869), is believed to have been the "intellectual and emotional" product of his relationships with Taylor.[36] Although Mill conceded that wives enjoyed better treatment than enslaved people, he believed that women's oppression was more insidious. *The Subjection of Women* emphasized that "no slave is a slave to the same lengths, and in so full a sense of the word, as a wife is."[37]

This reveals the degree to which postbellum commentators, from influential British philosophers to controversial American radicals, contributed to an intertextual web that assumed as much as it worked to construct a woman-as-slave worldview. Following the epigraphs in works by women reformers, these quotations steadily came to reinforce each other. In addition to Mill, Heywood went on to cite other contemporaries such as Woodhull. The woman-slave analogy existed at the foundations of their collective theorization about the condition of women. Heywood concluded his pamphlet by embracing the possibilities of love, proclaiming that only when individuals defied their "slave masters" would the "bonds of affection be welcomed, for the yokes which Cupid imposes 'are easy and their burden light.'"[38] In extended works as much as through relatively brief comments, advocates of free love contributed to a reform culture that was effectively beginning to undermine the severity of chattel slavery and a more accurate collective memory of its legacy.

[33] Heywood, *Cupid's Yokes*, 6, 8, 23.
[34] J.S. Mill, *The Subjection of Woman* (London: Longmans, Green, Reader, and Dyer, 1869), 147–148; Heywood, *Cupid's Yokes*, 6, 8.
[35] Barbara Caine, *Victorian Feminists* (Oxford: Oxford University Press, 1992).
[36] Susan Mendus, "John Stuart Mill and Harriet Taylor on Women and Marriage," *Utilitas* 6, no. 2 (1994): 287–299.
[37] Mill, *Subjection of Woman*, 57.
[38] Heywood, *Cupid's Yokes*, 23.

The woman-slave analogy became equally central to concerns about the marriage market amongst elite women. Although the matrimonial exchange of women did not accurately reflect social practices, it was a popular idea that illuminated the societal changes associated with the expansion of capitalism.[39] The marriage market conceptually expanded upon the antebellum idea that women were "bought and sold" to shape late-nineteenth-century reform discourse. Women's rights reformers and suffragists used the woman-slave analogy to condemn white women's domination by white men, while free love advocates often described women's obligation to engage in marital sex as sexual slavery.[40] "Compelled to market themselves as slaves," one contributor to *Woodhull and Claflin's Weekly* observed, "woman ... is in haste to dispose of herself, as she is a perishable commodity, ... whether wanted for wife or prostitute."[41] The self-possession and autonomy that married women lacked was equally lost for women who literally sold themselves in the market economy. For suffragist Anna Howard Shaw, the world was "a market-place in which women are bought and sold," because women, upon marriage, lost their name and legal rights, and therefore "occupied the same position to her husband as the slave to his master."[42]

The changing use of the woman-slave analogy across the postbellum era was detrimental to the maintenance of the fragile cross-racial reform network that had prospered during the antebellum era. As early as the 1850s, reform discourse and popular culture contributed to a rhetorical shift from black slavery to white slavery, a transformation which came to influence the manner in which white reformers employed discourses of slavery following slave emancipation. This represented a complex impulse: to ignore or undermine the legacy of chattel slavery, but simultaneously, to appropriate it fully for purposes other than racial uplift. The new meanings and implications of the woman-slave analogy, either implicitly or outright, might be considered a key inhibitor for building any sustained cross-racial coalitions across the postbellum women's movement.

---

[39] Margit Stange, *Personal Property: Wives, White Slaves, and the Market in Women* (Baltimore: Johns Hopkins University Press, 1998).
[40] Freedman, *Redefining Rape*, 52–53, 67.
[41] E.S. Wheeler, "The Woman Market," *Woodhull and Claflin's Weekly*, 24 February 1872.
[42] Anna Howard Shaw, "The National-American Convention of 1894," in *History of Woman Suffrage* [hereafter *HWS*], Vol. IV, eds. Susan B. Anthony and Ida Husted Harper (Indianapolis: The Hollenbeck Press, 1902), 230.

Remembering Chattel Slavery

In the decades after the Civil War, African Americans neither explicitly censured nor unequivocally endorsed the changing manner in which their white contemporaries had come to embrace the woman-slave analogy. Understanding that the subjugation of women was far from the only extant form of oppression, African Americans recognized the logic of racism that had informed this rhetoric for decades. However, the 1890s also witnessed more African-American reformers than ever before begin to mobilize discourses of slavery to describe the experiences of formerly enslaved women as well as the contemporary situation of freedwomen. This was at once a continuation of the tradition established by reformers such as Sojourner Truth and Frederick Douglass and a response to the skewed and increasingly hyperbolic claims of many white reformers. African-American women, in particular, periodically embraced this rhetoric to describe certain aspects of women's oppression, both amongst women of color and free people of African descent.

The ideal of racial uplift dominated African-American religious and civil organizations, especially the black women's club movement, at the turn of the twentieth century. Evelyn Brooks Higginbotham describes racial uplift as working toward goals that were both progressive and conservative. The 1880s and 1890s witnessed the beginnings of Jim Crow segregation, the systematic legislative and extrajudicial disenfranchisement of African-American men, and a rapid increase in lynching across the South. In response, African-American women challenged racism through religious organizations at the same time as advocating for self-help and mutual aid through equal education, greater employment opportunities, and women's enfranchisement. Collectively, their approach revealed the inextricability of race and gender, as well as class, in black women's lives.[43] While racial uplift created the "discursive ground" through which African-American women could explore and dispel negative stereotypes, it also "remained locked within hegemonic articulations of gender, class and sexuality."[44] Yet, as Brittney C. Cooper argues, respectability discourse

---

[43] Evelyn Brooks Higginbotham, *Righteous Discontent: The Women's Movement in the Black Baptist Church, 1880–1920* (Cambridge, MA: Harvard University Press, 1993), 26; Deborah Gray White, *Too Heavy a Load: Black Women in Defense of Themselves, 1894–1994* (New York: W.W. Norton, 1999), 25–55.

[44] Evelyn Brooks Higginbotham, "African-American Women's History and the Metalanguage of Race," *Signs: Journal of Women in Culture and Society* 17, no. 2 (1992): 271.

"constituted one of the earliest theorizations of gender within newly emancipated Black communities." Although many black clubwomen valued their privacy, a new generation of "race women" intellectuals began to discuss their feelings and personal experiences of bodily violation. It was through this embodied discourse, Cooper suggests, that African-American women sought to "politicize their interior lives and feelings."[45]

The 1890s was, in Frances Ellen Watkins Harper's words, a "woman's era" during which African-American women came together to analyze and organize around questions that "addressed all aspects of the social organization of oppression."[46] The decade began with the posthumous publication of Octavia V. Rogers Albert's groundbreaking work, *The House of Bondage; or, Charlotte Brooks and Other Slaves* (1890). Born to enslaved parents in 1853, the young Octavia experienced slave emancipation as a child. As a young woman, Albert went on to work as a teacher in rural Georgia, during which she began to record the stories of the older freedpeople in her community. By chronicling the voices and stories of the women and men who had personally experienced the hardship, violence, and trauma of chattel slavery, Albert produced what amounted to one of the earliest oral histories of the institution. Thus, more than 40 years prior to the Work Projects Administration's oral narratives of the 1930s, Albert had documented formerly enslaved people's own recollections. This is all the more remarkable, Anne C. Bailey observes, as the development and publication of *The House of Bondage* represented the "rarest of circumstances—an ex-slave who becomes an interpreter of her own experience and the experience of others."[47]

Hereafter, African-American women began to explore the parallels between the eras of chattel slavery and freedom. Reflecting on the legacy of sexual exploitation under chattel slavery, black women novelists used a comparison between free women and enslaved women to illuminate these concerns in the present. Other reformers similarly used discourses of slavery to consider social questions, including women's enfranchisement.

[45] Brittney C. Cooper, *Beyond Respectability: The Intellectual Thought of Race Women* (Urbana: University of Illinois Press, 2017), 12–19, 40–41.

[46] Hazel V. Carby, "'On the Threshold of Woman's Era': Lynching, Empire, and Sexuality in Black Feminist Theory," *Critical Inquiry* 12, no. 1 (1985): 265; Martha S. Jones *All Bound Up Together: The Woman Question in African American Public Culture, 1830–1900* (Chapel Hill: University of North Carolina Press, 2007), 171.

[47] Anne C. Bailey, *African Voices of the Atlantic Slave Trade: Beyond the Silence and the Shame* (Boston: Beacon Press, 2005), 101–107, esp. 102.

Periodically, journalists embraced this rhetoric to condemn lynching as much as to denounce those who remained apathetic or complacent as white southerners' violence intensified. Importantly, African-American women's lives, genealogies, and fictions contradicted the claims of so many generations of feminist foremothers: the idea that all women were born to slavery. That black women did sometimes use rhetoric which was comparable to that of white women, however, remains largely overlooked. African Americans, as Carla L. Peterson astutely emphasizes, certainly invoked chattel slavery "not as an analogy but as a historical reality that affected black women's lives."[48] This trend, however, was not absolute. Rather than merely acknowledging that African Americans "rarely" embraced the woman-slave analogy, it is worth reconsidering the contexts in which they did.[49] The moments at which African Americans mobilized discourses of slavery in order to describe that which was not chattel slavery can be usefully reconsidered in light of the extent to which their contemporaries persisted with the woman-slave analogy.

Antebellum women such as Sarah Forten and Sarah Mapps Douglass transformed the practice of metempsychosis by linking the experiences of free blacks in the North to that of enslaved people of African descent in the South.[50] Among abolitionists, many of whom became preoccupied with the irony of near-white people of African descent being subject to chattel slavery, antislavery discourse had sometimes embraced prostitution as a euphemism for the rape of enslaved women.[51] As Frederick Douglass proclaimed in 1850, millions of enslaved women were "consigned to a life of revolting prostitution":

> It is also known that slave women, who are nearly white, are sold in those markets, at prices which proclaim ... the accursed purposes to which they are to be devoted. Youth and elegance, beauty and innocence, are exposed for sale upon the auction block; while villainous monsters stand around, with

---

[48] Carla L. Peterson, "'And We Claim Our Rights': The Rights Rhetoric of Black and White Women Activists before the Civil War," in *Sister Circle: Black Women and Work*, ed. Sharon Harley and the Black Women and Work Collective (New Brunswick: Rutgers University Press, 2002), 131.

[49] Louise Michele Newman, *White Women's Rights: The Racial Origins of Feminism in the United States* (New York: Oxford University Press, 1999), 6.

[50] Gay Gibson Cima, *Performing Anti-Slavery: Activist Women on Antebellum Stages* (Cambridge: Cambridge University Press, 2014), 91–122.

[51] Freedman, *Redefining Rape*, 30.

pockets lined with gold, gazing with lustful eyes upon their prospective victims.[52]

Conscious of the degree to which chattel slavery had institutionalized the racial and sexual violence which continued unabated, a new generation of African-American women developed connections between their contemporary experiences and that of previous generations of enslaved women.[53]

As a result, the legacy of chattel slavery shaped much postbellum African-American literature. In response to the racism of the Jim Crow era, some black women novelists reinvigorated the tragic mulatta trope.[54] Frances Harper and Pauline E. Hopkins, in particular, mobilized the collective memory of chattel slavery to denounce African-American women's continued vulnerability to rapacious white men in novels structured around narratives that spanned the antebellum and postbellum eras. This occurred to emphasize the experiences of enslaved women in the antebellum era as much as to bear witness to the persistence of sexual violence against freedwomen.

Harper's novel *Iola Leroy; or, Shadows Uplifted* (1892) explored these themes through the character of Iola, a mixed-race child of the planter aristocracy. This novel, in its focus on a mixed-race woman of the planter class, echoed Hannah Crafts' earlier manuscript, *The Bondwoman's Narrative* (1850s), and extended its implications to the postbellum era. *Iola Leroy* transitions between narratives set in the postbellum and antebellum eras. Prior to the Civil War, Leroy Sr's death leads to the discovery of Iola's mixed-race parentage. As one scholar notes, this development relegates Iola to the "status of sexual object for which no indignity is too great."[55] Although this character has the "proud pose of Leroy," Harper wrote, the attorney Louis Bastine surmises her to be "a most beautiful creature" whose ancestry and feminine beauty would "bring $2000 any day in a New Orleans market."[56] For Iola, the possibility of sale and sexual

---

[52] "Frederick Douglass Discusses Slavery," in *A Documentary History of the Negro People in the United States*, Vol. II, ed. Herbert Aptheker (New York: Citadel Press, 1951, 1969), 309–313.

[53] Feimster, *Southern Horrors*, 43–61.

[54] Venetria K. Patton, *Women in Chains: The Legacy of Slavery in Black Women's Fiction* (Albany: State University of New York Press, 2000), 93–95.

[55] Ibid., 94.

[56] Frances Ellen Watkins Harper, *Iola Leroy; or, Shadows Uplifted* (Boston: Beacon Press, 1892/1987), 100.

assault is predicated on the legacy of chattel slavery, her racial heritage, and the market value accorded to mixed-race women. Thus, black women novelists used the collective memory of chattel slavery to emphasize that white supremacy continued to engender the exploitation and victimization of freedwomen on account of both race and sex.

Hopkins, too, revealed the way in which elite white men continued to take sexual advantage of African American and mixed-race women. Her novel *Contending Forces: A Romance Illustrative of Negro Life North and South* (1900) was also structured so that the postbellum narrative drew on an antebellum backstory. Both the threat and enactment of physical and sexual violence shaped what Jennifer Putzi describes as African-American women's "embodied subjectivity" in these parallel narratives.[57] The antebellum narrative featured the character of Grace Monfort, the wife of a slaveholding planter from Bermuda. Two poor, white troublemakers speculate about her racial ancestry; her complexion may be "creamy in its whiteness," they maintain, yet they conjecture that Grace is not "a genooine white 'ooman." When she refuses the rival planter Anson Pollock's romantic attentions, Grace is tied up and subjected to a brutal beating. After an overseer "satiated his vengeful thirst" upon Grace, he "cut the ropes which bound her"—a scene which recalls the power relations between master and slave, rather than the men and women of the planter elite.[58] Grace, like Iola, is only objectified and brutalized after her race is questioned; yet unlike Iola, she disappears soon after for her supposed act of racial passing.[59] A parallel postbellum narrative features the character of Mabelle, a mixed-race 14-year-old girl, who is raped by her white uncle. Afterward, Mabelle becomes the center of a financial exchange between half-brothers:

> "Well," said he, "whatever damage I have done I am willing to pay for. But your child is no better than her mother or her grandmother. What does a woman of mixed blood, or any Negress, for that matter, know of virtue? It is my belief that they were a direct creation by God to be the pleasant companions of men of my race. Now, I am willing to give you a thousand dollars and call it square."[60]

---

[57] Jennifer Putzi, "'Raising the Stigma': Black Womanhood and the Marked Body in Pauline Hopkins's *Contending Forces*," *College Literature* 31, no. 2 (2004): 2.

[58] Pauline E. Hopkins, *Contending Forces: A Romance Illustrative of Negro Life North and South* (Boston: Colored Co-operative Publishing, 1900), 40–41, 69–70.

[59] Patton, *Women in Chains*, 94; Putzi, "'Raising the Stigma'," 9–10.

[60] Hopkins, *Contending Forces*, 260–261.

The "contending forces" of the novel's title were a result of these connections between womanhood, chattel slavery, and prostitution. By describing mixed-race characters such as Grace and Mabelle who could not be granted the sexual self-ownership reserved for white women, Hopkins condemned the fact that freedwomen should continue to be considered in terms of the market economy even following the abolition of chattel slavery.

Other African-American women expressed these concerns even more resolutely at the World's Congress of Representative Women, held in conjunction with the 1893 World's Columbian Exhibition in Chicago. Anti-lynching advocate Ida B. Wells encouraged a boycott of the World's Columbian Exhibition due to what she and others viewed as the likelihood of the racist cultural misrepresentation of African Americans at the event. Women's organizations, too, were dissatisfied with how the event's organizers approached their cause. This led to the organization of the World's Congress of Representative Women, at which six black women—Harper, alongside Fannie Barrier Williams, Anna Julia Cooper, Fanny Jackson Coppin, Hallie Quinn Brown, and Sarah J. Early—made addresses.[61] Frederick Douglass, who, in his later years, had built connections with the younger generation of African-American reformers and mentored women such as Ida B. Wells and Mary Church Terrell, also made an appearance.[62] In spite of Wells' concerns, Douglass also became involved in planning what was described as the "Colored People's Day" at the World's Columbian Exhibition.[63]

At the World's Congress, each considered how questions of race, gender, and class related to the experiences of African-American women, in the past context of chattel slavery and the present context of lynching. Of all these women, Harper was the elder stateswoman, whose career as an abolitionist, poet, and novelist the younger Brown commended in her own remarks. On the world's stage, Harper continued a strategy that African-American suffragists, herself included, had pioneered during the 1870s: to emphasize their own greater need for the vote than white women.[64] In her

---

[61] Claudine Raynaud, "African American Women's Voices at the 1893 Chicago World's Fair," in *Women in International and Universal Exhibitions, 1876–1937*, eds. Rebecca Rogers and Myriam Boussahba-Bravard (London: Routledge, 2017).

[62] Cooper, *Beyond Respectability*, 60–61.

[63] Leigh Fought, *Women in the World of Frederick Douglass* (Oxford: Oxford University Press, 2017), 281–284.

[64] Rosalyn Terborg-Penn, *African American Women in the Struggle for the Vote, 1850–1920* (Bloomington: Indiana University Press, 1998), Chapter 4.

1893 address, Harper considered the ongoing question of women's enfranchisement, maintaining that "the social and political advancement which woman has already gained bears the promise of … emancipation." Such a description of women's need for enfranchisement must be contextualized in terms of the woman-slave analogy, given the degree to which discourses of slavery—as well as their inverse, discourses of emancipation—had dominated across the nineteenth-century women's rights and suffrage movements. As Harper concluded, "I know that no nation can gain its full measure of enlightenment and happiness if one-half of it is free and the other half is fettered."[65]

The other African-American women's addresses both echoed and anticipated the novels by Harper and Hopkins, as the structure of each explored the connections in black women's experiences between the antebellum and postbellum eras. Williams, a clubwoman and member of the black elite, alluded to the exploitation of enslaved women, who had been too overwhelmed and structurally disempowered to "struggle to emancipate themselves from the demoralization of [chattel] slavery." Although Williams could "appreciate the offensiveness of all references to American slavery," she believed that its influence could not be ignored by those who sought to address racist stereotypes about black women's promiscuity. In freedom, Williams emphasized, African-American women were flourishing in the realms of religion, education, and social reform; yet she also drew attention to the racial discrimination they continued to experience. As Williams reminded her spectators, "the thousands of colored women in the North were free from the vicious influences of slavery," compared with "once-enslaved women," who continued to strive to "emancipate themselves from the demoralization of their enslavement." This generation of African Americans as well as the next, Williams insisted, would be defined by "self-emancipating women."[66]

By chronicling the histories of formerly enslaved women, these African Americans claimed their own past. Yet their addresses at the World's Congress can also be read as a pointed response to the manner in which white reformers had come to use discourses of slavery—and perhaps even to how their audiences, largely comprising white women, were accustomed to hearing such rhetoric applied. The intent of these black women's comments

---

[65] Harper, "Woman's Political Future," 434, 436.
[66] Fannie Barrier Williams, "The Intellectual Progress of the Colored Women of the United States since the Emancipation Proclamation," in *World's Congress*, 696–711.

differed from that of so many white women, who habitually failed to differentiate between women's experiences along the lines of race and class. Echoing Williams, Brown even more decisively asserted: "For two hundred and fifty years the negro woman of America was bought and sold as a chattel." It was only after the Civil War—which had "broken" the "gyves [fetters] and chains on [the] wrists and ankles" of the enslaved—that the African-American woman "stepped forth ... a free woman."[67] Brown's proclamations not only attested to the strength of African-American women, but also served as a reminder to white women that their own oppression was not, in fact, tantamount to chattel slavery, and never had been. By declaring exactly which category of woman had been enslaved during the antebellum era, African-American women implicitly disputed the notion that all women were born to slavery.

However, African Americans did not wholly refute the rhetorical framework that the woman-slave analogy offered. Cooper challenged privileged white women to consider how their own gender and class interests often came at the expense of oppressed peoples, a project she pursued in *A Voice from the South* (1892).[68] "I speak for the colored women of the South," Cooper asserted, continuing these efforts in her address at the World's Congress. Although she conceded that white women, too, experienced oppression, Cooper insisted that this was different from that of black women: "The white woman could at least plead for her own emancipation; the black woman, doubly enslaved, could but suffer and struggle and be silent."[69] Cooper may have been motivated to meet white women on their own rhetorical ground; in doing so, she could indicate that white women were only singly "enslaved," or singly oppressed, whereas black women were doubly so. It was through this framework, one that discourses of slavery offered, that Cooper strove to highlight these multiple forms of oppression, centralized around the experiences of African-American women as the actual victims of chattel slavery.

Other African Americans used discourses of slavery in the context of debates about lynching, in what amounted to deeply multilayered textual maneuvers. Ida B. Wells had been born to enslaved parents in 1862, nearly a decade after Octavia Albert. The 1890s constituted the peak of her anti-

---

[67] Hallie Q. Brown, "Discussion of the Same Subject," in *World's Congress*, 724–725.
[68] Carby, "'On the Threshold of Woman's Era'," 266.
[69] A.J. Cooper, "Discussion of the Same Subject," in *World's Congress*, 712.

lynching crusade, beginning with her journalism and followed by the publication of *Southern Horrors: Lynch Law in All Its Phases* (1892) and her series of transatlantic reform lectures.[70] *The Red Record* (1895), another influential anti-lynching work, featured a preface by Frederick Douglass. In the final chapter of this work, Wells paid homage to abolitionist poet James Russell Lowell. *The Red Record* reprinted his 1843 antislavery poem, "Stanzas on Freedom," in which Lowell had used discourses of slavery to implicate errant northerners in the crimes of chattel slavery. "To those who still feel they have no obligation in the matter," Wells wrote of lynching, "we commend the following lines of Lowell":

> Men! whose boast it is that ye
> Come of fathers brave and free,
> If there breathe on earth a slave
> Are ye truly free and brave?
> If ye do not feel the chain,
> When it works a brother's pain,
> Are ye not base slaves indeed,
> Slaves unworthy to be freed?

> Women! who shall one day bear
> Sons to breathe New England air,
> If ye hear without a blush,
> Deeds to make the roused blood rush
> Like red lava through your veins,
> For your sisters now in chains,
> Answer! are ye fit to be
> Mothers of the brave and free?

> Is true freedom but to break
> Fetters for our own dear sake,
> And, with leathern hearts, forget
> That we owe mankind a debt?
> No! true freedom is to share
> All the chains our brothers wear,
> And, with heart and hand, to be
> Earnest to make others free!

---

[70] Mia Bay, *To Tell the Truth Freely: The Life of Ida B. Wells* (New York: Hill and Wang, 2009).

> There are slaves who fear to speak
> For the fallen and the weak;
> They are slaves who will not choose
> Hatred, scoffing, and abuse,
> Rather than in silence shrink
> From the truth they needs must think;
> They are slaves who dare not be
> In the right with two or three.[71]

Although Lowell had used discourses of slavery to describe both free men and women, his poem had directly connected northern women to their southern "sisters now in chains" in the same discourse that had been embraced by countless abolitionist women. Resituating this poem in this 1890s context, Wells remobilized both antebellum antislavery discourse and abolitionist strategy to suggest that those who failed to condemn lynching were themselves also culpable. Wells implied, too, that freedpeople with poor morals could indeed be rendered enslaved, mentally, thus reprising Maria Stewart's 1830s sentiment that there existed "no chains as galling as the chains of ignorance—no fetters so binding as those that bind the soul."[72] In reprinting Lowell's poem in *The Red Record*, Wells also used the same strategies as earlier abolitionist women, who used poetry to preface and thus frame their own works.[73]

Such direct connections to antebellum abolitionism were not limited to Wells. The works of Angelina Weld Grimké, the mixed-race great-niece of Sarah Grimké and Angelina Grimké Weld, devoted renewed vigor to alleviating racial and gender oppression amongst African-American women. Her father, Archibald Henry Grimké, had become only the second African American to graduate from Harvard Law School, with the support of his aunts. Born in 1880, only a year after the elder Grimké Weld passed on, the young Angelina grew up as her famous great aunt's namesake in a cultural milieu dominated by Boston's elite cross-racial reform networks.

---

[71] Ida B. Wells-Barnett, *The Red Record: Tabulated Statistics and Alleged Causes of Lynching in the United States, 1892–1893–1894* (Chicago and New York: Miss Ida B. Wells and Open Road Integrated Media, 1895/2015), 117–118.

[72] *Meditations from the Pen of Mrs. Maria W. Stewart* (Washington: Enterprise Publishing Company, 1879), 57–58.

[73] The epigraph to Lydia Maria Child's *Brief History of the Condition of Women: In Various Ages and Nations* (1835), for example, read "I am a slave, a favored slave," words from Lord Byron's 1814 poem, *The Corsair*. In her antislavery tract, *An Appeal to the Women of the Nominally Free States* (1838), Angelina Grimké also quoted the poetry of Sarah Forten.

An educator, poet, and playwright, Weld Grimké remained attached to the memory of her enslaved grandmother, Nancy Weston Grimké. An early experience of thwarted love, after which Gloria T. Hull suggests that she "foreswore lasting intimacy," led to much of her unpublished poetry exploring themes of lesbian love. Her most famous work, *Rachel: A Play in Three Acts* (1920), first staged in 1916, explored themes relating to lynching and racial discrimination.[74] Weld Grimké's short stories also appeared in Margaret Sanger's *Birth Control Review*; one featured in a 1919 edition entitled "The New Emancipation: The Negros' Need for Birth Control, as Seen by Themselves."[75] This reflected the expansive manner in which countless white reformers had come to describe various new social movements—many of which related to women's oppression— as a "new emancipation," believing that such movements were a renewal of antebellum abolitionism.

Nearly a century after the trailblazing abolitionist addresses in which the elder Grimké sisters had pioneered the use of the woman-slave analogy in the United States, the younger Angelina Weld Grimké offered a perspective toward both chattel slavery and women's rights that was not so different from that of her great aunts. In one poem, she considered the nature of freedom specifically in the context of chattel slavery's legacy:

> But we, their children, bone of them and blood
> Bound by new fetters, tortured still, have seen
> A light: We know that soul and mind are free
> That sorrow, tears and evil all are good;
> We know it matters not what we have been
> But this, and always this: What we shall be.[76]

---

[74] Gloria T. Hull, *Color, Sex, and Poetry: Three Women Writers of the Harlem Renaissance* (Bloomington: Indiana University Press, 1987), 21–22, Chapter 3; Katharine du Pre Lumpkin, *The Emancipation of Angelina Grimke* (Chapel Hill: University of North Carolina Press, 1974), 220–227. Angelina Weld Grimké was related to many famous figures within Boston's interracial network of reformers: her great uncle, Theodore D. Weld, outlived his wife Angelina by 16 years; Sarah Forten was the aunt of her aunt, Charlotte Forten Grimké. For the extended family network, see: Janice Sumler-Lewis, "The Forten-Purvis Women of Philadelphia and the American Anti-slavery Crusade," *Journal of Negro History* 66, no. 4 (1981): 281–288.

[75] Angelina W. Grimké, "The Closing Door," *Birth Control Review*, September and October 1919.

[76] Carolivia Herron, ed. *Selected Works of Angelina Weld Grimké* (Oxford: Oxford University Press, 1991), 103–104.

Other overtures to the elder Grimké sisters appeared in an undated speech entitled "The Social Emancipation of Women," in which Weld Grimké considered the situation of women in the early twentieth century. "Women's social emancipation," she argued, "is not an independent movement but is dependent upon her other emancipations, educational, economical, political, etc." Despite women's recent progress, Weld Grimké emphasized the degree to which the legal establishment, education, and employment continued to place double standards upon women. Thus, she saw her own generation as the beneficiaries of what only amounted to a "partial Emancipation," especially in terms of marriage. Her description of the institution in the "olden days" characterized the wife as "a toy and often a household servant."[77] This turn of phrase directly evoked Sarah Grimké's own antebellum works, which Weld Grimké could perhaps even have accessed through the family archive. Indeed, Sarah Grimké had described men's regard for "[f]ashionable women" as "pretty toys or as mere instruments of pleasure," and women "as the upper servant in the domestic relations" when married.[78] Marriage had indeed transformed since the nineteenth century, Weld Grimké believed, as she observed that men were beginning to take greater responsibility for household duties. "[S]till," she maintained, "I am sorry to say, woman after marriage is still very often little more than a slave."[79]

Weld Grimké, as a poet, educator, and playwright, may have been more guarded in her use of the woman-slave analogy than her white nineteenth-century predecessors. It is nevertheless apparent that, during the 1890s and beyond, other African-American novelists, reformers, and commentators exhibited a willingness to use discourses of slavery to describe the condition of women. This was, crucially, almost always to highlight the specific situation of African-American women in the specific context of chattel slavery and its ongoing legacy, enabling black women to contrast their own situation with that of white women. In this context, the woman-

---

[77] Angelina Emily Weld Grimké, "The Social Emancipation of Women," n.d., in Weld-Grimké Family Papers, William L. Clements Library, University of Michigan, Women and Social Movements in the United States, 1600–2000. Thanks to Isobelle Barrett Meyering for acquiring this source.

[78] Sarah Grimké, *Letters on the Equality of the Sexes, and the Condition of Woman: Addressed to Mary S. Parker* (Boston: Isaac Knapp, 1837/1838), 47; Sarah Grimké, "The Education of Woman," n.d., in *The Feminist Thought of Sarah Grimké*, ed. Gerda Lerner (New York: Oxford University Press, 1998), 83.

[79] Weld Grimké, "Social Emancipation."

slave analogy functioned to elucidate the situation of African-American women—specifically as women and African Americans—thus working to underscore the degree to which their oppression derived from gender, race, and class.

Another African-American woman who would pursue such a project was Mary Church Terrell. At the beginning of the twentieth century, she returned again and again to her ever-developing understanding of chattel slavery and its history. Cooper suggests that Terrell embraced her "personal ties to the history of enslavement to signify her racial identity and to inform her subjectivity as a *free woman*." As a child, the young Mary Church had experienced what Cooper describes as "a moment of rupture" when, during a history lesson at school, she realized that she was the descendant of formerly enslaved parents.[80] If not for the Civil War, Terrell emphasized in her 1904 address to the International Council of Women, "instead of addressing you as a free woman to night, in all human probability I should be on some plantation in one of the southern states of my country, manacled body and soul in the fetters of a slave." In some respects, this address echoed her 1898 remarks at the fiftieth anniversary of the National American Woman Suffrage Association (NAWSA). However, in 1904, she was instead addressing European rather than American spectators. Terrell characterized herself, quite specifically, as the "only woman who will speak from this platform whose parents were actually held as chattels and who but for the kindly intervention of a beneficent would herself be a slave." Despite this irrefutable declaration, Terrell also emphasized that she rejoiced "not only in the emancipation of my race, but in the almost universal elevation of my sex."[81]

The 1904 International Council of Women took place in Berlin, Germany. A polyglot fluent in English, French, and German, as well as Latin and Greek, Terrell astutely decided to deliver her address in German. The Europeans in attendance were manifestly surprised to learn that she was, in fact, a woman of color; this strategic maneuver, Cooper argues, allowed Terrell to transcend linguistic differences and thus to "refract the audience's gaze." The genre of autobiography therefore offered Terrell "a

---

[80] Cooper, *Beyond Respectability*, 77.
[81] Mary Church Terrell, Address to be Delivered at the International Congress of Women in Berlin, Germany, 13 June 1904, Mary Church Terrell Papers: Speeches and Writings, 1866–1953, Library of Congress.

site of intersectional theorizing."[82] It is equally important to emphasize the degree to which discourses of slavery offered the framework through which Terrell produced such a theorization. As much as American reformers were accustomed to the rhetorical flourish the woman-slave analogy so often provided, European women would have been familiar with discourses of slavery and discourses of emancipation being mobilized slightly differently. German women, for example, had discussed *frauenemancipation* as a concept representative of women's rights and enfranchisement as early as the 1840s.[83] Thus, those who witnessed Terrell's 1904 address would likely have been exposed to the distinct manner in which this rhetoric was mobilized in social movements across Europe. For most Europeans, however, this rhetoric was never quite as explicitly linked to chattel slavery—either in American or European imperial contexts—as it was amongst those in the United States. Concomitant with Terrell's ability to "refract the audience's gaze," then, was her desire to alert her spectators to their very different personal histories. In characterizing the extant possibilities of her own life as one of enslavement, Terrell, too, refuted the claim that all women were born to slavery. Explicitly suggesting that she herself could very well have been born enslaved, Terrell effectively told her white spectators that they could not have been.

At the other end of the political spectrum were those who embraced discourses of slavery to criticize the social and cultural mores of free African-American communities. The writings of William Hannibal Thomas, a conservative mixed-race journalist and legislator, denigrated the character of African-American women. His book *The American Negro: What He Was, What He Is, and What He May Become* (1901) suggested that "not only are fully ninety per cent of the negro women of America lascivious by instinct and in bondage to physical pleasure, but that the social degradation of our freedwomen is without a parallel in modern civilization."[84] Described by Estelle B. Freedman as "an unrepresentative figure," Thomas nonetheless expressed views that correlated with that of

[82] Cooper, *Beyond Respectability*, 77–81.

[83] Bonnie S. Anderson, "*Frauenemancipation* and Beyond: The Use of the Concept of Emancipation by Early European Feminists," in *Women's Rights and Transatlantic Antislavery in the Era of Emancipation*, eds. Kathryn Kish Sklar and James Brewer Stewart (New Haven: Yale University Press, 2007), 82–96.

[84] William Hannibal Thomas, *The American Negro: What He was, What He is, and What He May Become; a Critical and Practical Discussion* (New York: The Macmillan Company, 1901), 195.

those white southerners who continued to perpetuate antebellum stereotypes about black women's lack of sexual morality as a justification for sexual violence.[85]

The moments at which African Americans made recourse to the woman-slave analogy cannot be dismissed as a series of anomalies. When reconsidered alongside the abundant and myriad ways in which white reformers mobilized the woman-slave analogy, the manner in which African Americans used discourses of slavery to describe the situation of women emerges as both familiar and distinct. African-American women's literature exposed the real—rather than imagined—histories of enslaved women and the ongoing consequences of interracial sexual violence. The intent was to highlight the oppression of African-American women, enslaved and free, as well as to reclaim the history of chattel slavery. At the same time, African Americans not only partook in, but, to varying degrees, perpetuated a reform culture that had become dominated by a woman-as-slave worldview.

Remembering Abolitionism in White Slavery Narratives

In 1910, the US Congress passed the White Slave Traffic Act, also known as the Mann Act, to prohibit the trafficking of women across state lines for immoral purposes. This legislation led to more than 2000 arrests by law enforcement officials over the next eight years.[86] Gretchen Soderlund describes white slavery as "a social construct, a model for understanding commercial sex exchanges that entered the late Victorian and Progressive public spheres by way of mass-distributed cultural productions."[87] Its specious nature aside, many believed that white slavery was a more urgent social question than lynching, despite the reality of violence and racial segregation experienced by so many African Americans. The rhetoric used to frame this legislation represents the point at which the authorities began to take seriously the criticisms that women reformers, predominantly white women, had been developing for nearly a century. This legislative

---

[85] Freedman, *Redefining Rape*, 81.
[86] Brian Donovan, *White Slave Crusaders: Race, Gender, and Anti-vice Activism, 1887–1917* (Urbana: University of Illinois Press, 2006), 1.
[87] Gretchen Soderlund, *Sex Trafficking, Scandal, and the Transformation of Journalism, 1885–1917* (Chicago: University of Chicago Press, 2013), 5.

response suggests that the rationale for the woman-slave analogy—as specifically envisioned in the rhetoric of white slavery—had finally gained a degree of political and cultural acceptance. However, this also precipitated an even greater focus on the subjugation of white women, more surveillance of those women who did wish to engage in sex work, and further disregard for the situation of women of color, who continued to be at the greatest risk of sexual violence.

After the Civil War, slave emancipation transformed the meaning of prostitution and redefined it as a social problem that was symbolically inseparable from ideas about slavery and freedom.[88] This took place alongside the conceptual shift from black slave to white slave in popular culture, which, as the case of the Circassian Beauty revealed, reshaped ideas about who could be an enslaved person and what constituted an enslaved class. Historians suggest that the concept of white slavery had most often been associated with labor exploitation during the antebellum era; however, it had gained sexual connotations and, increasingly, an association with prostitution as early as the 1840s.[89] Although some suggest that these epistemic connections developed more unevenly, such ideas were well-established by the late nineteenth century.[90] The 1880s witnessed mounting concerns about the prospect of women laboring beyond the home. A belief that working women were in particular danger of becoming prostitutes coalesced to create what Sharon E. Wood describes as "an old image with a new gender: the white slave."[91]

The longer history of the woman-slave analogy offers yet another degree of context for what came to be described as the white slavery panic. An international phenomenon by the early twentieth century, it emerged as a transatlantic concern at a moment when white reformers were beginning to recast discourses of slavery in order to censure the subjugation of white women alone. The sensational revelations in W.T. Stead's 1885 exposé, "The Maiden Tribute of Modern Babylon," suggested that the market economy and its pernicious influence was causing girls and young

[88] Amy Dru Stanley, *From Bondage to Contract: Wage Labor, Marriage, and the Market in the Age of Slave Emancipation* (Cambridge: Cambridge University Press, 1998), 218–219.

[89] David R. Roediger, *The Wages of Whiteness: Race and the Making of the American Working Class* (London: Verso, 1991/2007), 72; Donovan, *White Slave Crusaders*, 18–19.

[90] Mara L. Keire, *For Business and Pleasure: Red-Light Districts and the Regulation of Vice in the United States, 1890–1933* (Baltimore: Johns Hopkins University Press, 2010), 70–73; Soderlund, *Sex Trafficking*, 2–6.

[91] Sharon E. Wood, *The Freedom of the Streets: Work, Citizenship, and Sexuality in a Gilded Age City* (Chapel Hill: University of North Carolina Press, 2005), 79, 8, 257. For a comparable analysis of this genealogy, see: Amy Lippert, "The Visual Pedagogy of Reform: Picturing White Slavery in America," *Journal of Urban History* (ahead-of-print 2019): 1–31, esp. 7–9.

women to become vulnerable to prostitution. Stead's series of articles, originally published in London's *Pall Mall Gazette*, described the phenomenon as "a veritable slave trade" flourishing in the "heart of London." "Slavery has gone. A slave trader is treated as *hostis humani generis* [an enemy of humankind]," he stated, in reference to the abolition of chattel slavery. "May we not hope, therefore, … [to] greatly reduce … the plague of prostitution?"[92] These claims particularly resonated with those Americans who had been abolitionists and antislavery sympathizers, refocusing their attention to that class—women—whose subjugation the Fifteenth Amendment had purportedly ignored.[93]

Stead's journalistic exposé anticipated what would come to be known as the "new abolitionism."[94] A strategy embraced amongst many anti-vice reformers was to render the white slave panic either locally or nationally specific. In the United States, Mara L. Keire argues, one approach was to situate the phenomenon in economic terms, emphasizing its commercial business interests; envisioning the red-light district as a marketplace of women; and focusing on indentured servitude as a form of debt peonage (or debt bondage).[95] However, the white slavery panic could be made even more nationally specific through the collective memory of other formative national experiences: chattel slavery, the antebellum antislavery movement, the Civil War, the Emancipation Proclamation, slave emancipation, and the Reconstruction amendments. This new generation of "moral entrepreneurs," Soderlund suggests, continued the work of the antebellum antislavery movement; their rhetoric drew on national and global ideas about racialized chattel slavery and sometimes even famous abolitionist iconography, such as the "Am I Not a Woman and a Sister?" emblem.[96] Anti-vice reformers aimed to generate support for the "new abolitionism" by mobilizing the nineteenth-century antislavery movement's symbolism in their addresses, pamphlets, and novels, including the specter of the "Great Emancipator," President Abraham Lincoln.[97] The earlier success of the antislavery movement inspired the use of antislavery and abolition as analogies—an approach Frederick Douglass himself had favored in his later suffrage addresses. Anti-vice reformers, like some African-American

[92] W.T. Stead, "We Bid You Be of Hope," *Pall Mall Gazette*, 6 July 1885.
[93] Soderlund, *Sex Trafficking*, 68.
[94] Donovan, *White Slave Crusaders*, Chapter 2.
[95] Keire, *For Business and Pleasure*, Chapter 4.
[96] Soderlund, *Sex Trafficking*, 6–7.
[97] Donovan, *White Slave Crusaders*, esp. 34–35.

reformers, structured both fictional and nonfictional white slavery literature around the collective memory of chattel slavery and the Civil War.

White slave narratives are said to have "peaked around 1910," the year in which the White Slave Traffic Act was introduced.[98] The characteristics of these novels, however, owed much to antebellum reformist literature, especially Harriet Beecher Stowe's *Uncle Tom's Cabin*, which dominated popular culture across 1852–1853 and remained a potent transatlantic cultural force thereafter.[99] This bestselling novel had long held a pivotal position in offering inspiration to other reform novelists. Mary Gove Nichols' semiautobiographical *Mary Lyndon; or, Revelations of a Life* (1854), for example, provoked comparisons to Stowe's novel. A free love advocate who condemned the many facets of women's oppression, Nichols envisaged *Mary Lyndon* as "an *Uncle Tom's Cabin* for women," while the abolitionist and women's rights reformer Henry B. Blackwell, who personally repudiated free love, recognized Nichols in the characteristics of its heroine.[100] Antebellum southern women had also found inspiration in the slave narrative, although their proslavery novels focused on the lives and trials of elite southern slaveholders rather than their enslaved property.[101] Based on the character archetype of the fugitive slave, as epitomized in Stowe's novel, the fugitive wife trope also went on to define much women's rights and free love literature between the late 1850s and early 1870s. Amongst suffragists from the west coast to the east, including Elizabeth Cady Stanton and Abigail Scott Duniway, the fugitive wife echoed throughout women's rights debates about marriage and divorce.

Subsequently, many white slave narratives found inspiration in these antislavery sources. As Brian Donovan details, anti-vice and temperance reformers such as Jane Addams and Frances E. Willard styled their own efforts as an extension of Stowe's antislavery legacy. Reginald Wright Kaufmann's novel *The House of Bondage* (1910) is described as "perhaps the closest imitator of *Uncle Tom's Cabin*." Its narrative followed a white teenager from rural Pennsylvania who is abducted and victimized by a Jewish procurer of white slaves, then by a French brothel madam. *The House of Bondage* appropriated various character names and storylines

[98] Freedman, *Redefining Rape*, 157.
[99] Meer, *Uncle Tom Mania*; Jo-Ann Morgan, *Uncle Tom's Cabin as Visual Culture* (Columbia: University of Missouri Press, 2007).
[100] Passett, *Sex Radicals*, 30, 19–20.
[101] Russ Castronovo, "Incidents in the Life of a White Woman: Economies of Race and Gender in the Antebellum Nation," *American Literary History* 10, no. 2 (1998): 239–265.

from Stowe's original: for example, Stowe's villain is the slaveowner Simon Legree and Kaufmann's is the brothel madam Rose Legérè.[102] But this novel's title also quite literally copied that of a far more recent antislavery work: Octavia V. Rogers Albert's 1890 documentary history of chattel slavery, *The House of Bondage*, itself a testimony to the fortitude of formerly enslaved African Americans. Beyond the memory of chattel slavery, Kauffman alluded to other types of labor exploitation, including the continued abuse of African laborers in European colonies and of white laborers across the globe. As Kauffman reflected, "the slaves of Rose Legérè were as much slaves as any mutilated black man of the Congo, or any toil-cramped white man in a factory."[103]

But which type of exploitation did these anti-vice reformers consider to be more egregious? Ernest A. Bell's book *Fighting the Traffic in Young Girls; or, War on the White Slave Trade* (c. 1910) illustrates the degree to which the anti-vice movement undermined the legacy of chattel slavery, as its subtitle positioned white slavery as "The Greatest Crime in World's History." "No white slave need remain in slavery in this state of Abraham Lincoln," Bell reflected, "who made the black slaves free."[104] Other novels, such as Anne Lee's *A Woman in Revolt* (1913), explored the phenomenon by evoking the legacy of the Civil War. When the character of Dr Rathbourne gives an address about white slavery, he denounces the "white slave driver" and questions how this figure could keep "a young, helpless girl in this horrible bondage, more atrocious and indefensible than that for which the Civil War was fought."[105] This style of analysis sidelined the concerns of women of color outright, although some anti-vice reformers did concede that such terminology had the potential to be misleading. "The term white slavery, perhaps, is a misnomer," Clifford G. Roe admitted in a NAWSA pamphlet in 1911, "since the traffic reaches to every race and color." However, the erstwhile focus on the "abolition" of the "white slave market" amongst anti-vice reformers meant the vast majority of criticisms assumed that white girls and women were most—and perhaps even

---

[102] Donovan, *White Slave Crusaders*, 35–36.

[103] Reginald Wright Kauffman, *The House of Bondage* (Upper Saddle River: The Gregg Press, 1910), 69.

[104] Ernest A. Bell, *Fighting the Traffic in Young Girls; or, War on the White Slave Trade* (Chicago: G.S. Ball, c. 1910), 194.

[105] Anne Lee, *A Woman in Revolt* (New York: Desmond FitzGerald, 1913), 311, 305.

exclusively—vulnerable to the "traffic in girls for immoral demands."[106] By producing a rhetorical binary between antebellum chattel slavery and postbellum white slavery, anti-vice reformers minimized the brutality of the former in order to focus unequivocally on popular beliefs about white women's contemporary victimization.[107]

These tendencies resonated throughout anti-vice literature, becoming most fully developed in the work of Jane Addams. Her research was based on a Juvenile Protection Association report that described narratives about sexual exploitation in terms of white slavery.[108] The structure of Addams' key work, *A New Conscience and an Ancient Evil* (1912), developed a binary between chattel slavery and prostitution that would resonate throughout. The "new conscience," for Addams, was an awareness of prostitution; and the "ancient evil" was slavery itself. "Chapter 1: An Analogy" pursued an overt comparison between chattel slavery and what Addams considered to be the "twin of slavery"—white slavery. Although she described the comparison as a structural shortcoming, noting that it is "always easy to overwork an analogy," Addams continued to provide an elaborate history of the antebellum antislavery movement in order to give immediacy to this new reform imperative. Addams used chattel slavery and its representation in Stowe's *Uncle Tom's Cabin* to describe what she perceived as the similarities between the Underground Railroad, a secret network of antebellum safehouses established to assist fugitive slaves, and the "rescue homes and preventive associations" of the Progressive Era. Believing that the "sexual commerce" in large cities provided the "economic basis" for white slavery, Addams persistently returned to discourses of slavery to emphasize how "the chastity of women is bought and sold." While she distanced "commercialized vice" from the legal questions surrounding marriage and divorce, Addams nonetheless sought to induce sentimental reflection on the subject, highlighting the "overwhelming pity" surrounding the "white slave traffic," which supposedly affected "thousands of young girls, many of them still children."[109] In the process,

---

[106] Clifford G. Roe, *What Women Might Do with the Ballot: The Abolition of the White Slave Traffic* (New York: National American Woman Suffrage Association, 1911), 1.

[107] Donovan, *White Slave Crusaders*, 32–34; Soderlund, *Sex Trafficking*, 6–7.

[108] Janet Beer and Katherine Joslin, "Diseases of the Body Politic: White Slavery in Jane Addams 'A New Conscience and an Ancient Evil' and Selected Short Stories by Charlotte Perkins Gilman," *Journal of American Studies* 33, no. 1 (1999): 6.

[109] Jane Addams, *A New Conscience and an Ancient Evil* (New York: The Macmillan Company, 1912), 4–6, 9–11.

Addams followed the conclusions of countless white reformers in that she described white slavery as more egregious than chattel slavery.

Maude E. Miner's anti-vice manifesto, unambiguously titled *The Slavery of Prostitution: A Plea for Emancipation* (1916), described itself as "an earnest study of what I consider without sensationalism or exaggeration to be the *slavery of prostitution*." Her treatise offered a definition of what she believed constituted slavery in these circumstances. Importantly, this was a vision quite distinct from what defined chattel slavery. Women and girls were not, Miner suggested, "except in rare instances, physically enslaved; but through loss of freedom of will and of action, they have been bound to prostitution." It was the victim's "demoralization of character" that became the source of their "moral enslavement." And this, according to Miner, was worse than chattel slavery. "More insidious and deadly than any physical bondage," she intimated, "is this moral servitude." The archetypical "newcomer to prostitution" was "a runaway girl," who she described in similar terms to the fugitive wife. Often "deserted by a man who promised to marry her," she becomes pregnant, is reviled by family, and thrust upon her own resources.[110] Anti-vice reformers collectively maintained that white women were most—and perhaps even only— affected by the white slave trade, a claim which correlated with their conclusion that forced prostitution was worse than chattel slavery.

Remembering Social Reformers

Frederick Douglass appeared at the 1893 World's Columbian Exhibition as an elder statesman of the nineteenth century's social movements. Looking toward an era when "all discriminations against men and women on account of color and sex ... will pass away," Douglass offered a brief address to the World's Congress of Representative Women, where he was the only man to speak as part of its General Congress.[111] The commemoration of the lives, labors, and rhetoric of Douglass and his contemporaries soon offered yet another opportunity to reflect upon the analogies between abolitionism and women's rights, woman and slave, and the rights contingent upon distinctions of sex and race. The meaning and implications of the comparisons, which Douglass had both questioned and embraced as

---

[110] Maude E. Miner, *The Slavery of Prostitution: A Plea for Emancipation* (New York: The Macmillan Company, 1916), ix, 22–23. Emphasis in original.

[111] Frederick Douglass, *World's Congress*, 717.

early as the 1840s, continued to have great resonance amongst later generations of reformers.

At the turn of the twentieth century, the younger generation of reformers began to memorialize their forebears. The Nineteenth Amendment, which extended the elective franchise to women in 1920, was popularly described as the Susan B. Anthony Amendment.[112] Among both black and white women, local as well as national organizations such as the Julia Ward Howe Republican Women's Club in Providence, Rhode Island, and the Susan B. Anthony League came into existence.[113] The Lucy Stone League, established in 1921, followed in the footsteps of its namesake by advocating for women who wished to retain their maiden name after marriage.[114] Beyond initiatives such as these, however, the commemorative efforts of reformers reveal the significance that both the woman-slave analogy and the sex-race analogy had gained across the many nineteenth-century social movements dedicated to women's rights.

The *History of Woman Suffrage*, published in six volumes between 1881 and 1922, emerged as one of the most influential examples of activists chronicling the history of their own movement. It was edited by such celebrated and influential suffragists as Elizabeth Cady Stanton, Susan B. Anthony, Matilda Joslyn Gage, and Ida Husted Harper. The historical narrative it constructed, however, offered a far from neutral interpretation. As Lisa Tetrault argues, the *History of Woman Suffrage* reimagined the history of the women's movement. Beginning with the 1848 women's rights convention in Seneca Falls, New York, these volumes privileged the National Woman Suffrage Association (NWSA) at the expense of the American Woman Suffrage Association and disregarded the contributions of most African Americans. However, this narrative was also constructed at Stanton's own expense, especially after her political and religious radicalism began to alienate her coadjutors during the 1890s. Anthony, in contrast, became an increasingly perceptive and recognizable suffragist, allowing her to astutely emerge at the heart of the movement's historical memory.[115]

---

[112] Elaine Weiss, *The Woman's Hour: The Great Fight to Win the Vote* (New York: Viking, 2018), 8.

[113] Terborg-Penn, *African American Women*, 103–104; Simon Schama, *Landscape and Memory* (New York: Vintage Books, 1996), 387–389.

[114] Claudia Goldin and Maria Shim, "Making a Name: Women's Surnames at Marriage and Beyond," *Journal of Economic Perspectives* 18, no. 2 (2004): 143–160.

[115] Lisa Tetrault, *The Myth of Seneca Falls: Memory and the Women's Suffrage Movement, 1848–1898* (Chapel Hill: University of North Carolina Press, 2014).

7 "SLAVERY REDIVIVUS": FREE LOVE, RACIAL UPLIFT... 293

What began with Anthony herself turned into self-perpetuating commemorative efforts that continued across the twentieth century and even today.[116]

Despite the organizational conflicts it elided, the *History of Woman Suffrage* revealed the centrality of the woman-slave analogy as it had been mobilized by white women reformers. As a result, these volumes highlighted the countless ways in which women's rights reformers and, in particular, white suffragists had used and abused discourses of slavery for half a century and more. It arguably foregrounded the voices of those African-American women whose rhetoric had reflected that of white suffragists most closely.[117] However, many other, if often far smaller, commemorative efforts emerged in conjunction with and following this masterful work, not least the eulogies and memorialization that began amongst the reformers themselves. This again revealed the significance of the woman-slave analogy for those reformers who sought to commemorate their own efforts as well as that of their friends and coadjutors. Collectively, these sites of memorialization echoed the rhetoric not only of celebrated reformers, but also of many of the specific causes to which they had dedicated themselves.

As early as 1869, some commentators began to describe the reformers associated with the women's rights and suffrage movements as "Lady Emancipators."[118] This recalled the antebellum words of Paulina Wright Davis, who, in 1853, had described herself and her fellow women's rights reformers as the "abolitionists of slavery among women," comments which had been quickly endorsed by *Frederick Douglass' Paper*.[119] In the years after the Civil War, these reflections would become increasingly central as antebellum reform luminaries began to pass on. Often, reform eulogists focused on how abolitionist women aimed to alleviate oppression in its many forms: not only through the abolition of chattel slavery and slave emancipation, but also amongst women.[120] This style of memorialization

---

[116] Christine A. Kray, Tamar W. Carroll, and Hinda Mandell, eds. *Nasty Women and Bad Hombres: Historical Reflections on the 2016 U.S. Presidential Election* (Rochester: University of Rochester Press, 2018).

[117] Terborg-Penn, *African American Women*, 31, 35.

[118] "Emancipation of Turkish Women," *Revolution* (from the *Messenger Franco American*), 21 May 1868.

[119] "The Moral Character of Woman," *Una*, 1 June 1853; "WOMAN," *Frederick Douglass' Paper*, 10 June 1853.

[120] Ana Stevenson, "The 'Great Doctrine of Human Rights': Articulation and Authentication in the Nineteenth-Century US Antislavery and Women's Rights Movements," *Humanity: An International Journal of Human Rights, Humanitarianism, and Development* 8, no. 3 (2017): 430–431.

necessarily echoed the words of antebellum reformers themselves, specifically their own use of the woman-slave analogy. At the 1879 memorial for Angelina Grimké Weld, for example, Lucy Stone recalled how Sarah Grimké, who had passed away in 1873, espoused "one great purpose to 'remember those in bonds as bound with them.'" Angelina herself, the abolitionist Elizur Wright reminisced, had labored for abolitionism as well as to eliminate the "tyranny and prejudice which have always hitherto consigned her sex to ... absolute thralldom."[121]

Remembering the lives of women reformers through the lens of a woman-as-slave worldview continued well into the twentieth century. It was a project to which Douglass himself contributed. In his final autobiography, *The Life and Times of Frederick Douglass* (1892), he famously stated that the "cause of the slave has been peculiarly woman's cause." Commemorating Lucretia Mott and her contemporaries, Douglass foregrounded some of the ideas that had animated not only their antislavery efforts, but also the women's rights movement. "Sympathetic in her nature," he reflected, "it was easy for Mrs. [Lydia Maria] Child to 'remember those in bonds as bound with them,'" noting also how his own abolitionism led him toward the woman question:

> Observing woman's agency, devotion, and efficiency in pleading the cause of the slave, gratitude for this high service early motivated me to give favorable attention to ... what is called "woman's rights" and caused me to be denominated a woman's-rights man.

Attributing his own conversion to conversations with Stanton, Douglass repeated what he had asserted many times over—as early as the late 1840s in his abolitionist newspaper, the *North Star*. In the final years of his life, Douglass continued to both assert and broaden his vision of what constituted oppression beyond the limits of chattel slavery alone. "War, slavery, injustice and oppression, and the idea that might makes right," he reflected, meant that many individuals "have had practically no rights which the strong have felt bound to respect." Douglass thus echoed the words of Chief Justice Roger B. Taney in the *Dred Scott v. Stanford* decision of 1857. Again, asserting his ongoing support for woman suffrage, Douglass

---

[121] Theodore Dwight Weld, *In Memory: Angelina Grimké Weld* (Boston: George H. Ellis, 1880), 25, 23.

offered an analogy between the prospect of women's enfranchisement and the disenfranchisement of African Americans.[122]

On the day of his passing in February 1895, Douglass had been feted by Susan B. Anthony and Anna Howard Shaw at a meeting of the National Council of Women in Washington, DC.[123] The most famous self-emancipated abolitionist of the nineteenth century became the object of much memorialization. At a Douglass Memorial Meeting in 1899, for example, the African-American educator Rosa Hazard Hazel reflected: "The woman who would battle for the freedom of the slave soon found that ... she herself worked with fettered limbs, and unworthily, until her own individuality was recognized, her own freedom accomplished." Hazel's reflections both privileged discourses of slavery and endorsed the sex-race analogy. "In the chemistry of his own soul," she believed, Douglass had discovered an "affinity between the rights of the negro and the rights of woman." His example, Hazel averred, must remain an inspiration for African-American men. On account of their own experiences of oppression, she believed that such men had "less excuse for an attitude of indifference to the political inferiority of woman, in that his own escape from bondage has been largely due to her efforts."[124]

At the 1908 centennial anniversary of Seneca Falls County, a year that also celebrated the sixtieth anniversary of the Seneca Falls women's rights convention, Mary Church Terrell commemorated the life of Frederick Douglass. In doing so, she reiterated some of the proclamations that Douglass himself had made throughout his life, as well as the perspective Hazel had espoused nearly a decade earlier. Proudly describing herself as "a woman like Elizabeth Cady Stanton," Terrell emphasized that she was also a woman who "belong[s] to the race of which Frederick Douglass was such a magnificent representative":

> I know what it means to be circumscribed, deprived, handicapped and fettered on account of my sex. But I assure you that no where in the United States have my feelings been so lacerated, my spirit so crushed, my heart so

---

[122] Frederick Douglass, *Life and Times of Frederick Douglass* (Boston: De Wolfe & Fiske Co., 1892), 570–571, 574–576; *Dred Scott v. Sanford*, 1857.

[123] S. Jay Walker, "Frederick Douglass and Woman Suffrage," *The Black Scholar* 14, no. 5 (1983): 18–25; Fought, *Women in the World*, 290.

[124] "Mrs. Rosa H. Hazel at Douglass Memorial Meeting, St. Paul, Minnesota," *Twin City American*, 4 May 1899, in *Frederick Douglass on Women's Rights*, ed. Philip S. Foner (New York: Da Capo Press, 1976/1992), 172–174.

wounded, no where have I been so humiliated and handicapped on account of my sex as I have been on account of my race.[125]

Although Terrell essentially agreed with many white women reformers in her assertion that a woman could be "fettered on account of [her] sex," she emphasized that the oppressions derived from sex and race were not, in fact, equal. Terrell had effectively "assumed the role of the racial or minorities protagonist," a strategy she used frequently in her advocacy of woman suffrage.[126]

Other commemorative tributes reflected the more pernicious meanings that had come to be associated with the woman-slave analogy in recent decades. Zula Maud Woodhull, for example, the daughter of Victoria Woodhull, recalled how her mother "took up the part of helpless woman, who stupidly acquiesces in her position as the white slave of man."[127] Increasingly, these sites of memory not only reiterated discourses of slavery, but also uncritically accepted the belief that nineteenth-century women, as much as freedpeople, had been enslaved and in need of emancipation. This occurred when the National Woman's Party (NWP) feted Margaret Fuller, the transcendentalist who had penned *Woman in the Nineteenth Century* (1845) but died prematurely well before the women's movement really gained momentum. Only three years after the ratification of the Nineteenth Amendment of 1920, which enfranchised all women but left African-American women and men effectively disenfranchised, the NWP remembered Fuller for "emancipating a class whose period of slavery was to mark its ending through her activity and her far-reaching influence."[128] Public and press memorials such as these collectively accepted and reinforced the influence of the woman-slave analogy, which had defined a century's reform efforts dedicated to alleviating women's oppression.

These tendencies became most prominent in the celebration of Susan B. Anthony. To describe her life's work, both the mainstream and reform press drew upon a variety of ideas about freedom and slavery in the United

---

[125] Mary Church Terrell, "Frederick Douglass," 1908, Centennial Anniversary of Seneca County and Auxiliary Papers, Seneca Falls Historical Society, in Ibid., 176–179.

[126] Terborg-Penn, *African American Women*, 68.

[127] Zula Maud Woodhull, biographical sketch of Victoria Woodhull, n.d., Victoria Woodhull Papers, Box 3: Manuscript Fragments, Boston Public Library.

[128] Lavinia Egan, "Margaret Fuller—Feminist and Literateur," *Equal Rights: Official Weekly of the National Woman's Party*, 22 September 1923, Margaret Fuller Papers, Houghton Library, Harvard University.

States. After Anthony's passing in March 1906, Terrell emphasized how she had worked "indefatigably" as an abolitionist at a memorial held in New York City. "The debt of gratitude which white women owe Susan B. Anthony is great enough," Terrell stated, "but the representatives of a race which bowed under the yoke of a cruel bondage in addition to bearing the burdens of a handicapped sex owe her a debt of gratitude that cannot be estimated in words." Terrell's comments were qualified by race to specifically elucidate the differential emphasis that white reformers placed on white versus black women's enfranchisement. However, Terrell still believed that Anthony, as a reformer, had devoted herself to "promot[ing] the cause of freedom." Anthony had worked in fulfilling the AASS's "holy mission to secure freedom for the oppressed, until the shackles had fallen from the last slave," she asserted.[129] And while Terrell's comments were explicit, noting that this took place in Anthony's capacity as an antebellum abolitionist, others may not have been so judicious in their interpretation. Indeed, Anthony herself would have taken Terrell's particular turn of phrase, "until the shackles had fallen from the last slave," as a reference both to formerly enslaved people of African descent as well as women—most especially disenfranchised women.

Days later, Anthony's long-time biographer and collaborator Ida Husted Harper wrote another obituary for her friend and coadjutor. The memorial would be accompanied by a masthead featuring the suffragist leaning down to a supplicant woman, recalling the supplicant slave from the "Am I Not a Woman and a Sister" abolitionist emblem of the 1830s.[130] In this masthead, however, the black supplicant slave is replaced by a white woman. Another memorial cast Anthony as a "Liberator," most assuredly in regard to her work as a suffragist rather than as an abolitionist.[131] This continued well into the twentieth century when the *New York Times Magazine* described Anthony's "slogan" as having been "Woman is in Chains."[132] The centrality of this particular catchphrase has not endured,

[129] Mary Church Terrell, "Remarks Made at the Memorial Service Held in Honor of Susan B. Anthony in New York City, March 25th, 1906," 1–2, Mary Church Terrell Papers: Speeches and Writings, 1866–1953, Library of Congress.

[130] Ida Husted Harper, "The Passing of Susan B. Anthony," *Collier's*, 31 March 1906, Susan B. Anthony Papers, Series I: Biographical Material and Writings, 1935/n.d., Sophia Smith Collection.

[131] "Susan B. Anthony: Liberator," Susan B. Anthony Papers, Series I: Biographical Material and Writings, 1935/n.d., Sophia Smith Collection.

[132] R.F. Dibble, "She Blazed the Trail for Suffrage: Now a Shrine Will Honor Susan B. Anthony, Whose Slogan Was: 'Woman is in Chains'," *New York Times Magazine*, 12 April 1925.

as the phrase that Anthony biographers would later describe as her "talismanic words" were "Failure Is Impossible."[133] It nonetheless indicates the degree to which various iterations of the woman-slave analogy permeated the cultural memory of the woman suffrage movement. Another 1938 headline, alongside a photograph of Anthony, claimed that "Women Throw Off Shackles, Win Vote, Rise to Political Power in Sixty Years."[134]

Many twentieth-century commemorations posited that Anthony had worked toward the emancipation of women, just as George Washington had emancipated the United States from the political slavery of the British Crown and Abraham Lincoln had emancipated African Americans from chattel slavery. A *Washington Post* article declared that Anthony shared "Similarity of Characteristics With Washington and Lincoln."[135] During her birthday month of February, and sometimes even on her birthday itself, Anthony was routinely compared to both of these men. On its February 1947 magazine cover, one magazine declared Washington, Lincoln, and Anthony to be "The Three Great Emancipators."[136] Rosa Arnold Powell, a former secretary and treasurer of the Susan B. Anthony League during the 1920s, campaigned for a decade to have Anthony's likeness carved into Mount Rushmore alongside the four former presidents Jefferson, Roosevelt, Washington, and Lincoln.[137] Years after Powell had given up on her ultimately unsuccessful campaign, she listed Anthony as a great "American Emancipator," alongside Washington and Lincoln, in the 15 February 1956 edition of the *Christian Science Monitor*.[138]

These efforts collectively indicate the difficulties that twentieth-century women reformers encountered in their attempts to ensure the efforts of

---

[133] Kathleen Barry, *Susan B. Anthony: A Biography of a Singular Feminist* (New York: New York University Press, 1988), Chapter 13; Ida Husted Harper, *The Life and Work of Susan B. Anthony*, Vol. 3 (Indianapolis: The Hollenbeck Press, 1908), 1409, 1442.

[134] "Women Throw Off Shackles, Win Vote, Rise to Political Power in Sixty Years," *Minneapolis Journal*, 24 November 1938, Folder A: 107, Rosa Arnold Powell Collection, Schlesinger Library.

[135] Ida Husted Harper, "Biographer Lauds Susan B. Anthony's Work for Suffrage," *Washington Post*, 15 February 1925, Susan Brownell Anthony Scrapbook, 1905–1906, Reel 6, The Papers of Susan B. Anthony, Library of Congress Manuscript Division.

[136] "The Three Great Emancipators," *The American Soroptimist*, February 1947, Folder A: 107, Rosa Arnold Powell Collection, Schlesinger Library.

[137] Schama, *Landscape and Memory*, 385–392.

[138] Rosa Arnold Powell, "American Emancipators Honored Together," *Christian Science Monitor*, 15 February 1956, Folder A: 107, Rosa Arnold Powell Collection, Schlesinger Library.

their forebears were adequately commemorated. Mobilizing the woman-slave analogy as journalistic hyperbole, memorial articles directly echoed the claims of the nineteenth-century reformers themselves. However, using discourses of slavery to situate Susan B. Anthony's achievements relative to presidents Washington and Lincoln might be seen to only have had vacillating success, as genuine efforts to commemorate the suffragists only really launched during the 1960s and 1970s.[139] The memorialization of nineteenth-century reformers more often contributed to the forgetting of chattel slavery and the appropriation of discourses of slavery for the benefit of white women alone.

Conclusion

The reconfiguration of discourses of slavery across the postbellum era was indebted to the collective memory of antebellum chattel slavery, which came to be mobilized as an impetus for new social movements. However, using the woman-slave analogy to describe the subjugation of women, especially in the context of sexual violence, had competing results amongst the reformers of the Progressive Era. Free love advocates and anti-vice reformers, alongside many white suffragists, positioned the prostitution of white women as more extreme than antebellum chattel slavery, conveniently sidelining the continued subjugation of freedpeople. African-American novelists and reformers, however, used this collective memory to interrogate the connections between oppressions derived from race, gender, and class.

Why, by the 1890s, did so many more African Americans come to express a newfound propensity to embrace the woman-slave analogy? The entrance of more African-American women into the public sphere may simply have resulted in more opportunities for individuals to express a woman-as-slave worldview. It may also be attributed to a greater willingness to use discourses of slavery to describe that which is not chattel slavery in the decades that followed slave emancipation. Equally significant, however, is the fact that African-American women constantly interrogated the very recent reality of chattel slavery in conjunction with new analyses of black women's oppression. "The consciousness of being fully free has not yet come to the great masses of colored women," Fannie Barrier Williams reflected in 1900. "To feel that you are something better than a

[139] Tetrault, *Myth of Seneca Falls*, 193–196.

slave, or a descendant of an ex-slave, to feel that you are a unit in the womanhood of a great nation and a great civilization, is the beginning of self-respect and the respect of your race."[140] However, the broader focus on the need to ameliorate women's oppression on the basis of gender alone, rather on the basis of sex and race, meant that few white reformers were willing to embrace a similar approach.

---

[140] Fannie Barrier Williams, "The Club Movement among Colored Women of America," in Booker T. Washington, *A New Negro for a New Century: An Accurate and Up-to-Date Record of the Upward Struggles of the Negro Race* (Chicago: American Publishing House, 1900), 383, 404.

CHAPTER 8

"Lady Emancipators": Conclusion

In 1906, following the passing of the famous abolitionist and suffragist Susan B. Anthony, the president of the National Association of Colored Women, Mary Church Terrell, penned a eulogy in *The Voice of the Negro*:

> The debt of gratitude which women ... owe Miss Anthony is great enough to be sure. But the representatives of that race which but fifty years ago bowed under a yoke of cruel bondage ... in addition to bearing the burdens of a handicapped sex, owe her a dept of gratitude which cannot be expressed in words.[1]

Terrell, whose life was dedicated to racial uplift, civil rights, and woman suffrage, reserved her use of discourses of slavery to describe the experience of African Americans, herself included. Observing the achievements of Anthony's own life, Terrell contemplated the important resonances between those social movements dedicated to antislavery and women's rights. W.E.B. DuBois' book *Dark Water: Voices from within the Veil* (1920) also concluded that the "uplift of women is, next to the problem of the color line and the peace movement, our greatest modern cause."

---

[1] Mary Church Terrell, "Susan B. Anthony, The Abolitionist," *Voice of the Negro* (June 1906): 411.

© The Author(s) 2019
A. Stevenson, *The Woman as Slave in Nineteenth-Century American Social Movements*, Palgrave Studies in the History of Social Movements, https://doi.org/10.1007/978-3-030-24467-5_8

DuBois regarded the connections between these movements, of "woman and color," as having "deep meaning."[2]

By the early twentieth century, influential African-American reformers such as Terrell and DuBois had come to embrace the sex-race analogy as an evocative expression of the connections between social movements dedicated to sex and race—and sometimes even to elucidate the oppression engendered by both. A century earlier, however, most women reformers had approached its precursor, the woman-slave analogy, very differently. Through metempsychosis, the abolitionist women of the 1830s began to imagine themselves as experiencing a state of slavery in very nearly strictly abolitionist circumstances. Some then considered the extent to which they, as women, were suffering gender-based prejudice and discrimination within the American Anti-Slavery Society. Their successors in the women's rights movement then contemplated the degree to which a larger proportion of women—namely, married women—might also be enslaved. Hereafter, dress reformers, labor reformers, suffragists, and free love advocates declared the possibility that a far wider proportion of women than ever before—all women, in fact—could consider themselves to be an "enslaved" class. In the midst of this transformation, the Civil War era changed the circumstances under which reformers were operating. Those women reformers who had convinced themselves of being another enslaved class did not experience Reconstruction in the same manner as formerly enslaved people of African descent. In the wake of slave emancipation, suffragists, free love advocates, and anti-vice reformers increasingly argued that all women faced a situation far more dire than chattel slavery had ever been.

In their antebellum analyses of the woman question, some white reformers and many black reformers had remained attentive to the distinctive situation of enslaved people of African descent. African Americans, however, never forgot about chattel slavery or its unfinished legacy. Some illustrated a willingness to use discourses of slavery to analyze the literal and metaphorical exploitation of enslaved women, the subjugation of wives, the rigors of fashion, labor exploitation, disenfranchisement, and the general condition of women, especially black women. Most crucially, these analyses always remained in perspective, as African-American reformers contextualized different forms of oppression so as not to undermine the severity

[2] W.E.B. Du Bois, *Dark Water: Voices from within the Veil* (New York: Harcourt, Brace & Co., 1920), Chapter 7.

of chattel slavery. In the process, these reformers came to evoke a greater preference for the sex-race analogy than the woman-slave analogy, potentially because the former was both less offensive and possibly more believable than the latter. At the turn of the twentieth century, African-American reformers did not abandon analogy; instead, many continued to embrace it as a literary device through which activism grounded in concerns about race, gender, and sometimes class could inform one another.

If most antebellum reformers had conceded that chattel slavery was the most severe form of oppression, its abolition in 1865 created a watershed moment. Few white reformers, following slave emancipation, continued to embrace the woman-slave analogy in a manner that remained attentive to the influence of race or class in addition to that of gender. Instead, they focused on the sense of sameness borne of legal subjugation and patriarchy. But what did this do for their cause? As David Brion Davis argues of wage slavery, "analogies with chattel slavery may ... have retarded the development of a vocabulary that could depict more subtle forms of coercion, oppression, and class rule."[3] The same must be said of the woman-slave analogy, a rhetorical device that inhibited a more meaningful discourse for analyzing women's oppression. Despite its limitations, the analogy did operate as a literary device as well as a reform and political strategy through which many reformers began to pursue a theoretical analysis of the woman question. Interpreting the long history of the woman-slave analogy illuminates the degree to which white women used this rhetoric to focus on their own situation, as well as the manner in which African Americans explored the connections between race, gender, and class. It also suggests that the history of the woman-slave analogy needs to be situated in terms of the longer history of feminist theory.

ANTICIPATING INTERSECTIONALITY?

Intersectionality has become a key framework for the analysis of the intersections that exist between multiple axes of oppression. It emerged as a criticism of the activist and scholarly analyses that had failed to consider how different forms of oppression—including that derived from gender, race, class, sexuality, ethnicity, and nation—intersect. It was only by the 1980s that scholars really began to appreciate that minority-group

---

[3] David Brion Davis, "Reflections on Abolitionism and Ideological Hegemony," *American Historical Review* 92, no. 4 (1987): 809.

analogies, including between sex and race, were inefficient when applied to women's history as "explanatory concepts."[4] More than a century earlier, the woman-slave analogy had existed as a particularly prominent example of this very failure in reform discourse.

A term developed by critical race legal scholar Kimberlé Crenshaw between 1989 and 1991, intersectionality is now viewed as one of the most important interventions in both feminist theory and critical race studies.[5] Crenshaw, together with Sumi Cho and Leslie McCall, has recently described intersectionality as an "analytic sensibility" that informs a scholar's analysis, rather than a methodological or theoretical approach per se:

> If intersectionality is an analytic disposition, a way of thinking about and conducting analyses, then what makes an analysis intersectional is not its use of the term "intersectionality", nor its being situated in a familiar genealogy, nor its drawing on lists of standard citations. Rather, what makes an analysis intersectional—whatever terms it deploys, whatever its iteration, whatever its field or discipline—is its adoption of an intersectional way of thinking about the problem of sameness and difference and its relation to power.[6]

This renewed attention toward questions of sameness and difference echoes Carla L. Peterson's analysis of analogy in the antebellum era.[7] It prompts a reconsideration of why certain reformers had, in previous centuries, embraced analogy in the first place, as well as reflections about what took place in the intervening centuries to challenge and transform how scholars and activists approach analogy.

[4] Joan Kelly-Gadol, "The Social Relation of the Sexes: Methodological Implications of Women's History," in *Feminism and Methodology: Social Science Issues*, ed. Sandra G. Harding (Bloomington: Indiana University Press, 1987), 19.

[5] Kimberlé Crenshaw, "Demarginalizing the Intersection of Race and Sex: A Black Feminist Critique of Antidiscrimination Doctrine, Feminist Theory and Antiracist Politics," *University of Chicago Legal Forum* 139 (1989): 139–167; Kimberlé Crenshaw, "Mapping the Margins: Intersectionality, Identity Politics, and Violence against Women of Color," *Stanford Law Review* 43, no. 6 (1991): 1241–1299.

[6] Sumi Cho, Kimberlé Williams Crenshaw, and Leslie McCall, "Toward a Field of Intersectionality Studies: Theory, Applications, and Praxis," *Signs: Journal of Women in Culture and Society* 38, no. 4 (2013): 785–810.

[7] Carla L. Peterson, "'And We Claim Our Rights': The Rights Rhetoric of Black and White Women Activists before the Civil War," in *Sister Circle: Black Women and Work*, ed. Sharon Harley and the Black Women and Work Collective (New Brunswick: Rutgers University Press, 2002).

Historically, many different analytic and methodological frameworks have been used to understand and theorize the connections between gender, race, and class. As Anna Carastathis explains, intersectionality emerged as the product of black activist women's participation in social movements across the twentieth century. Together, these activists "identified the manifold manifestations of oppression, discrimination, and violence that structure the conditions in which women of colour live in the United States, Britain, and other white settler and imperial states."[8] Earlier generations of African Americans, from late-nineteenth-century race women to twentieth-century communists, had also signaled a desire to illuminate and interrogate the connections between different forms of oppression.[9] This ethos found greater articulation in the context of the civil rights and women's movements during the 1960s and 1970s. The emergence of Frances Beal's analysis of "double jeopardy" and the Third World Women's Alliance's articulation of "triple jeopardy" in the early 1970s offered antecedents to the concept that sociologist Deborah K. King described as "multiple jeopardy" in 1988.[10] Other black feminist theorists would begin to interrogate "interlocking systems of oppression" during the 1980s and early 1990s.[11] It is important, Carastathis emphasizes, to appreciate that none of these theoretical approaches were one and the same; each was characterized by a slightly different focus or intent. Collectively, however, they constituted the theoretical precursors to the analytical framework of intersectionality.[12]

[8] Anna Carastathis, *Intersectionality: Origins, Contestations, Horizons* (Lincoln: University of Nebraska Press, 2016), 15.
[9] Brittney C. Cooper, *Beyond Respectability: The Intellectual Thought of Race Women* (Urbana: University of Illinois Press, 2017); Carol Faulkner and Alison M. Parker, eds. *Interconnections: Gender and Race in American History* (Rochester: University of Rochester Press, 2012); Namita Goswami, Maeve O'Donovan, and Lisa Yount, eds. *Why Race and Gender Still Matter: An Intersectional Approach* (London: Pickering & Chatto, 2014); Erik S. McDuffie, *Sojourning for Freedom: Black Women, American Communism, and the Making of Black Left Feminism* (Durham: Duke University Press, 2011).
[10] Frances Beal, "Double Jeopardy: To Be Black and Female," in *The Black Woman: An Anthology*, ed. Toni Cade Bambara (New York: New American Library, 1970); Keeanga-Yamahtta Taylor, ed. *How We Get Free: Black Feminism and the Combahee River Collective* (Chicago: Haymarket Books, 2017); Deborah K. King, "Multiple Jeopardy, Multiple Consciousness: The Context of a Black Feminist Ideology," *Signs: Journal of Women in Culture and Society* 14, no. 1 (1988): 42–72.
[11] Patricia Hill Collins, *Black Feminist Thought: Knowledge, Consciousness, and the Politics of Empowerment* (London: Routledge, 1990), 222.
[12] For a fuller reconstruction and analysis of this genealogy, see: Carastathis, *Intersectionality*, Chapter 1.

This brief history of intersectionality and its immediate theoretical precursors suggests that an acknowledgment of the intersections between different forms of oppression occurred long before there was terminology to explain the phenomenon more precisely. Did analogical reasoning, even if expressed only through a brief or fledgling awareness, begin to perform this work in previous decades? Some scholars suggest that it did. Sociologist Nira Yuval-Davis, for example, positions bell hooks' groundbreaking work of black feminist theory, *Ain't I a Woman* (1981), and most especially its criticism of the analogue feminists had pursued between the "situation of women and the situation of blacks," as one of the important points of genesis for the theory that would become intersectionality.[13] Another step backward from hooks' criticism of the sex-race analogy suggests that the woman-slave analogy may have been a site of obfuscation amongst nineteenth-century reformers as much as it was a point of origin for theorizing multiple intersecting axes of oppression. Indeed, as Patricia Hill Collins and Sirma Bilge argue, analogy might initially appear "benign" because it represents the "first step in intersectional engagement where two sides recognize one another's struggles in a move to solidarity," but it simultaneously obscures those whose experiences lie at the intersection.[14]

Much of the woman-slave analogy's mobilization represented a disingenuous move toward interracial and cross-class solidarity across the nineteenth century. Reaching toward an analogy of chattel slavery and racial oppression allowed white reformers to undermine the abuses of chattel slavery, particularly following slave emancipation. Their constant recourse to the woman-slave analogy destabilized what could be, in other contexts, quite comprehensive analyses and criticisms of the woman question. And while African-American reformers did not necessarily refute either the woman-slave analogy or the sex-race analogy, they collectively rejected the racism of their white contemporaries. This led African Americans to reconfigure discourses of slavery to describe women's rights, especially black women's rights, on their own terms. This suggests that the rhetorical phenomenon itself was not always the main source of tension between reformers. What was really being interrogated was the differing approaches to the analogy, especially the question of whether black women or white women should

---

[13] Nira Yuval-Davis, "Intersectionality and Feminist Politics," *European Journal of Women's Studies* 13, no. 3 (2006): 193.

[14] Patricia Hill Collins and Sirma Bilge, *Intersectionality* (Cambridge: Polity Press, 2016), 109–111.

be at the center of its expression. These very contestations might therefore be recovered as yet another point of genesis for the many theoretical antecedents to intersectionality.

The woman-slave analogy offered nineteenth-century reformers a framework through which to begin to consider the existence of multiple axes of oppression. This was a process whereby the analyses of African Americans emerged as the most consistently radical—and intersectional. The contestations that resulted from different approaches to the woman-slave analogy can be productively reconfigured as one of the catalysts for later analytical, methodological, and theoretical approaches. Intersectionality does not rely on, but in fact transcends, the long feminist history of reasoning through analogy.

The Competing Legacies of the Woman-Slave Analogy

This is not to suggest that white women were the intellectual progenitors of intersectionality itself. Quite the opposite, in fact, was the case. The crucial link that now exists between critical inquiry and critical praxis was, for so many nineteenth-century reformers, often missing.[15] The analyses of white reformers collectively reveal a deep and abiding willingness to ignore how race and class compounded gender-based oppression. The analyses as well as the reform imperatives developed amongst the majority of white reformers were principally, although not exclusively, devoid of intersectional considerations. However, it is equally revealing to appreciate the degree to which proslavery commentators and lawmakers expressed a desire to maintain and perpetuate the status quo of racial and gender subordination. Resituating a woman-as-slave worldview in this cultural and intellectual tradition serves as a cautionary tale for how contradictory political projects can influence theoretical positionings.

Elizabeth Cady Stanton, Susan B. Anthony, and Frederick Douglass emerge as the most consistent champions of a woman-as-slave worldview, although each used it to differing ends. However, those who existed on the fringes of these social movements, such as Hannah Crafts and Laura Curtis Bullard, equally found meaning in discourses of slavery. Women's rights print culture revealed the degree to which the analyses of famous

[15] Ibid., 31–33.

reformers influenced the rank-and-file. Stanton and Anthony's constant recourse to the woman-slave analogy offered the most insistent and repetitive example of a willful failure to link critical inquiry with critical praxis. Both women had a background in the antislavery movement, although Anthony's abolitionism was more firmly established. Despite this, both abandoned what could have become intersectional imperatives following the Civil War. Much of the racism that Stanton and Anthony espoused had its foundations in their embrace of the woman-slave analogy or, later, the sex-race analogy. In contrast, the less-renowned free love advocate Warren Chase was more attentive to the differences between the situation of working-class and middle-class women as well as that of enslaved women of African descent. Yet, as nuanced as such a discussion had the potential to be, his manifesto, *The Fugitive Wife: A Criticism on Marriage, Adultery and Divorce* (1861), undermined the possibilities of his own analysis by reiterating—both implicitly and explicitly—that marriage was worse than chattel slavery.

African-American reformers most consistently developed what scholars increasingly describe as the antecedents of intersectionality. Recent prehistories of intersectionality rightly center on African-American women and men such as Maria W. Stewart, Sojourner Truth, Frederick Douglass, Anna Julia Cooper, Ida B. Wells, Fannie Barrier Williams, Mary Church Terrell, and W.E.B. Du Bois.[16] What needs to be emphasized, however, is the consistency with which discourses of slavery appeared at the center of the analyses that scholars are now beginning to read as intersectional. Cooper, for example, claimed in 1893 that "the black woman, doubly enslaved, could but suffer and struggle and be silent," her words directly anticipating later concepts such as double jeopardy and triple jeopardy.[17] Du Bois, too, found resonance in social movements dedicated to both "woman and color," an approach reflected in the National Association for the Advancement of Colored People's magazine, the *Crisis*.

---

[16] Kathryn T. Gines, "Race Women, Race Men, and Early Expressions of Protointersectionality, 1830s–1930s," in *Why Race and Gender Still Matter*; Kristin Waters, "Past as Prologue: Intersectional Analysis from the Nineteenth Century to the Twenty-First," in *Why Race and Gender Still Matter*; Vivian M. May, *Anna Julia Cooper, Visionary Black Feminist: A Critical Introduction* (New York: Routledge, 2007); Wanda A. Hendricks, *Fannie Barrier Williams: Crossing the Borders of Region and Race* (Urbana: University of Illinois Press, 2013); Cooper, *Beyond Respectability*, 6–7, 33–86.

[17] A.J. Cooper, "Discussion of the Same Subject," in *World's Congress of Representative Women*, ed. May Wright Sewell (Chicago: Rand, McNally & Company, 1894), 712.

If race and sex constituted what Cooper described as double enslavement and what DuBois perceived as having "deep meaning," some white women added to this the experience of disenfranchisement. Stanton herself had tentatively reflected that the disenfranchised freedwoman of color "was doomed 'to triple bondage that man never knows.'"[18] Her words alone meant little, however, without the conviction of a broader reform agenda dedicated to developing and maintaining interracial reform coalitions. Stanton's unpublished reflections, unlike Cooper's very public proclamation at the 1893 World's Congress of Representative Women, must be situated in terms of her disingenuous concern for freedwomen. The repeated recourse to the woman-slave analogy suggests that some white women were, in fact, beginning to realize and perhaps even seeking to understand the connections between oppression derived from gender, race, and class. The crucial difference was that, increasingly, these white women desired their rights and the vote for themselves alone and did not always care about any intersectional alliances beyond these goals.

Women's rights reformers, suffragists, and feminists have routinely compared the condition of women to that of enslaved people, servants, and workers since the eighteenth century. Yet, as Carole Pateman argues, none of these comparisons have served to capture the nature of patriarchal subjection.[19] One of the greatest inadequacies of analogy amongst antebellum women's rights reformers was, as Hélène Quanquin describes it, a "failure to describe and convey the reality of women's condition on its own terms."[20] It was equally a collective and systematic failure amongst white women to look beyond the condition of women of their own race, class, and free status. The analyses borne of the woman-slave analogy only ever worked to convince a subset of reformers that women were, indeed, oppressed; in addition, the white slavery panic led to a very specific and short-lived legislative embrace of this rhetoric during the early twentieth century. When their theoretical positioning was based in these terms, women's

---

[18] Elizabeth Cady Stanton, "Reconstruction," unpublished manuscript speech, Elizabeth Cady Stanton Papers, Library of Congress, in Ellen Carol DuBois, *Feminism and Suffrage: The Emergence of an Independent Women's Movement in America, 1848–1869* (Ithaca: Cornell University Press, 1978), 69.

[19] Carole Pateman, *The Sexual Contract* (Stanford: Stanford University Press, 1988), 117.

[20] Hélène Quanquin, "'There Are Two Great Oceans': The Slavery Metaphor in the Antebellum Women's Rights Discourse as a Redescription of Race and Gender," in *Interconnections*, 76.

rights reformers often focused more on describing the rightness of the analogy itself than on seeking to rethink the status of women entirely.

The theorization of questions relating to gender, race, and class through the framework of the woman-slave analogy produced diverse and contradictory results. It reveals how a variety of nineteenth-century Americans grappled conceptually with an idea yet to be defined, and how many white reformers would come to sideline and then abandon its radical implications after the Civil War. Although the very existence of the woman-slave analogy reflected a growing recognition of and desire to understand the connections between different forms of oppression, its actual mobilization ultimately failed to achieve its desired ends: to describe the subjugation of women effectively, lead women toward a greater understanding of their own oppression, and encourage them to seek their own rights. The rate at which so many white reformers abandoned intersectional principles remains a cautionary tale. When historians, scholars, and activists consider the ethics of feminist analysis today, it is essential to observe the ease with which so many nineteenth-century reformers dismissed the intersectional possibilities of the woman-slave analogy in favor of advocating for the rights of white women alone.

BIBLIOGRAPHY

PRIMARY

ARCHIVAL COLLECTIONS

AMERICAN ANTIQUARIAN SOCIETY

Abby Kelley Foster Papers, 1836–1891, https://www.americanantiquarian.org/abby-kelley-foster-papers-finding-aid.

BOSTON PUBLIC LIBRARY

Victoria Woodhull Papers, Box 3: Manuscript Fragments.

ELIZABETH CADY STANTON & SUSAN B. ANTHONY PAPERS PROJECT, RUTGERS UNIVERSITY

Declaration of Sentiments and Resolutions, Seneca Falls, New York, 19–20 July 1848, http://ecssba.rutgers.edu/docs/seneca.html.

HOUGHTON LIBRARY, HARVARD UNIVERSITY

Margaret Fuller Papers.

© The Author(s) 2019
A. Stevenson, *The Woman as Slave in Nineteenth-Century American Social Movements*, Palgrave Studies in the History of Social Movements, https://doi.org/10.1007/978-3-030-24467-5

Library Company of Philadelphia

Chase, Warren. *The Fugitive Wife: A Criticism on Marriage, Adultery and Divorce* (Boston: Bela Marsh, 1861).
Heywood, E.H. *Cupid's Yokes: Or, the Binding Forces of Conjugal Life* (Princeton: Co-Operative Publishing Co., 1877).

Library of Congress

Mary Church Terrell Papers: Speeches and Writings, 1866–1953.
Susan Brownell Anthony Scrapbook, 1905–1906, Reel 6, The Papers of Susan B. Anthony, Library of Congress Manuscript Division.
Terrell, Mary Church. *The Progress of Colored Women* (Washington, DC: Smith Brothers Printers, 1898), https://cdn.loc.gov/service/rbc/lcrbmrp/t0a13/t0a13.pdf.

Massachusetts Historical Society

Adams Family Papers: An Electronic Archive, https://www.masshist.org/digitaladams/archive/.
Caroline Wells Healey Dall Papers.

U.S. National Archives and Records Administration

The Emancipation Proclamation, 1 January 1863, *National Archives*, https://www.archives.gov/exhibits/featured-documents/emancipation-proclamation.

Schlesinger Library, Harvard University

Papers of Elizabeth Cady Stanton and Susan B. Anthony.
Susan B. Anthony Papers.
Rosa Arnold Powell Collection.
Caroline Wells Healey Dall Papers.

Sophia Smith Collection, Smith College

Suffrage Collection.
Garrison Family Papers, Series IX: Wright Family.
Susan B. Anthony Papers, Series I: Biographical Material and Writings, 1935/n.d.

NEWSPAPERS

ACCESSIBLE ARCHIVES, HTTPS://WWW.ACCESSIBLE-ARCHIVES.COM/
Frederick Douglass' Paper
Godey's Lady's Book
Liberator
National Anti-Slavery Standard
North Star

GOOGLE BOOKS, HTTPS://BOOKS.GOOGLE.COM/
Ladies' Home Journal
Medical Tribune: A Monthly Magazine
Sartain's Union Magazine of Literature and Art
Water-Cure Journal

GREEN LIBRARY, STANFORD UNIVERSITY
Lily
Knickerbocker
New Northwest
Sibyl
Una
Woodhull and Claflin's Weekly

HAITI TRUST: DIGITAL LIBRARY
Birth Control Review, https://catalog.hathitrust.org/Record/000675880.
Crisis, https://catalog.hathitrust.org/Record/000502434.
Harper's New Monthly Magazine, https://catalog.hathitrust.org/Record/008919716.

INTERNET ARCHIVE
Genius of Universal Emancipation, https://archive.org/details/geniusuniversal01garrgoog.
Illustrated London News, https://archive.org/details/illustratedlondov37lond.
Massachusetts Magazine, https://archive.org/details/massachusettsbap11bald.

314 BIBLIOGRAPHY

Library of Congress

Anti-Slavery Bugle, http://www.loc.gov/chroniclingamerica/lccn/sn8303 5487/issues.
Congressional Globe, https://memory.loc.gov/ammem/amlaw/lwcglink.html.
New National Era, http://www.loc.gov/chroniclingamerica/lccn/sn8402 6753/issues.

Schlesinger Library, Harvard University

Revolution

Sophia Smith Collection, Smith College

Woman's Journal

The W.T. Stead Resource Site, https://www.attackingthedevil.co.uk

Paul Mall Gazette

The Voice of Industry, http://www.industrialrevolution.org

Voice of Industry

Books and Edited Collections

Addams, Jane. *A New Conscience and an Ancient Evil* (New York: The Macmillan Company, 1912), https://archive.org/details/newconscienceand00adda.
Alcott, Louisa May. *Work: A Story of Experience* (New York: Schocken Books, 1873/1977).
Anthony, Susan B. and Ida Husted Harper, eds. *History of Woman Suffrage*, Vol. IV (Indianapolis: The Hollenbeck Press, 1902), https://www.gutenberg.org/ebooks/29870.
Aptheker, Herbert, ed. *A Documentary History of the Negro People in the United States*, Vol. II (New York: Citadel Press, 1951/1969).
Astell, Mary. *Some Reflections Upon Marriage* (London: R. Wilkin, 1700/1706), https://digital.library.upenn.edu/women/astell/marriage/marriage.html.
Barnes, G.H. and D.L. Dumond, eds. *Letters of Theodore Dwight Weld, Angelina Grimke Weld, and Sarah Grimke, 1822–1844*, Vol. II (Gloucester: Peter Smith, 1965).
Beecher, Henry Ward. *Star Papers; or, Experiences of Art and Nature* (Boston: Phillips, Sampson & Co., 1855), https://archive.org/details/starpapersorexpe00inbeec.

BIBLIOGRAPHY 315

Bell, Ernest A. *Fighting the Traffic in Young Girls; or, War on the White Slave Trade* (Chicago: G.S. Ball, c. 1910), https://archive.org/details/fightingtraffici00bell.

Birney, Catherine H. *The Grimké Sisters: Sarah and Angelina Grimké: The First American Women Advocates of Abolition and Woman's Rights* (Boston: Lee & Shepard, 1885), https://archive.org/details/grimksisterssara00birn.

Blackstone, William. *Commentaries on the Laws of England*, Vol. I (Oxford: Clarendon Press, 1765), https://archive.org/details/BlackstoneVolumeI.

Blackwell, Alice Stone. *Lucy Stone: Pioneer of Women's Rights* (Charlottesville: University Press of Virginia, 1930), https://books.google.co.za/books/about/Lucy_Stone.html?id=sdGGAAAAMAAJ.

Blake, Lillie Devereux. *Fettered for Life; or, Lord and Master: A Story of To-Day* (New York: The Feminist Press, 1874/1996).

———. *Woman's Place To-Day* (New York: John W. Lovell Company, 1883), https://archive.org/details/womansplacetoda00blakgoog.

Blassingame, John W., ed. *Slave Testimony: Two Centuries of Letters, Speeches, Interviews, and Autobiographies* (Baton Rouge: Louisiana State University Press, 1977).

Blassingame, John and C. Peter Ripley, eds. *The Frederick Douglass Papers: Series One—Speeches, Debates, and Interviews*, Vol. I (New Haven: Yale University Press, 1979).

Bradford, Sarah H. *Scenes in the Life of Harriet Tubman* (Auburn: W.J. Moses, 1869), https://archive.org/details/scenesinlifeofha1869brad.

Brown, William Wells. *Clotel; or, the President's Daughter: A Narrative of Slave Life in the United States* (New York: Dover Publications, 1853/2004).

———. *Clotelle; or, the Colored Heroine* (Boston: Lee & Shepard, 1867), https://archive.org/details/clotelleorcolore00browrich/.

Bullard, Laura Curtis. *Christine; or, Woman's Trials and Triumphs* (New York: De Witt & Davenport, 1856), https://books.google.co.za/books/about/Christine.html?id=7a9BAAAAYAAJ.

Carpenter, Cari M., ed. *Selected Writings of Victoria Woodhull: Suffrage, Free Love, and Eugenics* (Lincoln: University of Nebraska Press, 2010).

Cavendish, Margaret. *Orations of Divers Sorts, Accommodated to Divers Places* (London, 1662), http://ota.ox.ac.uk/tcp/headers/A53/A53051.html.

———. *The World's Olio*, 2nd ed. (London: A. Maxwell, 1653/1655), https://quod.lib.umich.edu/cgi/t/text/text-idx?c=eebo;idno=A53065.0001.001.

Chestnut, Mary Boykin. *A Diary from Dixie: Mary Boykin Chestnut*, ed. Ben Ames Williams (Boston: Houghton Mifflin Company, 1905/1949/1980).

Child, L. Maria. *Brief History of the Condition of Women: In Various Ages and Nations* (New York: C.S. Francis & Co., 1845), https://books.google.co.za/books?id=saR89EZ8pHoC&source.

———, ed. *Incidents in the Life of a Slave Girl* (Boston: The Author, 1861), https://docsouth.unc.edu/fpn/jacobs/jacobs.html.

Crafts, Hannah. *The Bondwoman's Narrative*, ed. Henry Louis Gates, Jr. (New York: Warner Books, c. 1850, 2002).

Crew, Danny O. *Suffragist Sheet Music: An Illustrated Catalogue of Published Music Associated with the Women's Rights and Suffrage Movement in America, 1795–1921* (Jefferson: McFarland & Company, 2002).

Dall, Caroline Wells Healey. *The College, the Market, and the Court: Or, Woman's Relation to Education, Labor and Law* (Boston: Lee & Shepard, 1867), http://www.gutenberg.org/ebooks/43657.

Davis, David Brion, ed. *Antebellum American Culture: An Interpretative Anthology* (University Park: Pennsylvania State University Press, 1979).

Davis, Paulina W., ed. *A History of the National Woman's Rights Movement, for Twenty Years* (New York: Journeymen Printers' Co-operative Association, 1871), https://www.loc.gov/resource/rbnawsa.n6134/.

Douglass, Frederick. *My Bondage and My Freedom* (New York: Miller, Orton & Mulligan, 1855), https://www.gutenberg.org/ebooks/202.

———. *Life and Times of Frederick Douglass* (Boston: De Wolfe, Fiske & Co., 1892), https://docsouth.unc.edu/neh/dougl92/dougl92.html.

Du Bois, W.E.B. *Dark Water: Voices from Within the Veil* (New York: Harcourt, Brace & Co., 1920), https://www.gutenberg.org/ebooks/15210.

Dumond, Dwight L., ed. *Letters of James Gillespie Birney*, Vol. I (New York: D. Appleton-Century Co., 1938), https://books.google.co.za/books/about/Letters_of_James_Gillespie_Birney_1831_1.html?id=pXPhAAAAMAAJ.

Ecob, Helen Gilbert. *The Well-Dressed Woman: A Study in the Practical Application to Dress of the Laws of Health, Art, and Morals* (New York: Fowler & Wells, Co., 1893), https://archive.org/details/welldressedwoman00ecob.

Fitzhugh, George. *Sociology for the South, or the Failure of Free Society* (Richmond: A. Morris, 1854), https://archive.org/details/sociologyforsout00fitz.

Flower, B.O., ed. *Arena*, Vol. 4 (Boston: The Arena Publishing Co., 1891), https://archive.org/details/ArenaMagazine-Volume04.

———. *Fashion's Slaves* (Boston: The Arena Publishing Co., 1892), https://archive.org/details/fashionsslaves00flow.

Foner, Philip S., ed. *American Labor Songs of the Nineteenth Century* (Urbana: University of Illinois Press, 1975).

———. *Frederick Douglass on Women's Rights* (New York: Da Capo Press, 1976/1992).

———, ed. *The Factory Girls* (Urbana: University of Illinois Press, 1977).

Foster, Frances Smith, ed. *A Brighter Coming Day: A Frances Ellen Watkins Harper Reader* (New York: The Feminist Press, 1990).

Fuller, Margaret. *Woman in the Nineteenth Century* (New York: W.W. Norton, 1845/1997).

Gordon, Ann D., ed. *The Selected Papers of Elizabeth Cady Stanton and Susan B. Anthony*, Vol. I: In the School of Anti-slavery, 1840 to 1866 (New Brunswick: Rutgers University Press, 1997a).

———. *The Selected Papers of Elizabeth Cady Stanton and Susan B. Anthony*, Vol. II: Against an Aristocracy of Sex, 1866 to 1873 (New Brunswick: Rutgers University Press, 1997b).

Grimké, Angelina E. *Appeal to the Christian Women of the South* (New York: American Anti-Slavery Society, 1836), https://archive.org/details/appealtochristia1836grim.

———. *An Appeal to the Women of the Nominally Free States*, 2nd ed. (Boston: Isaac Knapp, 1838a), https://archive.org/details/appealtowomenofn00anti.

———. *Letters to Catherine E. Beecher, in Reply to an Essay on Slavery and Abolitionism, Addressed to A.E. Grimké* (Boston: Isaac Knapp, 1838b), https://archive.org/details/letterstocatheri00grim.

Grimké, Sarah M. *Letters on the Equality of the Sexes, and the Condition of Woman: Addressed to Mary S. Parker* (Boston: Isaac Knaap, 1837/1838), https://archive.org/details/lettersonequalit00grimrich.

Hale, Sarah Josepha. *Traits of American Life* (E.L. Carey & A. Hart, 1835), https://archive.org/details/traitsamericanl01halegoog.

Hamilton, Gail. *Woman's Wrongs: A Counter-Irritant* (Boston: Ticknor and Fields, 1868), https://archive.org/details/womenswrongscoun00hamiuoft.

Harper, Frances E.W. *Minnie's Sacrifice, Sowing and Reaping, Trial and Triumph: Three Rediscovered Novels*, ed. Frances Smith Foster (Boston: Beacon Press, 2000).

Harper, Ida Husted. *The Life and Work of Susan B. Anthony: Including Public Addresses, Her Own Letters and Many from Her Contemporaries During Fifty Years*, Vol. I (Indianapolis: The Bowen-Merrill Company, 1898), https://archive.org/details/lifeworkofsusanb01harp.

Hentz, Caroline Lee. *Eoline; or, Magnolia Vale; or, the Heiress of Glenmore* (Philadelphia: T.B. Peterson & Brothers, 1852a), https://archive.org/details/eolinemagnolia00hentrich.

———. *Linda; or, the Young Pilot of the Belle Creole* (Philadelphia: T.B. Peterson & Brothers, 1850), https://archive.org/details/lindaoryoungpil00inhent.

———. *Marcus Warland; or, the Long Moss Spring* (Philadelphia: T.B. Peterson & Brothers, 1852b), https://archive.org/details/marcuswarlandorl00hentuoft.

Herron, Carolivia, ed. *Selected Works of Angelina Weld Grimké* (Oxford: Oxford University Press, 1991).

Higginson, Thomas Wentworth. *Cheerful Yesterdays* (Boston: Houghton Mifflin Company, 1898), https://archive.org/details/cheerfulyesterd00higgoog.

———. *Woman and Her Wishes; An Essay: Inscribed to The Massachusetts Constitutional Convention* (Boston: Robert F. Wallcut, 1853), https://archive.org/details/womanandherwish00higgoog.

History of Pennsylvania Hall, Which was Destroyed by a Mob, On the 17th of May, 1838 (Philadelphia: Merrihew and Gunn, 1838), https://archive.org/details/DKC0124.

Howe, Julia Ward. *The Hermaphrodite*, ed. Gary Williams (Lincoln: University of Nebraska Press, 2004).
Kauffman, Reginald Wright. *The House of Bondage* (Upper Saddle River: The Gregg Press, 1910).
Lasser, Carol and Marlene D. Merrill, eds. *Friends and Sisters: Letters between Lucy Stone and Antoinette Brown Blackwell, 1846–1893* (Urbana: University of Illinois Press, 1987).
Lee, Anne. *A Woman in Revolt* (New York: Desmond FitzGerald, 1913), https://archive.org/details/awomaninrevolt00leegoog.
Lewis, Charlton T. and Charles Short. *A Latin Dictionary; Founded on Andrews' Edition of Freund's Latin Dictionary* (Oxford: Clarendon Press, 1879/1984), https://archive.org/details/latindictionaryf00andr.
Locke, John. *Two Treatises of Government* (London: Awnsham and John Churchill, 1698), https://books.google.co.za/books?id=qlgnNQAACAAJ&source.
Lockley, Fred. *Conversations with Pioneer Women*, ed. Mike Helm (Eugene: Rainy Day Press, 1981).
Lundy, Benjamin, ed. *The Poetical Works of Elizabeth Margaret Chandler: With a Memoir of Her Life and Character* (Philadelphia: Lemuel Howell, 1836), https://archive.org/details/poeticalworksofe00chanrich.
Luther, Seth. *An Address to the Working Men of New England, on The State of Education, and on the Condition of the Producing Classes in Europe and America* (New York: George H. Evans, 1833), https://books.google.co.za/books?id=PHdGAAAAYAAJ&source.
Meditations from the Pen of Mrs. Maria W. Stewart (Washington: Enterprise Publishing Company, 1879), https://archive.org/details/meditationsfromp00stew.
Meltzer, Milton and Patricia G. Holland, eds. *Lydia Maria Child: Selected Letters, 1817–1880* (Amherst: University of Massachusetts Press, 1982).
Memminger, C.G. *Lecture Delivered Before the Young Men's Library Association of Augusta, April 10th, 1851* (Augusta: W.S. Jones, Newspaper, Book and Job Printer, 1851), https://archive.org/details/lecturedelivered00memm.
Mill, J.S. *The Subjection of Woman* (London: Longmans, Green, Reader, and Dyer, 1869), https://www.gutenberg.org/files/27083/27083-h/27083-h.htm.
Miner, Maude E. *The Slavery of Prostitution: A Plea for Emancipation* (New York: The Macmillan Company, 1916).
Montesquieu, Baron de. *The Spirit of the Laws*, eds. and trans. Anne M. Cohler, Basia C. Miller, and Harold S. Stone (Cambridge: Cambridge University Press, 1748/1989), https://archive.org/details/MontesquieuTheSpiritOfLawsCambridgeIntegral.
Phelps, Elizabeth Stuart. *What to Wear?* (Boston: James R. Osgood and Company, 1873), https://archive.org/details/whattowear01phelgoog.

Proceedings of the General Anti-slavery Convention: Friday, June 12th, to Tuesday, June 23rd, 1840 (London: British and Foreign Anti-slavery Convention, 1841), https://archive.org/details/oates71027137.

Proceedings of the Meeting of the Loyal Women of the Republic, Held in New York, May 14, 1863 (New York: Phair & Co., 1863), https://archive.org/details/proceedingsofmee00wome.

Proceedings of the National Women's Rights Convention, Held at Cleveland, Ohio, on Wednesday, Thursday and Friday, October 5th, 6th, and 7th, 1853 (Cleveland: Gray, Beardsley, Spear, 1854), https://archive.org/details/proceedingsnati08convgoog.

Proceedings of the Woman's Rights Convention, Held at Worcester, October 23rd & 24th, 1850 (Boston: Prentiss & Sawyer, 1851), https://www.loc.gov/item/93838286/.

Rankin, John. *Letters on American Slavery* (Boston: Garrison & Knapp, 1833), https://archive.org/details/ASPC0005144300.

Reid, Marion. *A Plea for Woman: Being a Vindication of the Importance and Extent of Her Natural Sphere of Action* (New York: Farmer & Daggers, 1845), https://books.google.co.za/books?id=QMNYAAAAcAAJ&dq=A+Plea+for+Woman&source=gbs_navlinks_s.

Reynell, Charles Weatherby. *Black and White Slaves* (London: Office of "The Examiner", 1872).

Robinson, Harriet H. *Loom and Spindle: Or, Life Among the Early Mill Girls* (Boston: Thomas Y. Crowell & Company, 1898), https://archive.org/details/loomspindleorlif00robi.

Roe, Clifford G. *What Women Might Do with the Ballot: The Abolition of the White Slave Traffic* (New York: National American Woman Suffrage Association, 1911), https://archive.org/details/whatwomenmightdo00roecuoft.

Rousseau, Jean Jacques. *The Social Contract & Discourses*, trans. G.D.H. Cole (New York: E.P. Dutton and Co., 1762/1782/1913), https://oll.libertyfund.org/titles/rousseau-the-social-contract-and-discourses.

Saunders, William L., ed. *The Colonial Records of North Carolina*, Vol. 1: 1662–1712 (Raleigh: P.M. Hale, 1886), https://archive.org/details/colonialrecordso01nort.

Sewell, May Wright, ed. *World's Congress of Representative Women* (Chicago: Rand McNally & Company, 1894), https://archive.org/details/worldscongressof00worluoft.

Simpson, Stephen. *The Working Man's Manual: A New Theory of Political Economy, on the Principle of Production the Source of Wealth* (Philadelphia: Thomas L. Bonsal, 1831), https://archive.org/details/workingmansmanu00simpgoog.

Sklar, Kathryn Kish, ed. *Women's Rights Emerges within the Antislavery Movement, 1830–1870: A Brief History with Documents* (New York: St. Martin's Press, 2000).

Smedes, Susan Dabney. *Memorials of a Southern Planter* (Baltimore: Cushings & Bailey, 1887), https://archive.org/details/memorialsofsouthsmed.

Southworth, E.D.E.N. *Retribution; or, The Vale of Shadows: A Tale of Passion* (Philadelphia: T.B. Peterson, 1856), https://books.google.co.za/books?id=c608AAAAYAAJ&source=gbs_navlinks_s.

———. *Retribution. The Missing Bride; or, Miriam the Avenger* (Philadelphia: T.B. Peterson & Brothers, 1855), https://archive.org/details/miriamavengerorm00soutiala/.

Stanton, Elizabeth Cady. *Eighty Years and More: Reminiscences 1815–1897* (New York: T. Fisher Unwin, 1898), http://www.gutenberg.org/ebooks/11982.

———. *History of Woman Suffrage*, Vol. II (Rochester: Susan B. Anthony, 1881a), http://www.gutenberg.org/ebooks/28039.

———. *History of Woman Suffrage*, Vol. III (Rochester: Susan B. Anthony, 1886), http://www.gutenberg.org/ebooks/28556.

Stanton, Elizabeth Cady, Susan B. Anthony, and Matilda Joslyn Gage, eds. *History of Woman Suffrage*, Vol. I (Rochester: Susan B. Anthony, 1881b), http://www.gutenberg.org/ebooks/28020.

Stanton, Theodore and Harriot Stanton Blatch, eds. *Elizabeth Cady Stanton as Revealed in Her Letters, Diary and Reminiscences* (New York: Harper & Brothers, 1922), https://archive.org/details/elizabethcadysta01stan.

Stowe, Harriet Beecher. *Uncle Tom's Cabin; or, Life Among the Lowly* (London: George Routledge & Co., 1852), https://books.google.co.za/books?id=K4pDAAAAcAAJ&dq.

Sumner, Helen. *Report on the Condition of Women and Child Wage Earners in the United States*, Vol. 9: History of Women in Industry in the United States (Washington: Government Printing Office, 1910), https://archive.org/details/reportonconditio09unitrich.

Taylor, Clare, ed. *British and American Abolitionists: An Episode in Transatlantic Understanding* (Edinburgh: Edinburgh University Press, 1974).

The Bible (New Revised Critical Edition).

Thomas, William Hannibal. *The American Negro: What He Was, What He Is, and What He May Become; a Critical and Practical Discussion* (New York: The Macmillan Company, 1901), https://archive.org/details/americannegrowha00thom.

Tolles, Frederick B., ed. *Slavery and "the Woman Question": Lucretia Mott's Diary of Her Visit to Great Britain to Attend the World's Anti-slavery Convention of 1840*, Supplement No. 23 to the *Journal of the Friends' Historical Society* (Haverford: Friends' Historical Association, 1952).

Train, George Francis. *The Great Epigram Campaign in Kansas: Championship of Women* (Leavenworth: Prescott & Hume, 1867), https://babel.hathitrust.org/cgi/pt?id=uiug.30112004283799.

Walker, Mary E. *Hit* (New York: The American News Company, 1871), https://books.google.co.za/books/about/Hit.html?id=Qk4WAAAAYAAJ&redir_esc=y.

Ward, Jean M. and Elaine A. Maveety, eds. *"Yours for Liberty": Selections from Abigail Scott Duniway's Suffrage Newspaper* (Corvallis: Oregon State University Press, 2000).
Washington, Booker T. *A New Negro for a New Century: An Accurate and Up-to-Date Record of the Upward Struggles of the Negro Race* (Chicago: American Publishing House, 1900), https://archive.org/details/newnegrofornewce00wash.
Weld, Theodore Dwight. *In Memory: Angelina Grimké Weld* (Boston: George H. Ellis, 1880), https://archive.org/details/inmemoryangelin00weldgoog.
Wells-Barnett, Ida B. *The Red Record: Tabulated Statistics and Alleged Causes of Lynching in the United States, 1892–1893–1894* (Chicago and New York: Miss Ida B. Wells and Open Road Integrated Media, 1895/2015).
Wollstonecraft, Mary. *A Vindication of the Rights of Woman* (London: J. Johnson, 1792/1796), https://quod.lib.umich.edu/e/ecco/004903441.0001.000?view=toc.
———. *Maria; or, The Wrongs of Woman* (Philadelphia: James Carey, 1798/1799), https://quod.lib.umich.edu/cgi/t/text/text-idx?c=evans;idno=N26724.0001.001.
Woolson, Abba Gould. *Dress-Reform; A Series of Lectures Delivered in Boston, on Dress as It Affects the Health of Women* (Boston: Roberts Brothers, 1874), https://archive.org/details/dressreformserie00wooluoft.

ARTICLES AND BOOK CHAPTERS

"A Week in the Mill," *The Lowell Offering* (Lowell: Misses Curtis and Farley, 1845).
Anthony, Susan B. "Status of Woman, Past, Present, and Future," *Arena* 17 (May 1897): 901–908.
———. "WOMAN: The Great Unpaid Laborer of the World," c. 1848, in *Voices from Women's Liberation*, ed. Leslie B. Tanner (New York: Mentor, 1970).
Child, L. Maria. "The Quadroons," in *The Liberty Bell*, ed. Friend of Freedom (Boston: Massachusetts Anti-slavery Fair, 1842).
Dibble, R.F. "She Blazed the Trail for Suffrage: Now a Shrine Will Honor Susan B. Anthony, Whose Slogan Was: 'Woman is in Chains'," *New York Times Magazine*, 12 April 1925, https://www.nytimes.com/1925/04/12/archives/she-blazed-the-trail-for-suffrage-now-a-shrine-will-honor-susan-b-a.html.
Flower, B.O. "Fashion's Slaves," *Arena* 4 (September 1891): 401–430.
Gouges, Olympe de. "The Declaration of the Rights of Woman," 1791, in *Women in Revolutionary Paris, 1789–1795: Selected Documents*, eds. Darline Gay Levy, Harriet Branson Applewhite, and Mary Durham Johnson (Urbana: University of Illinois Press, 1979).
Grimké, Angelina W. "The Closing Door," *Birth Control Review*, September and October 1919.

Grimké, Angelina Emily Weld. "The Social Emancipation of Women," in Weld-Grimké Family Papers (Folder 147, Moorland-Spingarn Research Center, Howard University), William L. Clements Library, University of Michigan, n.d., https://search.alexanderstreet.com/view/work/bibliographic_entity%7Cbibliographic_details%7C3180702.
Harper, William. "Memoir on Slavery," *Southern Literary Journal* 3, no. 2 (1838): 81–97.
H.F., "Editorial," *The Lowell Offering* (Lowell: Misses Curtis and Farley, 1845).
Leech, John. "Bloomerism—An American Custom," *Punch* 21 (1851): 141.
"Letter: From Harriet Martineau, London, July 9, 1847," in *The Liberty Bell*, ed. Friends of Freedom (Boston: National Anti-slavery Bazaar, 1849).
L.S.M. "Carey on the Slave Trade," *Southern Quarterly Review* 9, no. 17 (January 1854): 115–184, https://quod.lib.umich.edu/m/moajrnl/.
———. "Enfranchisement of Women," *Southern Quarterly Review*, no. 5 (April 1852): 322–341, https://quod.lib.umich.edu/m/moajrnl/.
May, Samuel J. "The Rights and Condition of Women: A Sermon, Preached in Syracuse, Nov., 1845," *Woman's Rights Tracts*, no. 1 (1853): 1–16, http://memory.loc.gov/ammem/naw/nawshome.html.
National Council of Women of the United States. "Symposium on Women's Dress, Part I," *Arena* 6 (October 1892): 488–507.
Parkman, Francis. "The Failure of Universal Suffrage," *North American Review* 127, no. 263 (1878): 1–20.
———. "The Woman Question Again," *North American Review* 130, no. 278 (1880): 303–321.
Russell, Frances E. "A Brief Survey of the American Dress Reform Movements of the Past, with Views of Representative Women," *Arena* 6 (August 1892): 325–340.
Stanton, Elizabeth Cady. "Our Girls," 1880, http://voicesofdemocracy.umd.edu/stanton-our-girls-speech-text/.
Stowe, Harriet Beecher. "Sojourner Truth, The Libyan Sibyl," *Atlantic Monthly* 11 (April 1863): 473–481.
Terrell, Mary Church. "Susan B. Anthony, The Abolitionist," *Voice of the Negro* (June 1906): 411.
Vogel, Lise. "Their Own Work: Two Documents from the Nineteenth-Century Labor Movement," *Signs: Journal of Women in Culture and Society* 1, no. 3 (1976): 794–802.
Wheatley, Phillis. "To the Right Honorable William, Earl of Dartmouth, His Majesty's Principal Secretary of State for North-America," in *The Collected Works of Phillis Wheatley*, ed. John Shields (New York: Oxford University Press, 1988).
"Woman's Emancipation," *Punch* 21 (1851): 3.

SECONDARY

BOOKS

Abruzzo, Margaret. *Polemical Pain: Slavery, Cruelty, and the Rise of Humanitarianism* (Baltimore: Johns Hopkins University Press, 2011).

Abzug, Robert H. *Passionate Liberator: Theodore Dwight Weld and the Dilemma of Reform* (New York: Oxford University Press, 1980).

Allen, Robert L. and Pamela P. Allen. *Reluctant Reformers: Racism and Social Reform Movements in the United States* (Washington: Howard University Press, 1974).

Amireh, Amal. *The Factory Girl and the Seamstress: Imagining Gender and Class in Nineteenth-Century American Fiction* (New York: Garland Publishing, 2000).

Amott, Teresa and Julie Matthaei. *Race, Gender, and Work: A Multicultural Economic History of Women in the United States* (Boston: South End Press, 1991).

Anderson, Bonnie S. *Joyous Greetings: The First International Women's Movement, 1830–1860* (Oxford: Oxford University Press, 2000).

Bailey, Anne C. *African Voices of the Atlantic Slave Trade: Beyond the Silence and the Shame* (Boston: Beacon Press, 2005).

Bailyn, Bernard. *The Ideological Origins of the American Revolution* (Cambridge, MA: Harvard University Press, 1967).

Barry, Kathleen. *Susan B. Anthony: A Biography of a Singular Feminist* (New York: New York University Press, 1988).

Bay, Mia. *To Tell the Truth Freely: The Life of Ida B. Well* (New York: Hill & Wang, 2009).

Baym, Nina. *Woman's Fiction: A Guide to Novels by and About Women in America, 1820–1870*, 2nd ed. (Urbana: University of Illinois Press, 1978/1993).

Bennett, Andrew and Nicholas Royle. *An Introduction to Literature, Criticism and Theory*, 4th ed. (London: Routledge, 1960/2014).

Bennett, Judith M. *History Matters: Patriarchy and the Challenge of Feminism* (Philadelphia: University of Pennsylvania Press, 2006).

Blight, David W. *Race and Reunion: The Civil War in American Memory* (Cambridge: Belknap Press, 2001).

Bogdan, Robert. *Freak Show: Presenting Human Oddities for Amusement and Profit* (Chicago: University of Chicago Press, 1988).

Boisseau, Tracey Jean and Tracy A. Thomas, eds. *Feminist Legal History: Essays on Women and Law* (New York: New York University Press, 2011).

Bolt, Christine. *The Women's Movements in the United States and Britain from the 1790s to the 1920s* (Amherst: University of Massachusetts Press, 1993).

Boydston, Jeanne. *Home and Work: Housework, Wages, and the Ideology of Labor in the Early Republic* (Oxford: Oxford University Press, 1990).

Breward, Christopher. *The Culture of Fashion: A New History of Fashionable Dress* (Manchester: Manchester University Press, 1995).
Broeck, Sabine. *Gender and the Abjection of Blackness* (Albany: State University of New York Press, 2018).
Bynum, Victoria E. *The Long Shadow of the Civil War: Southern Dissent and Its Legacies* (Chapel Hill: University of North Carolina Press, 2010).
Caine, Barbara. *Victorian Feminists* (Oxford: Oxford University Press, 1992).
Carastathis, Anna. *Intersectionality: Origins, Contestations, Horizons* (Lincoln: University of Nebraska Press, 2016).
Caraway, Nancie. *Segregated Sisterhood: Racism and the Politics of American Feminism* (Knoxville: University of Tennessee Press, 1991).
Carey, Brycchan, Ellis Markman, and Sara Salih, eds. *Discourses of Slavery and Abolition: Britain and Its Colonies, 1760–1838* (Basingstoke: Palgrave Macmillan, 2004).
Cayleff, Susan E. *Wash and Be Healed: The Water-Cure Movement and Women's Health* (Philadelphia: Temple University Press, 1987).
Chafe, William H. *Women and Equality: Changing Patterns in American Culture* (New York: Oxford University Press, 1977).
Chakkalakal, Tess. *Novel Bondage: Slavery, Marriage, and Freedom in Nineteenth-Century America* (Urbana: University of Illinois Press, 2011).
Charteris-Black, Jonathan. *Politicians and Rhetoric: The Persuasive Power of Metaphor*, 2nd ed. (Basingstoke: Palgrave Macmillan, 2011).
Chaumette, Xavier. *Le Costume tailleur: La culture vestimentaire en France au XIXème siècle* (Paris: Esmond Edition, 1995).
Christian, David. *Maps of Time: An Introduction to Big History* (Berkeley: University of California Press, 2005).
Cima, Gay Gibson. *Performing Anti-Slavery: Activist Women on Antebellum Stages* (Cambridge: Cambridge University Press, 2014).
Claybaugh, Amanda. *The Novel of Purpose: Literature and Social Reform in the Anglo-American World* (Ithaca: Cornell University Press, 2007).
Clinton, Catherine. *The Plantation Mistress: Woman's World in the Old South* (New York: Pantheon Books, 1982).
Cobb, Jasmine Nichole. *Picture Freedom: Remaking Black Visuality in the Early Nineteenth Century* (New York: New York University Press, 2015).
Collins, Patricia Hill. *Black Feminist Thought: Knowledge, Consciousness, and the Politics of Empowerment* (London: Routledge, 1990).
Collins, Patricia Hill and Sirma Bilge. *Intersectionality* (Cambridge: Polity Press, 2016).
Cook, Adrian. *The Armies of the Streets: The New York City Draft Riots of 1863* (Lexington: University Press of Kentucky, 1974).
Cooper, Brittney C. *Beyond Respectability: The Intellectual Thought of Race Women* (Urbana: University of Illinois Press, 2017).

Corrigan, John Michael. *American Metempsychosis: Emerson, Whitman, and the New Poetry* (New York: Fordham University Press, 2012).
Cott, Nancy F. *Public Vows: A History of Marriage and the Nation* (Cambridge, MA: Harvard University Press, 2000).
———. *The Bonds of Womanhood: "Woman's Sphere" in New England, 1780–1835* (New Haven: Yale University Press, 1977).
Crane, Diana. *Fashion and Its Social Agendas: Class, Gender, and Identity in Clothing* (Chicago: The University of Chicago Press, 2000).
Crozier-De Rosa, Sharon and Vera Mackie. *Remembering Women's Activism* (Oxon: Routledge, 2019).
Cunliffe, Marcus. *Chattel Slavery and Wage Slavery: The Anglo-American Context, 1830–1860* (Athens: University of Georgia Press, 1979).
Cunningham, Patricia A. *Reforming Women's Fashion, 1850–1920* (Kent: Kent State University Press, 2003).
Cunningham, Patricia Anne and Susan Voso Lab, eds. *Dress and Popular Culture* (Bowling Green: Bowling Green State University Press, 1991).
Davis, Angela Y. *Women, Race & Class* (London: The Women's Press, 1981).
Davis, David Brion. *Inhuman Bondage: The Rise and Fall of Slavery in the New World* (Oxford: Oxford University Press, 2006).
Davis, Sue. *The Political Thought of Elizabeth Cady Stanton: Women's Rights and the American Political Traditions* (New York: New York University Press, 2010).
DeCredico, Mary A. *Mary Boykin Chestnut: A Confederate Woman's Life* (Lanham: Rowman & Littlefield Publishers, 1996).
Dillon, Elizabeth Maddock. *The Gender of Freedom: Fictions of Liberalism and the Literary Public Sphere* (Stanford: Stanford University Press, 2004).
Dixon, Chris. *Perfecting the Family: Antislavery Marriages in Nineteenth-Century America* (Amherst: University of Massachusetts Press, 1997).
Donovan, Brian. *White Slave Crusaders: Race, Gender, and Anti-Vice Activism, 1887–1917* (Urbana: University of Illinois Press, 2006).
Drescher, Seymour and Stanley L. Engerman, eds. *A Historical Guide to World Slavery* (New York: Oxford University Press, 1998).
Drescher, Seymour. *Abolition: A History of Slavery and Antislavery* (Cambridge: Cambridge University Press, 2009).
Dublin, Thomas. *Women at Work: The Transformation of Work and Community in Lowell, Massachusetts, 1826–1860*, 2nd ed. (New York: Columbia University Press, 1979/1981).
DuBois, Ellen Carol. *Feminism and Suffrage: The Emergence of an Independent Women's Movement in America, 1848–1869* (Ithaca: Cornell University Press, 1978).
duCille, Ann. *The Coupling Convention: Sex, Text, and Tradition in Black Women's Fiction* (New York: Oxford University Press, 1993).
Dudden, Faye E. *Fighting Chance: The Struggle over Woman Suffrage and Black Suffrage in Reconstruction America* (Oxford: Oxford University Press, 2011).

Dunbar, Erica Armstrong. *A Fragile Freedom: African American Women and Emancipation in the Antebellum City* (New Haven: Yale University Press, 2008).
Earle, T.F. and K.J.P. Lowe, eds. *Black Africans in Renaissance Europe* (Cambridge: Cambridge University Press, 2005).
Engs, Ruth Clifford. *The Progressive Era's Health Reform Movement: A Historical Dictionary* (Westport: Greenwood Publishing, 2003).
Farrell, Grace. *Lillie Devereux Blake: Retracing a Life Erased* (Amherst: University of Massachusetts Press, 2002).
Farrell, Michael P. *Collaborative Circles: Friendship Dynamics and Creative Work* (Chicago: University of Chicago Press, 2001).
Faulkner, Carol. *Lucretia Mott's Heresy: Abolition and Women's Rights in Nineteenth-Century America* (Philadelphia: University of Pennsylvania Press, 2011).
Faulkner, Carol and Alison M. Parker, eds. *Interconnections: Gender and Race in American History* (Rochester: University of Rochester Press, 2012).
Feimster, Crystal N. *Southern Horrors: Women and the Politics of Rape and Lynching* (Cambridge, MA: Harvard University Press, 2009).
Ferguson, Moira. *Subject to Others: British Women Writers and Colonial Slavery, 1670–1834* (New York: Routledge, 1992).
Fischer, Gayle V. *Pantaloons & Power: A Nineteenth-Century Dress Reform in the United States* (Kent: The Kent State University Press, 2001).
Folsom, Joseph K. *The Family and Democratic Society* (New York: John Wiley & Sons, 1943).
Foner, Eric. *Free Soil, Free Labor, Free Men: The Ideology of the Republican Party Before the Civil War* (Oxford: Oxford University Press, 1970/1995).
Foner, Philip S. *Women and the American Labor Movement: From Colonial Times to the Eve of World War I* (New York: The Free Press, 1979).
Foster, Frances Smith. *Witnessing Slavery: The Development of Ante-Bellum Slave Narratives* (Westport: Greenwood Press, 1979).
Foster, Helen Bradley. *"New Raiments of Self": African American Clothing in the Antebellum South* (Oxford: Berg, 1997).
Fought, Leigh. *Women in the World of Frederick Douglass* (Oxford: Oxford University Press, 2017).
Fox-Genovese, Elizabeth. *Within the Plantation Household: Black and White Women of the Old South* (Chapel Hill: University of North Carolina Press, 1988).
Freedman, Estelle B. *Redefining Rape: Sexual Violence in the Era of Suffrage and Segregation* (Cambridge, MA: Harvard University Press, 2013).
Frost, Linda. *Never One Nation: Freaks, Savages, and Whiteness in U.S. Popular Culture, 1850–1877* (Minneapolis: University of Minnesota Press, 2005).

Gac, Scott. *Singing for Freedom: The Hutchinson Family Singers and the Nineteenth-Century Culture of Reform* (New Haven: Yale University Press, 2007).
Gaspar, David Barry and Darlene Clark Hine, eds. *More Than Chattel: Black Women and Slavery in the Americas* (Bloomington: Indiana University Press, 1996).
Gelles, Edith B. *First Thoughts: Life and Letters of Abigail Adams* (New York: Twayne Publishers, 1998).
Genovese, Eugene D. *The Political Economy of Slavery: Studies in the Economy and Society of the Slave South*, 2nd ed. (Middletown: Wesleyan University Press, 1989).
Giddings, Paula J. *When and Where I Enter* (New York: HarperCollins, 1984/2009).
Ginzberg, Lori D. *Elizabeth Cady Stanton: An American Life* (New York: Hill & Wang, 2010).
———. *Women and the Work of Benevolence: Morality, Politics, and Class in the Nineteenth-Century United States* (New Haven: Yale University Press, 1990).
Glenn, Evelyn Nakano. *Unequal Freedom: How Race and Gender Shaped American Citizenship and Labor* (Cambridge, MA: Harvard University Press, 2002).
Glymph, Thavolia. *Out of the House of Bondage: The Transformation of the Plantation Household* (New York: Cambridge University Press, 2008).
Goodman, Paul. *Of One Blood: Abolitionism and the Origins of Racial Equality* (Berkeley: University of California Press, 1998).
Goswami, Namita, Maeve O'Donovan, and Lisa Yount, eds. *Why Race and Gender Still Matter: An Intersectional Approach* (London: Pickering & Chatto, 2014).
Green, Elna C. *Southern Strategies: Southern Women and the Woman Suffrage Question* (Chapel Hill: University of North Carolina Press, 1997).
Griffith, Elisabeth. *In Her Own Right: The Life of Elizabeth Cady Stanton* (New York: Oxford University Press, 1984).
Harding, Sandra, ed. *Feminism and Methodology: Social Science Issues* (Bloomington: Indiana University Press, 1987).
Hartman, Saidiya V. *Scenes of Subjection: Terror, Slavery, and Self-Making in Nineteenth-Century America* (New York: Oxford University Press, 1997).
Hendricks, Wanda A. *Fannie Barrier Williams: Crossing the Borders of Region and Race* (Urbana: University of Illinois Press, 2013).
Hersh, Blanche Glassman. *The Slavery of Sex: Feminist-Abolitionists in America* (Urbana: University of Illinois Press, 1978).
Higginbotham, Evelyn Brooks. *Righteous Discontent: The Women's Movement in the Black Baptist Church, 1880–1920* (Cambridge, MA: Harvard University Press, 1993).
Hofstadter, Douglas and Emmanuel Sander. *Surfaces and Essences: Analogy as the Fuel and Fire of Thinking* (New York: Basic Books, 2013).

hooks, bell. *Ain't I a Woman: Black Women and Feminism* (Boston: South End Press, 1981).
———. *Feminist Theory: From Margin to Centre* (Boston: Beacon Press, 1984).
Hull, Gloria T. *Color, Sex, and Poetry: Three Women Writers of the Harlem Renaissance* (Bloomington: Indiana University Press, 1987).
Hull, Gloria T., Patricia Bell Scott, and Barbara Smith, eds. *All the Women are White, All the Blacks are Men, but Some of Us are Brave: Black Women's Studies* (New York: The Feminist Press, 1982).
Humez, Jean M. *Harriet Tubman: The Life and the Life Stories* (Madison: University of Wisconsin Press, 2006).
Husband, Julie. *Antislavery Discourse and Nineteenth-Century American Literature: Incendiary Pictures* (New York: Palgrave Macmillan, 2010).
Jacobs, Wilbur R. *Francis Parkman, Historian as Hero: The Formative Years* (Austin: University of Texas Press, 1991).
Jeffrey, Julie Roy. *Abolitionists Remember: Antislavery Autobiographies and the Unfinished Work of Emancipation* (Chapel Hill: University of North Carolina Press, 2008).
———. *The Great Silent Army of Abolition: Ordinary Women in the Antislavery Movement* (Chapel Hill: University of North Carolina Press, 1998).
Jones, Jacqueline. *Labor of Love, Labor of Sorrow: Black Women, Work, and the Family, from Slavery to the Present* (New York: Basic Books, 1985).
Jones, Martha S. *All Bound Up Together: The Woman Question in African American Public Culture, 1830–1900* (Chapel Hill: University of North Carolina Press, 2007).
Jones-Rogers, Stephanie E. *They Were Her Property: White Women as Slave Owners in the American South* (New Haven: Yale University Press, 2019).
Kasson, Joy S. *Marble Queens and Captives: Women in Nineteenth-Century American Sculpture* (New Haven: Yale University Press, 1990).
Kaufmann, Miranda. *Black Tudors: The Untold Story* (London: Oneworld Publications, 2017).
Keire, Mara L. *For Business and Pleasure: Red-Light Districts and the Regulation of Vice in the United States, 1890–1933* (Baltimore: Johns Hopkins University Press, 2010).
Kelley, Mary. *Learning to Stand & Speak: Women, Education, and Public Life in America's Republic* (Chapel Hill: University of North Carolina Press, 2006).
Kessler-Harris, Alice. *Out to Work: A History of Wage-Earning Women in the United States* (Oxford: Oxford University Press, 1982/2003).
Kohn, Denise M., ed. *Christine; or, Woman's Trials and Triumphs* (Lincoln: University of Nebraska Press, 1856/2010).
Kraditor, Aileen S. *The Ideas of the Woman Suffrage Movement, 1890–1920* (New York: Anchor Books, 1965/1971).

Kray, Christine A., Tamar W. Carroll, and Hinda Mandell, eds. *Nasty Women and Bad Hombres: Historical Reflections on the 2016 U.S. Presidential Election* (Rochester: University of Rochester Press, 2018).

Laas, Virginia Jeans. *Love and Power in the Nineteenth Century: The Marriage of Violet Blair* (Fayetteville: University of Arkansas Press, 1998).

LeFlouria, Talitha L. *Chained in Silence: Black Women and Convict Labor in the New South* (Chapel Hill: University of North Carolina Press, 2015).

Lerner, Gerda. *The Creation of Feminist Consciousness: From the Middle Ages to Eighteen-Seventy* (New York: Oxford University Press, 1993).

———. *The Creation of Patriarchy* (New York: Oxford University Press, 1986).

———. *The Feminist Thought of Sarah Grimké* (New York: Oxford University Press, 1998).

———. *The Grimké Sisters from South Carolina: Pioneers for Women's Rights and Abolition* (Chapel Hill: University of North Carolina Press, 1967/2004).

———. *The Majority Finds Its Past: Placing Women in History* (New York: Oxford University Press, 1979/2005).

Levander, Caroline Field. *Voices of the Nation: Women and Public Speech in Nineteenth-Century American Literature and Culture* (New York: Cambridge University Press, 1998).

Logan, Shirley Wilson. *"We are Coming": The Persuasive Discourse of Nineteenth-Century Black Women* (Carbondale: Southern Illinois University Press, 1999).

Lounsbury, Richard C., ed. *Louisa S. McCord: Political and Social Essays* (Charlottesville: University Press of Virginia, 1995).

Lumpkin, Katharine du Pre. *The Emancipation of Angelina Grimke* (Chapel Hill: University of North Carolina Press, 1974).

Lystra, Karen. *Searching the Heart: Women, Men, and Romantic Love in Nineteenth-Century America* (Oxford: Oxford University Press, 1989).

Mabee, Carleton. *Sojourner Truth: Slave, Prophet, Legend* (New York: New York University Press, 1993).

Macfarlane, Alan. *Marriage and Love in England: Modes of Reproduction, 1300–1840* (Oxford: Blackwell, 1986).

Makdisi, Saree. *William Blake and the Impossible History of the 1790s* (Chicago: University of Chicago Press, 2003).

Marilley, Suzanne M. *Woman Suffrage and the Origins of Liberal Feminism in the United States, 1820–1920* (Cambridge, MA: Harvard University Press, 1996).

Matthews, Glenna. *The Rise of Public Woman: Woman's Power and Woman's Place in the United States, 1630–1970* (New York: Oxford University Press, 1992).

Mattingly, Carol. *Appropriate[ing] Dress: Women's Rhetorical Style in Nineteenth-Century America* (Carbondale: Southern Illinois University Press, 2002).

May, Vivian M. *Anna Julia Cooper, Visionary Black Feminist: A Critical Introduction* (New York: Routledge, 2007).

Mayeri, Serena. *Reasoning from Race: Feminism, Law, and the Civil Rights Revolution* (Cambridge, MA: Harvard University Press, 2011).

McClintock, Anne. *Imperial Leather: Race, Gender, and Sexuality in the Colonial Contest* (New York: Routledge, 1995).

McDuffie, Erik S. *Sojourning for Freedom: Black Women, American Communism, and the Making of Black Left Feminism* (Durham: Duke University Press, 2011).

McFadden, Margaret H. *Golden Cables of Sympathy: The Transatlantic Sources of Nineteenth-Century Feminism* (Lexington: The University Press of Kentucky, 1999/2015).

Meer, Sarah. *Uncle Tom Mania: Slavery, Minstrelsy, and Transatlantic Culture in the 1850s* (Atlanta: University of Georgia Press, 2005).

Merish, Lori. *Archives of Labor: Working-Class Women and Literary Culture in the Antebellum United States* (Durham: Duke University Press, 2017).

Midgley, Clare. *Women against Slavery: The British Campaigns, 1780–1870* (London: Routledge, 1992).

Million, Joelle. *Woman's Voice, Woman's Place: Lucy Stone and the Birth of the Woman's Rights Movement* (Westport: Praeger, 2003).

Molineux, Catherine. *Faces of Perfect Ebony: Encountering Atlantic Slavery in Imperial Britain* (Cambridge, MA: Harvard University Press, 2012).

Moore, Clive. *Kanaka: A History of Melanesian Mackay* (Port Moresby: University of Papua New Guinea Press, 1985).

Morgan, Jo-Ann. *Uncle Tom's Cabin as Visual Culture* (Columbia: University of Missouri Press, 2007).

Morrison, Toni. *Playing in the Dark: Whiteness and the Literary Imagination* (New York: Vintage, 1993).

Myrdal, Gunnar. *An American Dilemma: The Negro Problem and Modern Democracy* (New York: Harper & Brothers Publishers, 1944).

Newman, Louise Michele. *White Women's Rights: The Racial Origins of Feminism in the United States* (New York: Oxford University Press, 1999)

Nichols, Heidi L. *The Fashioning of Middle-Class America: Sartain's Union Magazine of Literature and Art and Antebellum Culture* (New York: Peter Lang, 2004).

Okker, Patricia. *Our Sister Editors: Sarah J. Hale and the Tradition of Nineteenth-Century American Women Editors* (Athens: University of Georgia Press, 1995).

Otele, Olivette. *African Europeans: An Untold History* (London: Hurst Publishers, 2019).

Painter, Nell Irvin. *Sojourner Truth: A Life, a Symbol* (New York: W.W. Norton & Company, 1996).

———. *The History of White People* (New York: W.W. Norton & Company, 2010).

Parker, Alison M. *Articulating Rights: Nineteenth-Century American Women on Race, Reform, and the State* (DeKalb: Northern Illinois University Press, 2010).

Passett, Joanne E. *Sex Radicals and the Quest for Women's Equality* (Chicago: University of Illinois Press, 2003).
Pateman, Carole. *The Sexual Contract* (Stanford: Stanford University Press, 1988).
Patterson, Orlando. *Slavery and Social Death* (Cambridge, MA: Harvard University Press, 1982).
Patton, Venetria K. *Women in Chains: The Legacy of Slavery in Black Women's Fiction* (Albany: State University of New York Press, 2000).
Pennebaker, James W., Dario Paez, and Bernard Rimé, eds. *Collective Memory of Political Events: Social Psychological Perspectives* (Mahwah: Lawrence Erlbaum Associates, 1997).
Peterson, Carla L. *"Doers of the Word": African-American Women Speakers and Writers in the North* (New Brunswick: Rutgers University Press, 1995).
Piepmeier, Alison. *Out in Public: Configurations of Women's Bodies in Nineteenth-Century America* (Chapel Hill: University of North Carolina Press, 2004).
Plasa, Carl and Betty J. Ring, eds. *The Discourse of Slavery: From Aphra Behn to Toni Morrison* (Oxon: Routledge, 1994).
Rabban, David M. *Free Speech in Its Forgotten Years, 1870–1920* (Cambridge: Cambridge University Press, 1997).
Raimon, Eve Allegra. *The "Tragic Mulatta" Revisited: Race and Nationalism in Nineteenth-Century Antislavery Fiction* (New Brunswick: Rutgers University Press, 2004).
Rakow, Lana F. and Cheris Kramarae, eds. *The Revolution in Words: Righting Women, 1868–1871* (London: Routledge, 1990).
Roediger, David R. *The Wages of Whiteness: Race and the Making of the American Working Class* (London: Verso, 1991/2007).
Romero, Lora. *Home Fronts: Domesticity and Its Critics in the Antebellum United States* (Durham: Duke University Press, 1997).
Rose, Margaret A. *Parody: Ancient, Modern and Post-modern* (Cambridge: Cambridge University Press, 1993).
Royster, Jacqueline Jones. *Traces of a Stream: Literacy and Social Change among African American Women* (Pittsburgh: University of Pittsburgh Press, 2000).
Ryan, Susan M. *The Grammar of Good Intentions: Race and the Antebellum Culture of Benevolence* (Ithaca: Cornell University Press, 2003).
Samuels, Shirley, ed. *The Culture of Sentiment: Race, Gender, and Sentimentality in Nineteenth-Century America* (New York: Oxford University Press, 1992).
Sánchez-Eppler, Karen. *Touching Liberty: Abolition, Feminism, and the Politics of the Body* (Berkeley: University of California Press, 1993).
Santamarina, Xiomara. *Belabored Professions: Narratives of African American Working Womanhood* (Chapel Hill: University of North Carolina Press, 2006).
Schama, Simon. *Landscape and Memory* (New York: Vintage Books, 1996).
Scott, Anne Firor. *The Southern Lady: From Pedestal to Politics, 1830–1930* (Chicago: The University of Chicago Press, 1970).

Sears, Clare. *Arresting Dress: Cross-dressing, Law, and Fascination in Nineteenth-Century San Francisco* (Durham: Duke University Press, 2015).
Seidman, Steven. *Romantic Longings: Love in America, 1830–1980* (New York: Routledge, 1991).
Sellers, Charles. *The Market Revolution, Jacksonian America: 1815–1846* (New York: Oxford University Press, 1991).
Sinha, Manisha. *The Slave's Cause: A History of Abolition* (New Haven: Yale University Press, 2016).
Sklar, Kathryn Kish and James Brewer Stewart, eds. *Women's Rights and Transatlantic Antislavery in the Era of Emancipation* (New Haven: Yale University Press, 2007).
Smith, John David and J. Vincent Lowery, eds. *The Dunning School: Historians, Race, and the Meaning of Reconstruction* (Lexington: University Press of Kentucky, 2013).
Soderlund, Gretchen. *Sex Trafficking, Scandal, and the Transformation of Journalism, 1885–1917* (Chicago: University of Chicago Press, 2013).
Speicher, Anna M. *The Religious World of Antislavery Women: Spirituality in the Lives of Five Abolitionist Lecturers* (New York: Syracuse University Press, 2000).
Spelman, Elizabeth V. *Inessential Woman: Problems of Exclusion in Feminist Thought* (Boston: Beacon Press, 1988).
Spongberg, Mary. *Writing Women's History since the Renaissance* (Basingstoke: Palgrave Macmillan, 2002).
Stancliff, Michael. *Frances Ellen Watkins Harper: African American Reform Rhetoric and the Rise of a Modern Nation State* (New York: Routledge, 2011).
Stange, Margit. *Personal Property: Wives, White Slaves, and the Market in Women* (Baltimore: Johns Hopkins University Press, 1998).
Stanley, Amy Dru. *From Bondage to Contract: Wage Labor, Marriage, and the Market in the Age of Slave Emancipation* (Cambridge: Cambridge University Press, 1998).
Stanley, Autumn. *Mothers and Daughters of Invention: Notes for a Revised History of Technology* (New Brunswick: Rutgers University Press, 1995).
Steele, Valerie. *The Corset: A Cultural History* (New Haven: Yale University Press, 2001).
Sterling, Dorothy. *Ahead of Her Time: Abby Kelley and the Politics of Antislavery* (New York: W.W. Norton & Company, 1991).
———. *We are Your Sisters: Black Women in the Nineteenth Century* (New York: W.W. Norton & Company, 1984).
Stewart, James Brewer. *Wendell Phillips: Liberty's Hero* (Baton Rouge: Louisiana State University Press, 1986).
Strasser, Susan. *Never Done: A History of American Housework* (New York: Pantheon Books, 1982/2000).

Summers, Leigh. *Bound to Please: A History of the Victorian Corset* (Oxford: Berg, 2001).
Swaminathan, Srividhya and Adam R. Beach, eds. *Invoking Slavery in the Eighteenth-Century British Imagination* (London: Routledge, 2016).
Taylor, Keeanga-Yamahtta. ed. *How We Get Free: Black Feminism and the Combahee River Collective* (Chicago: Haymarket Books, 2017).
Terborg-Penn, Rosalyn. *African American Women in the Struggle for the Vote, 1850–1920* (Bloomington: Indiana University Press, 1998).
Tetrault, Lisa. *The Myth of Seneca Falls: Memory and the Women's Suffrage Movement, 1848–1898* (Chapel Hill: University of North Carolina Press, 2014).
Thistle, Susan. *From Marriage to the Market: The Transformation of Women's Lives and Work* (Berkeley: University of California Press, 2006).
Tise, Larry E. *Proslavery: A History of the Defense of Slavery in America, 1701–1840* (Athens: University of Georgia Press, 1987/2004).
Tracey, Karen. *Plots and Proposals: American Women's Fiction, 1850–1890* (Urbana: University of Illinois Press, 2000).
Walters, Ronald G. *American Reformers: 1815–1860* (New York: Hill and Wang, 1978/1997).
Ware, Vron. *Beyond the Pale: White Women, Racism, and History* (London: Verso, 1992/2015).
Weinstein, Cindy. *Family, Kinship, and Sympathy in Nineteenth-Century American Literature* (Cambridge: Cambridge University Press, 2006).
———. *The Literature of Labor and the Labors of Literature: Allegory in Nineteenth-Century American Fiction* (Cambridge: Cambridge University Press, 1995).
Weiss, Elaine. *The Woman's Hour: The Great Fight to Win the Vote* (New York: Viking, 2018).
Welter, Barbara. *Dimity Convictions: The American Woman in the Nineteenth Century* (Athens: Ohio University Press, 1976).
Wheeler, Marjorie Spruill. *New Women of the New South: The Leaders of the Woman Suffrage Movement in the Southern States* (Oxford: Oxford University Press, 1993)
———, ed. *One Woman, One Vote: Rediscovering the Woman Suffrage Movement* (Troutdale: NewSage Press, 1995).
White, Deborah Gray. *Ar'n't I a Woman? Female Slaves in the Plantation South*, Rev. ed. (New York: W.W. Norton & Company, 1985/1999).
White, R.S. *Natural Rights and the Birth of Romanticism in the 1790s* (Basingstoke: Palgrave Macmillan, 2005).
Williams, Heather Andrea. *Help Me to Find My People: The African American Search for Family Lost in Slavery* (Chapel Hill: University of North Carolina Press, 2012).

Winter, Kari J. *Subjects of Slavery, Agents of Change: Women and Power in Gothic Novels and Slave Narratives, 1790–1865* (Athens: University of Georgia Press, 1992).
Withey, Lynne. *Dearest Friend: A Life of Abigail Adams* (New York: Free Press, 1981).
Wood, Sharon E. *The Freedom of the Streets: Work, Citizenship, and Sexuality in a Gilded Age City* (Chapel Hill: University of North Carolina Press, 2005).
Wosk, Julie. *Women and the Machine: Representations from the Spinning Wheel to the Electronic Age* (Baltimore: Johns Hopkins University Press, 2001).
Yalom, Marilyn. *A History of the Wife* (New York: Perennial, 2001).
Yee, Shirley J. *Black Women Abolitionists: A Study in Activism, 1828–1860* (Knoxville: University of Tennessee Press, 1992).
Yellin, Jean Fagan. *Women and Sisters: The Antislavery Feminists in American Culture* (New Haven: Yale University Press, 1989).
Zackodnik, Teresa C. *Press, Platform, Pulpit: Black Feminist Publics in the Era of Reform* (Knoxville: University of Tennessee Press, 2011).
Zaeske, Susan. *Signatures of Citizenship: Petitioning, Antislavery, and Women's Political Identity* (Chapel Hill: University of North Carolina Press, 2003).

ARTICLES AND BOOK CHAPTERS

Adéèkó, Adéléké. "Signatures of Blood in William Wells Brown's *Clotel*," *Nineteenth-Century Contexts: An Interdisciplinary Journal* 21, no. 1 (1999): 115–134.
Anderson, Bonnie S. "*Frauenemancipation* and Beyond: The Use of the Concept of Emancipation by Early European Feminists," in *Women's Rights and Transatlantic Antislavery in the Era of Emancipation*, eds. Kathryn Kish Sklar and James Brewer Stewart (New Haven: Yale University Press, 2007).
Anderson, Clare. "Convicts and Coolies: Rethinking Indentured Labour in the Nineteenth Century," *Slavery & Abolition: A Journal of Slave and Post-Slave Studies* 30, no. 1 (2009): 93–109.
Bannerji, Himani. "Mary Wollstonecraft, Feminism and Humanism: A Spectrum of Reading," in *Mary Wollstonecraft: And 200 Years of Feminisms*, ed. Eileen Janes Yeo (London: Rivers Oram Press, 1997).
Beal, Frances. "Double Jeopardy: To Be Black and Female," in *The Black Woman: An Anthology*, ed. Toni Cade Bambara (New York: New American Library, 1970).
Beer, Janet and Katherine Joslin. "Diseases of the Body Politic: 'White Slavery in Jane Addams' 'A New Conscience and an Ancient Evil' and Selected Short Stories by Charlotte Perkins Gilman," *Journal of American Studies* 33, no. 1 (1999): 1–18.

Bell, Vikki. "On Metaphors of Suffering: Mapping the Feminist Political Imagination," *International Journal of Human Resource Management* 24, no. 4 (1995): 507–519.

Berkeley, Kathleen Christine. "Elizabeth Avery Meriwether, 'An Advocate for Her Sex': Feminism and Conservativism in the Post-Civil War South," *Tennessee Historical Quarterly* 43, no. 4 (1984): 390–407.

Berlin, Ira. "Who Freed the Slaves? Emancipation and Its Meaning," in *Union and Emancipation: Essays on Politics and Race in the Civil War Era*, eds. David W. Blight and Brooks D. Simpson (Kent: Kent State University Press, 1997).

Bhana, Surendra. "Indenture in Comparative Perspective," *Safundi: The Journal of South African and American Studies* 9, no. 2 (2008): 215–224.

Botting, Eileen Hunt and Christine Carey. "Wollstonecraft's Philosophical Impact on Nineteenth-Century American Women's Rights Advocates," *American Journal of Political Science* 48, no. 4 (2004): 707–722.

Boydston, Jeanne. "The Woman Who Wasn't There: Women's Market Labor and the Transition to Capitalism in the United States," *Journal of the Early Republic* 16, no. 2 (1996): 183–206.

Brandt, Brenda M. "Arizona Clothing: A Frontier Perspective," *Dress* 15, no. 1 (1989): 65–78.

Bric, Maurice. "Debating Slavery and Empire: The United States, Britain and the World's Anti-slavery Convention of 1840," in *A Global History of Anti-slavery Politics in the Nineteenth Century*, eds. William Mulligan and Maurice Bric (Basingstoke: Palgrave Macmillan, 2013).

Brown, Gregory S. "The Self-Fashionings of Olympe De Gouges, 1784–1789," *Eighteenth-Century Studies* 34, no. 3 (2001): 383–401.

Brown, Kathleen M. "Brave New Worlds: Women's and Gender History," *William and Mary Quarterly* 50, no. 2 (1993): 311–328.

Bunker, Gary L. "Antebellum Caricature and Woman's Sphere," *Journal of Women's History* 3, no. 3 (1992): 6–43.

Carby, Hazel V. "'On the Threshold of Woman's Era': Lynching, Empire, and Sexuality in Black Feminist Theory," *Critical Inquiry* 12, no. 1 (1985): 262–277.

———. "White Woman Listen! Black Feminism and the Boundaries of Sisterhood," in *The Empire Strikes Back: Race and Racism in 70s Britain*, ed. Centre for Contemporary Cultural Studies (London: Routledge, 1982).

Castronovo, Russ. "Incidents in the Life of a White Woman: Economies of Race and Gender in the Antebellum Nation," *American Literary History* 10, no. 2 (1998): 239–265.

Chambers, Jacqueline M. "'Thinking and Stitching, Stitching and Thinking': Needlework, American Women Writers, and Professionalism," in *Famine and Fashion: Needlewomen in the Nineteenth Century*, ed. Beth Harris (Hampshire: Ashgate, 2005).

Cho, Sumi, Kimberlé Williams Crenshaw, and Leslie McCall. "Toward a Field of Intersectionality Studies: Theory, Applications, and Praxis," *Signs: Journal of Women in Culture and Society* 38, no. 4 (2013): 785–810.

Clark, Elizabeth B. "Matrimonial Bonds: Slavery and Divorce in Nineteenth-Century America," *Law and History Review* 8, no. 1 (1990): 25–54.

———. "'The Sacred Rights of the Weak': Pain, Sympathy, and the Culture of Individual Rights in Antebellum America," *Journal of American History* 82, no. 2 (1995): 463–493.

Clarke, Frances M. "Forgetting the Women: Debates over Female Patriotism in the Aftermath of America's Civil War," *Journal of Women's History* 23, no. 2 (2011): 64–86.

Crenshaw, Kimberlé. "Demarginalizing the Intersection of Race and Sex: A Black Feminist Critique of Antidiscrimination Doctrine, Feminist Theory and Antiracist Politics," *University of Chicago Legal Forum* 139 (1989): 139–167.

———. "Mapping the Margins: Intersectionality, Identity Politics, and Violence against Women of Color," *Stanford Law Review* 43, no. 6 (1991): 1241–1299.

Davis, Adrienne. "'Don't Let Nobody Bother Yo' Principle': The Sexual Economy of American Slavery," in *Sister Circle: Black Women and Work*, eds. Sharon Harley and the Black Women and Work Collective (New Brunswick: Rutgers University Press, 2002).

Davis, David Brion. "Declaring Equality: Sisterhood and Slavery," in *Women's Rights and Transatlantic Antislavery in the Era of Emancipation*, eds. Kathryn Kish Sklar and James Brewer Stewart (New Haven: Yale University Press, 2007).

———. "Reflections on Abolitionism and Ideological Hegemony," *American Historical Review* 92, no. 4 (1987): 797–812.

DuBois, Ellen Carol. "Outgrowing the Compact of the Fathers: Equal Rights, Woman Suffrage, and the United States Constitution, 1820–1878," *Journal of American History* 74, no. 3 (1987): 836–862.

———. "Taking the Law Into Our Own Hands: Bradwell, Minor, and Suffrage Militance in the 1870s," in *One Woman, One Vote: Rediscovering the Woman Suffrage Movement*, ed. Marjorie Spruill Wheeler (Troutdale: NewSage Press, 1995).

———. "The Nineteenth-Century Woman Suffrage Movement and the Analysis of Women's Oppression," in *Capitalist Patriarchy and the Case for Socialist Feminism*, ed. Zillah Eisenstein (New York: Monthly Review Press, 1979).

———. "Ernestine Rose's Jewish Origins and the Varieties of Euro-American Emancipation in 1848," in *Women's Rights and Transatlantic Antislavery in the Era of Emancipation*, eds. Kathryn Kish Sklar and James Brewer Stewart (New Haven: Yale University Press, 2007).

Farrell, Grace. "Afterword," in *Fettered for Life; or, Lord and Master: A Story of To-Day*, ed. Lillie Devereux Blake (New York: The Feminist Press, 1874/1996).

Ferguson, Moira. "Mary Wollstonecraft and the Problematic of Slavery," *Feminist Review* 42 (1992): 82–102.

Ferguson, Susanne. "Foreword," in *A Plea for Woman*, ed. Marion Reid (Edinburgh: Polygon, 1843/1988).

Fischer, Gayle V. "A Matter of Wardrobe? Mary Edwards Walker, a Nineteenth-Century American Cross-dresser," *Fashion Theory: The Journal of Dress, Body & Culture* 2, no. 3 (1998): 245–268.

———. "'Pantalets' and 'Turkish Trowsers': Designing Freedom in the Mid-Nineteenth-Century United States," *Feminist Studies* 23, no. 1 (1997): 110–140.

Fitzpatrick, Tara. "Love's Labor's Reward: The Sentimental Economy of Louisa May Alcott's 'Work'," *NWSA Journal* 5, no. 1 (1993): 28–44.

Folbre, Nancy. "The Unproductive Housewife: Her Evolution in Nineteenth-Century Economic Thought," *Signs: Journal of Women in Culture and Society* 16, no. 3 (1991): 643–684.

Foner, Eric. "Free Labor and Nineteenth-Century Political Ideology," in *The Market Revolution in America: Social, Political, and Religious Expressions, 1800–1880*, eds. Melvyn Stokes and Stephen Conway (Charlottesville: University Press of Virginia, 1996).

Freeman, Elizabeth. "'What Factory Girls Had Power to Do': The Techno-Logic of Working-Class Feminine Publicity in *The Lowell Offering*," *Arizona Quarterly: A Journal of American Literature, Culture, and Theory* 50, no. 2 (1994): 109–128.

Furstenberg, François. "Beyond Freedom and Slavery: Autonomy, Virtue, and Resistance in Early American Political Discourse," *Journal of American History* 89, no. 4 (2003): 1295–1330.

Gallagher, Charles A. "Color-Blind Privilege: The Social and Political Functions of Erasing the Color Line in Post Race America," *Race, Gender & Class* 10, no. 4 (2003): 22–37.

Gilman, Sander L. "Black Bodies, White Bodies: Toward an Iconography of Female Sexuality in Late Nineteenth-Century Art, Medicine, and Literature," *Critical Inquiry* 12 (1985): 204–242.

Gines, Kathryn T. "Race Women, Race Men, and Early Expressions of Protointersectionality, 1830s–1930s," in *Why Race and Gender Still Matter: An Intersectional Approach*, eds. Namita Goswami, Maeve O'Donovan, and Lisa Yount (London: Pickering & Chatto, 2014).

Goldin, Claudia and Maria Shim. "Making a Name: Women's Surnames at Marriage and Beyond," *Journal of Economic Perspectives* 18, no. 2 (2004): 143–160.

Gordon, Ann D. "Stanton on the Right to Vote: On Account of Race or Sex," in *Elizabeth Cady Stanton, Feminist as Thinker: A Reader in Documents and Essays*, eds. Ellen Carol Dubois and Richard Cándida Smith (New York: New York University Press, 2007).

Gould, Stephen Jay. "American Polygeny and Craniometry before Darwin: Blacks and Indians as Separate, Inferior Species," in *The "Racial" Economy of Science: Toward a Democratic Future*, ed. Sandra Harding (Bloomington: Indiana University Press, 1993).

Goyal, Yogita. "The Logic of Analogy: Slavery and the Contemporary Refugee," *Humanity: An International Journal of Human Rights, Humanitarianism, and Development* 8, no. 3 (2017): 543–546.

Hacker, Helen. "Women as a Minority Group," *Social Forces* 30 (1951): 60–69.

Hamand, Wendy F. "The Woman's National Loyal League: Feminist Abolitionists and the Civil War," *Civil War History* 35, no. 1 (1989): 39–58.

Harde, Roxanne. "'One-Hundred-Hours': Elizabeth Stuart Phelps' Dress Reform Writing," in *Styling Texts: Dress and Fashion in Literature*, eds. Cynthia Kuhn and Cindy Carlson (New York: Cambria Press, 2007).

Hartog, Hendrik. "Lawyering, Husbands' Rights, and 'the Unwritten Law' in Nineteenth-Century America," *Journal of American History* 84, no. 1 (1997): 67–96.

Helvenston, Sally. "Fashion on the Frontier," *Dress* 17, no. 1 (1990): 141–155.

Henderson, Christina. "Sympathetic Violence: Maria Stewart's Antebellum Vision of African American Resistance," *MELUS* 38, no. 4 (2013): 52–75.

Higginbotham, Evelyn Brooks. "African-American Women's History and the Metalanguage of Race," *Signs: Journal of Women in Culture and Society* 17, no. 2 (1992): 252–274.

Hogeland, Lisa M. "*Invisible Man* and Invisible Women: The Sex/Race Analogy of the 1970s," *Women's History Review* 5, no. 1 (1996): 31–53.

Jabour, Anya. "'No Fetters but Such as Love Shall Forge': Elizabeth and William Wirt and Marriage in the Early Republic," *Virginia Magazine of History and Biography* 104, no. 2 (1996): 211–250.

Jeffrey, Julie Roy. "Permeable Boundaries: Abolitionist Women and Separate Spheres," *Journal of the Early Republic* 21, no. 1 (2001): 79–93.

Kellow, Margaret M.R. "The Oriental Imaginary: Constructions of Female Bondage in Women's Antislavery Discourse," in *The Problem of Evil: Slavery, Race, and the Ambiguities of American Reform*, eds. Steven Mintz and John Stauffer (Amherst: University of Massachusetts Press, 2007).

Kelly-Gadol, Joan. "The Social Relation of the Sexes: Methodological Implications of Women's History," in *Feminism and Methodology: Social Science Issues*, ed. Sandra Harding (Bloomington: Indiana University Press, 1987).

Kendall, Joan. "The Development of a Distinctive Form of Quaker Dress," *Costume* 19 (1985): 58–74.

Kennon, Donald R. "'An Apple of Discord': The Woman Question at the World's Anti-slavery Convention of 1840," *Slavery & Abolition: A Journal of Slave and Post-Slave Studies* 5, no. 3 (1984): 244–266.

Kerr, Andrea Moore. "White Women's Rights, Black Men's Wrongs, Free Love, Blackmail, and the Formation of the American Woman Suffrage Association," in *One Woman, One Vote: Rediscovering the Woman Suffrage Movement*, ed. Marjorie Spruill Wheeler (Troutdale: NewSage Press, 1995).

Kesselman, Amy. "The 'Freedom Suit': Feminism and Dress Reform in the United States, 1848–1875," *Gender and Society* 5, no. 4 (1991): 495–510.

King, Deborah K. "Multiple Jeopardy, Multiple Consciousness: The Context of a Black Feminist Ideology," *Signs: Journal of Women in Culture and Society* 14, no. 1 (1988): 42–72.

Klassen, Pamela E. "The Robes of Womanhood: Dress and Authenticity among African American Methodist Women in the Nineteenth Century," *Religion and American Culture* 14, no. 1 (2004): 39–82.

Kohn, Denise M. "Laura Jane Curtis Bullard (1831–1912)," *Legacy: A Journal of American Women Writers* 21, no. 1 (2004): 74–82.

Kreger, Erika M. "The Nineteenth-Century Female Humorist as 'Iconoclast in the Temple': Gail Hamilton and the Myth of Reviewers' Disapproval of Women's Comic-Ironic Writings," *Studies in American Humor* 3, no. 11 (2004): 5–38.

Kunzle, David. "Dress Reform as Antifeminism: A Response to Helene E. Roberts's 'The Exquisite Slave: The Role of Clothes in the Making of the Victorian Woman'," *Signs: Journal of Women in Culture and Society* 2, no. 3 (1977): 570–579.

Kwan, Peter. "The Metaphysics of Metaphors: Symbiosis and the Quest for Meaning," *UMKC Law Review* 71, no. 2 (2002): 325–330.

La Rue, Linda. "The Black Movement and Women's Liberation," *The Black Scholar* 1, no. 7 (1970): 36–42.

Lewis, Jan. "'Of Every Age Sex & Condition': The Representation of Women in the Constitution," *Journal of the Early Republic* 15, no. 3 (1995): 365–393.

Lindhorst, Marie. "Politics in a Box: Sarah Mapps Douglass and the Female Literary Association, 1831–1833," *Pennsylvania History: A Journal of Mid-Atlantic Studies* 65, no. 3 (1998): 263–278.

Lippert, Amy. "The Visual Pedagogy of Reform: Picturing White Slavery in America," *Journal of Urban History* (ahead-of-print 2019): 1–35.

Martin, Vicki L. "E.D.E.N. Southworth's Serial Novels *Retribution* and *The Mother-in-Law* as Vehicles for the Cause of Abolition in the *National Era*: Setting the Stage for *Uncle Tom's Cabin*," in *E.D.E.N. Southworth: Recovering a Nineteenth Century Popular Novelist*, eds. Melissa J. Homestead and Pamela T. Washington (Knoxville: University of Tennessee Press, 2012).

Mas, Catherine. "She Wears the Pants: The Reform Dress as Technology in Nineteenth-Century America," *Technology and Culture* 58, no. 1 (2017): 35–66.

Mattina, Anne F. "'Corporation Tools and Time-Serving Slaves': Class and Gender in the Rhetoric of Antebellum Labor Reform," *Howard Journal of Communications* 7, no. 2 (1996): 151–168.

McCurry, Stephanie. "The Two Faces of Republicanism: Gender and Proslavery Politics in Antebellum South Carolina," *Journal of American History* 78, no. 4 (1992): 1245–1264.

McDaneld, Jen. "Harper, Historiography, and the Race/Gender Opposition in Feminism," *Signs: Journal of Women in Culture and Society* 40, no. 2 (2015): 393–415.

———. "White Suffragist Dis/Entitlement: The Revolution and the Rhetoric of Racism," *Legacy: A Journal of American Women Writers* 30, no. 2 (2013): 243–264.

Mellor, Anne K. "Sex, Violence, and Slavery: Blake and Wollstonecraft," *Huntington Library Quarterly* 58, no. 3/4 (1995): 345–370.

Mendus, Susan. "John Stuart Mill and Harriet Taylor on Women and Marriage," *Utilitas* 6, no. 2 (1994): 287–299.

Midgley, Clare. "British Abolition and Feminism in Transatlantic Perspective," in *Women's Rights and Transatlantic Antislavery in the Era of Emancipation*, eds. Kathryn Kish Sklar and James Brewer Stewart (New Haven: Yale University Press, 2007).

Miers, Suzanne. "Slavery: A Question of Definition," *Slavery & Abolition: A Journal of Slave and Post-Slave Studies* 24, no. 2 (2003): 1–16.

Mitchell, Mary Niall. "The Real Ida May: A Fugitive Tale in the Archives," *Massachusetts Historical Review* 15 (2013): 54–88.

Nadelhaft, Jerome. "The Englishwoman's Sexual Civil War: Feminist Attitudes towards Men, Women, and Marriage 1650–1740," *Journal of the History of Ideas* 43, no. 4 (1982): 555–579.

Neal, David. "Free Society, Penal Colony, Slave Society, Prison?" *Australian Historical Studies* 22, no. 98 (1987): 497–518.

Nelson, Jennifer Ladd. "Dress Reform and the Bloomer," *Journal of American and Comparative Cultures* 23, no. 1 (2000): 21–25.

Nelson, Robert K. "'The Forgetfulness of Sex': Devotion and Desire in the Courtship Letters of Angelina Grimke and Theodore Dwight Weld," *Journal of Social History* 37, no. 3 (2004): 663–679.

Offen, Karen. "How (and Why) the Analogy of Marriage with Slavery Provided the Springboard for Women's Rights Demands in France, 1640–1848," in *Women's Rights and Transatlantic Antislavery in the Era of Emancipation*, eds. Kathryn Kish Sklar and James Brewer Stewart (New Haven: Yale University Press, 2007).

———. "Women and the Question of 'Universal' Suffrage in 1848: A Transatlantic Comparison of Suffragist Rhetoric," *NWSA Journal* 11, no. 1 (1999): 150–177.

Olney, James. "'I Was Born': Slave Narratives, Their Status as Autobiography and as Literature," *Callaloo* 20 (1984): 46–73.

Ostrowski, Carl. "Slavery, Labor Reform, and Intertextuality in Antebellum Print Culture: The Slave Narrative and the City-Mysteries Novel," *African American Review* 40, no. 3 (2006): 493–506.

Palmer, Phyllis Marynick. "White Women/Black Women: The Dualism of Female Identity and Experience in the United States," *Feminist Studies* 9, no. 1 (1983): 151–170.

Park, Roberta J. "'All the Freedom of the Boy': Elizabeth Cady Stanton, Nineteenth-Century Architect of Women's Rights," *International Journal of the History of Sport* 18, no. 1 (2001): 7–26.

Peterson, Carla L. "'And We Claim Our Rights': The Rights Rhetoric of Black and White Women Activists before the Civil War," in *Sister Circle: Black Women and Work*, ed. Sharon Harley and the Black Women and Work Collective (New Brunswick: Rutgers University Press, 2002).

Petrov, Julia. "'A Strong-Minded American Lady': Bloomerism in Texts and Images, 1851," *Fashion Theory: The Journal of Dress, Body & Culture* 20, no. 4 (2016): 381–413.

Piper, Alana Jayne. "'Woman's Special Enemy': Female Enmity in Criminal Discourse During the Long Nineteenth Century," *Journal of Social History* 49, no. 3 (2016): 671–692.

Prude, Jonathan. "To Look Upon the 'Lower Sort': Runaway Ads and the Appearance of Unfree Laborers in America, 1750–1800," *The Journal of American History* 78, no. 1 (1991): 124–159.

Putzi, Jennifer. "'Raising the Stigma': Black Womanhood and the Marked Body in Pauline Hopkins's *Contending Forces*," *College Literature* 31, no. 2 (2004): 377–402.

Quanquin, Hélène. "'There are Two Great Oceans': The Slavery Metaphor in the Antebellum Women's Rights Discourse as a Redescription of Race and Gender," in *Interconnections: Gender and Race in American History*, eds. Carol Faulkner and Alison M. Parker (Rochester: University of Rochester Press, 2012).

Ray, Angela G. and Cindy Koenig Richards. "Inventing Citizens, Imagining Gender Justice: The Suffrage Rhetoric of Virginia and Francis Minor," *Quarterly Journal of Speech* 93, no. 4 (2007): 375–402.

Raynaud, Claudine. "African American Women's Voices at the 1893 Chicago World's Fair," in *Women in International and Universal Exhibitions, 1876–1937*, eds. Rebecca Rogers and Myriam Boussahba-Bravard (London: Routledge, 2017).

Reese, Renford. "Canada: The Promised Land for U.S. Slaves," *Western Journal of Black Studies* 35, no. 3 (2011): 208–217.

Rierson, Sandra L. "Race and Gender Discrimination: A Historical Case for Equal Treatment under the Fourteenth Amendment," *Duke Journal of Gender Law & Policy* 1, no. 89 (1994): 89–117.

Ritvo, Harriet. "Pride and Pedigree: The Evolution of the Victorian Dog Fancy," *Victorian Studies* 29, no. 2 (1986): 227–253.

Roediger, David. "Race, Labor and Gender in the Languages of Antebellum Social Protest," in *Terms of Labor: Slavery, Serfdom, and Free Labor*, ed. Stanley L. Engerman (Stanford: Stanford University Press, 1999).

Sanborn, Geoffrey. "'People Will Pay to Hear the Drama': Plagiarism in *Clotel*," *African American Review* 45, no. 1–2 (2012): 65–82.

Sears, Richard. "Working Like a Slave: Views of Slavery and the Status of Women in Antebellum Kentucky," *Register of the Kentucky Historical Society* 87, no. 1 (1989): 1–19.

Schueller, Malini Johar. "Analogy and (White) Feminist Theory: Thinking Race and the Color of the Cyborg Body," *Signs: Journal of Women in Culture and Society* 31, no. 1 (2005): 63–92.

Scott, Donald M. "Abolition as a Sacred Vocation," in *Antislavery Reconsidered: New Perspectives on the Abolitionists*, eds. Lewis Perry and Michael Fellman (Baton Rouge: Louisiana State University Press, 1979).

Scott, Joan Wallach. "French Feminists and the Rights of 'Man': Olympe De Gouges's Declarations," *History Workshop* 28 (1989): 1–21.

Shammas, Carole. "Re-assessing the Married Women's Property Acts," *Journal of Women's History* 6, no. 1 (1994): 9–30.

Siegel, Reva B. "Home as Work: The First Woman's Rights Claims Concerning Wives' Household Labor, 1850–1880," *Yale Law Journal* 103, no. 5 (1994): 1073–1218.

Sklar, Kathryn Kish. "'Women Who Speak for an Entire Nation': American and British Women Compared at the World Anti-slavery Convention, London, 1840," *Pacific Historical Review* 49, no. 4 (1990): 453–499.

Smith, Craig Bruce. "Claiming the Centennial: The American Revolution's Blood and Spirit in Boston, 1870–1876," *Massachusetts Historical Review* 15 (2013): 7–53.

Smith, Jeffrey E. "'Turning the World Upside Down': The Life and Words of Frances Dana Gage," in *Feminist Frontiers: Women Who Shaped the Midwest*, ed. Yvonne Johnson (Kirksville: Truman State University Press, 2010).

Spencer-Wood, Suzanne M. "A Feminist Theoretical Approach to the Historical Archaeology of Utopian Communities," *Historical Archaeology* 40, no. 1 (2006): 152–185.

Spillers, Hortense. "Mama's Baby, Papa's Maybe: An American Grammar Book," *Diacritics* 17, no. 22 (1987): 64–81.

Stanley, Amy Dru. "Conjugal Bonds and Wage Labor: Rights of Contract in the Age of Emancipation," *Journal of American History* 75, no. 2 (1988): 471–500.

———. "Home Life and the Morality of the Market," in *The Market Revolution in America: Social, Political, and Religious Expressions, 1800–1880*, eds. Melvyn

Stokes and Stephen Conway (Charlottesville: University Press of Virginia, 1996).

Stepan, Nancy Leys. "Race and Gender: The Role of Analogy in Science," *Isis* 77, no. 2 (1986): 261–277.

Stevenson, Ana. "'Bloomers' and the British World: Dress Reform in Transatlantic and Antipodean Print Culture, 1851–1950," *Cultural & Social History* 14, no. 5 (2017a): 621–646.

———. "The Gender-Apartheid Analogy in the Transnational Feminist Imaginary: *Ms.* Magazine and the Feminist Majority Foundation, 1972–2002," *Safundi: The Journal of South African and American Studies* 19, no. 1 (2018): 93–116.

———. "The 'Great Doctrine of Human Rights': Articulation and Authentication in the Nineteenth-Century US Antislavery and Women's Rights Movements," *Humanity: An International Journal of Human Rights, Humanitarianism, and Development* 8, no. 3 (2017b): 413–439.

———. "The Novel of Purpose and the Power of the Page": Breaking the Chains That Bind in *Fettered for Life*," *Crossroads* 6, no. 2 (2013): 104–114.

———. "'Symbols of Our Slavery': Fashion and Dress Reform in the Rhetoric of Nineteenth-Century American Print Culture," *Lilith: A Feminist History Journal* 20 (2014): 5–20.

Stimpson, Catharine. "'Thy Neighbor's Wife, Thy Neighbor's Servants': Women's Liberation and Black Civil Rights," in *Woman in a Sexist Society: Studies in Power and Powerlessness*, eds. Vivian Gornick and Barbara K. Moran (New York: Basic Books, 1971).

Strange, Lisa S. "Dress Reform and the Feminine Ideal: Elizabeth Cady Stanton and the 'Coming Girl'," *Southern Communication Journal* 68, no. 1 (2002): 1–13.

Strassel, Annemarie. "Designing Women: Feminist Methodologies in American Fashion," *WSQ: Women's Studies Quarterly* 41, no. 1 & 2 (2013): 35–59.

Stuard, Susan Mosher. "Ancillary Evidence for the Decline of Medieval Slavery," *Past and Present*, 149 (1995): 3–28.

Sumler-Lewis, Janice. "The Forten-Purvis Women of Philadelphia and the American Anti-slavery Crusade," *Journal of Negro History* 66, no. 4 (1981): 281–288.

Summers, Leigh. "Yes, They Did Wear Them: Working-Class Women and Corsetry in the Nineteenth Century," *Costume* 36 (2002): 65–74.

Thomas, Tracy A. "Elizabeth Cady Stanton and the Notion of a Legal Class of Gender," in *Feminist Legal History: Essays on Women and Law*, eds. Tracey Jean Boisseau and Tracy A. Thomas (New York: New York University Press, 2011).

Threedy, Debora. "Slavery Rhetoric and the Abortion Debate," *Michigan Journal of Gender & Law* 2 (1994): 3–26.

Tolles, Frederick B. "'Of the Best Sort but Plain': The Quaker Aesthetic," *American Quarterly* 11, no. 4 (1959): 484–502.

Torrens, Kathleen M. "All Dressed Up with No Place to Go: Rhetorical Dimensions of the Nineteenth Century Dress Reform Movement," *Women's Studies in Communication* 20, no. 2 (1997): 189–210.

Urwin, Tiffany. "Dexter, Dextra, Dextrum: The Bloomer Costume on the British Stage in 1851," *Nineteenth Century Theatre* 28, no. 2 (2000): 91–113.

Wahl-Jorgensen, Karin. "Letters to the Editor as a Forum for Public Deliberation: Modes of Publicity and Democratic Debate," *Critical Studies in Media Communication* 18, no. 3 (2001): 303–320.

Walker, S. Jay. "Frederick Douglass and Woman Suffrage," *The Black Scholar* 14, no. 5 (1983): 18–25.

Warner, Deborah Jean. "Fashion, Emancipation, Reform, and the Rational Undergarment," *Journal of the American Costume Society* 4 (1978): 24–29.

Waters, Kristin. "Past as Prologue: Intersectional Analysis from the Nineteenth Century to the Twenty-First," in *Why Race and Gender Still Matter: An Intersectional Approach*, eds. Namita Goswami, Maeve O'Donovan, and Lisa Yount (London: Pickering & Chatto, 2014).

Weiner, Marli F. "The Intersection of Race and Gender: The Antebellum Plantation Mistress and Her Slaves," *Humboldt Journal of Social Relations* 13, no. 1/2 (1986): 374–386.

Weinstein, Cindy. "'What Did You Mean?': Marriage in E.D.E.N. Southworth's Novels," *Legacy: A Journal of American Women Writers* 27, no. 1 (2010): 43–60.

Wellman, Judith. "The Seneca Falls Women's Rights Convention: A Study of Social Networks," *Journal of Women's History* 3, no. 1 (1991): 9–37.

Wilson, Carol and Calvin D. Wilson. "White Slavery: An American Paradox," *Slavery & Abolition: A Journal of Slave and Post-Slave Studies* 19, no. 1 (1998): 1–23.

Yuval-Davis, Nina. "Intersectionality and Feminist Politics," *European Journal of Women's Studies* 13, no. 3 (2006): 193–209.

Zaeske, Susan. "The 'Promiscuous Audience' Controversy and the Emergence of the Early Woman's Rights Movement," *Quarterly Journal of Speech* 81, no. 2 (1995): 191–207.

UNPUBLISHED THESES

Lewis, Helen Matthews. "The Woman Movement and the Negro Movement: Parallel Struggles for Rights" (Doctor of Philosophy, University of Virginia, 1949).

Index[1]

A
Abolition
  chattel slavery, 41, 43, 50, 52, 60, 71, 107, 109, 177, 196, 214, 219, 248, 252, 258, 265, 276, 287–288, 293
  transatlantic slave trade, 37, 61
Abolitionism
  Garrisonian, 51
  immediate abolition, 15, 41, 43, 49, 50, 52, 67, 86, 175
Abolitionist sisterhood, 39–50
Adams, Abigail, 40, 209, 210
Adams, John, 40, 209, 210
Adams, John Quincey, 211
Adams, William, 54
Addams, Jane, 288, 290, 291
Africa, vii, 35
Afric-American Female Intelligence Society, 185
African Americans
  chattel slavery (*see* Chattel slavery)
  free blacks, 44, 162, 186, 209, 273
  freedmen, 110–111, 195, 221–226, 230, 237, 248
  Freedmen's Bureau, 110, 194
  freedwomen, 18, 110, 111, 195, 226, 227, 259, 271, 275, 284
  literacy, 188
  manhood suffrage, 197, 208–209, 221–223, 226–227, 233
  marriage (*see* Marriage)
  men, 66, 194–196, 199, 221, 224, 228, 235, 240, 251, 256, 264, 271, 295
  mixed-race women, 79–80, 97–98, 103, 231–233, 259–260, 274–276, 280–283
  race women, 272, 305
  racial uplift (*see* Social movements)
  reformers, 19, 68, 70, 204, 216, 226, 227, 237, 244, 245, 271, 276, 287–288, 299, 302, 303, 306, 308

---

[1] Note: Page numbers followed by 'n' refer to notes.

© The Author(s) 2019
A. Stevenson, *The Woman as Slave in Nineteenth-Century American Social Movements*, Palgrave Studies in the History of Social Movements, https://doi.org/10.1007/978-3-030-24467-5

346 INDEX

African Americans (*cont.*)
    self-emancipated, 17, 18, 61, 70, 97, 104, 196, 200, 260, 295
    slave marriage (*see* Marriage)
    women, 4, 6, 8, 17, 18, 20, 43, 64, 66, 70, 93, 97, 111, 114, 142–143, 157, 159, 185–187, 191, 194, 196, 200, 217–218, 222, 224, 226–228, 234, 236–237, 244, 247–252, 255–256, 258, 259, 271–278, 280, 282–285, 293, 296, 299, 308
Albert, Octavia V. Rogers, 272, 278, 289
Alcott, Louisa May, 199–201, 247
Allender, Nina, 253, 254
All the Women Are White, All the Blacks Are Men, but Some of Us Are Brave: Black Women's Studies, 7, 266n25
American and Foreign Anti-Slavery Society (AFAAS), 50
American Anti-Slavery Society, 41, 44–48, 50–54, 58–60, 62–65, 213, 221, 263, 297, 302
American Colonization Society, 50
American Equal Rights Association (AERA), 107, 174, 195, 197, 224–231
American Freedman's Inquiry Commission, 194
American Free Dress League, 149
The American Negro: What He Was, What He Is, and What He May Become, 284
American Revolution, 39, 209, 242, 243
American Slavery as It Is: Testimony of a Thousand Witnesses, 171
American South, 10, 14, 24, 26, 37, 87, 163, 265

American Woman Suffrage Association (AWSA), 145, 229–231, 247, 292
"Am I Not a Woman and a Sister," 10, 41, 44, 287, 297
Analogy, 1–20, 24, 34, 37, 40, 52, 57, 62–64, 69–70, 77–78, 81, 84, 86, 88, 90, 96, 97, 114, 140, 142, 144, 195, 220, 228, 234, 235, 241, 251, 255, 265, 267, 268, 273, 290, 295, 303, 304, 306, 307, 309, 310
Ancient world
    slavery, 27
    social hierarchy, 27
Antebellum era, 2, 12n36, 16, 18, 19, 39, 71, 90, 95–97, 99, 101, 109, 112, 118, 144, 146, 156, 161, 174, 182, 188, 194, 209, 227, 238, 250, 256, 270, 274, 278, 286, 304
Anthony, Susan B., 57, 60, 64, 84, 85, 106, 107, 109, 134, 135, 146, 149, 178, 190, 196–199, 203, 207, 220, 223, 224, 229, 230, 235–237, 243, 245, 250, 255, 256, 292, 293, 295–299, 301, 307, 308
    abolitionism, 308
    illegal voting, 237
    memorialization, 293, 295, 299
    suffrage, 85, 107, 149, 190, 197, 198, 213, 223, 224, 229, 235, 237, 243, 245, 256, 298, 301
Anti-abolitionists, 15
Anti-Fashion Convention, 151
Antislavery, 2
    jealousy about the success of slave emancipation, 209, 287
    petition campaigns, 41, 196, 210, 220
    See also Social movements

Anti-Slavery Bugle, 190, 191, 193
Anti-Slavery Standard, 46–47, 54–55, 190, 215–216, 224–228, 263
Anti-Slavery Convention of American Women, 42
Anti-suffrage, *see* Social movements
Anti-vice, 19–20, 68, 259, 287–291, 299, 302
"new abolitionism," 287–291
See also Social movements
Appeal to the Christian Women of the South, 45, 177
Appeal to the Colored Citizens of the World, 41
An Appeal to the Women of the Nominally Free States, 45, 280n73
Arena, 153, 156
Astell, Mary, 27, 31, 35, 184
Atlantic Monthly, 143, 190, 194
Authentic Anecdotes of American Slavery, 42
Avery, Alida C., 151

B
Bagley, Sarah G., 170, 173
Barnum, P.T., 261–263
Barry, Francis, 85
Beal, Frances, 305
"double jeopardy," 305
Beecher, Catharine, 212
Beecher, Rev. Henry Ward, 108, 129
Behn, Aphra, 32
Bell, Ernest A., 289
Benevolent paternalism, 86, 89, 94, 95, 166
The Bible, 90
Birney, James, 175
Birth Control Review, 281
Blackface minstrelsy, *see* Popular culture

Black Power, *see* Social movements
Blackstone, Sir William, 29
Blackwell, Alice Stone, 124, 156
Blackwell, Henry B., 76–77, 124, 150, 181, 230, 249, 288
Blake, Lillie Devereux, 112, 113, 181, 257
Blake, William, 35, 36
Bloomer, Amelia, 14, 65, 74, 117, 127, 128, 130, 131, 134, 156
Bloomer costume, 117–118, 126–146, 156–157
backlash against, 44, 131–135
different appellations, 130–131
transatlantic circulation, 129–134
"Bloomerism–An American Custom," 131–133
Bloss, William C., 214
The Bondwoman's Narrative, 97, 98, 274
Boston Anti-Slavery Bazaar, 38, 54
Boston Female Anti-Slavery Society, 45
Botts, Mary, 260
Brief History of the Condition of Women: In Various Ages and Nations, 27
Brisbane, Albert, 165, 166
Britain, 23–26, 39, 50–57, 61–62, 122, 131–134, 141, 163–164, 209–210, 305
British and Foreign Anti-Slavery Society, 50
British Empire, 37, 265
Brown, Hallie Quinn, 276, 278
Brown, John, 140
Brown, Mary Onley, 237
Brown, Rev. Antoinette, 76, 179, 181
Brown, William Wells, 80, 92, 110, 111, 260
Bullard, Laura Curtis, 83, 84, 102, 182, 200, 307

348 INDEX

Buxton, Priscilla, 37
Buxton, Thomas Fowell, 37
Byron, Lady, 53
Byron, Lord, 56, 280n73

C
Cady, Judge Daniel, 75
Canada, 99, 102, 104, 108–110
Caribbean, 14, 37, 39, 52
Cary, Mary Ann Shadd, 236, 251
Cavendish, Margaret, Duchess of Newcastle, 31
Chandler, Elizabeth Margaret, 43, 44, 46, 58
Chapman, Maria Weston, 54
Chase, Warren, 103–105, 108, 265, 268, 308
Chattel slavery, 27, 29–67, 69–72, 74, 76–83, 85–98, 104, 106–107, 109–110, 112–114, 135–144, 154–156, 184–196, 257–285, 287–291, 293–300, 302–303, 306
   American South, 10, 14, 24, 26, 265
   analogous to marriage, 30, 238, 239
   bondswoman as "abject icon," 77
   Caribbean, 14, 39, 52
   colonial chattel slavery, 34
   "emancipation anxiety," 261
   enslaved labor, 30, 37, 200
   fugitive slaves, 99–114
   harshest category of oppression, 15
   Jezebel stereotype, 93
   legacy of chattel slavery, 196, 269, 270, 274, 275, 281, 282, 289, 302
   North Star, 294
   Ottoman Empire, 14
   "sexual economy," 97
   slave emancipation, 19, 20, 106, 156, 220, 258, 266, 267, 293, 299, 306
   transatlantic slave trade, 26, 27, 39
   Underground Railroad, 290
Chestnut, Mary Boykin, 89, 90, 92
Child, Lydia Maria, 27, 42, 46, 47, 56, 79, 80, 92, 188, 294
Christian Science Monitor, 298
Christine; or, Woman's Trials and Triumphs, 83–84, 102–103, 182–183, 200–201
Circassian Beauty, *see* White slavery
Citizenship
   civil citizenship, 208
   political citizenship, 208
Civil rights, *see* Social movements
Civil War (American), 2, 12, 19, 23, 41, 67, 71, 83, 85, 90, 98, 99, 103, 106, 107, 110, 118, 125n38, 135–144, 152, 174, 184, 194–204, 208, 215, 216, 219, 221, 237, 238, 256, 258, 260, 261, 263–264, 271, 274, 278, 283, 286–289, 293, 302, 308, 310
Clarkson, Thomas, 50
Clay, Laura, 249
Clotel; or, The President's Daughter, 80, 110, 260
Clotelle; or, The Colored Heroine, 110
Cobbe, Frances Power, 269
Collective memory, 258, 264, 269, 274, 275, 287, 288, 299
The College, the Market, and the Court: Or, Woman's Relation to Education, Labor and Law, 184
Collins, Emily Parmley, 199, 246
Collins, John A., 61
Collins, Lydia M., 117
Colonial slavery, *see* Chattel slavery

Colonization, 63
Colver, Nathaniel, 52
Commentaries on the Laws of England, 29
Contending Forces: A Romance Illustrative of Negro Life North and South, 275
Contract theory
 sexual contract, 16, 26, 29
 social contract, 26, 29
Convict labor, 8, 161, 187
Cook, Coralie Franklin, 251, 252
Cooper, Anna Julia, 66, 276, 278, 308, 309
Coppin, Fanny Jackson, 276
Corsets, *see* Fashion
Courtship, *see* Marriage
Craft, Ellen, 260
Crafts, Hannah, 97, 98, 274, 307
Crenshaw, Kimberlé, 304
Crisis, 251, 255, 308
Critical race theory, 304
Cross-dressing, *see* Fashion
Cupid's Yokes: Or, the Binding Forces of Conjugal Life, 268
Curtis, Harriot, 168

D

Dall, Caroline Wells Healey, 180, 184, 245
Dark Water: Voices from within the Veil, 301
Davis, Paulina Wright, 2, 13, 57, 63, 65, 81, 125, 179–181, 217, 229, 293
de Gouges, Olympe, 33
de Scudéry, Madeleine, 30
Déclaration des droits de la femme et de la citoyenne (Declaration of the Rights of Woman and the Female Citizen), 33

Déclaration des droits de l'homme et du citoyen (Declaration of the Rights of Man and the Male Citizen), 33
Declaration of Independence, 62, 210, 213
Declaration of Sentiments, *see* American Anti-Slavery Society
Declaration of Sentiments and Resolutions, 62
Discourse, 9–10, 14, 17, 26, 31, 32, 37–40, 42, 64, 72–73, 79, 89, 90, 103, 118, 130, 133, 136, 140, 142, 145–146, 153, 154, 156–157, 170, 178, 181, 210, 214, 226–227, 241, 251, 254, 256, 261, 265, 270–273, 277, 280, 284, 303, 304
 discourses of slavery, 1–2, 12, 14–15, 17–20, 30–31, 33, 36–38, 40, 48, 56, 60–63, 65–66, 68, 70, 72–73, 77, 80, 84, 88, 91, 98, 102, 110–111, 114, 118, 120–121, 123, 125–126, 128–129, 131, 133–137, 139, 142–146, 148–149, 151, 153, 157, 159–160, 162, 165–166, 168, 170–172, 184–186, 194–198, 200–201, 203–204, 209, 214, 216, 219, 225–226, 231, 238, 242, 245–248, 250, 258, 264–266, 268, 271–273, 277–280, 282, 284–286, 290, 293, 295–296, 299, 301–302, 306–308
Divorce, 29, 81, 102–103, 108–110, 230, 265, 267, 288, 290, 308
 wife selling, 29
 See also Marriage
Domesticity, 45, 74, 89, 159–204
Dorsey, Louisa, 183
Dorsey, Thomas, 183

Douglass, Frederick, 17, 25, 38, 59, 61–64, 99, 173, 180, 183, 184, 190, 214, 218, 229, 232, 244, 245, 248, 249, 252, 271, 273, 276, 279, 287, 291, 294, 295, 307, 308
  abolitionism, 291
  memorialization, 295
  newspapers, 25, 62, 63, 294
  relationship with Elizabeth Cady Stanton, 307
Douglass, Rosetta, 183, 184
Douglass, Sarah Mapps, 44, 273
Dred Scott v. Sanford, 109, 228, 234, 235, 294
Dress reform
  philosophies, 144
  See also Social movements
Dress-Reform, 149
Du Bois, W.E.B., 308
Duniway, Abigail Scott, 110, 151, 201, 288
Dunning School, 264

E
Early, Sarah J., 276
Eastern harem, 34, 37, 95
Eastman, Mehitable, 173
Education, 30, 31, 34, 154, 246, 271, 277, 282
  girls, 30
Egypt, 37–38, 231
Emancipation anxiety, *see* Chattel slavery
Emancipation Day, 37
Emancipation Proclamation, 10, 105, 146, 220, 231, 252, 257, 260, 263, 287
Emancipation Suit, *see* Fashion
Emancipation Union Under-Flannel, *see* Fashion
Emancipation Waist, *see* Fashion

English Civil War, 30
Eoline; or, Magnolia Vale; or, the Heiress of Glenmore, 92–93
Epigraph, 55, 56, 141, 269
An Essay on Slavery and Abolitionism, with reference to the Duty of American Females, 212
"Europe Supported by Africa and America," 35
Examiner, 265

F
Factory Girl, 165, 169
Farley, Harriet, 168
Fashion
  analogous to chattel slavery, 186, 239
  antifashion, 117–157
  bifurcated garments, 132
  corsets, 119–120, 145, 148–149, 152, 153
  cross-dressing, 133, 147
  Emancipation Suit, 145, 150
  Emancipation Union Under-Flannel, 145
  Emancipation Waist, 145
  fashionable dress, 117–128, 135, 136, 139–151, 153, 157
  health, 118, 120, 123–125, 128, 131, 135, 138, 153
  Quaker fashion, 123
  "slaves to fashion," 120
  technological transformation, 119, 124
  "tyranny of fashion," 123, 123n31, 135, 150
  undergarments, 119, 144–157
Fashion's Slaves, 153, 203
Fawcett, Millicent Garrett, 269
Fellows, Elvina Apperson, 101
Female Labor Reform Association, 170
Factory Tracts series, 170

Female Literary Society of
  Philadelphia, 44
Female operatives, *see* Labor; Lowell,
  Massachusetts
Feminism, *see* Social movements
Feminist theory, 2, 6, 303–306
Fern, Fanny (Sara Willis), 181
*Fettered for Life; or, Lord and Master:
  A Story of To-Day*, 112
*Fighting the Traffic in Young Girls; or,
  War on the White Slave Trade*, 289
Fitzhugh, George, 87
Flower, B.O., 153, 154, 156, 157
Folsom, Joseph K., 3
Forten, Sarah, 43, 273, 280n73,
  281n74
Foster, Abby Kelley, 58–59, 75–76,
  122, 177, 242
Foster, Stephen S., 75, 150, 227
France, 30n24
Frederick Douglass' Paper, 17, 63, 293
Freedmen's Bureau, 110, 194
Free labor, *see* Labor
Free love, *see* Social movements
Free soil, 140, 143
French Revolution, 33, 34
Fugitive Slave Law, 71, 99, 101, 104,
  107, 179, 260
*The Fugitive Wife: A Criticism on
  Marriage, Adultery and Divorce*,
  103, 104, 265, 265n23, 308
Fugitive wife trope, 71, 99–114, 156,
  182–183, 259, 288, 291, 308
Fuller, Margaret, 177, 296
  memorialization, 296

G

Gage, Frances Dana, 180, 181, 190,
  192–194, 226, 237, 243, 247
Gage, Matilda Joslyn, 57, 190, 207,
  243, 292

Garrison, William Lloyd, 41, 44, 46,
  50, 53, 54, 67, 185–186, 251, 263
Genius of Universal Emancipation, 43
Germany, 283
Gilbert, Olive, 188
Gilded Age, 153
Gilman, Charlotte Perkins, 183
Gleason, Rachel Brooks, 128
Godey's Lady's Book, 120, 123, 136
Gordon, Kate, 249
Graham, Sylvester, 125
The Greek Slave, 23, 24, 26, 37, 67,
  154–156
Greenwood, Grace (Sarah Jane
  Lippincott), 152, 181
Grimké, Angelina Weld, 280–283
Grimké, Archibald Henry, 280
Grimké, Nancy Weston, 281
Grimké, Sarah, 5–7, 44–49, 51, 54,
  57, 58, 67, 73–74, 112,
  122–123, 125, 170–171, 175,
  176, 186, 192, 211–212,
  218–219, 236, 238, 239,
  280–282, 294
Grimké [Weld], Angelina, 5, 44–49,
  51, 54, 57, 58, 65, 67, 74,
  122–123, 125, 156, 170–171,
  175–177, 192, 211–212,
  219–220, 236, 238–239, 282,
  293–294

H

Hacker, Helen, 3
Haitian Revolution, 261
Hale, Sarah Josepha, 123
Hamilton, Gail (Mary Abigail Dodge),
  240, 241
Harper, Frances Ellen Watkins, 14, 66,
  87, 111, 142, 185, 187–188,
  231, 232, 248, 252, 257,
  274–277

352 INDEX

Harper, Ida Husted, 292, 297
Harper, William, 86–87, 98
Harper's Bazaar, 115–116, 154–156, 203
Harper's Ferry, 140
Harper's New Monthly Magazine, 132, 134
Harper's Weekly, 154
Hazel, Rosa Hazard, 295
Health reform, 118, 125, 138, 153
Hebrews 13:13, 42
Hentz, Caroline Lee, 69, 90–98, 112, 246, 268
Herald of Freedom, 54
The Hermaphrodite, 125n39
Heyrick, Elizabeth, 41, 52
Heywood, Angela, 268
Heywood, E.H., 85, 268–269
History of Woman Suffrage, 57, 190, 213–214, 226, 236, 243, 247, 250–251, 292–293
Hit, 152
Hopkins, Pauline E., 66, 274–277
The House of Bondage, 288–289
The House of Bondage; or, Charlotte Brooks and Other Slaves, 272, 288–289
The House of Mirth, 183
Howe, Julia Ward, 125, 145, 230, 241, 292
 memorialization, 292
Human rights, 215, 224–225
Husbands, 78, 81, 82
 as slaveowner, 78, 81, 82
Hutchinson Family Singers, *see* Music
Hutchinson, John, 243
Hydrotherapy, 125

I
Ida May: A Story of Things Actual and Possible, 260
Illustrated London News, 130

Immediate, Not Gradual Abolition, 41
Incidents in the Life of a Slave Girl, 61, 67–68, 97–98, 122
Indentured servitude, 8, 287
Independent, 190
Industrialization, 161, 166, 174, 246
International Council of Women, 283
Intersectionality, x, 303–308
Iola Leroy; or, Shadows Uplifted, 274–275, 285

J
Jackson, Mercy B., 149
Jacobs, Harriet, 61, 67, 97, 98, 122, 180, 188, 260
Janin, Albert, 111
Janin, Violet Blair, 111–112
Jefferson, Thomas, 33, 80, 298
Jim Crow era, 259, 264, 271, 274, 285
Jonas, Rosalie, 251
Julia Ward Howe Republican Women's Club, 292

K
Kaufmann, Reginald Wright, 288–289
Kelley, Abby, *see* Foster, Abby Kelley
King, Deborah K., 7
 "multiple jeopardy," 305
Knight, Anne, 56
Ku Klux Klan, 246

L
Labor
 analogous to chattel slavery, 186
 "cotton lords," 172
 domestic labor, 163, 166, 174, 178, 179, 187, 203
 drudgery, 183, 185
 female operatives, 166–173, 182, 194, 203, 204

free labor, 159–204
immigrant labor, 172
men's labor, 163, 199
millinery, 151
reform labor, 174
seamstresses, 103, 182, 183
wage labor, 160, 161, 163, 168, 184, 187
wage slavery, 41, 61, 162, 163, 178, 184, 198, 303
women's labor, 159–161, 166–168, 173, 174, 176, 180–182, 184, 186, 193–195, 198, 200, 201, 203, 204
Labor reform, *see* Social movements
Ladies' Department
Liberator, 41–44, 76, 172, 175, 186, 190, 212, 263
Voice of Industry, 170, 172
Ladies' Home Journal, 120, 145
Lafayette, Gilbert du Motier Marquis de, 33
Lawmakers, 3, 15, 68, 106, 107, 207, 212, 217, 222, 235, 307
Lee, Anne, 289
Legal establishment, 29, 79, 109, 282
L'Esclavage des Noirs (Black Slavery), 33
Letters on the Equality of the Sexes, and the Condition of Women, 6, 47, 212
Liberator, 41–44, 76, 175, 186, 190, 212, 263
The Liberty Bell, 38
The Life and Times of Frederick Douglass, 294
Lily, 65, 76, 77, 85, 123, 127, 128, 140, 178, 181
Lincoln, Abraham, 231, 252–256, 287, 289, 298–299
  assassination, 221

Emancipation Proclamation, 10, 105, 146, 220, 231, 252, 257, 260, 263, 287
Linda; or, the Young Pilot of the Belle Creole, 69, 91–92, 94
Literary public sphere, 30, 32, 61
Literature
  antislavery, 31, 61, 70, 78–80, 86, 92, 94, 95, 97, 99, 103, 260
  women's rights, 83, 86, 101–103, 112, 182, 184, 200
Locke, John, 29, 30, 67
Logan, Adella Hunt, 250n163, 251
London, 23, 32, 50, 51, 57, 117, 129, 131, 138, 265, 287
London Female Anti-Slavery Society, 37
Love, x, 14, 19, 20, 32, 34, 60, 68, 71–73, 76, 77, 79, 81, 84–87, 93, 95, 96, 99, 101, 103, 104, 112–114, 118, 123, 151, 201, 236, 257–300, 302, 308
Lowell, Francis Cabot, 166
Lowell, James Russell, 279, 280
Lowell, Massachusetts
  female operatives, 166–173, 182, 203–204
  Lowell Bloomer Institute, 131
  mill girls, 167–169, 171, 179
  textile factories, 172
Lowell Offering, 168, 170, 171
Lucy Stone League, 292
Lundy, Benjamin, 43
Luther, Seth, 165
Lynching, 7, 259, 261, 271, 273, 276, 278–281, 285

M
Mahan, Asa, 65
Maiden name, *see* Marriage
Marcus Warland; or, the Long Moss Spring, 96

Marriage
  amongst African Americans, 104, 110, 114
  analogous to chattel slavery, 238
  based on romantic love, 72, 73
  companionate marriage, 72, 73, 75, 84, 102, 113
  contract, 71, 76, 78–81, 83, 86, 106, 111, 180
  courtship, 69, 70, 98, 112
  coverture, 30, 40, 111
  divorce, 29, 81, 102, 103, 108–110, 230, 265, 267, 288, 290, 308
  engagement, 73, 96, 113
  maiden name, 292
  marriage market, 270
  marriage protests, 76, 77
  married women, 11, 13–14, 28, 29, 69–114, 201, 203, 208, 215–216, 218–219, 259, 270, 282, 302
  as sinful, 74
  slave marriage, 70, 90, 93, 104, 106, 108–110
  true marriage, 72, 77, 172
Marriage market, *see* Marriage
Married Women's Property Acts, 72, 105, 180, 184, 216, 219
Martineau, Harriet, 37, 38, 95, 156
Mary Lyndon; or, Revelations of a Life, 288
May, Rev. Samuel J., 125, 179
McCord, Louisa S., 238–241, 246
McFarland, Abby Sage, 108, 109
McFarland, Daniel, 108
McFarland-Richardson trial, 108
Memminger, C.G., 87
Meriweather, Elizabeth Avery, 246–247
Metaphor, 9–12, 17, 27, 32, 34, 40, 70, 99, 141, 168, 241, 302

Metempsychosis, 43, 44, 49, 58–60, 59n135, 67, 70, 75, 177, 178, 190, 211, 273, 302
Middle-class women, *see* Women
Mill, John Stuart, 269
Miller, Albert E., 77
Miller, Elizabeth Smith, 126, 127, 134
Millinery, *see* Labor
Miner, Maude E., 291
Minnie's Sacrifice, 231–232
Minor, Francis, 233–235
Minor v. Happersett, 234, 235
Minor, Virginia, 233–235, 242
Mirabeau, Honoré, 33
The Missing Bride; or, Miriam the Avenger, 95–96
Missouri Woman Suffrage Association, 233
Mott, Lucretia, 50–54, 54n113, 56, 57, 66, 72, 122, 127, 224, 250, 294
Murray, Judith Sargent, 40
Music
  antislavery, 243
  Hutchinson Family Singers, 243
  women's rights, 243
My Bondage and My Freedom, 184
Myrdal, Gunnar, 3

N
Narrative of Sojourner Truth; A Bondswoman of Olden Time, 190
Narrative of Sojourner Truth; A Northern Slave, 189
Nast, Thomas, 154
National American Woman Suffrage Association (NAWSA), 249, 250, 250n163, 252, 253, 256, 283, 289
National Anti-Slavery Standard, 47, 54, 190, 263

National Association for the
  Advancement of Colored People
  (NAACP), 251, 252, 255, 308
National Association of Colored
  Women (NACW), 250, 301
National Council of Women, 295
National Dress Reform Association
  (NDRA), 135, 136, 140, 144,
  146, 149, 157
National Era, 94, 99
National Labor Union, 198
National Negro Race Conference, 255
National Typographical Union, 198
National Woman's Party (NWP),
  252–254, 296
National Woman Suffrage Association
  (NWSA), 146, 149, 230, 231,
  236, 242, 249, 256, 292
  schism, 231
Native Americans, 7, 30, 35, 243
Negro's hour, *see* Wendell Phillips
Nell, William C., 214
*A New Conscience and an Ancient
  Evil*, 290–291
New Departure, *see* Suffrage
New England, 57, 159, 161, 166,
  167, 171, 172, 174, 175, 199,
  246, 268, 279
New England Women's Club
  (NEWC), 145, 148, 149
  Dress Reform Committee, 145, 149
New National Era, 244
New Northwest, 151
Newspapers
  editors, 117, 123, 127–129,
    136–137, 147, 157, 180, 226,
    244
  reform, 76, 138, 151, 215
New York City, 45, 191, 195, 198,
  224, 250, 261, 262, 297
New York Freeman, 248
New York Times, 108

New York Times Magazine, 297
New York Tribune, 108, 128
New-York Daily Tribune, 190
Nichols, Mary Gove, 128, 288
Nichols, Thomas Low, 27
North American Review, 241, 245
North star, 99–102
North Star (newspaper), 25–26,
  62–64, 192, 294

O
Oberlin College, 65, 183
O'Connell, Daniel, 50
"One Hundred Years Hence," 243,
  244
Oneida Community, *see* Utopian
  communities
Opium, 14
Oppression
  forms of, 2, 3, 15, 18, 20, 38, 48,
    60, 65, 76, 98, 99, 141, 150,
    172, 188, 196, 214, 227, 243,
    249, 258, 259, 267, 271, 278,
    302, 303, 305, 306, 310
  harshest category (*see* Chattel
    slavery)
Orientalism, 33–34, 37–38, 95–96
Oroonoko; or, The Royal Slave, 32
Ottoman Empire, 14
*Our Nig: Sketches from the Life of a
  Free Black, in a Two-Story White
  House, North, showing that
  Slavery's Shadows Fall Even There*,
  92

P
Pall Mall Gazette, 287
Parkman, Francis, 241, 245, 249
Parody, 137–139
Pease, Elizabeth, 56

Peterson's Magazine, 120, 136
Petition campaigns, *see* Antislavery
Phelps, Elizabeth Stuart, 148, 149, 156
Philadelphia, 43, 51, 82, 91, 122, 145, 183, 238
Philadelphia Female Anti-Slavery Society, 44
Phillips, Wendell, 53, 57, 221, 223, 224, 226, 232, 241
"Negro's hour," 223, 226
Philosophy
classical philosophy, 28
enlightenment philosophy, 38, 86
Pillsbury, Parker, 63, 64, 192, 197, 224, 227, 232
Pittsburgh, Pennsylvania, 63, 129, 190
Plantation mistress, *see* Women
The Planter's Northern Bride, 91
A Plea for Woman, 55
Poems on Various Subjects, Religious and Moral, 32
The Poetical Works of Elizabeth Margaret Chandler, 45–46, 58
Polygenesis, 87
Popular culture, 31–32, 61, 69–71, 81–83, 90–103, 114, 123–124, 201–203, 221–222, 246, 251, 259–263, 270, 286, 288–291
blackface minstrelsy, 243–244, 261
cartoons, 23–26, 81–83, 120–121, 131–134, 154–156, 163–164, 201–203, 221–222, 251–253
comic valentines, 81–83, 120–121, 201–203
engravings, 35, 130
literature, 90–103, 251, 288–291
Postbellum era, 12, 78, 81, 109, 114, 209, 230, 235, 246, 259, 264, 270, 274, 277, 299
Powell, Rosa Arnold, 298
Powers, Hiram, 23, 24, 37, 95, 154–156, 261

Prescod, Samuel Jackson, 52
Print culture, 17, 77–86, 97, 101, 103, 112, 118, 126, 128, 130, 132, 168, 170, 182, 265, 307
Progressive Era, 290, 299
Proslavery, 3, 15, 20, 69, 70, 86–98, 106, 114, 147, 162, 163, 201, 238–239, 246, 265, 268, 288, 307
Prostitution, 85, 103, 107, 267, 273, 276, 285–291, 299
analogous to chattel slavery, 186, 239, 291
euphemism for the rape of enslaved women, 273
Providence, Rhode Island, 165, 292
Punch, 23, 25, 131, 133
Purvis, Robert, 232, 233

Q
"The Quadroons," 79
Quakers, or the Religious Society of Friends, 41, 43–46, 51–56, 122–123, 125, 231–232
Hicksite, United States, 51
Orthodox, Britain, 51
Orthodox, United States, 51
Quaker fashion (*see* Fashion)

R
Rachel: A Play in Three Acts, 281
Racial uplift, *see* Social movements
Radical Republicans, 197n154, 220, 221, 223, 263
Rank-and-file reformers, 13, 19, 20, 99, 136–138, 157, 160, 177, 266
Rankin, Rev. John, 59
Rape, *see* Sexual violence
Ray, Charlotte E., 251
Reconstruction amendments, *see* US Constitution

Reconstruction era, 12, 19, 20, 110, 194, 207, 221, 228, 237, 256
The Red Record: Tabulated Statistics and Alleged Causes of Lynching in the United States, 279–280
Reid, Marion, 55, 56, 66
Religious Society of Friends, *see* Quakers, or the Religious Society of Friends
Remond, Charles Lenox, 53–54, 61
Retribution: A Tale of Passion, 94
Revolution, 84–85, 107–109, 146–147, 196–199, 227, 229–235
Revolutionary era, 139, 209, 242
Richardson, Albert, 108
Robinson, Harriet H., 173
Rockford; or, Sunshine and Storm, 112
Roe, Clifford G., 289
Rogers, Nathaniel Peabody, 54, 58
Rose, Ernestine, 215, 220
Rousseau, Jean Jacques, 26
Royal African Company, 30
Russell, Frances E., 151, 153, 156

S
Safford-Blake, Mary J., 149
Sanborn, Franklin B., 143
Sartain's Union Magazine of Literature and Art, 120, 129
Satire, 132, 137–138
Saturday Visiter, 63–64, 190, 192
Seamstress, *see* Labor
Seneca Falls, New York, 62, 117, 127, 213–214, 250, 292, 295
Sex, 3, 7, 8, 10, 11, 15, 20, 46, 64, 85, 104, 110, 128, 131, 147, 150, 209, 210, 215–238, 240, 246, 250–252, 256, 257, 270, 275, 283, 285, 286, 291, 294–297, 300–302, 304, 309

Sex-race analogy, 3–4, 219, 223, 228, 233, 237, 241, 242, 250, 251, 255, 256, 258, 292, 295, 302–303, 306–307
Sexual violence
  rape of enslaved women, 273
  sexual victimization, 271–285
Shaw, Anna Howard, 270, 295
Shelley, Percy Bysshe, 55
Sibyl, 65, 136–142, 150, 157
Simpson, Stephen, 162
"Sisterhood of Reforms," 2, 13, 136
Slave emancipation, 10, 19, 20, 49, 71, 105–106, 109, 110, 145–146, 155–156, 160, 185, 187, 201, 204, 208–209, 216, 219–221, 224, 231, 238, 239, 242, 244, 250, 252–256, 258, 260–261, 263–270, 272, 286–287, 293, 299–300, 302–303, 306
Slave narrative
  by African Americans, 61, 67–68, 92, 97–102, 184–185, 188–190
  "stolen slave narrative," 90–92, 98
  white slave narrative, 285–291
Slaveowners, 30, 44, 78, 79, 81, 82, 142, 179, 289
Slavery
  analogy, 26–28, 30, 31, 33–35, 38–41, 61–62, 67, 209–210
  born to slavery, 20, 27, 31–32, 55, 57, 60, 66–68, 273, 277–278, 284
  metaphor, 17–18, 27, 31–33, 39–40, 70–71, 140–141, 168
"Slavery Redivivus," 257–300
Slavery Abolition Act, 10, 37
The Slavery of Prostitution: A Plea for Emancipation, 291

"A Slave's Appeal," 218–219
Smedes, Susan Dabney, 88
Smith, Gerrit, 75, 126, 180
Social movements
   abolitionism, 11, 15, 33, 41–42, 46–53, 57, 60, 63–65, 67, 69–70, 86, 91, 94–95, 140, 162–163, 175, 188, 189, 192, 212–213, 219–221, 263–264, 268, 280–281, 285–291, 293–294, 307–308
   antislavery, 2–3, 14–15, 19, 20, 23–114, 118, 124, 129, 138, 141, 143, 157, 160, 162–163, 169–173, 176–185, 187, 187n116, 192, 196–197, 197n154, 199, 210–214, 220, 223, 224, 238–239, 241, 243–244, 246, 249, 260–261, 263–264, 268, 273–274, 279–280, 287–291, 294, 301–302, 308
   anti-suffrage, 238–242
   black power, 8
   civil rights, 8, 214–215, 218–219, 225, 263, 301, 305
   dress reform, x, 19, 20, 68, 77, 117–157, 173
   feminism, 1–20, 70, 301–310
   free love, 19, 20, 68, 71, 84–86, 99, 101, 103–105, 113, 114, 118, 151, 201, 236, 259–270, 288, 302, 308
   health reform, 118, 124–125, 128, 135, 138, 153
   labor reform, 19, 159–173, 178–179, 187–201, 230, 259, 268
   racial uplift, 19, 20, 68, 248, 271–285, 301
   southern suffrage, 199, 238–240, 246–247, 249
   suffrage, 19, 20, 57–58, 68, 76–77, 83, 85, 107, 118, 145–152, 189–199, 207–256, 265n23, 266–269, 277, 283–284, 287, 292–302
   temperance, 14, 17, 40–41, 52, 60, 117, 141, 153–154, 188, 192, 221, 246, 268, 288–289
   transatlantic social movements, 21, 23–68, 133–134, 171–172, 179–180, 214, 265–266, 278–279, 283–287
   women's liberation, 8
   women's rights, 1–20, 50–68, 71–86, 99–114, 117–119, 122, 125–129, 133–136, 138–141, 143–145, 148–149, 151–153, 157, 160, 172–174, 176, 178–180, 182–184, 189–196, 200–201, 203, 204, 207–208, 208n5, 210, 212–217, 219–227, 220n53, 229–230, 235, 237, 239, 242–246, 250–251, 255–257, 264–268, 270, 276–277, 281, 284, 288, 291–295, 301–302, 306–307, 309–310
Society in America, 37
"A Solution of the Southern Question," 249
Some Reflections Upon Marriage, 27, 31
Southern Horrors: Lynch Law in All Its Phases, 278–279
Southern Literary Journal, 86–87
Southern Quarterly Review, 239–240
Southern Strategy, *see* Suffrage
Southern suffrage movement, *see* Social movements
Southwold: A Novel, 112
Southworth, E.D.E.N., 90–91, 94–97, 181–182

Stanton, Elizabeth Cady, 51, 54,
  56–57, 60, 62, 66–67, 69, 74–75,
  80–86, 96–97, 101–102,
  107–110, 120, 126–128,
  134–135, 146–147, 149–152,
  156, 196–199, 213–214,
  216–238, 241, 245, 250, 268,
  288, 292–295, 307–309
  relationship with Frederick
    Douglass, 62, 213–214,
    217–218, 229, 244–245,
    294–295, 307–308
Stanton, Henry B., 50, 75
Stead, W.T., 286–287
Stewart, Maria W., 185, 186, 195, 308
Stone, Huldah, 173
Stone, Lucy, 24–25, 67–68, 74,
  76–77, 101–102, 127, 134–136,
  139, 156, 177–178, 212–213,
  224–225, 229–231, 236–237,
  241–243, 250
  maiden name (*see* Marriage)
  memorialization, 292–294
Stowe, Harriet Beecher, 80, 91, 94,
  99–100, 103, 142–143, 163,
  181–182, 190, 193–194, 260,
  288–291
Sturge, Joseph, 51–52
The Subjection of Women, 269
Suffrage
  disenfranchisement, 61–62, 107,
    150–151, 197–198, 208–212,
    215, 218, 221–222, 227, 231,
    235–237, 243, 247–252, 256,
    258–259, 265, 271–272,
    294–295, 302–303, 309
  disenfranchisement analogous to
    chattel slavery, 107, 176
  educated suffrage, 245–246, 249
  enfranchisement, 20, 61–62,
    150–151, 194–199, 207–256,
    258–259, 263–265, 268–269,
    271–272, 276–277, 283–284,
    294–297, 302–303, 309
  manhood suffrage, 196–197, 199,
    208–209, 221–238, 244–245,
    249, 287
  New Departure, 233–238
  performative acts of voting,
    236–237
  "Southern Strategy," 242–256
  universal suffrage, 20, 189–197,
    215–216, 223–226, 228–229,
    231–232, 234, 249, 252–255
  woman suffrage, 107, 196–199,
    207–256, 294–298, 301–302
  Wyoming, 233–234
Suffragist, 253–254
Susan B. Anthony Amendment, 292
Susan B. Anthony League, 292, 298
Swisshelm, Jane Grey, 63–65, 129,
  192, 192n137

T
Taney, Chief Justice Roger B., 109,
  234–235, 294–295
Taxation
  taxation without representation,
    180, 242–243
Taylor, Harriet, 269, 269n36
T.B. Peterson & Brothers of
  Philadelphia, 91
Temperance, *see* Social movements
Terrell, Mary Church, 66, 250–251,
  276, 283–284, 283n81, 295–297,
  296n125, 301–302, 308
Textile factories, *see* Lowell,
  Massachusets
Third World Women's Alliance, 305
"triple jeopardy," 305
Thomas, William Hannibal, 284–285
Thompson, George, 44, 53, 57
Titus, Frances W., 188–189

Tragic mulatta trope, 78, 94–95, 102, 260, 274–276
Train, George Francis, 147, 197
Traits of American Life, 123–124, 123n31
Transatlantic, 20, 23–68, 129–134, 179–180, 278–279, 286–287
Transatlantic slave trade, *see* Abolition; Chattel slavery
Transatlantic social movements, *see* Social movements
Truth, Sojourner, 66, 117, 142–143, 143n109, 174, 177, 188–196, 225–227, 236–237, 247, 252, 255, 271, 308
  "A'n't I a woman?," 189–196
Tubman, Harriet, 143
"The Two Platforms,", 222

U
Una, 65, 76, 178–180, 215
Uncle Tom's Cabin; or, Life Among the Lowly, 80, 91, 99–100, 163, 260, 288, 290
Underground Railroad, *see* Chattel slavery
United States
  founding of the Republic, 14, 39–40, 161–162, 181, 207–210, 242
US Constitution
  Fifteenth Amendment, 199, 228–230, 233, 235–236, 244, 249, 287
  First Amendment, 210–212
  Fourteenth Amendment, 196–197, 207–208, 228–229, 233–236
  Nineteenth Amendment, 252, 292, 296
  Thirteenth Amendment, 10, 106–107, 196, 220–221, 223, 235, 263

US Supreme Court, 108–109, 234–236
Utopian communities, 124, 124n34
  Oneida Community, 124

V
Villard, Fanny Garrison, 251
A Vindication of the Rights of Men, 34
A Vindication of the Rights of Woman, 34–35, 67
Vineland, New Jersey, 236
A Voice from the South, 278
Voice of Industry, 170, 172–173
The Voice of the Negro, 301

W
Wage labor, *see* Labor
Wage slavery, *see* Labor
Walker, David, 41
Walker, Mary E., 77, 151–153
Waltham-Lowell system, *see* Francis Cabot Lowell
Washington Post, 298
Washington, DC, 90–91, 111, 207, 235–236, 244–245, 250, 295
Washington, George, 298–299
Water-Cure Journal, 125, 128, 131
Weld, Theodore Dwight, 45, 74, 123, 170–171, 176, 281n74, 293–294
Wells, Ida B., 276, 278–280, 308
Wharton, Edith, 183
What to Wear?, 148
What Women Might Do with the Ballot: The Abolition of the White Slave Traffic, 290–291
Wheatley, Phillis, 32, 61
Whitehead, Celia B., 150, 156
White slavery
  "Circassian Beauty," 261–263, 268
  labor, 161–164, 168–173, 259–260, 270, 286

prostitution, 265–270, 285–291, 296, 299–300
white slavery panic, 286–291, 309–310
White slavery panic, *see* White slavery
White Slave Traffic Act, 285–286, 288
Whittier, John Greenleaf, 176, 212–213
Willard, Frances E., 153, 160, 288
Williams, Fannie Barrier, 276–278, 299–300, 308
Wilson, Harriet, 92
Wives, 10–13, 28–29, 63–67, 69–116, 128–129, 154, 159–160, 163, 165–166, 168, 174–175, 179–180, 194–195, 203, 209–210, 217–218, 238–240, 246–248, 255–256, 264–265, 268–270, 281–282, 302–303
as slaves, 66, 72, 104, 109, 165
Wollstonecraft, Mary, 34–38, 60, 67, 95–96, 184
Woman-as-slave worldview, 3, 5, 12–20, 28, 37, 49, 56, 65, 84, 105–106, 134, 136–137, 141, 154, 173, 233, 238, 244–245, 264–269, 285, 294, 299–300, 307–308
Woman in All Ages and Nations, 27
A Woman in Revolt, 289
Woman question, 3, 19, 39–57, 83, 111, 157, 191–192, 236, 294, 302–303, 306–307
Woman's Christian Temperance Union, 153, 288
"Woman's Emancipation," 131–134
Woman's Journal, 76–77, 81, 112, 144, 145, 149–151, 230–231, 248–249
Woman's National Loyal League (WNLL), 220
Woman's Place To-Day, 257

Woman's Wrongs: A Counter-Irritant, 240–241
Women
born to slavery, 20, 27, 31–32, 55, 57, 60, 66–68, 273, 277–278, 284
elite southern women, 7, 70–71, 86–98, 114, 238–240, 246–247, 274–276, 288
enslaved women, 1, 5, 12, 13n37, 23–26, 28, 42, 45, 59, 61, 78–80, 90, 93–96, 142–143, 169, 184–196, 199–203, 212, 214–215, 225–227, 260, 261, 271–285, 302–303, 308
middle-class women, 119, 133, 148–149, 160, 173, 250–251, 307–308
mining industry, 132–133
plantation mistress, 7, 69–70, 88–98
remuneration, 147–148, 160, 165–170, 172, 178–180, 182–183, 197–199, 203–204
self-ownership, 13–14, 77–78, 86, 104–105, 113–114, 148–149, 179–181, 184, 267, 275–276
self-worth, 173–174, 177, 204
working-class women, 6, 68, 119, 131–133, 148–149, 159–204, 245–246
Women's history
as a discipline, 3, 79, 139, 304
of slavery, 27
Women's liberation, *see* Social movements
Women's rights, *see* Social movements
Women's rights conventions
1848, Rochester, New York, 214
1848, Seneca Falls, New York, 62, 117, 127, 213–214, 250, 292, 295

Women's rights conventions (*cont.*)
  1850, Worcester, Massachusetts, 63–64, 214–215, 239–240
  1851, Akron, Ohio, 189–194
  1852, Syracuse, New York, 17
  1853, Cleveland, Ohio, 65, 215–216
  1866, New York City, 195, 224–226
Women's Typographical Union, 199
Woodhull, Victoria, 85, 151–152, 201, 234–236, 267–269, 296
  memorialization, 299
Woodhull, Zula Maud, 296
Woodhull and Claflin's Weekly, 151, 236, 259, 267, 268, 270
Woolson, Abba Gould, 149, 156
The Word: A Monthly Journal of Reform, 268
Work: A Story of Experience, 199–201

Working Women's Association (WWA), 198–200
Working-class women, *see* Women
Work Projects Administration, 272
World's Anti-Slavery Convention, 50–58, 63–67, 75
World's Columbian Exhibition, 276, 291
World's Congress of Representative Women, 257, 276–278, 291, 308–309
Wright, Elizur, 294
Wright, Henry C., 175
Wright, Martha Coffin, 201
Wyoming, *see* Suffrage

Y
"*The Yellow Wallpaper*," 183